Solitary Star/

A BIOGRAPHY OF SAM HOUSTON

by Donald Braider/

G. P. Putnam's Sons, New York

For Suzanne and John Verdery,
with great love

Solitary Star

A BIOGRAPHY OF SAM HOUSTON

I

SAM HOUSTON was born March 2, 1793, at Timber Ridge, Rockbridge County, on the western side of the Blue Ridge Mountains of Virginia. He was the fifth child and the fifth son of Captain Samuel Houston and Elizabeth Paxton. Both of his parents were originally from the Tidewater section of the state. Both were descended from Scotch-Irish immigrants who had been lured to the New World by prospects of an eventually easy life in Britain's most fashionable American colony. There had been Houstons and Paxtons in Virginia since the middle of the eighteenth century.

Samuel Houston, the father, was a career militia officer, a brigade inspector. He owned considerable properties in northwestern Virginia, to which he and his bride had moved not long after their marriage. The captain was frequently not at home to oversee the planting, nurturing, and harvesting of the crops. His dabblings in local and state politics were hardly more rewarding than his ventures into agriculture. According to the vague accounts available, he was an archetypal gentleman-soldier-planter whose expenditures on a gracious way of life consistently exceeded his revenues. His accumulated debts would be settled only with bankruptcy or death. Moderately admired by his acquaintances, he was respected with similar reservations by those who served him. He was a likable, affable man, but he seemed to lack the kind of ferocious drive required to make a marked success of his life on the demanding frontier land of western Virginia.

Elizabeth Houston was much the stronger personality of the couple. A prolific producer of children, she was completely the mistress of the Timber Ridge household.

She brought a significant dowry of intelligence and fortitude as well as gold to her marriage with Captain Houston. All biographers, including her own son, Sam Houston, have portrayed Elizabeth as a powerful and indomitable soul, capable of facing exceptional hardships and of dealing with them according to precepts which owed as much to her Protestant Anglo-Saxon heritage as to her American upbringing. She was handsome, forthright, certain of her virtuous values, enormously energetic, and physically courageous. The life of the American frontier called upon every one of those assets in fullest measure.

The fifth Houston son owed approximately equal hereditary debts to his mother and his father. For though his character was essentially formed in a home dominated by the formidable Elizabeth, from whom he inherited qualities of personal and moral force, he derived from his somewhat quixotic father a strain of obstinate romanticism.[1]

By the time Sam was in his eighth year, his mother had given birth to four more children. The size of the Houston family was not at all unusual on the American frontier, where infant mortality was even higher than the worldwide norm of 50 percent. What *was* remarkable was that none of the Houston offspring perished in infancy (though two died before attaining their majority)—testimony to the relative prosperity of the Houstons and to the care and nourishment provided them by their mother.[2]

The Rockbridge County phase of the Houston saga was not particularly arduous for any member of the family. So long as the captain's credit held out, they could live comfortably, cared for by slaves who also tended their fields. In an age when specie was one of the least dependable forms of monetary exchange, lenders did not often force bankruptcy upon borrowers—especially if those debtors were substantial landowners and slaveholders.

Life in Rockbridge County, for the propertied class, had a sense of bucolic ease that was satisfying even if it did not quite come up to the level of graceful living enjoyed in Richmond or along the Atlantic shore of Virginia. Although a satisfactory school system was lacking, education among the more prosperous could be accomplished at home, because gentlemen of taste with aspirations to rustic fashion were expected to have libraries where their children (and particularly their sons) might improve their minds.

It was among his father's books that young Sam Houston acquired a lifelong interest in the classical literature of Greece and Rome. Surviving documents and his own autobiographical writings indicate *some* exposure to the rudiments of formal learning at Liberty Hall Academy, in Timber Ridge, from 1801 until 1806. There he was taught to read and write, but he was never able to master algebra and geometry. Nonetheless, he did finally master enough arithmetic to support a long and occasionally brilliant career in politics as an administrator.

It is doubtful that when he was only ten years old Sam Houston was much aware of his country's domestic difficulties or its complex international relations. Even those of the Commonwealth of Virginia would have escaped his attention. But the events that were shaping themselves at that time were to have an enormous effect on his later life.

In 1803, with President Jefferson's audacious acquisition of the Louisiana Territory from France, the configuration of American history was definitively altered. The Louisiana Purchase was not received happily by the Spanish, who claimed ownership to much of this immense uncharted area, and particularly that portion of Mexico that was Texas. Spain also controlled Florida and vast tracts of North America extending from the eastern border of modern-day Texas (the Sabine River), to the Pacific coast.

Residents of western Virginia, Kentucky, and Tennessee took it for granted that the Spanish, with assistance from several Indian nations, would declare war against the American Republic to prevent the assumption of a questionable title. Inhabitants of Rockbridge County and other sections of the land west of the Blue Ridge prepared eagerly for the anticipated conflict. The state militia underwent an urgent reorganization, which included the promotion of Captain Samuel Houston to the rank of major. This committed him to more active duty which kept him away from home for even longer intervals than usual.

Although the war failed to materialize, the cost of the major's travel (which he had to bear personally as an officer and gentleman), forced him to dispose of some of his property around Lexington and sell some of his slaves. In spite of this setback, however, the family was still comfortable financially.[3]

This era, for the United States generally, was one of economic stagnation and great political uneasiness, especially in the states which lay on the southwestern frontier. Part of this was owing to Great Britain's war against Napoleonic France. Sympathies of Americans were divided. Some saw in Bonaparte's daring attempt to master the European continent the possibility of breaking Britain's nearly absolute control of international maritime commerce. If Britain's power were broken by France, Americans would be free to bargain with other European countries and thus, perhaps, obtain more favorable prices for their products.

American hostility to the British cause was as much emotional as economic, however. Equally passionate was the sympathy generated for Napoleon, whom many Americans saw as the one who might salvage from the ruins of the French Revolution some form of constitutional government. Although he had proclaimed himself Emperor of the French, it was felt that he might spread the virtues of controlled monarchy to some of Europe's decadent tyrannies—notably Great Britain.

That Great Britain had been under constitutional rule since 1688 could not offset the fact that she was still nominally governed by George III, whose blind obduracy had been a prime cause of the American war for independence. Spain was technically the ally of Britain in the struggle against France. To injure Spain, therefore, was to injure George III. Furthermore, Britain's maritime blockade of continental European ports, coupled with her reckless practice of impressing American nationals into her naval service, exacerbated relations between the two countries.

Historians are generally agreed that residents of frontier states were stronger advocates of war than those dwelling near the Atlantic Seaboard. The latter argued that war was always more costly than peace, particularly against an enemy who was stronger. They added that Napoleonic tyranny was a much less benevolent policy than Britain's insistence on the maintenance of a balance of power on the Continent. Most persuasive of all was that trade with the British, however restricted, was better than no trade at all.

This trade-oriented position meant very little to inhabitants of the inland western-boundary territories. As their numbers increased, they became more and more pressed for space. Agricultural practices were wasteful and primitive. As land became exhausted or overcrowded, as poor whites (mainly from southern cotton lands on the Atlantic coast) began to pour westward, the demands for acreage increased. The need for practically limitless expanses of land to the west, territories defended only by Indians, made the prospect of war even more desirable.

Furthermore, the expansionists held that the Indians had forfeited all their rights to these virgin lands by allying themselves with enemies of the United States; the Spanish in the South and Southwest and the British-Canadians in the North and Northwest. There was also an important and fundamental racial prejudice against all red "savages" which pervaded the American frontier outlook. To deprive the Indians of their holdings was as natural as depriving African blacks of their freedom.

Thus, the roots of the War of 1812 were established in 1803 by the purchase of the Louisiana Territory. Northeastern politicians, acting almost as a single bloc, were successful for nearly ten years in preventing a declaration of war, but in retrospect it is evident that the energies accumulating on the frontier could not forever be restrained. British intransigence lit the fuse, but the cannon was loaded in the American West by men who had never laid eyes on a Briton.

During the next three years a fever for war spread from the Niagara frontier to Tennessee. It was greatly increased in 1806 by rumors of a major conspiracy plotted by Aaron Burr and some other notable New Yorkers. Accounts suggested various possibilities, the most grandiose of which envisaged the seizure of Texas and the installation of Burr, former American Vice President, as emperor of all of North America's huge southwestern sector.

That there *was* a Burr conspiracy is unquestioned, but its specific nature was never clarified at his dramatic trial for treason. It was clearly established that it had to do with a large area west of the Mississippi and included at least some of the Louisiana Territory. While tantalizing lies and half-truths circulated on both sides, frontier farmers eagerly awaited official word to mobilize for war against Britain. In Tennessee, lawyer Andrew Jackson was anxious to organize a force of 2,000 men. In western Virginia, Major Samuel Houston enthusiastically anticipated similar instructions. But 1806 was not to be the year of the war's beginning.

*   *   *

This atmosphere of controlled frenzy affected the lives of the major's children. As he entered his thirteenth year, Sam and his older brothers and their friends played the games of frontier soldiery. Such diversions were common and usually approved by adults along the hundreds of miles of border country of the American West.

There were visits to Houston relatives of the Blue Ridge region, one of whom lived near High Bridge—now Natural Bridge. Another, the Reverend Samuel, was a classics scholar who may have reinforced the teen-aged Sam's interest in the wisdom and adventures of the ancients. He was also a sometime traveler to Tennessee and had invented a reaper, out of which he hoped to make his fortune; unfortunately Cyrus McCormick, another farmer who lived in Rockbridge County, had devised a simpler and more efficient machine which became successful. The Reverend Samuel probably planted the idea of eventual emigration to Tennessee in the mind of Sam's father.

The school at Timber Ridge stood on land which Sam's father had donated for the purpose. Sam was a frequent truant, and the major could discipline him only when he was at home. Admonitions of mother and older brothers carried no weight. Sam did, however, tow *some* lines. On Sundays, for example, the Houstons en masse attended services at the nearby Timber Ridge church. But religion played no important role in their daily lives. Sam was not baptized until late in his life, and then under compulsions quite different from those of pure form.

The prospects of war, adumbrated by talk of the Burr plot, were conclusively dispelled in the summer of 1806. From the east banks of the Cumberland and Ohio rivers prospective soldier-colonists stocked flatboats which were to carry them south, they believed, to a dazzling destiny and a brand new start in life. At the same time young New York adventurer, Samuel Swartwout, set out on horseback for a secret rendezvous on the Sabine River. In his possession was a coded message in the hand of Aaron Burr. Apprehended in Virginia, Swartwout was imprisoned, Burr arrested, and the conspiracy dissolved. The possibilities of an immediate war were ended—to the great disappointment of most American Westerners and particularly Major Samuel Houston.[4]

In his fifties now, he discovered himself to be genuinely on the verge of bankruptcy. He decided to sell out his entire holding at Timber

Ridge, resign from the militia, and with what was left after his debts were cleared purchase a tract of land in Tennessee and migrate, along with thousands of his fellow countrymen who were heeding the call of the wilderness. Because he also found himself in failing health, Major Houston acted with dispatch. He contracted to sell Timber Ridge and negotiated for a grant of land in East Tennessee, where several Houston and Paxton families were already long established. He made his will, which he hoped would provide adequately in the event of his imminent death for his widow and children during the period of transition from Virginia to the new land.

Samuel Houston was not a man likely to die peacefully in his bed, nor did he. In September, 1806, after having accomplished all he reasonably could to assure his family's future, he rode off from Timber Ridge on his last mission as inspector of the Virginia militia. He died not long after his departure. His remains were brought to the property of his cousin, Matthew Houston, of High Bridge, and were interred in the local graveyard. As a notable of the region, he was honored by a substantial gathering of the western Virginia gentry, including his nine children and a widow who must now assume in name the role of family head she had previously performed in fact.

The major was not long in his grave before Elizabeth Houston sold every farm implement and piece of household furnishing she thought she could do without. The proceeds amounted to $3,600, a considerable sum when added to what was left after settlement of debts from the disposal of the Timber Ridge property. Early in the spring of 1807, the widow and her young began the journey south and west to the land her late husband had contracted for in Blount County, Tennessee. It stood about twelve miles west of Maryville, on a tributary of Baker's Creek. They arrived after three weeks of hard, steady travel.[5]

The Houstons reached their destination in a condition which the great majority of pioneers would have thought enviably affluent. They had nine horses, two Conestoga wagons, several slaves, and all of the absolute essentials for their new beginning in the wilderness. Yet, for a gentlewoman with nine children, the picture must not have appeared cheerful. Elizabeth was nearly fifty, and very much a lady; but she was singularly strongminded. She was, according to her son, Sam: "a heroine . . . an extraordinary woman . . . gifted with intellectual and moral qualities, which elevated her . . . above most of her sex. Her life shone with purity and benevolence, and yet she was nerved with a stern fortitude, which never gave way in the midst of wild scenes that checquered the history of the frontier settler."

She lost no time in registering her claim to about 420 acres of Blount County land at Maryville's courthouse. Maryville was hardly prepossessing, despite its comparative importance as the Blount County seat. The environs of Maryville supported about forty families. It was a crossroads trading center where two stage lines, one from Knoxville, the other from Nashville, converged and then extended south to Georgia and east to the Carolinas. Maryville boasted a solitary, roisterous hostelry and tavern, a smithy, a harnessmaker, a tannery, a grist mill, and a hatter. There were two or three general stores, one of which was soon to become partly the property of the newly arrived Houstons and operated by Sam's eldest brother, John. John Houston also became, in time, clerk of the county court. The courthouse and jail were the most imposing of the log-and-pitch buildings. In 1808, the year after the Houstons' settlement, the town was to see the opening of its first school, Porter Academy. James and Robert Houston, also Sam's brothers, became trustees of this institution.

The ease with which Elizabeth and her brood established themselves in their new setting was partly due to the presence of two other Houston families, who had come to Tennessee from eastern Virginia immediately after the Revolution. James Houston had been elected to the legislature of the state when it joined the Union in 1796. Jim Houston's fort, on Nine Mile Creek, was only five miles or so from the site Elizabeth had selected for the house which she and her children would occupy.

The fort had been built to withstand attack by Indians, but there had been no serious threat from the Creeks or the Western Cherokees for almost twenty years. After long, mutual harassment, treaties had been concluded. The whites received contracts to acquire land that comprised much of the present state of Tennessee—leaving what is now Alabama to the Creeks, and the land west of the Tennessee River to the Western Cherokees. In every instance the whites refused to honor the terms of those treaties. Long before the thirty-year scourge which ended so obscenely at Wounded Knee, the fate of the red man in North America had been sealed against him by white Europeans.

16

We do not know to what degree Sam Houston was aware of the plight of the Indians of the region during his first year in Tennessee. How, exactly, he came into contact initially with the Western Cherokee tribe that would play so important a part in his adolescent development and in his later career as well, is not known either.

The Houstons worked along with their slaves to clear their lands, to build their house and barns and slave quarters, to plant their fields, and to bring in the harvests. They added to their holdings of land and slaves. They prospered wonderfully. They mingled with other, longer-established settlers as well as with their Houston relations. A Paxton cousin had married another Houston and was living in Blount County, as were several former neighbors from Rockbridge County. The new life was demanding, but it was not lonely.

When Elizabeth Houston acquired an interest in the Maryville general store, she sent Sam to help his brothers John and James with its management. The boy had proved of little use on the plantation and showed little interest in retail merchandising. His nature seemed exceptionally perverse to his mother and older brothers. They could detect in his attitudes and behavior something of his father, whom they had respected and loved but affectionately despaired of in terms of practical achievement.

Hours when he was not in the store were passed at Porter Academy, just opened. As a student he was no better there than he had been at Timber Ridge. Casually kept records suggest that he passed no examinations whatever. He remained a faithful reader, however, and particularly treasured Pope's translation of *The Iliad*, which he had almost memorized by the time he was fifteen. He later claimed that he renounced formal learning at Porter Academy because it offered him no opportunity to study the classics, an allegation refuted by the records. Absorption of *The Iliad* was not the type of accomplishment deemed to be of great value in a wilderness area where literacy was scorned as useless to the principal concerns of most whites—survival and the expansion of one's holdings by whatever means possible.

Toward the end of his sixteenth year, Sam began to disappear, sometimes absenting himself for days. When he returned, he explained that he had wished to devote himself to uninterrupted reading. His mother reproached him for his refusal to do the work expected of him.

He was not intimidated. He was also annoyed by complaints from his brothers, who reasonably contended that since he was a shareholder in all the Houston enterprises, according to the terms of their father's will, he should not neglect his obligations. Houston's streak of obstinacy now manifested itself much more strongly than it had ever done before the major's death. The young alien became a rebel, and at sixteen, the adolescent had become a man.

Doubtless the mutual hostility that characterized family relations at this time accounted for Sam Houston's eventual rejection of all significant ties with his immediate family, even with his mother whom he so warmly portrayed in his memoirs. Later, during the period of his political prominence in Tennessee, he bestowed no favors on his brothers, and there is no record of his having more than casual communication with his mother, who survived into the 1830's. It was in Sam Houston's nature neither to forgive nor forget their reluctance to accept him as he was.

The Tennessee setting in which he was asked to conform was a rough one, plainly no place for a youth who was steeping himself in classical literature. But Sam Houston was exceptional physically as well as in his literary tastes. He was very tall, especially for the time. One report stated his height to be six feet six inches—about four inches taller than the notation in his passport and military records. He was fair-skinned, with russet hair, pale blue eyes, and rather soft, blurred features. He later described himself as having been at this time "wild and impetuous, but spotted by no crime."[6]

Explanations and descriptions of the youth are sparse and unreliable. Those who knew him well either did not write about him, or what they wrote was pious and dutiful and thus of dubious value, for by the time they got around to committing their memories of him to print, Sam Houston was a greatly celebrated figure. His enemies, of which he made many, were so virulent in their assaults on his nature that they are even less credible than his friends.[7]

Sam himself, in a political autobiography which he composed with the aid of journalist C. Edwards Lester, did not deign to speculate much about his childhood beyond the obvious and superficial. Consequently one remains perplexed by this lad of sixteen, as he was on the point of departing for the first major adventure of a long and adventurous life. All the facets of his character were now fairly well established—the soldier, the romantic lover, the land speculator, the lawyer, the politician, and the statesman he was to become. These qualities manifested themselves through an act of rebellion which he committed in the winter of 1809: the first of a prolonged series of self-exiles among the Cherokee.

II

S AM HOUSTON left behind no note when he slipped away from
Maryville, no explanation of his flight. On previous disap-
pearances, he had found refuge in the dense woodlands that lay not far
from his home, accompanied only by a volume of literature or ancient
history. He lived off the land. This time, however, as winter gave way
to spring, he had been absent two months before any word was
received of his whereabouts. White trappers who had been poaching
on Cherokee lands reported that Sam was living in the village of Chief
Oolooteka, near the point where the swollen, surging Tennessee River
converged with the lesser and muddier Hiwassee, which carried off the
thawed snows of the Great Smokies.

The youth's immediate desire had been simply to escape. He had
given no thought to any long-range plan, and certainly not to the social
or political implications of his visit with the Indians. There is no
evidence to suggest that he intended to become a "squaw man." By
1809 that style of life had fallen into disrepute among the civilizing
whites of the frontier. They no longer perceived the value of a
miscegenating white trader infiltrating Indian tribes for purposes of
subversion. Everywhere along the borders, the Indians were menaced
by the settlers, and yet, perversely, it was the Indians who were treated
as menaces.

Indian resistance, which mainly took the form of lightning raids, was
considered cruel and without provocation. Thus did settlers project
upon the Indians the vice of which they were themselves far guiltier. By
1809 this was an ugly, old story. To evince concern for the plight of the

Indians or for their rights was to invite the white man's scorn. To choose to live among them was to behave most bizarrely. How had Sam Houston come first to respect the Cherokees and, eventually, to take up residence among them? There is no conclusive answer, but it seems that he chose life among the Indians because Maryville had little to offer him. To his white contemporaries, this choice was undoubtedly degrading to his class and to his race.

Of all the tribes still located in the Southwest at that time, the Cherokees were the most adjusted to the customs of the whites. In the previous century they had done their best to accommodate themselves to the first Europeans to intrude upon their wilderness. Mainly Scotch and Irish, these visitors had been welcomed and soon found themselves folded into both the eastern and western branches of the great Cherokee family. By the beginning of the nineteenth century there had been so much intermarriage that even Cherokee chiefs were crossbreed descendants of the first whites.

Although the natives with whom Sam Houston now dwelt did not behave exactly according to precepts decreed by the intrusive settlers who lived just across the Tennessee, they tended to follow at least some of the proposed guidelines. They had become increasingly agrarian, because the game on their lands had been appallingly depleted by the white man's commercial hunting and trapping enterprises. Their dress was an odd combination of native and alien styles. Also, the chiefs and lesser leaders were often slaveholders in this period, the slaves being blacks who had been bartered for pelts or crops.

The Indians were hard though sporadic drinkers. While recent inquiries seem to dismiss the idea that they are peculiarly susceptible to alcoholism, it is known that whites induced them to deed away immense portions of their birthright while they were drunk. And in the evolution of America's genocidal policy toward the Indians, it became axiomatic that trade in spirts was dangerous (*after* they had been bilked of their land) because, when intoxicated, they became belligerent. For unscrupulous whites and half-breeds there was a lucrative traffic with the Indians in illicit spirits.

The natives had marijuana as an alternative source of pleasure. Whites used the fibrous stalks of this hemp for ropes on the boats that plied the lakes and rivers, but for the Indians the leaf rather than the stem was the object of interest. A much hardier plant than tobacco, marijuana was smoked in the ceremonial pipe, inducing the sort of

22

euphoria that undoubtedly is the source of the phrase "pipe of peace."

In 1809, the Cherokees understood well the precariousness of their position. The year before, Chief Oolooteka's brother, Tahlontusky, leader of another tribe of the western nation, had agreed to emigrate westward, to the Arkansas Territory (now Oklahoma) beyond the Mississippi, in exchange for promised indemnities of gold and trade. Oolooteka undoubtedly resented the transposition of his Cherokee name into English. He was known as John Jolly. It was degrading. It was meant to be. Oolooteka was a man of honor, good will, and forbearance, and he had every reason to see the whites as the scourge of the earth.

The boy of sixteen who made his appearance at the lodge of Oolooteka in the forest was welcomed, accepted, and soon made a full member of the tribe. He was awarded a Cherokee name, Colonneh—the Rover. (For unknown reasons Houston wrote that the meaning of his name was "Raven.") There was nothing extraordinary about this reception. The Western Cherokees had been as completely Europeanized as their eastern brothers. John Rogers, a Scotchman, had been one of the first "squaw men" of the American Southwest. He had taken Oolooteka's sister as his bride and got several children by her. Rogers' name was perpetuated in at least three of Sam's contemporaries—John, James, and Diana Rogers, all favorites of the chief. The boys became Houston's intimates, and the name of Rogers long endured. Will Rogers was proud of his Cherokee lineage.

According to Houston the early weeks in Oolooteka's lodge were idyllic. Writing three decades later he says he saw the Cherokees who had adopted him as incarnations of Rousseau's Noble Savage. He believed them to have been imbued with a clarity of vision unimpaired by the sophistications and sophistries that afflicted those descended purely from European stock. He was happier than he had ever been before.

His own brothers John and James were delegated by their mother to trudge to Oolooteka's wigwam to persuade the errant lad to return to his home. Houston's description of their meeting, in *The Only Authentic Memoir,* is too smug to be wholly dependable. He wrote that when his brothers made their appearance, he was lying beneath the boughs of a tree, reading Pope's *Iliad.* After hearing his mother's request, he claimed total preoccupation with a "translation from the Greek," and said he wanted to go on reading in peace. His brothers were not that easily put off. They persisted. Sam responded with derogatory comments on life at Maryville. He told them he "preferred measuring deer track to [measuring] tape." He liked "the wild liberty of the Red Man better than the tyranny of his brothers."

Choosing to overlook this outburst, John and James were confident that Sam would follow them back to Maryville. They were mistaken. He remained with Oolooteka's family for more than a year. Imaginative and alert, Sam Houston soon adapted many Indian customs and even mastered the Cherokee tongue. More relevant to his later life (and to the future of the tribe which had adopted him), he absorbed the psychology and philosophy of the Indian. He became son, brother, and friend. Eventually he would become the most outspoken, impatient, and implacable white advocate of the lost Indian cause in the United States in his own century. At perpetual peril to his political success, Houston remained faithful to the kinship engendered in his youth.

His return to Maryville, probably in the summer of 1810, was partly due to a desire to purchase gifts for the Cherokees and partly because of the same kind of impulse that had driven him from home—a surfeit, this time, of the quiet Cherokee life. He also had a natural curiosity about what might have gone on since his departure. The prodigal was warmly received. Mother and sisters, distressed by his threadbare state, made him new clothing before allowing him to visit Maryville.[1]

When he did go to town, however, his suitable dress failed to inhibit his conduct. With an older companion, John Cusack, he paid a long visit to the tavern, where both men got uproariously drunk. This was Sam Houston's first spree of public record. After leaving the tavern he and Cusack disrupted the drill of the local troop of militia, the Mounted Gunmen, by pounding loudly on a drum. They compounded this misdemeanor by resisting "with force . . . the Sheriff and Officer of the Court in the discharge of his duty. . . ." They had "transgressed against the peace and dignity of the State." Sobered up after a night in jail, they were released and brought to trial in the county court when it was next in session, September 29. Cusack was fined $10, Houston $5, fairly substantial penalties at the time. Cusack received the stiffer fine because he happened to be the commanding officer of the Mounted Gunmen whose parade he had interrupted. Both penalties were remitted when the court sat again.[2]

This casual brush with the law, and a general feeling of ennui with

24

civilization turned Sam Houston's eyes back toward the wilderness. With his presents and his new homespun suit, he returned to the Cherokees before the end of the year and remained with them until the autumn of 1811. He was as happy during his second visit as he had been in his first. Carrying himself "straight as an Indian," he continued to absorb the lore, the language, the mores, and the life-style of the Indians. They fully satisfied his adolescent passion for individuality within the framework of a code he could easily accept. While denying the authority of his family, which had been exerted without much effect, he willingly abided by the even stricter dicta of Oolooteka. In their later contacts, the chief and Houston maintained a relationship of respected parent and beloved son, though there were occasional lapses in the adopted child's decorum.

Later in 1811, despite his love for Cherokee ways, Sam was back in Maryville, again buying gifts, and again garbed in new clothing by his mother and sisters. This time he vowed to reside in the bosom of his family. However, he had a falling-out with his brothers over how he was to make himself useful and he was soon off once more across the Tennessee for a third long season with the Cherokees.[3]

In his nineteenth year, Sam Houston was a man by any standards. Strong and tall, fully accomplished in the Indians' methods of hunting, fishing, and trapping and also at their sports, he was also old enough to understand the sexual implications of the green-corn dance—a fertility rite performed in early summer by many tribes and taken very seriously. Population was an increasing problem among all the aboriginal nations. Because of conflict with the whites, they were becoming an endangered species. It is estimated, for instance, that Oolooteka's personal band totaled no more than three hundred. Yet this chief, in his forties now, was a highly respected sachem, a member of the Cherokee national council. He rarely attended annual meetings for he was convinced that no common Indian policy could prevail against the inexorable tide of whites who were fanning out in all directions from the Atlantic Seaboard. His advice to his own people was that they lie low, protect their lands as best they could in a peaceable way, and hope for the best—while expecting the worst.

We have an appealing self-portrait of young Sam Houston at about this time from *The Only Authentic Memoir:*

It was the moulding period of life, when the heart, just charmed into

25

the feverish hopes and dreams of youth, looks wistfully around on all things for light and beauty—"when every idea of gratification fires the blood and flashes on the fancy—when the heart is vacant to every fresh form of delight. . . ." The poets of Europe, fancying such scenes, have borrowed their sweetest images from the wild idolatry of the Indian maiden.[4]

The Indian maiden to whom so discreet an allusion is made was never named, but we may be certain she existed. Anxious to make a good impression on a nation which, he hoped, would name him to the Presidency of the United States, Senator Sam Houston of Texas left many shadows on his past in this account. He was not likely to scandalize his readers with tales of his first triflings with the heart of a woman. Yet it is virtually certain that his initiation occurred among the Cherokees, where such experiences were not frowned upon as they were at Maryville. Virginity was not considered important to the Indians and by 1812 Sam was more Indian than white. He undoubtedly accepted their sexual mores since he accepted their views about practically everything else. Polygamy was the rule of the Cherokees. Moreover, the line between promiscuity and polygamy was not sharply drawn. During the hunting seasons, braves abstained from sexual intercourse in the belief that it sapped their vigor. And in wartime they were celibate for the same reason. Though never at war during the period of Houston's long stays with them, the Cherokees were almost always hunting. Whether he followed the customs of his hosts in this respect or those of his own race is not known.

Apart from sharing hunting, sporting, and loving activities with the young Cherokees, he reported later that he helped to scout the subversive activities of Tecumseh, the Shawnee chief. After the death of his brother, Tenskwatawa, at the hands of American general William Henry Harrison at Tippecanoe in November, 1811, Tecumseh had gone to the Southwest seeking to ally the Cherokees and Creeks with the British-Canadians who knew that war with the United States was inevitable.

Tecumseh enjoyed no success in his effort to woo the Cherokees to the cause of Great Britain. They had seemingly been reconciled to life beside the American whites and could see no benefit in an alliance with the British. With the Creeks, however, the Shawnee chief was more successful. Though basically unfriendly to all whites, the Creeks found it easier to detest the Americans than the British or Spanish, for the Americans were nearer at hand and more threatening to the integrity of Creek territory.

Organization of relations between the United States and the Indians had yet to be established formally, though patterns were sufficiently set to be accurately predictable by the beginning of 1812. There were still no official trade agreements with the Western Cherokees. Trade in pelts was managed for Oolooteka's people by his nephew John Rogers, one of Sam Houston's closest friends. Having accompanied Rogers on some of his trading journeys, Houston acquired a familiarity with the Cherokees' problem that would serve both him and them well later on.

The young man had problems of his own. They came to a head early in 1812. He discovered that he owed $100 to Maryville merchants. Until he was able to meet these obligations, he could buy no more gifts to please his Cherokee friends. He observed in his memoirs that this was the reason for his third return to civilization. As he entered his twentieth year he had to find some means of gainful employment. His credentials were hardly dazzling, and the times were not propitious for job-hunting. Because employment was so difficult to find, Sam's older brother Robert had elected to follow his father's example by joining the Army. The Mounted Gunmen, still under the dubious leadership of Sam's erstwhile drinking companion, Captain John Cusack, were meeting more frequently. If war came, Maryville was determined to be ready.

Sam Houston was not in the least interested in pursuing a military career. He was not much more interested in work of any variety, but his financial situation demanded that he do something. He decided to open a school. His own education was not a very convincing recommendation to prospective pupils, but he was undeterred. The Houston name carried more weight than the most brilliant of scholastic records would have done.

His academy was to be situated about five miles from Maryville. He expected to attract children who found the daily journey to the county seat too taxing. He advertised that in May he would accept applicants for the sum of $8 per term, a tuition payable in equal parts of ready money, corn, and woven cotton material. The first and only session of Sam Houston's school opened on schedule. The term was to end in November, with the beginning of winter.

The school was housed in a log cabin. Although the venture seemed financially questionable it proved more of a success than the novice schoolmaster had dreamed. He had more applicants than he was able to accommodate, demonstrating the truth of the adage about the country of the blind where the one-eyed man is king. With little systematic schooling behind him, Sam Houston could only have given instruction on the most rudimentary level. His surviving letters, the first of them dating to 1813, reveal him to have been a most uncertain speller, an eccentric punctuator, but a potentially colorful stylist. But at least he knew more than his charges.[5]

Houston's school had been operating little more than a month when it was learned at Maryville that the United States had at last declared war against Great Britain. The news was jubilantly received. Felix Grundy, a Tennessee Congressman, had been a "War Hawk" leader. As the month of July began, Governor Willie Blount issued a proclamation asking that all able-bodied men volunteer for service in one of the two militia divisions being raised in East and West Tennessee. The men who enlisted gave the state its nickname, "Volunteer." Sam Houston was not among them, because patriotism would not excuse a man from his financial obligations. Besides, he felt a moral responsibility to complete the school term he had begun. His concerns, at the war's outset, were still purely personal.

However, he was surrounded by the intemperate rhetoric that accompanies the beginnings of all wars. The Major General of Tennessee, Andrew Jackson—politician, lawyer, and judge, as well as professional soldier—published a typically inflammatory statement:

> There is not one individual among the Volunteers who would not prefer perishing on the field of battle . . . than to return . . . covered with shame, ignominy, and disgrace! Perish our friends—perish our wives—perish our CHILDREN . . . nay, perish . . . every earthly consideration! But let the honor and name of the Volunteer service be untarnished.[6]

In homespun garments of dark blue or nut brown, or in buckskins, Captain Cusack's Mounted Gunmen were incorporated into the Eastern Division of the Volunteers and readied themselves for the honorable death to which Jackson's exhortation had invited them.

They marched off to Natchez, where they arrived early in the fall of 1812 to find that no enemy awaited them. What they discovered, instead, was the massive insufficiency of all kinds of supplies that resulted from the Army's dependence on civilian contractors. The demoralization of both Tennessee divisions was severe. No company's officers could predict, from one reveille to the next, how many of their men would be present. Desertion reached epidemic proportions. Morale was not greatly improved in that first autumn of the war by reports of British-Canadian-Indian military successes in the North.

The American record during the war's first year was not marked by a single significant triumph. Usually the Yankees surrendered in great numbers all along the boundary between the United States and Canada. The political, military, and logistical incompetence demonstrated by American officers and greedy civilians at every level, on sea well as land, was devastating.[7]

At the conclusion of Sam Houston's term as proprietor of a school, he realized his shortcomings as a teacher and decided that he had better try to perfect himself before proceeding further. With his debts paid and a modest cash surplus in hand, he enrolled once again at Porter Academy. His explanation was that he wanted to master mathematics in order to qualify for a commission in the Army—the first indication that he had such an aspiration. Unfortunately he boggled at the initial geometry problem handed him. He later observed that he found the subject "uninspiring."[8]

Isaac Anderson, senior master at Porter Academy, reminisced about Sam Houston as a student: "I often determined to lick him, but he could come up with such a pretty dish of excuses that I could not do it." It was not the first time, nor would it be the last, when Sam's charm carried him through. Exactly how long he stayed at Porter Academy is undetermined, but the date of his enlistment in the regular Army was March 1, 1813. He turned twenty the next day.[9]

The procedure for joining was not elaborate. A recruiting officer harangued anyone who would listen about the glories of military life. Accompanying him were a drummer and a bugler, sometimes a piper. On the head of the drum were some silver dollars. To take one of these signified one's intention to enlist. Sam Houston took a coin. Because he was a minor, he had to seek his mother's permission. We must assume she gave it with mixed feelings—relief and anxiety.

An anecdote recounted in *The Only Authentic Memoir* refers to this occasion. Elizabeth Houston, on learning of Sam's decision to enlist, presented him with a plain gold ring on whose interior surface was engraved the single word, "Honor." She placed it on his finger with the admonition that he wear it forever after. Houston recorded that this incident revealed everything about his mother and her hopes for him. Honor must always be for him the first and overriding consideration. He promised to obey her instructions. He was determined to return to her covered with glory.

Before the end of April, 1813, Sam Houston was a sergeant assigned to the 7th Infantry Regiment stationed at Knoxville. By mid-September, he was an ensign and transferred to the 39th Infantry.[10] Thus, in little more than a year, he had left the tranquil wilderness of the Cherokees, where he had been free from all of the white man's burdens, and entered the disciplined ranks of the regular Army—a transition experienced by the Western Cherokees themselves, whose position shifted from one of cautious neutrality to active belligerence, as allies of the United States. Oolooteka and the other sachems of that nation had reluctantly concluded that self-interest dictated this commitment. A group of Cherokee warriors affiliated themselves with Andrew Jackson's divisions. Half-breeds John and James Rogers served in these ranks as scouts.

Writing of this experience, Sam Houston asserted that concern for the safety of his country was the major factor contributing to his enlistment. However, reflections of this kind, especially when composed for political purposes, are suspect—particularly in the case of Sam Houston. For there is little in the meager record to suggest a budding soldier-patriot.

His rise through the ranks to officer status is much less surprising than his determination to enlist. He undoubtedly stood out, literally and figuratively, from the other recruits with whom he trained at Fort Hampton, near Knoxville. He was agile and physically courageous. He looked like a leader and, when the opportunity presented itself, he behaved like one.[11]

III

FIVE DAYS after the United States had made a formal declaration of war, the British (unaware of the declaration) agreed to stop the practices to which America took such vigorous exception. By July this modification of policy was known in Washington. Thus, the reasons for the war had been eliminated before a major military encounter took place. But there were other compelling grievances that had not been mentioned in the declaration of war. The conflict went on because American policy makers believed it would yield more land. The War Hawks imagined that Canada would want to become an American dependency; all that was required was the opportunity to sever the tie with Britain. And, of course, territorial aggrandizement by whatever means at the expense of the Indian—the policy followed by all white immigrants to North America since the sixteenth century— was the true cause of the War of 1812.

One of the main conflicts in the Southwest was with the Creek Indians over possession of what amounted to most of modern-day Alabama. Under the terms of a treaty duly ratified by both parties, the land was indisputably Creek. The Indians were angrily bewildered by the constant intrusion of whites on their preserves. The poachers themselves completely disregarded the terms of the treaty which specifically prohibited their activities.

Not nearly so docile as the Cherokees, the Creeks had resisted American infiltration with ferocity. With the help of Tecumseh they had come to an understanding with the British-Canadians that committed them to war against the United States in exchange for arms and military advice. The tribe was known to its enemies as the "Red Stick," a name based on the symbol of Creek hostility, a crimson-dyed war club. Under the command of Bill Weatherford, a half-breed, they had risen against any further American invasion of their lands. Minor skirmishes along the borders had sent white squatters scurrying to safety.

On August 30, 1813, Weatherford enacted a gruesome massacre of retribution on a settlement of whites at Fort Mims (now in Alabama). Though reports differ as to the numbers scalped and slaughtered, it was at least 400. The massacre galvanized the citizens of the Southwest and the troops under General Andrew Jackson. Jackson pursued Weatherford's Creeks and caught up with them on four occasions in the fall of 1813, gaining tactical victories twice and twice being fought to a draw by the frenzied Indians. With about 2,500 volunteers to the enemy's 1,000, the American general was made to appear inept. An additional recruitment of 5,000 troops was called for. These new men, however, were slow to reach their various rallying points. When they did, they were as inadequate as the volunteer officers who led them. These officers were mainly bankrupted gentlemen, hardly competent to train and discipline such a rabble. Also, Jackson was ill for much of the time during this campaign, and the results were discouraging.[1]

Shortly after his elevation to the rank of ensign, Sam Houston was made third lieutenant in the 39th Infantry, a unit that had yet to see action. The commander was Colonel John Williams, a man in his thirties who would become a United States Senator from Tennessee immediately after the war. Second in command was Lieutenant Colonel Thomas Hart Benton, who later moved to Missouri where he distinguished himself as a Senator. Benton could not have looked forward to the prospect of service under Jackson. He and his brother had quite recently been involved in a near-murderous tavern encounter with the hot-tempered Jackson over some ill-considered observation about the sanctity of Jackson's marital state. Both of the Bentons had been severely injured and Jackson still suffered from the wound Tom Benton had inflicted on him. However, personalities were to be set aside for the duration of the war.[2]

On February 3, 1814, the 39th Infantry entered Fort Strother, and there Sam Houston first set eyes on the man who would become his second foster father, Andrew Jackson. Jackson saw the arrival of this regular Army unit as much-needed reinforcements for his faltering mob of volunteers. Houston saw the chance to prove himself at last in actual combat.

The most pressing task of Houston's regiment was not to make war against the Creeks, but to help restore discipline among the intractable militia companies. The presence of regulars gave Jackson a chance to offer a strong demonstration of authority. He ordered the summary execution of a volunteer found guilty of deserting his post. This gesture greatly impressed Sam Houston.[3]

In the middle of March Jackson moved his force out of Fort Strother. Ten days of hard trudging across nearly fifty miles of Creek wilderness brought the troops to a place which the Indians called Tohopeka, a sharp bend in the Tallapoosa River which is known to history as Horseshoe Bend. Two thousand whites were deployed there for a battle which took place March 27. Jackson's artillery consisted of two small cannons. These opened fire at ten in the morning, but they were completely ineffectual against the green-log fortifications that Weatherford had hastily erected. The futile barrage was soon suspended.

There followed a pause which lasted for about two hours—a period arranged by mutual consent to allow the Creeks to evacuate their women and children from the hundred-acre battle area. Just after noon, the battle resumed. The regulars of the 39th Regiment were the first to try to storm the enemy battlements. Tradition has it that the officer who led this assault was Major Lemuel P. Montgomery (a Tennessean after whom the Alabama city was named). He was killed the moment he made his appearance over the top of the rampart.[4]

Immediately behind him came Third Lieutenant Sam Houston, his sword in the air. He cleared the top of the fortifications and jumped down into the howling Creeks, flailing his weapon about him. An arrow had pierced his groin as he was coming over the barricade. Soon this injury caused him to stumble and fall. While the fighting raged above him, Houston tried to extract the arrow. Unable to, he called to a fellow officer and pointing to the barbed shaft, he begged the man to pull it out so he could continue the fight. With great reluctance the man tried to help, but failed. He told the badly wounded Houston that he should seek aid from the regimental surgeon. However, at Houston's angry insistence (at sword's point, according to Houston's version of this incident), the officer yanked the arrow out. This resulted in such a

33

great flow of blood that Houston, clutching the gash with both hands, staggered off in search of medical assistance.

When the Creeks had been compelled to abandon most of their positions, Jackson regrouped his forces, jubilant in the certainty that he had an important victory in his grasp. As he moved from company to company inspecting and praising his men, he came upon the wounded figure of Sam Houston, his injury sufficiently bound to stop the bleeding. After learning of the young officer's condition and the circumstances in which he had been injured, Jackson warned him to give up all further combat for the day. Houston ignored these instructions. In his memoirs he stated that he might have been less reckless had he not vowed to his mother to make an account of himself before returning to Maryville.

By two in the afternoon, the Creeks had split themselves into small groups. Refusing to concede defeat, Weatherford ordered his braves to harass Jackson's flanks with bow and arrow and then retreat into the thick undergrowth on the fringes on the battleground.

Houston reported that "Not a [single Creek] warrior offered to surrender, even while the sword was at his throat." Sheer force of numbers prevailed. Jackson finally ordered a halt in the action at three. He sent an emissary to Weatherford with the message that all who gave themselves up would be disarmed and paroled to their homes, provided they promise not to fight the Americans again. The offer was refused. A fanatical passion possessed the Creeks. They were determined to repel the whites, once and for all, or die in the attempt.

Near dusk, all resistance had ceased except from a single improvised blockhouse at the base of a sharp declivity. Once more, Jackson offered the holdouts a chance to save their own lives by surrender. Once more they declined. He then requested volunteers to storm this final pocket of resistance. Sam Houston limped forward, his leg stiffened from the wound he had sustained only a few hours earlier. He placed himself at the head of a volunteer platoon and led it down the bank toward the Creeks. Without looking back, the tall young officer charged forward. He got to within a few yards of the prize when the enemy opened fire. One musket ball smashed a bone of his right forearm. Another lodged in the flesh of his right shoulder. The pain was excruciating, yet he managed to continue his solitary assault. Turning to encourage his platoon, he discovered no one near him. He wheeled about and stumbled back up the side of the ridge. When he reached the crest,

34

where Jackson had been looking on, much impressed by Houston's courage, he fell at last and lost consciousness. Asking the officer's name, the general promoted him on the spot to the rank of second lieutenant.[5]

While Houston was borne off on a litter to the surgeon, Jackson ordered flaming arrows and hot shot directed at the blockhouse. The Battle of Horseshoe Bend was over. Andrew Jackson had his salutary victory.

A formal peace treaty, by which the Creeks ceded two-thirds of their lands to the United States, was not concluded until August, but at least this aspect of the shoddy war was ended. It was the first of Jackson's two major triumphs and militarily the more important, since it ended the Creek alliance with the British. However, the general was to be far better remembered for his success at New Orleans, a battle that occurred three weeks after the terms of the Treaty of Ghent had been settled.[6]

The war was already over for Sam Houston. His very survival was something of a miracle. It is not documented that he actually received professional attention during the days immediately after the Battle of Horseshoe Bend and he himself has no memory of those days, for he was frequently unconscious. The morning after, he was carried to Fort Williams, sixty miles from the Tohopeka battle site. Since most other casualties had been taken to Fort Jackson, somewhat nearer, there is speculation that Houston's body may have been overlooked in the confusion and transported in a different direction before the mistake had been detected. He was accompanied on this long and uncomfortable journey by a pair of youthful militia officers who could have known nothing about medicine. Ironically, Houston benefited as a result, because if a doctor had attended him, his right arm might have been amputated.

More than a week passed before Houston was placed in a rustic field hospital in East Tennessee. His injuries were not treated much during the fortnight he spent there, but during this time he was surely proffered at least one of the two universal anodynes—raw whiskey or laudanum. He was delirious some of the time, and unable to keep down much of the barely adequate nourishment offered him. In early May, however, his condition had improved. He had managed to stay alive for six weeks. Then he began the arduous trip to Maryville, borne on a crude litter.[7] By the time he was carried to the door of his mother's

35

house at Baker's Creek, nearly two months had elapsed since the agonies of Horseshoe Bend. Elizabeth Houston had difficulty believing that this emaciated figure was the robust son who had left her fourteen months before. A "wonted expression" about his eyes was all she recognized.

In June he was sufficiently strong to go to Knoxville to consult a physician. When he arrived, he was so drained by the short trip from Maryville that the doctor discouraged him from seeking treatment on the ground that he did not have long to live. There was no point in incurring a debt that his next of kin must settle. Knoxville was not large enough to support a second doctor so Houston rented a room and rested there for two weeks. When he returned to be examined again, the physician found him improved and therefore more eligible for treatment—especially since it was now possible he would live to pay his own bill. But it is problematical whether it was the medical care or his own body's self-curative powers that restored Houston to comparative good health.

After three months at Knoxville, he left for Washington. He was still in considerable pain, but he had regained enough of his strength to make the long trip to the capital. There he hoped to obtain medical assistance from the Army. Along the way, he paused to visit relatives and friends in Virginia. When he reached Washington, he found its principal public buildings to be burned-out shells. After a brief, fierce campaign, the British had taken possession of the capital in late August and sacked it. The destruction of Washington, which was intended to break America's resolve to continue the war, had no appreciable effect on American policy makers. What disturbed them more was mounting evidence of discord among their own countrymen.

Throughout eastern New York and New England, protests against the war were increasingly shrill and well organized. The lure of land, which still fired frontier Americans, could not offset, in the eyes of most Easterners, the loss of revenue and the rise in unemployment that had resulted from the British blockade of American shipping.

When Sam Houston saw the ruin of Washington, his "blood boiled" and he "was occasioned the keenest pangs" that he "should be disabled at such a moment."[8] He may have been in the capital when news arrived of threats by representatives of New England states to secede from the Union if the war were not ended immediately. To a resident of a frontier state, such talk was incomprehensible. Before the end of

36

the year the convention of New Englanders at Hartford proposed stringent restrictions on federal power that would have made the government as weak as the Confederation that had proved unworkable in the first years of the Republic's existence.

A major element of Sam Houston's political philosophy was his abiding conviction in the need to preserve the Union. This was probably engendered during this visit to Washington. Discouraged by all he learned there, he turned back toward home, his wounds troubling him still, despite the care of the Army's best doctors. He was at Maryville by Christmastime.

Nearly two months later he learned that on Christmas Eve, at Ghent, American and British diplomats had concluded the draft of a peace treaty. By its terms the United States had lost the war. No mention was made of the complaints uttered so loudly thirty months before. Not a single acre of British or Canadian soil became American. Only the territory ceded by the Creeks could be regarded as a clear gain. Against this must be set the disproportionately high human and material sacrifices made for the cause. Also, the suspicions and hostilities generated by the unpopularity of the war in the North was reflected increasingly in North-South relations, which became more antagonistic during the next forty-five years. This disharmony of economic, political, and social interests led directly to the division of the Union in 1860.

With the war over, Sam Houston had anxieties about his future. The alternatives to continued military service were few and unpromising. He had already shown his inadequacies as a schoolmaster. He knew he would be even unhappier as a planter or shopkeeper. A profession demanded further education. In early March, from Maryville, he wrote his Congressman, John Rhea, and his Senator, Joseph Anderson, and the Secretary of War, James Monroe, to ask their assistance in keeping his commission in the regular Army. To Rhea he said, "I have fought & bled for my country in consequence of which I am in measure unfit for other business."[9] Whether as the result of these letters or the command decision of Andrew Jackson, Houston was retained in the Army. However, official notice to this effect was slow in reaching him and in the meantime, he had no illusions that his position was safe.

On April 25 he wrote his old friend Alexander Campbell of Rockbridge County that he did not yet know his fate. If he were demobilized, he thought he would remain in Knoxville, where he was currently stationed, "for it will be proper for me to pursue some course from a livelihood which will not be laborious as my wounds are not near well, and I suppose it will be impractical for a disbanded officer to marry, for [ex-officers] will be regarded as cloathes, out of fashion . . . I will not court any of the Dear Girles before I make a fortune. . . ." He expressed reluctant gratification over the news of peace, which he did not think dishonorable, but admitted that many officers would have preferred the war to continue. ". . . I would not want peace if I did not believe it was promoting the happiness of the community at large, but at any time I am willing to sacrifice my wish to the welfare of the Republic. . . ."[10] The man who carried this letter to Campbell was Robert McEwen, Houston's Tennessee cousin who became one of his most intimate friends.

Although the 39th Infantry was demobilized, Houston was finally offered a second lieutenancy in the 1st Infantry, then garrisoned at New Orleans. He was informed of his new status May 17. After equipping himself at Nashville, he set out with Edward Douglas White, a recent graduate of Nashville University, on a flatboat which took them as far as Natchez. There they boarded a paddle-wheeled steamer for the remainder of the journey to Louisiana. New Orleans was the most cosmopolitan city of the South, long the principal trading and port center of the region. Its reputation for gaiety and social activity made Houston look forward to his arrival. He was less pleased by the prospect of another operation on his shoulder to remove a musket ball which had been overlooked by surgeons who had previously treated him.[11]

This was not his only problem. There was a disagreement with the War Department over the effective date of his promotion to the rank of second lieutenant in 1814. In mid-February of 1816, he wrote a courteous but defensive letter to William H. Crawford, Secretary of War. After describing his feats at Horseshoe Bend, he referred Crawford to Andrew Jackson as witness to his courage and to the date of his commission. He concluded: "My reasons for not refering you to my former Col Williams . . . are He has ever been inimical to me, since I have joined the [39th] Regiment he has written letters to officers . . . calculated to prejudice them against me."[12] Why Colonel Williams was "inimical" to Houston is not certain, though his anger may have been owing to the interest Andrew Jackson had expressed in the young officer. The dispute over back pay was never satisfactorily resolved.

Before he heard from Crawford, Houston was sent to New York for further treatment of the shoulder injury. The doctors in the North removed the musket ball, but the healing was never complete. After recovering from the operation, Houston was furloughed home, arriving at Maryville in the summer of 1816. He stayed there long enough to fall in love with one of the "Dear Girles" before his fortune and position were firmly established. When he was summoned to Nashville to serve in the division commanded by Andrew Jackson, he was virtually, if not formally, engaged to marry a young woman whose identity remains concealed. In correspondence she is referred to only as "M——."[13]

He made the journey to Nashville just after Christmas. He was pleased to find himself serving again with the man he so admired. Whether it was the change of scene or merely absence, Sam Houston had second thoughts about marrying the mysterious "M——" from Blount County. Because of his wounds, which still caused him pain, he was assigned to the office of the divisional adjutant, where he became acquainted with the rudiments of paperwork, a talent which would be very useful to him in later years. In May, 1817, he was promoted to first lieutenant.[14]

Predictably enough, Houston was soon restive in this sedentary military life. He wanted either to move onward and upward or to get out of the Army. On the other hand, his conversations with General Jackson were useful to both men. They became more familiar and finally quite close to each other. Houston described his early years among the Western Cherokees, a topic which held much interest at that time for Old Hickory and for the War Department. The year before, Oolooteka and other chiefs of that branch of the Cherokee nation had signed a treaty by which they agreed to exchange all their holdings on the Tennessee River for land west of the Mississippi, in the Arkansas Territory. The Indians were now expressing doubts. They had been hearing of the difficulties encountered in the West by their brothers who had gone that way in 1808 under the leadership of Tahlontusky. The Indian Affairs Office of the War Department had repeatedly refused to honor the terms of the bargain.

Later in May, Return J. Meigs, a white Indian agent, wrote Jackson of plans for a parley with Oolooteka's tribe which, he was convinced, would go badly unless some regular Army troops were nearby.[15] He specifically recommended, as well, that Sam Houston attend the conference, since he was still greatly respected by Oolooteka. Jackson did not react hastily to Meigs' suggestion, though Houston would have welcomed an immediate order to leave Nashville. Not only was he bored with his bureaucratic chores, he was embarrassingly embroiled with "M——" from Blount County.

In early June he received a letter from a Maryville friend, Jesse Beene, to whom he had entrusted the thankless task of breaking off the engagement:

> When you cease to love her your heart will become vitrified & a marriage with any other person will be for *convenience* and not for happiness. . . . [She is] ready to leave mother home friends and every thing dear to her, and forsake them all, and go with you to the earth's remotest bounds. . . . I know you & I know that J. Beene is your friend & if I were to advise you it would be to marry M—— by moonshine or any other way the most handy. . . . *Weigh well the verdict you are about to pronounce.*[16]

Houston did not return to Maryville, in spite of his friend's suggestion, and so ended the first of what he later called his "love scrapes." He suffered for an inordinately long time from loving neither wisely nor too well.

Soon after receiving Beene's letter, Houston applied for reassignment outside of Tennessee. He remained at Nashville for some time, though his request would eventually be granted. He had time to join the Masons, but his motives seem to have been mainly social, not religious.[17] In the fall, Jackson asked the new Secretary of War, John C. Calhoun, to give Houston the assignment for which he was ideally suited—agent to the Cherokees of Oolooteka's band. His assignment was to persuade them of the necessity to leave as soon as possible for their new homeland across the Mississippi.

If he had any sense of being ordered to betray his friendship with the Cherokees, Houston did not admit to this in any surviving document. Despite the hardening experiences he had suffered, he had no way of foreseeing the grim consequences of the instructions he had received from Jackson. He left Nashville with the certainty that his Indian friends would be better off in the West, where there would be fewer whites to harass them.

In early November he was with Oolooteka, who welcomed him warmly. Houston's orders were to see that the Indians move from the lands they had signed away. He saw that he would have little difficulty persuading his foster father to make the desired relocation. The Western Cherokees departed soon afterwards, led by a party of thirty-one under John Rogers. It seemed to occur to no one—certainly not Houston himself—that the territory "given" to the Cherokees in exchange was already claimed by other Indian nations. Soon after his arrival, a second agreement was reached providing for substantial federal assistance to the Cherokees for their trip west. Though nominally representing the government, Houston sought every advantage for his departing friends. His influence made this contract the most favorable to the Indians of any negotiated in this period.[18]

At the end of November, 1817, Tennessee's governor, Joseph McMinn, wrote Secretary of War Calhoun that another group of Western Cherokees, led by Tahlontusky (already settled for nearly a decade in the Arkansas Territory), had arrived at Lookout Mountain bound for Washington to discuss the government's persistent refusal to honor the terms of an agreement made in 1808.[19] Sam Houston was ordered by McMinn and Andrew Jackson to join this delegation on their trip to the national capital, acting as guide and interpreter. Two months were to elapse before the group arrived at Washington.[20]

IV

HOUSTON REACHED Knoxville in early January, where he joined the Tahlontusky group and learned of their grievances. In essence, they were twofold: The treaty of 1808 had been negotiated with the entire Cherokee nation, whose principal territory was in Georgia. All annuities paid by the United States for the removal of the Tahlontusky tribe had been, in effect, paid to the eastern branch. Little of the promised gold had reached those who had made the sacrifice of evacuating their ancestral home. Tahlontusky sought government approval of his plan to secede from the Cherokee nation, thus to assure direct payment of the moneys due them. The second problem lay in the West. Tahlontusky's Cherokees found formidable resistance from the Indians already there. He wanted government assistance to assure tranquility among the nations settled in the Arkansas Territory.

He made a good impression on Governor McMinn, who wrote, "I hazard nothing that he is considered in the light of a king among his people." Such a conclusion did not prevent the governor from presuming that judicious bribery would resolve the problems. He felt, nevertheless, that the delegation deserved a full hearing in the capital. He succeeded in delaying the party at Knoxville for more than a month while he briefed Lieutenant Sam Houston on his mission. During this time McMinn came to admire him.

When he joined the Indian group, Houston donned full Cherokee regalia (adding some embellishments of his own), and in this colorful garb he led the delegation out of Knoxville in the middle of January. He was in much pain at the time, for his shoulder wound had

43

developed an abscess, but Houston had become accustomed to pain. The ceremonial leave-taking inspired McMinn to describe the party in another letter to Calhoun as "the equal, in point of respectability of Character, of appearance and Dress to any other I have ever seen of the Indian Tribes."

While Tahlontusky's people made their way to Washington, Oolooteka affixed his mark to a "memorial" addressed to Calhoun in which he abjectly assented to the government's demands. But he added proudly, "You must not think by removing we shall return to savage life. You have taught us to be Herdsmen and cultivators. . . . Our women will raise the cotton and the Indigo and spin and weave cloth to cloath our children. Numbers of our young people can read and write, they can read what they call the Preachers book. . . . By intermarriage with our white brethren we are gradually becoming one people." Though Houston was well on his way to the national capital when this document was sent to the Secretary of War, it is fairly certain he influenced its composition. In fact some of his biographers believe him to be its author.

By the end of January Oolooteka led the main party of his tribe, about 350 in all, on the first leg of the long trip to the Arkansas Territory. But three years later the younger John Rogers was still petitioning the government for reimbursement of expenses incurred in taking the Cherokee vanguard west. And as Sam Houston himself later discovered, the War Department was just as frivolous about keeping its word to Oolooteka as it had been with Tahlontusky.

John C. Calhoun was a gentleman from South Carolina fired by political ambition. However, his courtliness of manner gave him unusual distinction and his greeting of Tahlontusky and his group at the recently refurbished White House reflected his talent for courteous condescension. He explained that the government wanted nothing so much as the complete satisfaction of all Indian grievances. He was sure that the President, who awaited them in an adjoining room, would work things out to the pleasure of all sides. As Tahlontusky and his personal retinue prepared to leave for their first interview with the Great White Father, Houston was brusquely detained by Calhoun, who furiously demanded an explanation of the extraordinary attire he was wearing—buckskins and a Cherokee blanket, topped off by feathered headgear—hardly the uniform of a lieutenant on active duty.

It *was* bizarre. Houston attempted to explain that his appearance had not been inspired by a desire to make a spectacle of himself. By emulating the dress of the Cherokees, he had hoped to improve his effectiveness as an ambassador to the Indians. Calhoun was not convinced by the explanation and ordered Houston to change into regulation dress before making another public appearance.

Increasingly garbled accounts of this meeting were to haunt Houston for the rest of his life. Chafing under the Secretary's harshness of manner, he joined Tahlontusky and the other Cherokees in the next room for what was a merely formal reception by President Monroe. The nettled Houston was not eager to prolong the visit. Subsequent exchanges between the Cherokees and the War Department were conducted without his aid.[1]

The government's bargaining methods were callous but effective. Tahlontusky accepted a bribe of $1,000 in gold for his promise not to press his cause any further. Each of his Indian companions received $500. They were to return to the Arkansas Territory and keep their peace and that was that. For Sam Houston, however, there was more humiliation in store. About ten days after his first interview with Calhoun, he was summoned to the Secretary's presence to be informed that he had been charged with trafficking in black slaves during his parleys with Oolooteka the previous November. Specifically, he was supposed to have conspired with a group of white smugglers who were transporting slaves from Georgia and Florida for sale in the border states.[2]

The facts were inadequately documented, consisting wholly of second-hand evidence whose source, as it turned out, was the smugglers themselves, whose operations Houston had made an abortive effort to halt. Preoccupied with his dealings with the Indians, he had failed to report the incident to Washington. His accusers, resentful of his attempt to block the trade, had decided on the strategy of charging Houston with the crimes they were committing.[3]

Houston's reaction was one of shock and bitterness. After protesting his innocence to Calhoun, whom he regarded as his enemy, he took his case to the President. Despite the bad feelings, the Secretary of War was a punctiliously honorable man. He vowed an immediate investigation. It developed that the Senator who had lodged the complaint was in league with the smugglers, and within a fortnight Houston's name was cleared.

But total vindication was not enough for him. He wanted all who had borne false witness against him called to account. Had the charges been allowed to stand, he told Calhoun, his career could have been ruined. He wished to be congratulated publicly for having exposed the actual wrongdoers. He wanted an apology in writing from the War Department for the insult so gratuitously and impulsively offered him. He failed in these demands. Senators, for all practical purposes, were above the law and government departments rarely admit their mistakes.[4]

He was enraged, but he did not wholly lose his head. Throughout the month of February he continued to advise Tahlontusky. Only when the negotiations reached their final stage did Houston take the only action he felt appropriate.[5] On March 1, 1818, he composed a one-line letter of resignation from the Army effective at once.[6] He persisted in holding Calhoun personally responsible for the failure to secure complete and honorable satisfaction. In all his future dealings with the man who would be Vice President under Andrew Jackson, Houston was invariably hostile.

Before leaving Washington Houston saw to it that Tahlontusky and his friends were adequately provisioned for their 2,000-mile trip back home. An interesting but unverifiable footnote to his dealings with the War Department credits him with assisting another Cherokee chief, "The Bowl" (as he was called by the whites), in securing a patent to an 1,800-square-mile tract in Texas, north of Nacogdoches. Since Texas belonged to Mexico, it is difficult to see how Houston could have been involved. But whatever the circumstances, he was convinced that no Indian nation would be secure from white molestation as long as it remained on lands claimed by the United States. Thus it is conceivable that he may have advised The Bowl to settle in East Texas.[7]

Houston's resignation from the Army, five years to the day after his enlistment, left him with little to show for his military career. He had made an important enemy in Calhoun, which was a source of perverse satisfaction to him. It gave him a reason to feel sorry for himself. This gave him a reason to drink. He did both with enthusiasm.

He returned to Tennessee with Tahlontusky's party, and subsequently resigned his post of Indian subagent, thereby completing his break with authority in Washington. If this seems like an overreaction, it is strikingly similar to his adolescent response to demands imposed

46

by his mother and brothers. When realities refused to conform to patterns he liked, he hid from them. Similarly, his response to the smuggling charge and the War Department's failure to name the guilty party seems excessive. He lived in an age when slander and libel were accepted political devices. It was also a time when such occurrences could provoke duels. That Houston should have severed all connection with the government over a matter of honor was typical of him. This kind of conduct would endure, and his interpretation of "honor" would help to ravage his personal as well as his political life. He suffered from the worst affliction of which a politician could be victim—an exceptionally thin skin.

Retirement found Sam Houston in debt. In order to settle his obligations, he returned to Maryville and sold his entire interest in the family holdings there to his eldest brother, James, who was now well on his way to becoming the most stable and prosperous of the major's sons. This sale, and the collection of $17.75 due him from the federal government, failed to clear Sam of all his indebtedness, but he *was* able to prevent himself from being declared a bankrupt. Although back pay was due him from the War Department, it would be years before he collected it.[8]

With no leanings toward a particular career, he went to Nashville, where he had made some useful acquaintances the year before. Among these was Judge James Trimble, who offered to teach Sam the law in June, 1818.[9] Trimble, a friend of the Houstons from Rockbridge County days, proposed a course of study which Houston could complete in eighteen months if he pursued it with steady diligence. Nowhere is it recorded that Houston was presented with an alternative—not one, certainly, on more favorable terms (Trimble asked for no tuition fee).

Though he applied himself regularly to the study of law, Houston found time for an active social life. This included a close affiliation with Noah Ludlow, director and stage manager of the Dramatic Club of Nashville, an endeavor that brought together a remarkably varied group, many of whom enjoyed social and/or political prominence. Its members included Andrew Jackson and Felix Grundy. "Out of door business," according to Ludlow's memoirs, was the concern of John H. Eaton, a Jacksonian with an illustrious future. Of those who performed on stage, Ludlow thought little of the aspiring lawyer, "the largest if

47

not the most gifted with dramatic ability." But Houston played several roles. His triumph, after a fashion, was in a one-act afterpiece, *We Fly by Night,* in which he appeared as a drunken hotel porter.

Initially, Sam Houston was chary of the role. However, he was finally persuaded to play it by Eaton, who assured him that the audience would make no invidious connection between the bewigged Irish caricature onstage and the proper young lawyer's apprentice of real life. Houston's performance was sensational. Ludlow wrote that he had "never met a man who had a keener sense of the ridiculous . . . nor one who could more readily assume the ludicrous or the sublime."[10] From his brief theatrical success it is clear that his talents would serve him well in his later political life. His friends and supporters admired his performances as a public speaker—a quality greatly feared by his enemies. By the standards of the time he was a master of oratorical devices and constructions.[11]

The second half of 1818 was a period of intense activity for Houston. He became something of a prodigy. In December, with Judge Trimble's apprehensive blessing, he sat for his bar examination and passed it. What the judge had expected him to accomplish in eighteen months, he had done in six. Stunning as this achievement was, it put no bread on his plate. He required assistance and considerable credit. He found both in the small town of Lebanon, about thirty miles east of Nashville on the main road to the state capital of Murfreesboro. The Lebanon postmaster, Isaac Halladay, was also the principal local merchant. He rented Houston an office and advanced him all the necessities, with the understanding that the young lawyer would repay him when he was able.

Halladay introduced Houston to important men of eastern Davidson County, urging them to use his services. Many of them did. At the suggestion of Andrew Jackson, Governor McMinn named Houston adjutant general of the state, a militia assignment that took him often to the capital and other Tennessee towns. The post carried a modest honorarium and a degree of prestige. The need to travel gave Houston an opportunity to be seen and heard. He retained this office until the autumn of 1820.[12]

By this time the United States had acquired Florida, a transaction of vital importance for Houston's future. The shotgun purchase treaty solemnly acknowledged Spain's unequivocal title to Texas—an immense territory whose actual dimensions were unknown. The Sabine and Red Rivers were accepted as the eastern boundary with the United States, although this would be hotly disputed before another generation ripened.

With the Florida Purchase settled, Andrew Jackson spent more time at his home, the Hermitage, which lay not far off the road connecting Lebanon with Nashville. Since Houston frequently had to make professional journeys along that route, it was logical that he stop whenever possible at the general's handsome mansion. There is no reason to suppose that the rising young lawyer responded to Jackson's friendship for selfish or ambitious motives. The whole of Sam Houston's life shows remarkably little of the cynicism that is characteristic of successful politicians. That he almost always acted with a whole heart was one of his most endearing qualities. Houston loved the childless Rachel and Andrew Jackson. They themselves had always been drawn to the young, having none of their own. They had adopted several of Rachel's nieces and nephews, the most promising of these being Andrew Jackson Donelson, six years Houston's junior. Donelson had served as the general's aide during the Seminole Wars and was now studying for the bar. He and Houston always got on well.

The post of adjutant general carried the rank of colonel, and the sensible young attorney responded with style. The work involved was similar to the experience Houston had two years before at Nashville while still in the Army, examining the accounts and other records of the militia. There were innumerable confusions to be rectified, petitions to receive and dispose of. He found these duties congenial, having himself been victim of the Army's bureaucratic inefficiency and delay. In addition to this, his private practice was growing in proportion to his increasing popularity.

One visitor who called on Sam Houston at Lebanon in the early fall of 1819 was John Rogers. His half-breed "brother" had a sorry tale to tell. In spite of Houston's efforts two years earlier to insure Oolooteka's people a calm life west of the Mississippi, they had encountered many difficulties. The land itself was not as arable as the banks of the Hiwassee and the Tennessee. There were hostile neighbors, especially the Osages, Creeks, and Quapaws, who, resentful of the Cherokee intrusion, made frequent raids on their settlements. Reuben Lewis, the white agent to Oolooteka's band, was described by Rogers as a thief and had been pressured to resign, under threat of exposure to the War

49

Department. Rogers' mission was to induce Sam Houston to apply for the position as Lewis' successor.

Houston gave this proposition serious consideration. He notified Andrew Jackson at once who, in turn, wrote a long letter to Calhoun, still Secretary of War. "I . . . enclose . . . a letter from . . . Houston. . . . I have recommended him to accept the appointment of Agent. I have done this more with a view to the interest of the U. States than his own. . . . In the capacity of Agent he can draw to the Arkansas in a few years the whole strength of the Cherokee Nation now in the East . . ." The reference to the Eastern Cherokees touched on a situation that had a tragic and shameful resolution. By 1819 most of the Western Cherokees had already emigrated west. Only a single enclave remained in Tennessee. Eventually, in 1838, they were rudely evicted. Their doleful trek would be called the "Trail of Tears," an episode in which Sam Houston was not directly involved, but one that would blemish relations between Texas and the Indians until 1860.[13]

In October, 1819, not long after John Rogers' visit, Houston sought election for the first time. The office he ran for was attorney general of Davidson County. Since he had the backing of Andrew Jackson and McMinn, there was little question about the outcome. The post was equivalent to that of district attorney. His base of operations would be Nashville. His success marked him as a promising political figure and established him as a personality in Tennessee's largest town.[14]

It is difficult to understand why Houston encouraged John Rogers to think him receptive to the proposal that he become Cherokee agent, when he must have known that his name would be placed before the voters. Nor, for that matter, did Jackson explain why he recommended Houston to Calhoun when he was at the same time urging his candidacy for the Davidson County position. Perhaps they were trying to keep Houston's options open. If he lost the election, he could make the move to Arkansas—assuming that Calhoun offered the post to him. As it turned out, the Secretary of War did not make the offer and John Rogers returned to Oolooteka's wigwam empty-handed. But Sam Houston had something like a full plate before him for the first time in his life.[15]

In December, 1821, Houston resigned as attorney general of Davidson County to devote himself exclusively to his burgeoning private practice in Nashville. He was, according to his own account, "uniformly successful." Yet he admitted that his manner in court annoyed some of his more austere colleagues. What he lacked in finesse, evidently, he made up for in vigor and thoroughness of preparation.[16] Rarely did he lose a case and as his reputation grew, his prosperity increased. He set himself up in new and larger quarters. The day after Christmas, 1821, the *Nashville Banner* carried this notice: "Sam Houston attorney at law, Having removed to an office below A. Kingley's Esq. on Market Street, can be found at all times where he ought to be."[17]

Despite his devotion to his profession, he did not neglect his social life. In July, 1820, he had joined the Tennessee Antiquarian Society, the first learned association in that sector of the American frontier. The Society promoted general culture and education as well as preserving documents and relics of the state's short past. Houston was also an active socializer. His name appeared on many lists of dinner guests in the best houses and he was present at every ball, for he was an enthusiastic dancer. He became the most eligible bachelor in Nashville, particularly because he had been elected major general of the 2nd Division of the state militia after his resignation as adjutant general, mainly on the recommendation of Andrew Jackson. Thus Colonel Houston became General Houston, and was so called for the rest of his life.

When not working or about in society, Houston could usually be found in the tavern of the Nashville Inn, the hostelry which served as Old Hickory's state headquarters. Houston was a hard drinker, but there is no evidence at this point that the habit interfered with his success. In fact, by the relaxed standards of what was still a frontier society, he was perfectly decorous.

He first indicated an interest in Texas in 1822 when he and some friends made application for land in Texas. Since 1820, when the Spanish-controlled government of Mexico had announced a willingness to allow European and American nationals to settle the lands west of the Sabine, emigrants had passed through Tennessee on their way to this newest of promised lands. In 1821 New Englander Stephen T. Austin had reluctantly taken over the task of his dead father to establish a colony of 300 families in Texas. He advertised his plan in the newspapers of border towns from New Orleans northward. John A. Wharton, a man reasonably well known to Houston, had left Nashville in that year to seek *his* fortune in the great wilderness of Texas as an *empresario*—organizer of a colony similar to Austin's. He wrote back to Tennessee of his profitable experiences and urged others from Nashville to join him.

As far as Houston and other Tennesseans were concerned, involvement with Texas in 1822 was purely speculative. There was the possibility of making large amounts of money from investment in land. With a group of Nashville residents, Houston made formal application to the Mexican government for several grants of territory.[18] The laws governing these concessions demanded that they be colonized under the direction of an *empresario*. The question thus arises of who, among the applicants from Nashville, planned to assume the role. It may well have been Sam Houston, since he had no close ties to keep him in Tennessee. Despite his success in practice and the invaluable friendship with Jackson—who now aspired to the Presidency—he seemed still to have no really clear sense of purpose or direction. It may even be that Jackson urged the step, given his well-known belief that Texas had been part of the original Louisiana Purchase.

Thus, in his thirtieth year, Houston was still searching. He was a late bloomer. His progress seems doubly impressive, for he made it almost in spite of himself. He allowed life and events to happen to him, paying little critical heed to the implications of what he did or did not do. What eventually happened to this set of applications is unknown, but Houston lost interest, for the time being, in the subject of Texas.

His immediate situation was rosier than it had ever been. He found himself on the periphery of a national political campaign to secure Andrew Jackson's election to the Presidency. As a friend to Old Hickory and acquaintance of many Tennessee lawmakers, he lobbied for an official state endorsement of Jackson's candidacy for the election of 1824. On August 3, 1823, he wrote to Jackson from Murfreesboro that the state senate had unanimously recommended him. He was certain that his friend would be the successful candidate. Houston claimed to have no personal ambitions. "As to my own wishes they are only for the best interests & honor of my country[.]"[19]

The letter shows the degree to which Houston had been affected by his master's political doctrine. As the first national figure to espouse a creed that would eventually be called Populism, the general was also the country's first major demagogue. Demagogues have no trouble making enemies, but Jackson's friends, among them free-wheeling characters like John Eaton (at the time a Senator in Washington), did as much harm to his cause as good. Even within Tennessee, the Jacksonian monolith showed cracks that could cause the collapse of his seemingly indestructible political house. As the Presidential campaign began to gather momentum, candidates proliferated. At the height of the season, late in 1823 and early in 1824, there were five serious contenders. One of the most vigorous of these was Houston's enemy, John C. Calhoun, who was definitely no Populist.

As the old year gave way to the new, Houston informed Jackson that William H. Crawford, former Secretary of War now residing in Georgia, would be among the candidates, as would Henry Clay (Speaker of the House) from Kentucky, and the Bostonian who eventually won the election, John Quincy Adams.[20]

In January, 1823, a vitally important opportunity came to Houston largely because of Jackson's affection and regard for him. The seat in the United States House of Representatives from the Ninth Tennessee District was to fall vacant at the conclusion of that session, and Houston was named by Jackson and McMinn as their candidate for it. This support, as he acknowledged in a letter to the governor on February 15, was tantamount to election. He was almost obsequiously grateful and justifiably proud of the distance he had covered in recent years: "Five years since I came to [Nashville], without education more than ordinary—without friends—without cash—and almost without acquaintances—consequently without credit. And here among talents and distinction I have made my stand! or the people have made it for me. . . ."[21]

Tennessee's constitution ruled that the state must have a new governor, since McMinn could succeed himself only once. He therefore ran for the post of state Senator, while maintaining close attention to the main consideration of that year, Jackson's Presidential candidacy. In the election which made Sam Houston a Congressman, William Carroll was elected governor. A skillful manipulator of public opinion and at least ostensibly a strong Jacksonian, Carroll was playing a double game, for he was also supporting the candidacy of Henry Clay. He now assumed a role in shaping the career of Sam Houston. He saw in the attractive young attorney the sort of promise that all talented politicians admire—vivacity, personal style, the capacity to persuade the public of his sincerity, and, above all, absolute devotion to the interests of the man at the top.

The affection and admiration that Houston felt for Jackson were reciprocated by Old Hickory. Though the opportunistic Jackson used any means available in his drive for the Presidency, once he got there, he stood by his younger friend in painful circumstances where others found it much more politic to abandon him.

Volumes have been dedicated to Jackson's philosophy. So far as Houston was concerned, it could be reduced to a single, succinct formula: "The Constitution and the Union." Houston could, and did, often temporize on all other issues, even the fate of his beloved Indians. However, when the basic tenets of the United States Constitution seemed in jeopardy or when the integrity of the Federal Union was menaced, Sam Houston's stand was unwavering regardless of personal price.

In 1823, however, his sights were not aimed high. He was strictly Jackson's liege man. The general, nominally Governor of Florida since 1821, had kept the seat of his power in Tennessee. With an eye fixed on his ultimate goal, Jackson allowed himself to be elected to the United States Senate. Consequently, representative-elect Sam Houston made his way to Washington devoted to little beside furthering the Presidential career of Senator-elect Andrew Jackson. Little more than thirty years old, his life had been transfigured.

V

THE FIRST letter Sam Houston is known to have written from Washington was to Major Abram Maury, an ardent Jacksonian. The date was December 13, 1823. Houston complained about the Presidential campaign as reported by "so many smart Editors in this part of the country—I say smart because many of them are so sagacious that they will not state facts, but make them to suit their wishes." He believed that Jackson was gaining strength daily and would continue to gain.[1] His allusion to the inaccuracy of the press was even more appropriate than the complaints of contemporary politicians. Papers and pamphlets of every political shading were pored over by everyone interested in national affairs. To the illiterate masses, passages were read aloud. Editors and writers were not overscrupulous in distinguishing between fact and opinion. Though libel laws existed, resort to legal action was less common than duels. *Niles' Register* was the most respectable weekly published in Washington, and Houston sent Maury a clipping from this paper which he called "generally correct."

Letters provide the main documentation of Houston's years in Congress. He represented his constituents' private interests admirably, although his main concern during his first year was the election of Jackson. He did, however, depart from custom by making his maiden speech little more than a month after being seated. The topic was Greek independence, and his conviction was that the United States should encourage that country's efforts to secure her freedom from the Turks. The speech, probably extemporaneous, was extensive—as were most of Houston's public utterances.[2] In the late spring Houston returned to Tennessee to practice law and to campaign for Jackson, until he succumbed to a fever. By the end of August he was sufficiently recovered to write his cousin, John Houston, his appraisal of the electoral prospects: "Old Hickory will get the South and West—there is no doubt—& N. York will yet see that she cannot make Billy Crawford President—Jackson or Adams . . . will succeed, but I think Jackson will be the man. . . ."[3]

By the end of 1824 Houston was back in the national capital.

The electoral dilemma was the talk of Washington. Of the four candidates who actually entered the national election (Calhoun had withdrawn), Jackson and Adams emerged the leaders in the Electoral College. Old Hickory received 99 votes, Adams 84. The remainder was divided between Crawford (41) and Clay (37). Since the election, there had been time for the bartering of House votes and the inevitable testing of the political winds. Houston believed them to be blowing in Jackson's direction.

In late January, 1825, Houston's thoughts were intently but not exclusively concentrated on the election. He wrote A. H. Hughes, a Tennessee friend, a letter about a nameless South Carolina girl whose hand he was seeking in marriage:

> . . . For my *single* self I do not know yet the sweets of matrimony, but in March or April . . . next I will; unless something should take place not to be expected . . . or wished for! To have been married on my way here would not have answered a good purpose. My errand here is to attend to the business of my constituents, and not to spend "honey moons." *Everything in due season!*[4]

By early February Houston was a little less confident of the outcome of the election soon to be determined in the House. While Jackson was "certainly the President of the People," he was in some doubt about the views of his fellow legislators. "There is much excitement in Congress at this time as well as throughout the nation!"[5] The excitement turned mainly on what Henry Clay would advise his supporters to do. After weeks of soul-searching, he announced for Adams, a decision widely believed to have been purchased with the promise that he would be named Secretary of State. When this charge was printed, Clay challenged its anonymous author to reveal himself. There was a clamor for investigation, but the issue was not seriously pressed. It was generally felt that no one's linen was very clean.

On February 9 the House convened to elect the President. What was required was a simple majority of the states' votes—each state delegation having a single ballot. In his eagerness to lure the Ohio delegation into Jackson's camp, Houston assured that state's governor that Henry Clay could have any post he wanted in a Jackson administration.[6] This and other last-ditch efforts were to no avail. Adams won on the first ballot. To the consternation of Sam Houston, John C. Calhoun was elected Vice President—his prize for having withdrawn his candidacy.

Almost immediately after Adams' inauguration, Congress adjourned. Houston left for Cheraw, South Carolina, with plans to marry. A distinguished Houston scholar asserts that the couple had exchanged letters regularly during the Congressman's stay in the capital. If so, not a line survives. However, Houston left Washington for Cheraw in a state of high emotion:

> The night before I left Washington I slept none; nor the next night . . . did I close my eyes, but traveled the livelong night. Instead of being as I calculated 40 miles on my route to the South I have only come from Richmond to day 22 miles. My appointment is to be in Cheraw on the 20th. . . .[7]

When he reached Cheraw, Houston was immediately retained as counsel in an important probate case, and promised the stupendous fee of $1,000. But he did not marry the girl he had been so impatient to see. In a letter to John Houston of April 20, while on his way to Nashville, he offered explanations for the postponement, asserting that he would be back in Cheraw to marry "Miss M——" in the autumn. It is apparently coincidental that the two women Houston had so far been engaged to had names beginning with *M*.

Another concern of Houston's was that while in South Carolina he had received letters from Nashville *"indicating hostility to me."* Since he had to campaign for reelection, he prepared to deal with "these threats." There was a possibility that he would run for the governorship of Tennessee, "but at this crisis, I do not like to quit Congress, if my dear constituents wish to send me back again." He had explained his situation to "Miss M—— and she concluded to defer matters until fall."[8]

Having decided not to oppose Billy Carroll in the gubernatorial election, Houston was easily reelected to Congress from the Ninth District. More interesting was his decision not to marry the girl from Cheraw. He probably made an appearance at Marlboro, South Carolina, to represent his client in the probate case for which he was to receive the $1,000 fee. Whether or not he saw the young woman is problematical. He did not marry her, nor does reference to her appear in any subsequent correspondence. Despite disclaimers, it is clear that the obstacles to marriage were of his own invention.

We are able to name few women who figured in Houston's life until 1828. All correspondence between him and members of the opposite sex during his premarital years has either been destroyed or allowed to repose in attic trunks. For his part, Houston, who so scrupulously copied most of his official letters, saw fit not to follow this practice in private exchanges.[9]

He was back at Washington by early December, 1825, again making a record as a diligent representative of his constituents. In January he made casual reference to his unmarried state: "I am making myself less frequent in the Lady World than I have been. I must keep up my Dignity, or rather I must attend more to politics and less to love."[10] The need for more attention to politics probably related to a speech he was preparing, delivered in the House on February 2. The topic was a resolution regarding America's role in a congress of American countries soon to be held at the Isthmus of Panama. The gist of the bill, as finally amended by Daniel Webster and others, was that Congress had the right to more detailed information about diplomatic negotiations. A thoughtful address, its conclusion has a startlingly modern ring, for the underlying issue was executive privilege. The plea he made has become a familiar one: How could the Congress legislate intelligently unless the President took the legislature into his confidence?[11]

His second important speech was longer and much more vitriolic. It concerned Massachusetts' claim for reimbursement by the federal government for sums paid to the state's militia during the War of 1812. Houston opposed the bill on both personal and political grounds. To aid the native state of John Quincy Adams did nothing for Andrew Jackson. But more than that, he was personally stung by the role of Massachusetts in that war in which he had been so badly wounded. "If

Massachusetts had pursued a similar course [to that of Tennessee], not a voice would have been heard ... in opposition to this claim—she chose to pursue a different course, and it is but just that she should realize its consequences."[12] It was not the last time that Houston would comment on this matter. Ultimately the issue was resolved by a compromise.

In the first half of 1826 John Eaton was given the task of revising and updating *A Civil and Military History of Andrew Jackson,* in anticipation of the 1828 Presidential election. Sam Houston's name has been improbably attached to this campaign biography. The principal emendation was a sympathetic treatment of Old Hickory's part in the controversial Seminole Wars and the acquisition of Florida.[13]

We can only surmise whether or not there was a connection between Jackson's determination to seek election to the Presidency again and Houston's decision to run for the governorship of Tennessee in 1827. Houston made his decision in the spring of 1826 and made his desire known to the state's voters. As governor, he would be in a better position to influence Tennessee's course during the Presidential campaign, and he had Jackson's support for the race. Billy Carroll posed no problem, since the constitution decreed that he must step aside for at least one term. When Houston made his intention public, Felix Grundy and John Bell announced their plans to seek the Ninth District seat he was leaving.[14]

All this lay in the future, however. Jackson had resigned his Senate seat and been succeeded by John Eaton. His reason for returning to the Hermitage was purportedly one of weariness. Moreover, his wife refused to go to Washington with him. The likelier explanation was a wish to more effectively camouflage his maneuverings behind the scenes.

Without Jackson at his side, Houston found that his stay in the capital allowed him more political elbow room. Furthermore, whatever his resolve about devoting himself less to the "Lady World" and more to politics, he was reported to have been seen in society a great deal. One place he visited was Mount Vernon, the residence of Miss Mary Custis, heiress to that venerable house and great-granddaughter of George Washington's wife. If Houston was wooing Mary Custis, he was not successful. She married Robert E. Lee.

There was, however, another issue that did pose something of a threat. In March, Houston had asked President Adams to name B. Y. Currey to the postmastership of Nashville instead of John P. Erwin, editor of the *Nashville Banner* and brother to a son-in-law of Secretary of State Henry Clay. Houston attacked Erwin's character in his letter to Adams: "He has taken the benefit of the act of insolvency, and now lives in ease and affluence. He does not pay his debts, tho' all believe him able to do so. . . . He was detected by three respectable members of the State legislature . . . e[a]vesdropping at the window of a Gentleman of character, to whom he was politically opposed! . . . [He is] not a man of fair and upright moral character."[15]

Given the President's debt to Henry Clay, there was no doubt that he would sustain the appointment of Erwin. Not surprisingly, Houston's victim was soon apprised of the Congressman's attack and it was to be expected that he would take it personally. Houston's friends told him of Erwin's rage. Even before departing from Washington, the Congressman thought it wise to familiarize himself with the operation of a dueling pistol.[16]

In August, some time after his return to Nashville (which had just been designated the provisional capital of the state), Houston received a note from John Erwin demanding that he retract the imputations of his letter to Adams. Houston answered on August 18: "You point me to no particular charge against you at Washington, hence I am unable to return any particular reply. In opposing your appointment, I was acting in my official character. . . . On that occasion I did make statements 'impeaching the integrity of your conduct.' I then believed them true, and nothing has since transpired to induce an alteration in the opinion then entertained."

These were fighting words, and Houston knew it. He placed Erwin in the position of having to challenge him to a duel. According to the grotesque ritual, the challenger had to communicate with the challenged through an intermediary. The man Erwin selected was a professional duelist who styled himself Colonel John Smith, T. Nominally a resident of Missouri, Smith happened to be in Nashville at the time. Houston, conforming strictly to the formula, designated as his second another colonel whose name was McGregor.

Smith approached McGregor on Nashville's main square and informed him that he had a message for Houston from Erwin. McGregor responded (as he had been instructed) that he could not accept the communication because the bearer was not a resident of Tennessee.

Smith disappeared, returning soon afterward with General William A. White, a Nashville lawyer. Instead of handing Erwin's challenge to McGregor, White gave it to Houston. Houston refused to receive it, explaining to White, whom he knew slightly, that it must come to him through his second. He added, however, that he would accept a challenge from White if White were himself the challenger. Since the quarrel was not White's no challenge was offered.

The affair dragged on. Erwin had ostensibly resigned his editorship, but he still had access to the columns of the *Banner*. He used them to keep the controversy alive. On September 8 Houston received a note from the notorious Smith, asking if the fact of his being a nonresident was the Congressman's only reason for refusing a challenge from his hand. Houston replied the day he was given Smith's inquiry:

> In refusing to receive the challenge presented by you, my friend, Col. McGregor, was directed to object to you for the reason that you were not a resident of the state, and because the dispute between Erwin and myself was a home affair. [The refusal] was given . . . because I conceived the whole mess of political character, and being [among my] constituents, felt that it should be inter[fered in by] no one living out of the state. My [decision not] to wound your feelings or to court your [enmity] was deemed the most advisable . . . and [the] one necessary to be used. . . .
>
> The concluding part of your letter is wrong. [Col.] McGregor did not use the language you have [credited] to him. His remark was this: "I know [nothing of] him (Col. Smith)—I have heard him spoken [of as a] gentleman." This, I am advised, was the remark made to him by Gen White.[17]
>
> [Note: The mutilations of this letter are due to the fact that the only copy is a clipping too closely cropped from a newspaper. The ellipses have been filled by Amelia W. Williams and Eugene C. Barker, editors, *The Writings of Sam Houston*.]

Smith was obviously seeking a reason to challenge Houston in his own right. The Congressman wrote a letter, published in the *Banner* of September 13, explaining at exhaustive length the circumstances of the quarrel.[18] There was much more message-bearing in the next few days. The upshot of Smith's failure was that General White decided to challenge Houston in Erwin's stead, on the ground that a defenseless friend had been offended. With great reluctance, Houston assented. The date for this duel was to be September 22.

Houston took advantage of the intervening period to consult Andrew Jackson, an expert in dueling. Whether the advice he sought was political or practical is not known. Old Hickory counseled his younger friend to hold a bullet between his teeth and clamp down hard as he was taking aim. After practicing for some hours on a target set against a tree near the Hermitage, Houston adjourned with his friends to the farm of an acquaintance, Sanford Duncan, near the Kentucky border. The duel was to take place outside the state to avoid prosecution.

At daybreak on the appointed morning Houston's party crossed into Kentucky to meet White's faction. There is no report that John Erwin was present. The seconds agreed that single shots were to be exchanged at a distance of fifteen paces. At such close range, the bulky, tall Houston made an easy target. However, it was William White who fell, so seriously wounded that he was convalescent for several months. Although Houston was indicted for assault by a Kentucky grand jury, he never stood trial; nor was he even arrested. Indeed, he was treated by his supporters as a hero. He rejected this accolade, saying that he despised dueling and that he was gratified only that "my adversary was injured no worse."[19]

His dispute with Erwin settled, Houston soon found himself trying to resolve a similar problem for Andrew Jackson. A month after his duel with White, the Congressman had a letter from Old Hickory reporting angrily that Samuel L. Southard, Secretary of the Navy, had been quoted as deprecating Jackson's role in securing New Orleans against the British in late 1814. These remarks were supposed to have been uttered in the presence of Dr. J. H. Wallace, a strong Jacksonian, who had seen fit to pass them on. According to Wallace, Southard had implied that New Orleans would have fallen to the enemy had it not been for the quick thinking of Secretary of State James Monroe. The inference was that Southard thought Jackson an imprudent and incompetent commander.

Once again honor demanded satisfaction. Jackson requested Houston to carry to Washington a letter for the Secretary of the Navy. Houston was to demand an immediate reply which was to be forwarded at once to Jackson at the Hermitage.[20] The general's letter was handed to Houston unsealed, allowing him the assumption that he was to read it before making the delivery. On reaching Washington, Houston showed Jackson's letter to friends, who agreed with him that the tone was too peremptory. The Congressman wrote Old Hickory to this effect in mid-December, 1826, adding that it might be wise if Houston merely intervened with Southard in his behalf. "It is now a desirable matter with all your friends . . . to keep you out of collision . . . as to things said and done . . . and whatever action may be thought necessary . . . to proceed thro some friend." He added owlishly, "I trust . . . you will not for one moment suppose that my course has been dictated by an eye . . . to your political advancement, and that while I wou'd promote that, that I wou'd not suffer your character . . . as a man . . . and Patriot to rest under imputations of dishonor!" He concluded that if Jackson proposed to write Southard another letter, "I pray you . . . to let [it] be in the mildest, calmest tone of expression— The very fact of his conduct and statement . . . will most effectually damn him . . . and those united with him."[21]

Jackson's response of early January was a model of calm, suggesting to Old Hickory's friends that Houston had power over him which few others had. It seemed that the Southard matter would be allowed to drop. But it flared up again when James Monroe, accidentally or by design, permitted an old letter of his to come into Houston's possession. In this document, the ex-President seemed to concur in Southard's judgment about his role in the battle of New Orleans. Perhaps because it had been addressed to Calhoun, Houston sent this letter on to Jackson on January 13, with a covering note in which he explained that the unnamed gentleman who had given him the document made him promise to show it to Old Hickory.[22]

Receipt of the Monroe letter to Calhoun altered Jackson's view of the Southard matter. By return, he ordered Houston to deliver his original communication to the Secretary of the Navy, which Houston immediately did. Though not denying his allegations, Southard said that he had spoken only to improve the reputation of Monroe, not to denigrate Jackson. There, fortunately, the issue was permitted to rest.

However, if there had been doubts that Jackson was still in the political arena, his response in the Southard affair dispelled them. Besides, Jacksonian candidates for House and Senate seats had triumphed almost everywhere in the elections of the previous autumn. The evidence was overwhelming that the "Era of Good Feeling," which was supposed to have been the chief attribute of Monroe's eight-year administration, had not been maintained during the first half of Adams' tenure in office.

Economic and social problems beset the nation. Jackson's fiery Populism had proved its appeal even in the election of 1824, which he had lost. The results in 1826 made the Whigs and Federalists tremble. About the only question unanswered in the minds of Jacksonians in 1827 was the name of the man Old Hickory would select as his running mate the next year, for he had announced his intention to be a one-term President. One of the men frequently mentioned was the incumbent, Calhoun. Obviously, Sam Houston opposed the candidacy of a man he thought his enemy. He favored DeWitt Clinton of New York, a name found sympathetic by many of Jackson's closest friends. However it was not a problem demanding immediate resolution.[23]

When Sam Houston reached Nashville in the spring of 1827, he was already an announced candidate for the Tennessee governorship. He campaigned briefly but vigorously, especially in the western portion of the state, as Jackson advised him to do. From his mother's house at Baker's Creek he wrote John Houston on April 8 that he would be elected governor "by a large majority unless some vast accident" occurred.[24]

As he predicted, his election was assured. Before the voting he returned to Washington for a final visit as Congressman. From there he wrote a long letter to Jackson. One paragraph is notable: "All matters move on here as I wou'd have them to do, if I had my wishes in the way of putting down a corrupt aristocracy, who rely solely for power . . . on the influence of patronage! Desperation now seems to characterize every act of the *Ministry!*"[25] This from a man who had risen to his present position by the very system he so deplored when it was employed by the opposition. That these lines were addressed to the man who was to be renowned for saying, "To the victor belong the spoils," adds to the irony.

Houston's stay in the capital was brief. By July 13 he was back in Tennessee. His Whig opponent for the governorship, Newton Cannon, was supported by Jackson's enemies, chiefly Felix Grundy. Grundy proved a serious match even for the combined forces of Andrew Jackson, Billy Carroll (who planned to resume the governor's seat in 1829), and Houston himself, who performed well on rural stumps and in the squares of the larger towns, affecting a gaudy style of dress that attracted as much attention as his harangues.

When he was not campaigning that summer, he was busy making himself the toast of Nashville, a community of about 6,000 residents, including slaves. The principal gathering place in the new capital was a square that occupied a high bluff overlooking the Cumberland River. Flanking this broad, sparsely planted area were three structures of importance—the courthouse (which served as meeting place for the legislature), the City Hotel, rendezvous for the state's Whigs, and the Nashville Inn, Houston's residence and headquarters for the Jacksonians. The general had favored the removal of the capital from Murfreesboro because Nashville was only nine miles west of the Hermitage. With his followers near at hand, Old Hickory could more easily maintain control.

Nashville provided a variety of homely diversions—cockfighting, billiards, and Clover Bottom, the best-known flat-racing track in the Southwest. In the center of the square there were facilities for the administration of corporal punishment—stocks and a whipping post. Gallows were erected for special occasions. Dinner parties of some splendor and numerous balls were regular features in the night life of the capital. Sam Houston was still the most eligible bachelor of Tennessee, a position enhanced by the certainty that he would soon be governor. One of the young ladies whom he charmed was Anne Hanna. Her informal memoirs include an intriguing phrase about Houston: "Two classes of people pursued Sam Houston all his life—artists and women."[26] His interest in personal appearance suggests considerable vanity. Anne Hanna's mention of artists is germane at this juncture because Houston commissioned a miniature of himself before his departure from Washington. Soon after his election as governor, he ordered another portrait. He is not known to have ever refused an artist the chance to paint him. Later on, in Texas, he never declined an opportunity to be photographed. As for women, he seems only rarely to have embroiled himself so deeply that he had difficulty eluding marriage. Houston would be well into his thirty-sixth year before he married.

The election took place in August. Informed estimates had been that Houston would run best in West Tennessee, where the Jackson-Carroll machine was most popular. In the eastern portion of the state there was resentment over the shifting of the capital. The fact that Maryville was in the east was not considered important. The masterminds believed it was the support of the Populist machine which would assure his election. In the end, Newton Cannon received a surprisingly large vote in areas considered safe by the Jacksonians. And in the east, the polls were overwhelmingly favorable to Houston. It was his home base which provided the crucial margin. The final tally was 44,426 to 33,410—not a landslide, but an impressive demonstration of Houston's personal popularity. In the Ninth District, Jacksonian James K. Polk defeated Felix Grundy in the race for Houston's vacated Congressional seat.[27]

As soon as the result was known, Houston went to the Hermitage to share his victory with Old Hickory. He then proceeded to Knoxville to express his public gratitude for the support of the voters of East Tennessee. At a dinner in his honor more than fifty toasts were drunk, several of them proposed by the governor-elect.

William H. Wharton, brother of the Nashville lawyer who had petitioned the Mexican government for Texan land grants along with Houston and others, had journeyed to Texas in 1827 and was back in Nashville later in the year. He spoke with Houston of his experiences there, and of the glowing prospects for speculators. He also told of the Fredonia rebellion, an abortive uprising of aliens against the Mexican authorities. This attempt to seize power had repercussions that would, a couple of years later, inspire the darkest official suspicions about Houston's personal ambitions, because of the involvement of Houston's friends, the Western Cherokees.

There is little doubt that Wharton's description of Texas stuck in Houston's mind, but it seemed to have no immediate significance. He would soon be governor of Tennessee, and once Andrew Jackson had been elected President of the United States, he could easily expect to find himself even more happily situated. As September, 1827, drew to a close, Sam Houston prepared himself for the duties of his new office with a sense of certainty about the shape and security of his future.

Sam Houston delivered his inauguration address in the First Baptist Church of Nashville, October 1, 1827. It was one of his shortest. He described his rise from obscurity to the position he now occupied, and promised to "exert all my abilities in sustaining the rights of the people." He would support the Federal Constitution, "sensible of the sacred and important character of that instrument." Yet he would also maintain the authority and jurisdiction of the state, and would see that justice was administered with an even hand.[28]

A fortnight later he sent his initial message to the state legislature. It was a sensible paper in which he dealt with such mundane but vital matters as commerce, agriculture, and problems of public transport —advancing, in virtually all cases, programs that Billy Carroll had already instituted. Since the state was still almost entirely agrarian, the export of harvests and the import of manufactured goods as cheaply and rapidly as possible was essential. A good canal system seemed ideal.[29]

The federal government had been seeking permission from the Western Cherokees to construct a canal from Hiwassee to Coosa over Indian land. So far, General John Cocke, a commissioner from the War Department, had failed in his negotiations. Through Houston, he sought the Tennessee legislature's help in breaking the deadlock. The Indians objected to the government's cheap bid of $10,000 in specie. Here, for the first time, when Houston's personal and official preferences might be at odds over an Indian question, he sided with the whites. No records of the time indicate that he felt serious qualms. However, subsequent behavior suggests that he may have.[30]

The first three months of his administration passed without cause for special note, setting the tone for his whole tenure as governor. Since his primary object was the assurance of Jackson's election to the Presidency, this blandness is hardly astonishing. Houston would do nothing to draw attention to himself at the expense of Old Hickory. One wonders, therefore, why a correspondent who wrote James Monroe ten days after Houston's inauguration said that the governor of Tennessee was "a blustering bully man & *not* in the *confidential confidence* of Gen Jackson."[31] That Houston was not destined to become a member of Jackson's "Kitchen Cabinet" was true enough, but he definitely enjoyed the general's favor and intimacy. Moreover, Houston's power lay in his ability to keep Jackson's temper in check. It appears that Monroe's informant was thinking wishfully.

In the middle of March, John Floyd, a Virginia Jacksonian, wrote Houston that he must try to guide Old Hickory in a path that was more "studied." Floyd also observed that Secretary of State Clay was "a bargaining dog" who was responsible for important opposition mounted against Jackson's candidacy in Indiana and New York. He concluded with a wish that Houston might "long continue to enjoy the confidence of *the people,* the *true source of power.*"[32]

From February through the end of May, the press—at first in East Tennessee and eventually across the country—made continuous reference to the eccentric circumstances of Andrew Jackson's early marital condition, a topic he had often brawled and occasionally dueled over. "New evidence" was purported to have been discovered revealing that Old Hickory had wrenched his dear Rachel from the arms of her first husband and that he had lived with her in sin for three years before marrying her. The evidence for these charges was spurious. However they were so seriously regarded that Jackson's aides convened a committee of respected citizens at Nashville to examine the facts and give a dispassionate opinion as to their accuracy. Sam Houston was not in the group, though he had advised its formation. The conclusion was foregone, and when finally published, it probably changed few minds.[33]

Although popular, Houston was not universally revered. The Cumberland Lodge of Masons in Nashville chose the month of October, 1828, just prior to the Presidential election, to raise charges against him for expressing public doubt about the virtue of a fellow member, Postmaster John P. Erwin, and for having dueled with another Mason, William A. White. The hearing to consider these complaints was not long secret—nor was it likely that it could be. Houston was cleared of the allegation of libel. For having engaged in a duel with General White, however, he was suspended from all Masonic functions for a year, on the ground of having permitted a political disagreement to mar a Masonic relationship. Though surely intended to embarrass Andrew Jackson at a critical moment of the campaign, the maneuver failed. Houston's only real cause for dismay at the time was that Old Hickory had chosen Calhoun to be his running mate.

From the beginning, the election had been a two-man race between Jackson and the incumbent, John Quincy Adams. On specific issues, there was little to differentiate them. Hence, it was the contrasting personalities of Adams and Jackson which transfixed the national electorate. It would have been hard to find temperaments that clashed more sharply, at least as they were presented to the public. The popular image of Adams was one of inviolable personal and political rectitude—even though he had connived shamelessly with Henry Clay to steal the Presidency from Jackson. On the other hand Jackson's enemies had created an image of far greater flamboyance than the man himself justified—though they were accurate in depicting a frontier character, a rough diamond, if a diamond at all.

As it developed, the campaign proved the most scurrilous of record to that year. It was plain by early autumn that nothing said or printed against Jackson was going to prevent his election. He had put together an impressive vote-getting machine. Though the popular vote was not of landslide proportions—647,276 to Adams' 508,064, the count in the Electoral College gave Jackson a margin of better than 2 to 1. On November 24 the President-elect wrote a friend that he was gratified by the result. But he was uneasy. His wife, Rachel, whom he had protected so long and so fiercely against slander, was in failing health.[34]

VI

THE ELECTION of Andrew Jackson, for which Sam Houston had worked so diligently, effectively marked the end of their intimacy—though the governor had no way of knowing it at the time. While remaining friends, they were to follow paths that led in opposite directions. They would see each other again, but under circumstances much different from before.

Just when Sam Houston became friendly with the family of John Allen of Gallatin, Tennessee, is not known. Allen was a prosperous landowner and something of a patrician. The Allens had been settled much longer on their land than Houston's family had been on the plantation at Baker's Creek. There was excellent flat-racing at Gallatin and Jackson, always fond of the sport, was often John Allen's guest at his house on the Cumberland when the horses were running. Houston had begun visiting the Allen plantation when he was a Congressman.

At the time of his first stay, Allen's daughter Eliza was no more than fourteen. Already entangled with the girl from Cheraw, Houston paid little attention to her. Even for a man who had always shown a preference for women far younger than he, she was underage. When he became governor, however, Eliza was sixteen. Houston traveled the state a great deal, and he seems to have been a fairly frequent visitor of John Allen's in 1827 and 1828. His host thought highly of him, had high hopes for his political future, and always made him welcome. No record indicates what Eliza felt for this prominent personage nearly twice her age. But Sam Houston felt strongly enough about Eliza to stay with the Allens when he ought to have been campaigning for Andrew Jackson. He was infatuated with her. He wanted to marry her.

No picture of Eliza Allen has been discovered. It is said that after her second marriage she destroyed all images of herself and would not allow mirrors to be hung in her house.[1] We know from witnesses that she was diminutive and fragile. Fair, with blond hair and blue eyes, she must have been quite beautiful. Certainly, Sam Houston found her so. Before their marriage, that was all he knew of her.[2]

The first known suggestion of his intentions appeared in a letter to John Houston written November 10, 1828: "I am not married but it may be the case in a few weeks, and should it—*you* shall *hear* of it . . . before the newspapers can reach you."[3] The period of serious courtship was apparently brief. Houston declared his love for Eliza to her father before making it known to the girl. However, had she offered a reasonable objection to the proposal, it is certain that neither Houston nor her father would have insisted on the marriage. John Allen willingly gave his consent, then Eliza acceded.

No episode in Sam Houston's life is so obscure and confusing as his brief marriage with Eliza Allen. Since it was such a pivotal experience, both personally and politically, it must be considered in as much detail as possible. The difficulty is that few reliable details are available. Although the record has been wiped nearly clean there has been much speculation.

In *The Raven,* Marquis James states flatly that when Sam Houston asked for her hand, Eliza was already secretly betrothed to another. However, being well raised, she would do as her father bade her, even though she would cherish this earlier and deeper affection even after her marriage.[4] Though this was probably the case, the evidence for it is shaky. Whatever the case there was unquestionably a significant emotional conflict in Eliza. It may have been because of her love for another man or it could have been owing to Houston's nature. Although he appeared charming to those who knew him casually he was a complex and difficult man. Houston himself seemed unaware that any kind of problem existed when he contracted for Eliza's hand. If he had suspected any reluctance from her demeanor, he would not have pursued his course with such resolution.

A further confusing note is added by an extract of a letter of December 4 from Houston to Tennessee Congressman John Marable. After alluding to his own renown as a flirt, he went on: "I have as usual had 'a small blow up.' What the devil is the matter with the gals I cant say but there has been hell to pay. . . ." Although no reference is made to Eliza, a possible inference is that he had importuned her and been caught in the act. It is also possible that he had been reported by the girl to her parents. There is not a trace of enthusiasm in his observation that "it may be I will splice myself with a rib."

Such an extreme interpretation may be questionable. It is not likely that Houston would have compromised a member of such a prominent family however great his passion for her—unless he was drunk. But coming little more than three weeks after his much more ebullient letter to John Houston, the note to Marable causes one's eyebrows to rise. *Would* Sam Houston have been dallying with *another* woman at a time like this? Marquis James thought the governor's line to Marable merely "jocose," intended to "disguise the tenderness that was in the writer's heart." With equal justification, one may think the tone wry or rueful.

This is not to suggest that Sam Houston was not in love with Eliza. The November letter to his cousin makes it clear that his intention was marriage, not dalliance. On the other hand Houston had shied away from impending marriage before. Even if he had been apprehended by a member of the Allen family in a harmless but forbidden embrace, Eliza would be seen as a woman compromised. Thus John Allen could have presented Houston with an ultimatum. Regardless of the chain of events that led to it, the betrothal was announced by the Allens in mid-December and the wedding was to occur at Gallatin on January 22.[5]

Within a week of this news, Rachel Jackson died. She was buried on Christmas Eve in the garden of the Hermitage, whose planting she had directed and which was a source of great pleasure to her. Jackson was devastated by his loss and much embittered that his wife's final months had been blighted by a recrudescence of ugly gossip about their relationship.[6]

Yet Old Hickory rallied. Not long after the funeral, he spoke with Houston not only about the younger man's matrimonial plans (of which he heartily approved) but also about his political future. Houston told Jackson that he wanted to seek reelection to the office he held, despite the tacit understanding that he would step aside so that Billy Carroll could resume the post. Jackson was not startled by this announcement, but it placed him in a difficult position. He favored

Houston for the governorship because he was a more dependable ally. Yet he was under an obligation to Carroll. The only alternative was a vacancy in the United States Senate which Jackson had thought to award to Felix Grundy who, in spite of earlier treachery, had aided him in his drive for the White House. They decided that Houston was to seek an accommodation with Carroll. Perhaps he would accept the Senate seat, allowing Houston to run for reelection without effective opposition.

Carroll was not to be so easily placated. He refused to change his own plan. He believed, with reason, that Houston's success as governor was due in large measure to programs that he himself had originated. There was no accommodation. In fact Carroll chose January 21, the day before the Houston-Allen marriage, to announce his candidacy.[7]

The wedding took place at Gallatin. A second-hand account avers that Eliza wept while she was being dressed for the occasion and that when she allowed Houston to place the ring on her finger, her hands were trembling. The author of this anecdote reported that the couple spent their wedding night beneath John Allen's roof. Houston is supposed to have remarked on Eliza's unwonted anxiety, "which convinced him some secret had not been revealed. Before retiring he frankly told her of his suspicion, asked a frank confession and pledged that he should work her no injury. His frankness and firmness led to the confession that her affections had been pledged to another . . . and that filial duty had prompted her acceptance of his offer [of marriage]." This narrative was written by the Reverend George W. Samson, a Washington minister who knew Houston as a parishioner between 1846 and 1859, when he was Senator from Texas. Taken from an article that appeared in the New York *Tribune* in 1880, it is cited by Marquis James, who observed in a note that "[i]n some of his reminiscences of Houston, given in this article, the doctor's memory is at fault, [but] I believe the portion quoted is worthy of credence."

One must express reservations about Dr. Samson's assertion. Countless intimates of Houston's tried to elicit from him—when he was drunk as well as sober—an explanation of the events that led to the separation from Eliza. With stubborn regularity, he refused to utter a single illuminating word. Thus, there is no reason to suppose that he would reveal to Samson what he had been unwilling to tell others much closer to him for so long. Samson's version may be accurate, but

74

as it stands it is far from convincing, especially when juxtaposed with another account, also cited by James, from *A History of Tennessee and Tennesseeans*. This alludes to the morning of January 24, 1829, after Eliza and Sam Houston had spent the second night of their short marriage at the home of the governor's friend, Robert Martin. There was snow on the ground. Martha Martin, wife of the host, was looking out the window as her daughters were engaged in a snowball fight with Houston. Just then, according to her recollection, Eliza came down the stairs:

> I said to her, "It seems as if General Houston is getting the worst of the snow-balling; you had better go out and help him." Looking seriously at me Mrs. Houston said, "I wish they would kill him." I looked astonished to hear such a remark from a bride of not yet forty-eight hours, when she repeated in the same voice, "Yes, I wish from the bottom of my heart that they would kill him."[8]

If one accepts Dr. Samson's assurance of Houston's tenderness in securing a confession from Eliza, the venom with which she spoke to Martha Martin was perverse indeed. It seems more likely that the marriage occurred because Houston had compromised the girl. While not dismissing the possibility that she was in love with someone else, this explanation would account for the bitterness of her outburst to Martha Martin.

Another possibility is that the marriage was an impromptu affair. Some years earlier, Houston had deferred his plan to marry a girl from Cheraw because he would be campaigning for Congress, would have to leave her alone at Nashville for extended periods, and as yet had no home. The conditions in January, 1829, were identical. He was about to announce his candidacy for governor, and he was still without a home since there was no governor's mansion at Nashville. After taking office in 1827, Houston had resided in rooms of the Nashville Inn, and this is where he settled his wife, after spending a few nights with the family of his favorite Tennessee cousin, Robert McEwen.

Whatever impression Eliza made on Mrs. Martin, she revealed nothing to McEwen's wife, who observed that though the couple seemed not very gregarious, they were as affectionate toward each other as any married pair she had ever seen. She assumed that their reserve could be explained by the fact that they had so recently wed.

Hardly were the Houstons settled at the Nashville Inn before the governor announced, January 30, that he planned to contest Billy Carroll's candidacy. With the battle joined, Carroll's forces, indignant over what they called Houston's betrayal, seemed anxious not to draw the name of Andrew Jackson into the fray. Houston, though making no proclamation to this effect, let it be known that he had the support of the President-elect.

The styles of the two candidates were markedly different. Carroll was an expert arm-twister, Houston a gifted speaker. Moreover, Houston had gained much popularity as a campaigner for Jackson. There is little doubt that had he remained in the race, Houston would have won the election. This contest, however, was not to occur. Between January 30 and April 9, Houston was at his desk at Nashville, in his apartment with Eliza, or addressing crowds all over the state. We know nothing of his relationship with his wife during this period.

A. J. Donelson's younger brother, Daniel, noted that in March he had conversed with Houston and learned that the governor had a "grand scheme" for stirring up a revolution of the white settlers of Texas against the Mexican authorities. According to Donelson, Houston's principal agent in this enterprise was William Wharton, who had just returned to Texas to foment such an uprising. Wharton was to inform Houston when the time was right for him to make an appearance and assume personal leadership. The Donelson report, fanciful as it appears at first, may be an accurate reflection of Houston's desperate frame of mind, when taken in the context of a marriage that must have been very nearly on the rocks in March, 1829. He had discussed the prospects in Texas with William Wharton's brother, John, almost two years before. He had been interested in land speculation there as early as 1822. So a renewed concern, on the part of a man whose personal life was crumbling, is not completely far-fetched.

There is another possible explanation of the Donelson account: Houston may have talked to him while drunk, for alcohol was a serious difficulty for Houston at this time. What role this played in his faltering marriage is unknown, but when Houston drank, he drank too heavily, and when he drank too heavily, he doubtless gave voice to whims. We know that A. J. Donelson paid particular attention to his brother's letter only after Houston's separation from Eliza. At that time Donelson advised Andrew Jackson to have Houston placed under surveillance. By early April the governor's movements were being watched by a mysterious Irishman, H. Haralson, who first made Houston's acquaintance at the tavern of the Nashville Inn. Haralson sent regular reports to Donelson or John Eaton, the new Secretary of War.

Daniel Donelson heard from another source that Houston's campaign was making excellent progress: "I think Houston will beat Carroll—they have commenced their canvass & from this out will be busy— It is a poor business for men so high in office to be trudging about. I wish to God we had more Jacksons to put such things down." On April 8 Houston's cousin, Robert L. Caruthers, informed Donelson that "The [gubernatorial] contest will be pretty close in middle Ten. but Houston will get a small majority unless I am extending myself by my partiality. If I be right in this opinion there can be no doubt about the general result." In the unlikely event that Houston were defeated, Caruthers noted, he would have a better chance than Felix Grundy of securing the United States Senate seat that fell vacant from the Tennessee legislature. Tennessee Judge Jo C. Gould, an astute observer, gave the opinion at about this same time that Houston's reelection would assure him a future that might even lead him to the White House.[9]

But all these varying appraisals of Houston's political future failed to take into account the fact that he was on the brink of personal catastrophe. At precisely what date the appalling wave of despair broke over Eliza and Sam Houston we cannot tell. Nor is it probable that we shall ever know what occasioned the disaster—though there is a plethora of hypotheses. Marquis James, drawing on the memoirs of John T. Moore (whose sources seem to have been the Nashville gossip of the day), stated that Houston may have returned unexpectedly to their rooms from a campaign journey:

> What the scene was no one can know. It has been said that Eliza was weeping over old love-letters. It has been said she was in a man's arms—a supposition not favored by the evidence. In any event, provocation was such that Sam Houston accused his wife of infidelity.
>
> The fearful indictment had scarcely fallen from his lips when doubts assailed him. It was the old story of jealous rage and terrible suspicions: a moment of wild accusation and a lifetime of regret. Naturally, Eliza desired to clear her name. By mutual consent the matter was laid before

a third party and then, by means unexplained, the news reached the Allens [at Gallatin]. There was no repairing anything after that.[10]

The "third party" has never been identified. One possibility is the Reverend William Hume, who performed the marriage ceremony. He and Houston were friends; and as an intimate of the Allens, he might well have been the source of their information. When the fact of the breach was made known, Tennesseans supplied many explanations: Sixteen years after the Battle of Horseshoe Bend, the wound that Houston had sustained in his groin remained incompletely healed, and this was repulsive to his bride. Another explanation is that his frontier crudeness offended her—that his bluff sexual approach was better suited to tavern maids and Indian women.[11]

An article that appeared in a Texas newspaper in 1901 named as Eliza's luckless lover one Will Tyree, "a poor but promising lawyer who went to Missouri to build up a practice, intending to return and marry." According to the story the Allens prevailed on their daughter to make the more opportune match with Houston during Tyree's absence. She was, however, unable to conceal her true feelings from her new husband.[12] Whatever the occasion for the rupture, Houston agreed that she should go home. On April 9 he wrote the following letter to John Allen:

Mr. Allen   The most unpleasant & unhappy circumstance has just taken place in the family, & one that was entirely unnecessary at this time. Whatever had been my feelings or opinions in relation to Eliza at one time, I have been satisfied & it is now unfit that anything should be a[d]vertted to. Eliza will do me the justice to say that she believes I was really unhappy. That I was *satisfied & believed her virtuous,* I had assured her on last night & this morning. This should have prevented the facts ever coming to your knowledge . . . & that of Mrs. Allen. I would not for millions it had ever been known to you. But one human being knew anything of it from me, & that was by Eliza's consent & wish. I would have perished first, & if mortal man had dared to charge my wife or say [a]ught against her virtue I would have slain him. That I have & do love Eliza none can doubt,—that she is the only earthly object dear to me God will witness.

The only way this matter can now be overcome will be for us all to meet as tho it had never occurred, & this will keep the world, as it should

78

be, ignorant that such thoughts ever were. Eliza stands acquitted by me. I have received her ever as a virtuous wife, & as such I pray God I may ever regard her . . . & trust I ever shall.

She was cold to me, & I thought did not love me. She owns that such was one cause of my unhappiness. You can judge how unhappy I was to think I was united to a woman who did not love me. This time is now past, & my future happiness can only exist in the assurance that Eliza & myself can be happy & that Mrs. Allen & you can forget the past,—forgive all & find your lost peace & you may rest assured that nothing on my part shall be wanting to restore it. Let me know what is to be done.[13]

As events proved, nothing was to be done. The letter raises many unanswered questions. How was Eliza able to convince Houston of her fidelity and love? What were the circumstances that led him to the dreadful accusation—other than that she was cold to him? Only the most hardened cynic would propose that he wished a reunion because of its crucial importance to his reelection.

A further complication arose from the fact that Eliza was at the Nashville Inn when Houston wrote John Allen. The likelihood is that she went to Gallatin at about the same hour on April 9 that he sent the letter. Later on, when the letter was published by the Allens, the statement was made that it was dispatched after her departure. Houston vehemently denied this and there is no apparent reason to doubt him. However, upon Eliza's return John Allen informed his intimates and relations that Houston had sent his daughter home because he questioned her virtue. Houston never uttered a word in public or private about this. In *The Only Authentic Memoir,* reference to this marriage is terse. It was as "unhappy as it was short," owing to conditions "about which far more has been conjectured than known by the world."[14] It was John Allen who made the matter public, hoping to bring the governor down. His aspirations were realized.

Llerena Friend, the most conscientious of recent Houston scholars, supports Marquis James' explanation of the situation: "Impulsive and jealous, and humiliated by the knowledge that he had not been able to supplant another man in her affection, he exclaimed, 'Eliza, I would not permit you to be my slave and so will return you to your family.' He felt that only one person's happiness need be sacrificed and that Eliza would secure a divorce and marry her former fiance."[15] [Miss Friend does not support the quote ascribed to Houston.]

From the abject tone of his letter to Allen, we see plainly that Houston regretted his accusations against Eliza almost at once. He made a visit to Gallatin and requested his father-in-law's permission to talk with her. Having heard from his daughter of her husband's temper (presumably when he was drunk), Allen agreed on condition that one of his sisters remain in the room with the couple during the interview. The sister recorded her recollection many years later: "[Houston] knelt before [Eliza] and with tears streaming down his face implored forgiveness . . . and insisted with all his dramatic force that she return to Nashville with him. Had she yielded to these entreaties what the future may have brought them none can tell. As it was there were many years of sadness to be endured."[16]

We do not know the date of this meeting. On the afternoon of April 11 there was a political gathering at Cockrell's Springs, where Billy Carroll and the governor were to debate. Colonel Willoughby Williams, sheriff of Davidson County, had mustered a battalion of the state militia to add glamor to the occasion. A good friend of Houston's, Williams reported that the governor was in good spirits and noted that he had been cheered to learn that the crowd appeared to side firmly with him. Williams accompanied Houston most of the way back to Nashville, leaving him off at the home of John Boyd, a prominent supporter. At the time of their parting, the sheriff thought Houston very cheerful.

This was a remarkable performance, only forty-eight hours after writing that despairing letter to John Allen. We tentatively set the date of his abortive meeting with Eliza as Sunday, April 12, because if Houston had been definitively rejected by her sooner, he probably would not have gone through with the Cockrell's Springs debate.

Having seen Eliza and had his attempt at reconciliation turned aside, Houston rode back to Nashville and closeted himself at the inn, solaced by friends to whom he apparently confided nothing but the barest bones of the sorry affair. He also sought spiritual help. Specifically, he wanted to be baptized. He first asked Dr. Hume to perform the service. Hume refused. He then turned to the Reverend Obadiah Jennings, pastor of the Nashville Presbyterian Church, who also declined. The only other source of comfort was drink, and we may be reasonably sure that Houston stayed drunk for the next ten days.[17]

During this time he made two decisions of central significance to his life: He would resign the governorship and he would leave Nashville.

On April 16 he wrote General William Hall, Speaker of the Tennessee Senate (who would take his place until Carroll's inauguration). He asked Willoughby Williams to deliver the letter:

It has become my duty to resign the office of Chief magistrate of the state ... & to place in your hands the authority & responsibility ... which on such an event ... devolved on you by the provisions of our constitution.—

In dissolving the political connexion which has so long ... & in such a variety of forms existed between the people of Tennessee and myself, no private afflictions however deep or incurable ... can forbid an expression of the grateful recollections so eminently due to the kind partialities of an indulgent public.—From my earliest youth, whatever of talent was committed to my care ... has been honestly cultivated & expended for the common good; and at no period of a life which has certainly been marked by a full portion of interesting events ... have any views of private interests or private ambition been permitted to mingle in the higher duties of public trust.—In reviewing the past, I can only regret that my capacity for being useful was so unequal to the devotion of my heart, and it is one of the few remaining consolations of my life ... that even had I been blessed with ability to equal to my zeal, my countrys generous support in every vicissitude of my life ... has been more than equal to them both. ....

And although shielded by a perfect consciousness of undiminished claim to the confidence & support of my fellow citizens, yet delicately circumstanced as I am, & by my own misfortunes, more than by the fault or contrivance of any one, overwhelmed by sudden calamities, it is certainly due to myself & more respectful to the world ... that I should retire from a position which, in the public judgment, I might seem to occupy by questionable authority.—[18]

Even before the break with Eliza, Houston had been talking about Texas. When the time for decision was upon him, however, he changed his mind. The day before he made his resignation official, he was reported by an acquaintance to be planning to leave for the Arkansas Territory, to take up residence once again with the Cherokees of Oolooteka's band.[19]

Sheriff Williams gave Houston a description of the ugly mood that had invested Nashville when news of his separation and resignation

81

became generally known. The gossips, thriving on the paucity of information, tended to be strongly sympathetic to Eliza. All the tales of Houston's extravagances, even of his heroism in the War of 1812, were suddenly turned against him. His effigy was burned at Gallatin. *Niles' Register* reported that the militia had to be called out to prevent a similar occurrence in Nashville, where mobs gathered to menace the safety of the former governor, now in disgrace.[20]

Mrs. Emily Drennen, who seems to have known Houston reasonably well, wrote a friend shortly after his resignation:

> There is a dreadfull stir in the country and town about our governor—he was married two months ago and is now parted from his wife. There is a thousand tails afloat. He has resined, and poor fellow is miserable enough. I never can believe he has acted ungentlemanly untill I see him and know the trouth from himself for he was a man so popular I know it must be some thing dreadfull or he never would have left her. He is very sick and has been ever since. As soon as he gets well enough he intends leaveing the country never to return. He is comeing to see us before he leaves town and then I will know the trouth. And what is more astonishing none of [Eliza's] connection has been near. If he was in fault I should think some of them would resent it. He never has said anything to any one not even his brother about her. I suppose he has toald his most intimate friends for none of his friends blame him so when you here repoarts about him you may know they are not so. He has a good menny enemies and a great menny friends. He says time will show who is to blame. The reason he does not tell. I expect you are tyered of this but I feel so interested.[21]

Mrs. Drennen's reference to a brother of Sam Houston is the only note on record that he was in contact with a member of his immediate family during this great crisis. It is doubtful that he made the promised visit to the Drennens. If he made the call, he may have "put on the white-tanned skin of a pied heifer," which an intimate of the Allens said he wore in the streets, adding that Houston pretended to be mad. Like Mrs. Drennen's allusion to his being "very sick," the madness was probably intoxication. In *The Only Authentic Memoir,* C. Edwards Lester quotes Houston as saying that reports of angry mobs caused him to leave the safety of the inn and show himself in the square, where he was neither accosted nor jeered.[22]

82

For most of the week left to him in Nashville after his resignation, Houston stayed in his rooms with friends. His most constant companion was Dr. John Shelby of Sumner County, a man who had known Eliza Houston all her life. Throughout the night of April 22 these two men, with the aid of the devoted Willoughby Williams, burned Houston's personal correspondence. On the eve of his departure from Tennessee Houston must have had plenty to drink to ease his sorrow.

At dawn of April 23 Houston was brought by his two companions down the steep bluff from Nashville's main square to the steamboat landing on the Cumberland. There he was placed aboard the *Red Rover*, a vessel bound downriver. Only one man traveled with him, the ubiquitous Irishman, H. Haralson. Sam Houston signed the register under the name of Samuels.

VII

HARALSON WAS an ideal traveling companion for Houston. Just as fond of the bottle as the man he had been assigned to spy on, he was also an enthusiastic riverboat gambler. Houston's incognito status was brief. At Clarksville, about sixty miles downriver from Nashville, the *Red Rover* was boarded by two of John Allen's brothers who feared that Houston's departure from the capital would somehow reflect on the good name of their niece. To allay their apprehensions, Houston requested that they publish a notice in the Nashville papers to the effect that he would come back and challenge any person to a duel who dared question the virtue of his estranged wife. This apparently satisfied the Allens, for they left the boat before she proceeded farther. According to Edward Burleson, a Texan who claimed to have heard this story directly from Houston, no such advertisement ever appeared.[1]

Another account of this journey has it that Houston took along a male slave whom he lost in a poker game. However, according to *The Only Authentic Memoir* Houston and Haralson kept to themselves during the trip. No mention is made of a slave or of gambling, though excessive drinking is conceded.[2] Also Houston did not learn of Haralson's mission until after they had parted.[3]

The *Red Rover's* circuitous passage took her to the confluence of the Ohio with the Mississippi at Cairo, where the two men secured a flatboat for the trip south to the junction of the Arkansas. At Helena, it is reported, they met Jim Bowie, who had visited Texas the year before. Bowie apparently found it difficult to believe that the scruffy, drunken figure who questioned him so closely about Texas could be the great Sam Houston of Tennessee. (Another version of this meeting sets it aboard the *Red Rover.*)[4]

At some point in the two-week journey that terminated at Little Rock, up the Arkansas River, Houston told Haralson that he was having second thoughts about stopping with the Cherokees. Instead, he outlined an outlandish scheme for the establishment of an "empire" in the American Northwest. Haralson dutifully reported the drink-inspired plan to Secretary of War Eaton.

President Jackson, still unaware of the sensational change in Houston's circumstances, offered Billy Carroll an ambassadorship so that he might avoid the embarrassment of being defeated at the polls. Only on April 30 did word reach the White House of Houston's resignation —and from the tone of Jackson's letter of that date to John G. McLemore, it is apparent that he knew no more of the details than anyone else. "I have this moment heard a rumor of poor Houston's disgrace. My God, is the man mad?"[5]

Charles Noland, a Virginian visiting Little Rock, wrote his father that Houston had reached that town some days earlier. He was drinking heavily, and boasting that he would create a "Rocky Mountain alliance," of which he was to be the first emperor. At that same time Sam Houston was composing a letter to the President. The beginning set the tone: "Tho' an unfortunate . . . and doubtless . . . the most unhappy man now living, whose honor, so far as depends upon himself, is not lost, I can not brook the idea of your supposing me capable . . . of an act that would . . . blot the escut[c]heon of human nature!" This remark was induced by reports that Jackson might think Houston was considering "an interprize calculated to injure . . . or involve my country." He assured the President of his innocence. In his final paragraph he described his immediate plans. In two hours' time, he and Haralson would take the steamer for Oolooteka's wigwam. He hoped to hunt buffalo that summer, and urged Jackson to write him. "I will always be happy to hear from you. I need not tell you how sincerely and truly I wish you a successful and glorious administration."[6]

Houston and Haralson left Little Rock that day, with a new companion, John Litton. The trio boarded the *Facility,* which plied the Arkansas as far as Cantonment Gibson, the most distant main outpost of the great Arkansas Territory. On reaching Fort Smith the three men were so intoxicated that they began what has been repeatedly described as a "bacchian celebration." Careening around a great fire, they gradually removed articles of clothing, which they tossed into the blaze. When all three men were naked, they fell into a deep slumber. The next morning, as the *Facility* was readied to proceed upstream, Houston and Haralson reboarded the vessel with no compunction about leaving Litton without clothing and without funds.

As the boat neared her final destination, a soldier attempted to fire a signal gun but the weapon misfired, killing some members of the crew and damaging much of the cargo. Adding to the spectacle of the docking of the *Facility* at Cantonment Gibson was the fact that Sam Houston was very drunk.

Word that Houston was aboard the *Facility* had been brought to Cantonment Gibson by messengers.[7] Haralson and the ex-governor were allowed no time to sober up before being given a welcome by Oolooteka's Cherokees. The two had reached Cantonment Gibson under cover of darkness on May 20, give or take a day, and black slaves belonging to Oolooteka carried torches to light the chief's way to the steamboat landing. *The Only Authentic Memoir* describes the meeting: "It was night when the steamboat . . . arrived at [Webbers] [F]alls, two miles . . . from the dwelling of the Cherokee Chief. As the boat passed the mouth of the river, intelligence was passed to the old man that his adopted son . . . was on board. . . . [T]he chief came down to meet his son."[8]

Although he never articulated his reason for choosing the Cherokee nation for his place of exile, we may plausibly suppose that Houston knew of no other location where he would be made to feel welcome. The Western Cherokees had much to be discontent about, but Oolooteka's reception of the prodigal was warm, according to *The Only Authentic Memoir:*

> The old chief threw his arms around [Houston] and embraced him with great affection. "My son," said he, "eleven winters have passed since we met. My heart has wandered often where you were; and I heard you were a great chief among your people. Since we parted . . . I have heard that a dark cloud had fallen on the white path you were walking, and when it fell in your way you turned your thoughts to my wigwam. I am glad of it—it was done by the Great Spirit. . . . We are in trouble and the Great Spirit has sent you to give us council, and take trouble away from us. I know you will be our friend, for our hearts are near to you, and

you will tell our troubles to the great father, General Jackson. My wigwam is yours . . . rest with us."

Houston described Oolooteka's style of life in the new wilderness. "His wigwam was large and comfortable, and he lived in patriarchal simplicity and abundance. He had ten or twelve [black] servants, a large plantation, and not less than five hundred head of cattle. The wigwam of this aged chieftain was always open to visitors, and his bountiful board was always surrounded by welcome guests. He never slaughtered less than one beef a week . . . for his table." Thus, despite the difficulties the Western Cherokees had encountered on settling in this new land, they had adapted themselves well and, according to all available accounts, were at least as prosperous as they had been in Tennessee.[9]

Their main trouble was the hostility of other tribes, particularly the Osages and Creeks. Reports from the period refer to frequent raids between nations in which women and children were the most numerous victims. Another major problem was relations with the United States. The whites maintained a garrison at Cantonment Gibson to arbitrate intertribal quarrels, to prevent alcohol from falling into the hands of the Indians, and to regulate trade. Because of the corruption of the agent system little of this was carried out effectively. There was, as well, the problem of Washington's reluctance to remit payments due under various contracts. No doubt Oolooteka's welcome was partially inspired by his belief that Houston could facilitate transactions with the Indian Office of the War Department.

The day after Houston threw himself into Oolooteka's arms, Andrew Jackson, still suspicious of his younger friend's motives, wrote some lines in his daybook. He had been receiving reports from Haralson, who made no attempt to distinguish between Houston's drunken ramblings and his sober reflections. The President was alarmed and wanted to put himself on the record as having no part of any plot that Sam Houston might be formulating: ·

May 21, 1829—recd from Genl. Duff Green an extract of a letter (Doctor [John] Marable to Genl. G.) containing declaration of Gov. Houston . . . that he would conquer Mexico or Texas, and be worth two million in two years, &c. Believing this to be the effusion of a distempered brain, but as a precautionary measure I directed the Secretary of

88

War [John Eaton] to write and enclose to . . . [the] Govr of Arkansas, the extract, and instruct him if such illegal project should be discovered . . . to adopt prompt measure to put it down and give the government the earliest intelligence of such . . . enterprise with the names of all those who may be concerned therein.[10]

Duff Green was editor and publisher of the *United States Telegraph,* friendly to Jackson at this time but soon to become his bitter enemy. Since he had yet to receive Houston's reassuring communication of May 11 from Little Rock, the President's reaction to reports was one of simple prudence. From Nashville, Daniel Donelson added fuel to this fire; he wrote his brother in Washington that Houston's resignation had been part of his plan to overthrow Mexican rule of Texas.[11] Billy Carroll wrote the President on May 25, "The fate of Houston must have surprised you. . . . His conduct, to say the least, was very strange and charity requires us to place it to the account of insanity. I have always looked upon him as a man of weak and unsettled mind . . . incapable of fully meeting a reverse of fortune."[12]

Politically inspired though Carroll's indictment was, his appraisal of Houston cannot be dismissed. When faced with a predicament, he had more than once opted to run from it. His propensity to think of himself as persecuted when he was merely the victim of common political assault serves as evidence of neurosis. Chronic alcoholism exacerbated the condition. But even in a reflective mood, when he was no longer drinking, Houston could tell Lester that, "Seldom, if ever . . . in the history of this country has so malignant a persecution been waged against a public man." He only had to recall the campaign of vilification mounted against Andrew Jackson to find an example that made his own case seem mild.[13]

Oolooteka's wigwam was situated at a place the Cherokees called Tahlontusky, in memory of the chief's late brother. The village was a few miles from Cantonment Gibson, near Three Forks, where two lesser streams fed into the Grand River, a tributary of the Arkansas. It was the scene of festivities ordered by the chief to celebrate Houston's return. He found other old friends there—John and James Rogers and their recently widowed sister, Diana Rogers Gentry. She was to become a very important part of Houston's attempt to make sense out of the shambles of his life.

Oolooteka wanted his adopted son to be present at a Cherokee grand council meeting to take place at the end of June. Also invited was Colonel Matthew Arbuckle, commandant of Cantonment Gibson. Arbuckle, though not an unsympathetic figure, went along with the systematic bilking of the natives by white and half-breed agents, subagents, and "sutlers." Taking advantage of the Indians' distrust of specie, with which the government paid claims, these men made huge profits through exorbitant rates of exchange.[14]

Houston was drunk for the better part of every day and night. On one particularly painful occasion he disputed so violently with Oolooteka that he struck him and had to be subdued by a group of horrified braves. Later, he apologized publicly for this lapse. With surprising good temper he accepted the soubriquet affixed to him thereafter—"Big Drunk." It was a name that pursued Sam Houston into Texas, where it would haunt him for years.[15]

However, he remained sober when the need arose, and this was often. He was ideally suited to play the role of interpreter and peacemaker among the Cherokees, Creeks, and Osages, and to negotiate with the War Department on the Indians' behalf. But he was not the only sympathetic white in the region. Another was Auguste-Pierre Chouteau, who had come to the territory from Missouri and had been followed by a tribe of Osages because they thought so highly of him. He and Houston soon met and liked each other, though Chouteau was bemused by the Tennessean's style of dress.

W. S. Oldham had come to the territory from Tennessee to serve as a judge. He noted that Houston had gone native to such a degree that he "would never speak English to anyone and a deep melancholy caused him to avoid all intercourse with white men. . . . He was seen armed only with a bow and arrow. . . ."[16] Oldham's assertion is open to question, for though Houston lived mainly with the Cherokees for more than three years, he trafficked often with whites.

Owen P. White, a historian of early Texas, stated that during the first months of his stay in the territory, "no matter in what company he found himself . . . Sam Houston invariably brought up the subject of Texas as an independent country with himself at the head of it. . . ." Offering no substantiation for this allegation, White appears to have relied on accounts of Houston's drunken chatter. On the other hand, Houston certainly was always eager for news of Texas.

Before the meeting of the Cherokee grand council, Houston visited

Chouteau at his comfortable house. They discussed means of effecting a permanent peace among the three principal nations occupying the Arkansas Territory. During this stay, "a parcel of Osage Indians" arrived to complain to Chouteau that their white agent, John Hamtramack, was cheating them of the federal annuity. "They insisted," wrote Haralson to John Eaton, "that Genl Houston . . . and myself go with them to the [Osage] agency. We told them we would go to see what passed between them and their agent." Haralson also noted that Houston's plan was to go west after the hot weather, to set up his mountain kingdom. His masters, however, were less gullible than he. They soon assigned him elsewhere, and he vanished forever from Sam Houston's life as casually as he had entered it.[17]

The visit to Hamtramack's agency prevented Houston from taking part in the grand council meeting. Matthew Arbuckle sent two young officers as observers. To these men Oolooteka handed a message that said in part: "I invited my son Gov Houston here to listen to what I had to say . . . but my son had promised to attend a council of my Neighbors . . . I must do the best I can without him." Nothing important was resolved at this conference.

By June 21 Houston was back at Three Forks. On its way to him was a letter from Andrew Jackson, composed that day:

It has been communicated to me that you had the *illegal enterprise* in view of conquering Texas; that you had declared you would, in less than two years, be *emperor* of that country, by conquest. I must have really thought you deranged to have believed you had such a wild scheme in contemplation; and particularly . . . when it was communicated that the physical force to be employed was the Cherokee Indians! Indeed my dear sir, I cannot believe you have any such chimerical, visionary scheme in view. Your pledge of honor [in Houston's letter of May 11] to the contrary is a sufficient guaranty that you will never engage in any enterprise injurious to your country, or that you would tarnish your fame.[18]

While this Presidential vote of confidence was on its way, Houston remained under the surveillance of Matthew Arbuckle, a bachelor who maintained the frontier military tradition of being able to drink all night and fight all day. The two men caroused and talked freely. If the officer was seeking an insight into Houston's purpose he failed to discover anything that disturbed him. On June 22 a delegation of Creeks arrived at Cantonment Gibson with a communication for President Jackson. Their complaints were essentially the same as those registered by the Osages—that their agent, David Brearly, was a thief and that the Indian Office failed to attend to their interests. While Houston willingly endorsed this document, he would not attest to the validity of the allegations. The most serious, in the view of Jackson and Eaton, was that Brearly was trafficking in spirits with the Indians. It was acceptable for agents to deprive the red men of funds due them and even to starve them to death by exacting inflated prices in monopoly situations, but to allow them to get drunk was an unconscionable offense.

Two days after the arrival of the Creek emissaries, Houston penned a letter to John Eaton proposing solutions to some of the problems he had found since arrival in the territory. He recommended that Chouteau be charged with negotiating peace among the tribes and offered to assist in any way he could, without pay.[19] What impressed the Secretary of War and the President more than his advocacy of Chouteau was that Houston, in little more than a month, had succeeded in establishing amicable relations with the three major Indian nations settled in the territory. "Big Drunk" though he might be called, he was becoming a pivotal figure in the Southwest.

There was a Cherokee meeting at Bayou Maynard in July where younger chiefs, infuriated by harassment from other tribes, decided to retaliate in kind. Houston was helpless to prevent them.[20] According to some accounts, it was during this meeting that he saw Diana Rogers Gentry for the first time since his arrival in the Arkansas Territory. If this was the case, some months would elapse before they became a couple. Houston was not yet in the right frame of mind to entangle himself with another woman. The scalding memory of his marriage was too recent.[21] Occasional messages from Nashville reminded him that he was not forgotten there. John Wharton wrote that the tale of his Texan "plot" was not discredited in the Tennessee capital. "I have heard you intended an expedition against Texas. I suppose, if it is true, you will let your Nashville friends know of it."[22]

Houston went to Fort Smith in the middle of July to see what he could do to aid the Choctaws settled near there. Like other tribes they were having trouble with their agent. On July 22 he wrote John Eaton of their plight. For nearly two months there was no answer.

His weeks of travel had exposed him to a fever, probably malaria. He managed to make his way back to Oolooteka's wigwam, where he was lovingly nursed back to health. His recovery seemed complete by September 19. In the interim, he had received a letter from his old commander, Thomas Hart Benton, now an established politician in Missouri, who sent him two articles about the southwestern boundary question and urged Houston to turn to journalism. On September 19 Houston wrote a long letter to Andrew Jackson, stating that he had been near death. Concerning his activities he wrote: "To meliorate the conditions of the Indians, to suggest improvements to their growing institutions, to prevent fraud . . . and peculation . . . on the part of the Governments Agents . . . and to direct the feelings of the Indians in kindness to the Government, and inspire them with confidence in its justice . . . and magnanimity towards the Red People have been objects of my constant solicitude . . . and attention . . . since I have been among them!" He did not plan to stay much longer in the Arkansas Territory, where "there is no field for distinction—it is fraught with *factions;* and if my object were to obtain wealth, it must be done by fraud . . . and many perjuries would be necessary." He thought of moving to Natchez to reestablish his political career. "It is hard for an old Trooper . . . to forget the *note* of the *Bugle!*"[23]

This letter revealed a rebirth not only of concern for politics but for life itself. He was sending up a trial balloon in his reference to Natchez, well aware that he was still anathema in white civilization. Gone, however, were most traces of the self-pity that had marked so many of his letters during the previous six months.

VIII

NOT LONG after posting his letter to Jackson, Houston received another note from John Wharton, who proposed that he visit Texas: "It is a fine field for enterprise. You can get a grant of land, be surrounded by your friends, and what may not the coming of time bring about?"[1] There is no record of his replying to either of Wharton's letters. For the moment, he seemed content to stay in the Arkansas Territory.

His role as intermediary increased in importance at the end of October when Major E. W. du Val, white agent to the Western Cherokees, arrived to remit $50,000 due under various treaties. The mood of the Indians gathered at Three Forks was genial, but it turned to dismay when they learned that payment was to be in specie, not gold. Houston was also indignant, for he realized that the Indians would be much more easily cheated, since they thought paper money was worthless. Unscrupulous traders and smugglers closed in on the gathering at Oolooteka's village.[2]

An authorized trader himself by now, Houston thought he could do himself and the Indians a good turn if he could obtain government contracts to provide rations and supplies to Indians gradually being transferred from their lands in the United States to territories in the West under the provisions of the Indian Removal Act of 1830.[3] For this purpose he became a Cherokee citizen. He thought his new status would afford him certain trading privileges not shared by American whites.[4] He had concluded that his future lay in the West, but Houston's conduct at this time is marked by conclusions rapidly reached and rapidly abandoned. In October, 1829, he had been sure he would not be able to restore his personal and political fortunes in Tennessee. Not too long afterward he changed his mind.

Affiliation with the Cherokees did not suggest enmity for the United States. He had added to his loyalties, and in December he would try to prove that, when he accepted Oolooteka's suggestion that he go to Washington as his emissary. He hoped to discourage Andrew Jackson from driving the Eastern Cherokees out of Georgia and the remaining Western Cherokees from their little corner of Tennessee without providing additional land in the Arkansas Territory for these new-comers to live on comfortably. He also intended to plead for fairer financial treatment for the Indians and finally to secure an Indian provisioning contract.

He left Three Forks in mid-December, accompanied by half-breeds Walter Webber and John Brown. He donned Cherokee dress and took a steamer down the Arkansas. When he reached Fort Smith, agent E. W. du Val asked Houston if he planned to lodge a complaint against him in Washington. Houston admitted that it was likely. Thus forewarned, du Val prepared a defense for himself.

The party changed vessels on reaching the Mississippi. As the steamboat *Amazon* reached the border of Tennessee, on Christmas Eve, Houston was moved to write some nostalgic verse:

> There is a proud undying thought in man,
> That bids his soul still upward look,
> To fames proud cliff! And longing
> Look in hope to grace his name
> For after ages to admire, and wonder
> How he reached the dizzy, dangerous
> Hight, or where he stood, or how—
> Or if admiring his proud station fell
> And left a name alone!!
> This is ambition's range, and while it seeks
> To reach
> Beyond all earthy name,
> And stands where millions never
> Dared to look, it leaves content
>   . . . the
> Companions of a virtuous heart! . . .

There is a race of mortals wild . . .
Who range the desert free
And roam where floods
Their onward currents pour
In majesty, as free as Indian thoughts,
Who feel that happiness and
Content are theirs.
They owe no homage to written rules,
. . . no allegiance to idle forms
. . . which
Virtue dare not own!
But proud of freedom,
In their native words, they
. . . pitch their hopes of endless joys
In fields where games of never
Dying sort . . .
Delights the hunter's soul![5]

There is no indication that these lines were addressed to anyone in particular. They seem to be the private musings of a lonely man at night on the river during the Christmas season. Four days later, while the *Amazon* still paddled up waters flanking Tennessee, Houston wrote Judge John H. Overton, the state's chief justice, that he planned to visit Nashville on his way back from Washington. He assured the judge, who was a staunch Jacksonian, that he would do nothing to embarrass the President. As it developed, he was to step into a dense bed of nettles.[6]

Having left Webber and Brown along the way to make purchases for his new trading enterprise and to estimate costs of provisioning emigrating Indians, Houston reached Washington about January 12, 1830, and soon visited Andrew Jackson.[7] Tradition has it that their first meeting was at a diplomatic reception. However pleased to see his former protégé, the President may have been as bemused by his bizarre appearance as were other Washingtonians. "[H]e has been described as wearing . . . a white hunting-shirt brilliantly embroidered, yellow leggings and moccasins elaborately worked with beads, with a circlet of turkey feathers for his head. He let his hair grow and braided it in a long queue, which hung down his back, and wore his beard upon his chin in a 'goatee,' shaving the rest of his face." He had a miniature painted of himself during this stay in Washington.[8]

At a subsequent interview with Jackson, Houston raised the subject of maltreatment of Indians, and presented two letters to the Great White Father from Oolooteka. After examining these documents and listening to an impassioned speech on the topic, the President asked for a statement in writing. Houston complied almost at once.[9] As a result Jackson agreed to see that various Indian territories were clearly delineated. However, in most other respects, Houston's embassy was a failure, at least as far as Cherokee aspirations were concerned.

When Thomas McKenney, Chief of Indian Affairs in the War Department, published an advertisement for bids on an Indian rations contract in February, Houston was prepared. He had been introduced to some New York financiers, John Van Fossen in particular, who were interested in underwriting his project. The President's concern at the time was the security of the boundary separating Texas from the United States. He asked Houston to keep him informed about the activities of Mexican troops in this area when he returned to Arkansas.[10] He also discussed the Indian rations contract with Houston. Trouble began when Duff Green, owner of the *United States Telegraph* and now the administration's enemy, reported finding Jackson and Houston with Secretary of War John Eaton poring over maps and papers in a manner he considered conspiratorial. Later, he published a version of this incident in which he suggested that there was a plot to defraud the government by awarding the provisions contract to Houston, irrespective of lower bids that might be made. In fact, there was no collusion between Houston and Jackson or Eaton. Houston made several trips to New York, where he made final arrangements with the rich Jacksonian John Van Fossen to finance the contract. In the light of subsequent developments, a single paragraph of Houston's letter of April 4 to Van Fossen is pertinent:

> To act in good faith with all parties, and to get just as much from the Government as will indemnify us for the use of capital employed . . . and the labor bestowed, is what I wish; and further, to do ample justice to the Indians in giving them full ration . . . and of good quality, should we get the contract, must be regarded as a "sine qua non" with us.[11]

This is not the viewpoint of a greedy man. Yet Houston was at least partially responsible for a blunder made by McKenney and Eaton; he should have insisted that they wait for bids from the South. The excuse later offered for this omission was the need for haste. Unfortunately for Houston, some months later John Eaton concluded that no contract at all should be awarded. He was under considerable pressure from Congress and although the facts were not fully disclosed until two years afterward, the Secretary of War gave as the ostensible reason for canceling bids the fact that the Senate had yet to ratify the Indian Removal Act. It appeared a sound, strategic withdrawal. It is a cruel irony that Indians were being driven from their lands as if the act had been ratified.[12]

Long before John Eaton made his decision, Houston was on his way back to the Southwest. He returned by way of Tennessee, despite a warning that his life would be menaced were he to set foot in the state. Feeling still ran high over the "desertion" of Eliza.[13] Emotions had been kept at this level of intensity by the Allens and supporters of Billy Carroll. So long as Houston remained a controversial figure, there would be no danger of his attempting a political comeback. However, he was determined to return to Nashville. He wanted to find out for himself where he stood with his old constituents. Also, he was involved with Cherokee trader Ben Hawkins in a venture to purchase a large piece of land in a desolate section of the state where there was supposed to be gold.

There may have been other reasons for his return: the nostalgia he had felt as he passed the Tennessee banks on his journey to Washington as well as a sense of personal honor. Having in effect been challenged by the warning received in Washington, he accepted the risk in order to prove his courage. An even more important impetus that cannot be proved is Houston's feeling for his wife. Did he or did he not want her back? If he wanted her back, what might his motive have been? Was it purely personal, purely political, or a combination of these? We do not know.

Confusion marks many accounts of Houston's stay in Tennessee during late April and early May, 1830. Although *The Only Authentic Memoir* makes no reference to it, some biographers have suggested that Houston went from Nashville to Gallatin as soon as he left his baggage at the house of his cousin, Robert McEwen. Accounts vary, but there is some agreement that if a meeting of Sam and Eliza occurred, it was in the presence of other members of the Allen family—all of whom opposed a reunion. Houston himself suggested that his wife might have agreed to a reconciliation had the decision been hers alone. But we are not even certain that he proposed anything of the sort or that he even had the chance. It is known that during this period the Allens sent Eliza to Carthage, Tennessee, to visit her uncle Robert and to place her beyond Houston's reach. His own testimony is that he would not have her back, but when he came to this conclusion is obscure. In any case, reconciliation proved out of the question.

Houston left Tennessee with no further hope of salvaging his ruined personal life there or his political career. To ensure this the Allens and some of their Sumner County friends formed an "impartial" committee to determine whether or not, a full year after the separation, there was ground for impugning Eliza's virtue. The group was convened soon after Houston's arrival at Nashville and was prepared to publish its report by the end of April. However, the document was withheld from the press until he had actually departed.[14]

Hardly was he embarked on the steamboat *Nashville* before the Gallatin committee requested Tennessee editors to print a statement assuring all readers that Eliza Allen Houston was purity personified. Also made public was Houston's emotional letter to John Allen of April 9, 1829, with some interpretive comments that were bald distortions of the facts concerning the composition of the letter.

Not far down the Cumberland on May 18, Houston learned of what had happened and wrote Andrew Jackson his own version of the Allens' actions and the reasons behind them:

> You will ... have seen a useless publication against me by sundry respectable citizens of Sumner County. The object must have been to injure me, because it could not benefit others to review this subject at this time. They were anxious to publish my letter [to John Allen], and they have done it. They have stated untruly that it was written after the separation ... it was before. ... The letter was written under a state of vast excitement and with a view to quiet matters, until the election for Governor was over and a friend of the country elected Speaker of the Senate, when I would have resigned and left the world without the slightest noise, and left it in darkness ... as to the cause and all things connected with the whole matter.
>
> Therefore I said [in the Allen letter] I was "satisfied." I was as to the

course I would . . . and ought to pursue. It is stated [in the committee report] that my treatment induced her to return to her Fathers house for protection. This is utterly false and without foundation. . . . I would not claim . . . nor even wish sympathy to be extended to my case by mortal being. To me the thought of it is as cold as the breezes of Norway. I never sought to injure her with any one. To you, even *you*, Sir, in whose estimation I have been proud to stand most honorable and fair, I appeal to know of your heart . . . if I cast the slightest reflection upon her . . . or her immediate family. But I have drunk the cup, and the *dregs* only remain for me to consume. I feel well satisfied, nor will I ever permit myself to abandon the ground which I have assumed. I have sacrificed everything that was Glorious to my peculiar necessities & conscious honor . . . and rectitude only remain as my companions. They are old friends, and will not desert me in time to come.

The recent attack would not have been made upon me . . . if it had not been supposed that I was down in society. The affections of the people of Tennessee are with me, and if I would present myself to them again, they would shew the world that they have confidence in me . . . and care nothing about private matters, which they cannot understand.[15]

The matter continued to prey on his mind. Two days later, when he reached the mouth of the White River, he wrote William B. Lewis, Jackson's former secretary, now an auditor in the Indian Department. Two paragraphs are pertinent:

My honest belief is that if I would return to Tennessee I would beat [Billy Carroll] for Governor, but I am too poor!!! I have a knowledge, too, of the late publication at Gallatin, though it did not come until I had left Nashville . . . when they had lost all hopes of a reunion. . . .

They sent [Eliza] to Carthage lest she should come to Nashville . . . in spite of them and I would not receive her. If she had come this would have been the case, so I said to my friends from the time I arrived there. Great efforts . . . and strong hopes of fame were held out to me but . . . all of no use. Tho' the world can never know my situation and may condemn me[,] God will justify me![16]

The suggestion that he might successfully oppose Billy Carroll is purest bravado, as was his comment to Jackson about enjoying the affection of the people. Houston must have known it was impossible for him to stand for election so long as the odor of scandal still clung to his broken marriage. His plea of poverty had little relevance. Had he been a plausible candidate, he would have had no difficulty financing a campaign.

As a steamboat bore him up the Arkansas, Houston recognized at last that his marital and political ties with Tennessee had been definitively severed. This realization was of central importance to his future. Whatever misgivings he might have held about becoming involved with another woman had been banished. And if he were to have another political career, he must establish himself as a force on the frontier. He moved in both directions simultaneously.

He reached Cantonment Gibson toward the end of May to find that E. W. du Val had dismissed his old friend John Rogers as official Cherokee interpreter. Houston saw immediately to his reinstatement. Ultimately, du Val was driven from office and he died before the year was out.[17] Both the Indian rations contract issue and the ensuing Congressional investigation were being discussed at Cantonment Gibson when Houston arrived. His name and John Eaton's had been unfavorably linked in this connection.

On June 13 he wrote Eaton from Wigwam Neosho, his home at Three Forks, referring to an earlier letter in which he had proposed himself as agent to the Cherokees. He now withdrew the request. "If the situation were now offered to me *by you*—as a man of principle and honor I would feel bound to reject it . . . for reasons that have lately arisen. . . . [I]t has been stated . . . that I . . . sought to impose upon the Government on account of the Indian rations. . . ." He identified his accuser as Luther Blake, a trader-agent who had long been taking advantage of his position to profit enormously. Houston despised him; the feeling was mutual. Blake had been low bidder for the contract Van Fossen had sought with Houston's cooperation. In this letter, Houston exposed a conspiracy by Blake and his associates to defraud the government but nothing was to be salvaged now. He ended his letter with the information that he planned to write a series of articles for the *Arkansas Gazette*, "showing in what manner the agencies have been . . . and are managed in this quarter. The innocent will not suffer, the guilty ought not to escape. . . ."[18]

The pieces for the *Arkansas Gazette* began to appear June 22. They drew much bitter correspondence and enlivened the pages of that weekly for more than five months. They had the effect of making Houston a hero to the Indians of the territory and a villain to most of the whites. They represent the most scathing and comprehensive indictment of white American conduct, official and unofficial, with respect to the Indians to appear in print prior to the Civil War. Houston's first piece opened with a statement of intention: "To remedy trifling evils ... requires some effort! how much greater, then, must be the exertion necessary to overcome vast evils, when a whole community experience the anguish of hope deferred ... and promises violated or totally disregarded."[19]

On June 28 he wrote John Houston a letter which, in view of the first article to appear in the *Arkansas Gazette,* indicated his awareness that he might no longer remain the darling of Jackson or Eaton. "I cannot long be in favor at *Court*. The Old Chief will always like me ... and trust me truly—but ... the War Department and me will differ. Eaton is destroying himself by retaining [Thomas] McKenney [Chief of Indian Affairs] and [William B.] Lewis. ... They are two bright links in a chain of the most *hellish corruption!*"[20]

Critical as the articles were of government policy, Houston laid principal blame at the feet of McKenney, whom he held responsible for having withheld payment to the Indians of the grants, bounties, and annuities long overdue. Moreover, McKenney had an obligation to see that agents' accounts were properly and regularly audited, a duty he treated very casually.[21] Thus, Houston had declared war against the Indian Department.

By the middle of July, his trading post at Wigwam Neosho was in operation. He prospered modestly because he was a white to be trusted. Nonetheless, despite the receipt of revenues from commerce and the sale of salt in the Arkansas Territory, Houston's business ventures were not nearly as profitable as he anticipated. It would always be this way. He was simply not cut out to be a businessman. Although he had discovered this at Maryville during his adolescence, he never failed to venture quixotically into new schemes, for he never fully accepted his lack of talent and ingenuity in finance. He was too scrupulous and too unimaginative. He was too cautious to be a successful speculator. Although his sense of fair play and his honesty were severe inhibitions to his hopes for monetary gain, they were always assets in his political life. His most scurrilous enemies were unable to accuse him convincingly of financial wrongdoing.

The concluding installment of his articles was published in the *Gazette* September 8. His writings had, by now, attracted national attention and been extensively reprinted. Houston's aggressive attacks were a threat to the entire white establishment in the Arkansas Territory. Reply was inevitable. So strong, indeed, was the response of a man who signed himself "Tekatoka" that the editor of the *Gazette* refused to print it as part of the paper. Instead, he issued a special supplement in late October to hold himself immune from libel. Houston replied in his own name to "Tekatoka" (who was E. W. du Val). His tone was so corrosive that the editor was forced to publish it as a supplement as well. It appeared December 8, but by this time, du Val was dead.[22]

So ended Houston's career in Arkansas as a political journalist. The judgment of history must count the exercise only a partial failure. Houston was successful in his immediate purpose: the removal from office of a handful of scoundrels responsible for the crimes he had so tirelessly enumerated. In addition, some small benefits did accrue to the Cherokees and Osages, and Houston and Chouteau secured official positions. But basically little was done to ameliorate the conditions of the Indians in the Arkansas Territory.

However, for all the spleen he had vented in his articles, Sam Houston was probably happier than he had ever been in the previous thirty-seven years of his life. For, at last, he was loved.

Our information about Diana Rogers Gentry is maddeningly skimpy. Not even her age is known, though she was probably about ten years younger than Houston.[23] The only portrait of her is admittedly a product of pure imagination, much romanticized and evocative of a dusky Elizabeth Taylor playing Cleopatra. The moment when she began to share Sam Houston's life on a steady basis is not known.

She was the childless widow of David Gentry, a half-breed blacksmith who had come to Arkansas as early as 1817 and died in a skirmish with the Osages.[24] Thereafter she had lived under the protection of her uncle, Oolooteka, and her brothers—Houston's closest Cherokee friends. *The Only Authentic Memoir* is silent on the topic of Diana. The revelation of his relationship with her would not have aided his aspirations to the White House.

Conjecturing biographers have suggested that it was Diana who nursed Houston back to health when he was struck down by malaria for the first time in the summer of 1829. We know she lived in Oolooteka's village, perhaps in his wigwam, at that time, and that she was unencumbered emotionally. She would have been close to any intimate of Oolooteka's. Certainly, the circumstances were propitious for the development of a warm relationship between the handsome young widow and the bitter ex-governor who had left an estranged wife behind in Tennessee.

External evidence implies that only after Houston's return from Washington and Nashville did he and Diana set up housekeeping together in the structure he called Wigwam Neosho. Susceptible as he was to gossip, he would no doubt have conscientiously avoided the appearance of an entanglement so long as he had hopes of restoring his reputation and career—and even, perhaps, his marriage—in Tennessee. Also he would not have wanted to lead a Cherokee delegation to the national capital with rumors of sexual indiscretion trailing after him. Agent du Val would have liked nothing better than a chance to malign Houston, whom he knew was carrying serious charges against him.

The widow Gentry cannot have had many illusions about Sam Houston. She had seen him very sick and she had seen him very drunk. Yet she was drawn to him. The key to the successful arrangement they made seems to be that she was undemanding and subservient. Although there is abundant evidence that the Cherokees regarded the couple as man and wife, no record exists of a marriage ceremony. For Houston Diana was a wonderful and faithful mistress.

She is credited with having kept him from drinking himself to death—something a lonely, spiritually desperate man might well have done. She willingly put up with much nocturnal rowdiness and she was also aware, no doubt, that he was a bird of passage. He had gone off on many journeys since his arrival in Arkansas. He had left greatness behind him in Tennessee. There was surely greatness in his future. Although it would be two years before he made a final break with the Cherokee life, Diana may well have detected in his restless comings and goings all the clues she needed to realize that he would hardly settle permanently for life in the wilderness. She offered no objection. She accepted him exactly as she found him, and she loved him.

Did he love her? He was devoted to her and sorely needed her devotion to him. But he could not have given himself completely to his

105

relationship with her. Houston felt himself born to be a great public figure; he was extremely conscious, even when in the very depths of depression, of a sense of enormous destiny. He was too persistently aware of what we now call a "public image" to allow deep personal feelings to obstruct his political progress.

Diana was more concubine than wife, regardless of the Cherokee view of their affiliation. Houston depended on her loyalty, patience, and attentions, but he gave her in return little more than his sporadic presence and some sexual gratification. He seems to have used her, and she consented to this condition. When they parted late in 1832, Houston deeded all his property to Diana. It was the only tangible remembrance she had of him, for he had given her no children. After her death in 1836, she was buried near Cantonment Gibson. Later, her body was removed to the military cemetery. A headstone was set up over the grave, bearing the inscription: "Talahina, Indian wife of General Sam Houston." In death, the whites attributed an Indian name to her she never had.[25]

Despite his continuing interest in pursuing a political career, Sam Houston made no attempt to conceal from the public his liaison with Diana. Travelers of the time reported visits to Wigwam Neosho when she served as hostess. Within the privacy of that lodge, too, he found in her gentle and uncomplaining attentions a sort of tranquility he had never known before and would never know again. With Diana, for better or worse, Sam Houston could be and was completely himself. She was the only woman in his long life who ever allowed him this luxury.

IX

THE FIRST eight months of 1831 were not filled with incident for Houston nor did he seem much preoccupied with plans for the future. No letter from his hand in this period suggests that he intended leaving the Arkansas Territory, but we have reason to believe that Houston was not content at Wigwam Neosho. He was restless and in consequence he drank too much. The effect, as before, was to discredit him in the eyes of the Cherokees. In the spring, he sought election to the grand council and was defeated—the first electoral reverse he had ever suffered. The event embittered him. He threatened to quit Three Forks and set himself up among the Choctaws.[1] He talked once more of returning to Tennessee. But it was mainly talk. He was helpless in these months to alter dramatically his circumstances. The man of action was frustrated. Everything was too calm for him. His state was disquietingly comfortable. His trading post flourished. The Grand Saline salt marsh he had invested in was proving a modest success. He had hopes that the Tennessee land he owned with Ben Hawkins would yield gold. But nothing important was happening. Houston grew sullen—and he continued to drink.

At the end of April, George Vashon, who had replaced E. W. du Val as Cherokee agent, requested Eaton's permission to prevent Houston from interposing himself between the agent and the Indians. Vashon claimed that the government was poorly served by Houston, whose influence he called "pernicious."[2] Nothing came of this.

In the spring of 1831 Arkansas papers published yet another diatribe against Houston, again referring mainly to the rations contract dispute. He was in Tennessee when it came to his attention, presumably to look into his gold prospects there. At White River Landing, he boarded a paddle-wheeler bound north. Matthew Maury, a Virginian whose father was then American consul at Liverpool was a fellow passenger. Maury recorded extracts of Houston's almost incoherent babblings about the Indians, the nature of republican government, and his own dream for the future. It is impossible to prove that the speaker was drunk, but the substance of his remarks suggests it. Of the Indians, Maury quotes him as saying, "They steal from friend & foe, & tho' they were so friendly & so trusting to Genl. Houston . . . that they would not sign their treaty with the United States without consulting him, they sought all occasions of stealing his horses." After more whiskey had flowed, Houston was cited thus:

> My opinion . . . is that the U. S. can only hold together so long as there is an abundance of rich unoccupied wild land for settlers; because as soon as the population is at all dense we shall fall to pieces. I would run a line on the parallel of 33 or 34 to the Pacific Ocean, & say all north of it belongs to the U. S.; it would embrace Santa Fe and N. California, but we could easily get them by conquest or treaty, & I would have the U. S. establish a fort & settlement at the mouth of the Columbia. And by God Gentlemen (said he, striking the table) if they don't do it, & if I can get some capitalists to join me, I would easily collect 2 or 300 volunteers on the Western frontiers, & I would proceed to establish a colony myself at the mouth of the Columbia; . . . I should get plenty of settlers, & from our great distance we could & would maintain an independence of any power on earth.

Maury added in his journal that Houston "gave no symptoms of that general knowledge & information which the imagination would consider indispensable in a Governor of a State."[3]

His friends were also not much pleased by his state when he reached Nashville in the middle of July. During this visit he felt more an exile than ever before. He even rubbed salt in this wound by causing a local artist to portray him as the Roman emperor Gaius Marius standing amid the ruins of Carthage. On July 13, filled with self-pity and impotent rage, he uttered for publication this extraordinary proclamation:

. . . Now, know all men by these presents, that I, Sam Houston, "late Governor of the State of Tennessee," do hereby declare to all *scoundrels whomsoever* . . . that they are authorized to accuse, defame, calumniate, slander, vilify, and libel me to any extent, in *personal* or *private* abuse, and I do further proclaim, to whomever it may concern, that they are hereby *permitted* and *authorized* to write, indite, print, publish and circulate the same; and that I will in *no wise* hold them responsible to me in law, or honor. . . .[4]

The conclusion that he drafted this proclamation while drunk seems unquestionable. That he should have allowed it to see print (and much reprint) is evidence that he had again abandoned any new hope of ever resuscitating his career.

Houston did not long remain in Nashville after the publication of his paranoiac "proclamation." He returned to Wigwam Neosho and Diana.[5] He was not there many weeks. A letter from Maryville informed him that his mother was dying. He hastily departed for the plantation at Baker's Creek. However, Elizabeth Houston was dead before he reached her home. Although he made suitable comments about the proudness of her death in *The Only Authentic Memoir*, Houston probably only felt a slight loss. Not since the time of his recovery from his war wounds had he spent many nights beneath her roof. He was neither a dutiful son nor brother, when he had achieved success, and in failure, he did not turn to his family for help or solace. In letters to the cousins whom he loved, he rarely referred to them, and when he did, his tone was cool.

After paying respects to his mother's grave, Houston returned to Three Forks. At the end of October, he began to plan another trip to Washington to represent the Cherokees and to do some business for himself. In a letter he wrote to Lewis Cass, who had replaced John Eaton as Secretary of War, he revealed some doubt about what his reception would be in Washington. "Tho' I possess the most perfect *confidence* and *respect* for the present administration, I feel some delicacy in soliciting any favor or benefit in behalf of any person."

The Cherokee mission was about the same as it had been two years before. Houston led a fairly large party out of Three Forks that December. Not far from Fort Smith, he made the acquaintance of Alexis de Tocqueville and Gustave de Beaumont. The two Frenchmen were touring the Southwest after completing a study of the American penal system. De Tocqueville's impression of Houston was not favorable. He thought Houston's previous political success demonstrated the failings of popular sovereignty.[6]

The group passed through Tennessee to visit the few Western Cherokees remaining in that state, and also through Georgia, where they conferred with John Ross, intransigent leader of the Eastern Cherokee nation. Houston handed Ross a letter from Oolooteka:

> Our Eastern brethren have been induced to think we feel unfriendly towards them.... Those who have joined us in the West have been acclaimed our brothers.... And whenever you and your people should become disposed to join us in the West ... and partake of our exemption from the troubles we left behind, you will find a hearty welcome awaiting your arrival. My Brother chiefs! We have performed the arduous duties of the pioneers of our nation ... [O]ur troubles are over ... [L]et us as brother-chiefs unite to obtain for our people ... whatever may be deemed essential to the promotion of the future prosperity of our nation.[7]

We cannot determine whether the thoughts were Oolooteka's, but the style of the document was pure Houston. The letter failed to move John Ross, who persisted in his policy of total resistance to the authority of the federal government. At the time this resolution must have seemed admirable, but the great chief's stand resulted in tragedy for his people. The whites ultimately responded with terrible rage. The final result was the shameful Trail of Tears.

Houston was "legal adviser" to the delegation that reached Washington early in 1832. He lodged, as usual, at Brown's Hotel, where he entertained his cousin John and renewed political and social acquaintances. He had not been there long before the long-smoldering embers of the old rations contract affair were soon fanned into flame. Those immediately responsible were members of the "Indian Ring," a collection of rascals, including numerous whites who had been agents before Houston's protests in the press and to the War Department had caused their replacement. They wielded considerable influence and Houston's presence in the capital assured a debate on the topic in Congress.

In February and March he visited New York several times, where John Van Fossen introduced him to James Prentiss, a banker and principal of the Galveston Bay and Texas Land Company who undertook to subsidize the expenses of a Houston trip to Texas to investigate the possibilities of further land investment there. Though nothing finally came of the arrangement, Prentiss and Houston began a lengthy association and correspondence.

At the end of March Houston was in New York. He returned to Washington, probably on April 1. Two days later, he wrote this letter to Congressman William Stanbery of Ohio:

> I have seen some remarks in the *National Intelligencer* of the 2nd instant, in which you are represented to have said, "Was the Secretary of War [Eaton] removed in consequence of his attempt fraudulently to give to Governor Houston the contract for Indian rations?"
>
> The object of this note is to ascertain whether my name was used by you in debate, and, if so, whether your remarks have been correctly quoted.[8]

This set in motion a chain of circumstances that had the most galvanic effect on Houston's career. Stanbery had been accurately quoted in the paper. Houston's letter was tantamount to a challenge. Wholly forgotten was the proclamation published in Nashville the year before, granting immunity to all slanderers. Stanbery did not reply. Since any remark made on the floor of the House was privileged, Houston realized that he must seek redress by securing a statement from the Congressman that enjoyed no such protection. Stanbery, advised by his friends that Houston was seeking a direct confrontation outside the House, began to carry a pistol when he was on the streets of Washington.

On the night of April 13, at about eight, Houston was walking with Senator Buckner of Missouri and Congressman Blair of Tennessee. Blair recognized William Stanbery crossing beneath a streetlamp. Blair then disappeared, leaving Buckner the sole witness to what then transpired. Houston accosted Stanbery, identified him, and after calling him "a damned rascal," knocked him about the head with the handle of a hickory walking stick.

After recovering from his surprise, Stanbery defended himself. Though he was no match physically for the larger Houston, he had the advantage of two healthy arms, whereas Houston could use only one, the other still impaired by his war wound. The two men rolled about on the muddy street for some time, while Buckner looked on. Finally, Stanbery was able to reach for a pistol and stick its muzzle against his attacker's breast. He pulled the trigger. Buckner reported seeing a spark, but the sultry evening on Foggy Bottom had moistened his powder. The weapon failed to go off. Houston was spared. He staggered to his feet, flogged Stanbery several more times with his cane, and concluded by lifting the Congressman's feet into the air and kicking him on the bottom. Then he and Buckner left the scene.

Stanbery was sufficiently injured to take to his bed. He wrote Andrew Stevenson, Speaker of the House, protesting that he had been "attacked, knocked down by a bludgeon and severely wounded by Samuel Houston, late of Tennessee, for words spoken in my place in the House of Representatives." He was temporarily incapable of carrying out his official duties, he claimed, and held Houston to be guilty of a breach of House privilege. Stanbery's letter was read into the record and a motion was offered that Houston be arrested on the charge of contempt of the House. Despite James K. Polk's objection that the House had no authority for such an action, the resolution carried by a margin of 145 to 25.[9]

On April 16 Houston made an appearance in the House. The visitor's gallery was jammed. He requested a day's delay so that he might prepare a defense and was granted a respite of forty-eight hours. On the eighteenth, he stood once again before his former colleagues, this time represented by counsel—Francis Scott Key. However, he had no great need of a lawyer. His response to the initial interrogation established his line of defense:

> *Interrogatory.* Do you admit, or deny, that you assaulted and beat the said Stanbery, as he has represented. . . ?
>
> *Answer.* [Houston] The accused denies that he "assaulted and beat the said Stanbery. . . ." He admits that he felt a great indignation on reading the National Intelligencer remarks there stated to have been made on the floor of the House of Representatives by the said Stanbery, imputing to the accused, by name, a gross offence, of which he knew himself to be innocent, and the dissemination of which . . . throughout the country . . . was evidently calculated to affect his honor and character. Under these

circumstances, the accused was induced to inquire of said Stanbery, in respectful note, whether the report of what he had said was truly set forth in said paper; to which inquiry . . . said Stanbery refused to give any answer, in a manner calculated still further to injure the accused. The accused admits that he was greatly excited by these provocations . . . and that, under the influence of feelings thus excited, he did, on accidentally meeting the said Stanbery, assault and beat him, the accused being unarmed with any other weapon than a common walking cane, and believing the said Stanbery to be, as in fact he was, armed with pistols; that the meeting took place several hours after the adjournment of Congress, about 8 o'clock in the evening, and nearly half a mile from the Capitol, and on the opposite side of the avenue from where Mr. Stanbery's boarding house is situated; and that, at the time of this occurrence, he was neither seeking for, nor expecting to see the said Stanbery.

The accused denies that he intended to commit, or that he believed he was committing, any contempt towards the House of Representatives, or any breach of its privileges, or of the privilege of any of its members. He denies that the act complained of constitutes any such contempt or breach of privilege, and is prepared to justify his conduct, so far at least as the rights and privileges of this House and its members are concerned, by proof.[10]

The trial lasted nearly a month. Before its conclusion, it drove many more important items from the front pages of most newspapers. As Houston observed later on, the sensation of a contempt trial rescued him from obscurity and made him a national celebrity. With respect to his accusations against Houston in the matter of the rations contract, Stanbery admitted, under cross-examination by Houston, that he had no evidence of wrongdoing. So far as Houston was concerned, this admission vindicated him. He did not mind being convicted of contempt of the House, for he had cleared his name.[11]

Andrew Jackson summoned Houston to the White House and forcefully condemned him for the embarrassment which his impulsive behavior had caused the administration. The President then asked if his friend had nothing more than buckskins to wear at his trial. Houston confessed that he had no money to purchase clothing more acceptable to official Washington. Jackson is supposed then to have tossed him a silk purse and to have advised him to seek a stronger line of defense. The clothes were produced at once, but a better defense could not be found. Although the President was undoubtedly annoyed with Houston, he was quoted as wishing that there were a dozen men like Houston to deal with members of Congress who resisted his initiatives.[12]

On May 1 Houston wrote Prentiss that the trial was progressing slowly, "and tho I play the part of a *patient* man, I do not feel precisely so composed. . . . It is the test of a great principle, in which the liberty & reputation of every American citizen is involved, and I am proud to be its representative on the present occasion." Houston told the New Yorker that Francis Scott Key would summarize the defense, after which he would, if permitted, address the House himself.[13]

Suffering from a very large hangover contracted during a night of carousing with Tennessee cronies and with Andrew Stevenson, Speaker of the House, Sam Houston appeared in the chamber to complete his case. Given his rather fragile condition, he defended himself well. Although his speech was unconscionably long, his delivery was so spirited that sympathetic hearers were moved to applause.[14]

Several days of debate followed, much of it devoted to the question which the defendant had raised—a definition of privilege. At last there was a vote, 106 to 89, "that Samuel Houston has been guilty of a contempt in violation of the privileges of this House." He was to be reprimanded by the Speaker, a sentence duly administered May 14, but without much conviction, for Andrew Stevenson had supported Houston throughout the trial.

Once the verdict had been pronounced and the sentence executed, Houston thought himself free to leave. However, Congressman Stanbery, quite as vindictive as the defendant had depicted him in his closing statement, lodged a complaint with the capital police. The charge was assault. Houston was brought to trial and found guilty. He was fined $500. The conviction was anticlimactic, and attracted virtually no attention in the press.

Stanbery was not done yet. He moved in the House that a select committee be created to investigate the charge of fraud in the Indian rations question. The hearings dragged on through June, with Duff Green's *Telegraph* proclaiming the guilt of Houston and Eaton, and

Francis Blair's *Globe,* sympathetic to Jackson's administration, maintaining their innocence. The committee ultimately found the two men "entirely acquitted from all imputation of fraud."[15] The vote was not unanimous, and the testimony suggests that if Houston and John Van Fossen had been awarded the contract their profit would have been about $1,000,000. Further, Eaton's decision to reject all bids had plainly been inspired by a desire to spare the administration just the kind of bad press it now received. All the same, had such an award been made it would have saved the War Department a significant sum and might, in the bargain, have spared the lives of many Indians who received no rations at all during their migrations westward.

Houston emerged from the trials and committee hearings a national figure. His debt to Stanbery was enormous, and he never failed to acknowledge it in later years as a major turning point on his road back to glory.

Throughout the period of hearings and trials, Houston had been planning his trip to Texas and had reached an agreement with Prentiss whereby it would be partially financed by the sale of land scrip in holdings of the Galveston Bay and Texas Land Company. The feeling for urgency was increased by news that General Antonio López de Santa Anna's ascendancy over Mexico was arousing the concern of Great Britain, that country's principal creditor. A claim had been lodged by the British with the King of Spain, its main thrust a rejection of Mexican independence (accorded at gunpoint in 1823) and, consequently, of Mexico's right to grant *empresario* titles to land in Texas. Because practically all *empresarios* were Americans, Britain's attitude was intolerable to those who longed to attach the immensity of Texas to the United States.

Andrew Jackson, who had acknowledged the established boundary lines, had never in his heart accepted the principle. While he had consistently denied any design against Texas, he was now proving sympathetic to a discussion with Houston of plans that would assure Texan independence without involving the United States in any direct military confrontation with Mexico. It has been argued persuasively that in the implementation of Jackson's real but unuttered wish, Sam Houston was his chosen instrument. The role he would play was that of "revolutionary agent." He was to seek the aid of Indian warriors in a struggle to "liberate" Texas and, somewhat more vaguely, to report to the President on conditions as he found them. Although none of this was put in writing, it may be reasonably deduced from the Houston-Prentiss correspondence. Indeed, one may even infer that Houston's connection with the Galveston Bay and Texas Land Company was a cover for his subversive activities in Texas.

On June 16 Houston received an interesting letter from John Wharton, who was currently practicing law in New Orleans. After congratulating him on the outcome of the Stanbery affair, he noted that Houston might soon hear from Branch T. Archer, a Virginian who had been in Texas and who was "intimately acquainted with matters and things there, and is in the confidence of all the leading men. He is of the opinion that there will be some fighting there next fall . . . [H]e is very desirous that you should go there, and believes that you can be of more service than any other man. . . . Texas does undoubtedly present a fine field for fame [,] enterprise, and usefulness. . . ."[16]

Houston did not get away from Washington until July 12. On his way south he passed through Cincinnati, where his presence at a theatrical performance occasioned rioting—presumably because of his assault against Stanbery, the Ohio Congressman. Reaching Nashville toward the end of July, he found himself in need of ready cash, even though he had disposed of his interest in the Grand Saline for $6,500 before leaving Washington.[17] On July 31 Prentiss wrote from New York that he was unable to raise funds because of a cholera epidemic. All the prosperous men had left town.[18]

Houston could not leave Nashville until he had a passport, which he received on August 16. He spent some of his spare time at the Hermitage, where Jackson was summering. The principal topic was surely Texas. An interesting feature of the passport, designed to give him unimpeded passage through Indian country, was that it described him as a citizen of the United States. He was proceeding to Texas as an American, though his object was to amass as many as 10,000 Indian braves who would join their cause with that of the American whites in Texas.

In a letter to Prentiss of August 18 stating that he would have to remain in Nashville at least until the end of the month, for financial reasons, Houston concluded with a paragraph that came closer than anything he had previously written to defining his purpose in going to

Texas: "My opinion is that it would be of vast importance to have a person [there] who could look at matters . . . with a view to changes . . . which are necessary . . . before long in that country, and without which it can never be . . . what it ought to be. . . . Several persons have said to me that I was looked for . . . and earnestly wished for by the Citzens of Texas. . . . The people look to the Indians on Arkansas as auxilliaries, in the event of change— So I will pass that way and see my *old friends.*"[19]

Marquis James believed that Houston found time to see his estranged wife during his six-week stay in Tennessee. If such a meeting occurred, there is no record of it. There *is* one account, attributed to Eliza Houston's personal slave, that Houston bribed her merely to allow him to gaze (without speaking) on the woman responsible for the traumatic change in his circumstances. The problem about this second-hand anecdote is that it has no date. It must be considered apocryphal.[20] It is much more likely that Houston whiled away his free hours in the tavern of the Nashville Inn.

According to some accounts his departure was finally made possible by Andrew Jackson's loan of $500. It may be that in advancing him this sum, the President established himself as Houston's true patron, for the connection with Prentiss had been severed. During the ensuing weeks, Houston traveled to Three Forks, where he arrived no later than October 8. He announced to Oolooteka and Diana his intention to leave for a new life in Texas.

He made some visits of farewell. At Cantonment Gibson, he joined Matthew Arbuckle for an evening of conversation with Washington Irving. The talk must have touched at least casually on Houston's plan to visit Texas, but neither in *A Tour of the Prairies* nor in his journals did the celebrated writer mention this. He did, however, record a description of Sam Houston in the middle of his fortieth year: "Tall, well formed, fascinating man—low crown large brimmed white beaver [hat]—boots with brass eagle spurs—given to grandiloquence. A large & military mode of expressing himself . . . Old Genl [Nicks—a white trader] used to say God made [Houston] two drinks scant."[21]

On October 11 Houston returned to Wigwam Neosho.[22] The main topic of conversation among the Cherokees was the Prohibition Act of 1832, which forbade the traffic in spirits by Indians within their own supposedly autonomous lands. Although it is unlikely that Houston attended the council meetings in which this matter was formally discussed, he probably had a hand in drafting the so-called Drew Memorial protesting the government's action in seizing cargoes of whiskey which had been imported by the Cherokees before the bill had become law. This was his final contribution to the well being of the tribe that had treated him so lovingly for so long.

He must certainly have raised the question of Indian participation in a possible Texan uprising. The answer he received was not encouraging. What benefit would the natives derive from helping to pull white chestnuts out of the fire? Since his plans were not precise, Houston did not press the point. When he knew what had to be done, he would seek assistance. Now he would avoid controversy.

Jack Gregory and Rennard Strickland, authors of *Sam Houston with the Cherokees,* and the most knowledgeable scholars of this period of Houston's life, have summarized his contribution to the welfare of the Indians in the Arkansas Territory thus:

> Sam Houston accomplished more during these three years than many men do in a lifetime. During his years with the Cherokees, Houston made two trips to Washington to assist in negotiations with Jackson and the War Department, and his negotiations to end the warfare between the Osages and the Creeks and the Cherokees was the most successful in thirty years of attempted settlements. A long-range reform program in the Indian Agency system as well as removal of agents of questionable ability and honesty resulted from his intervention; through his political column in the *Arkansas Gazette* . . . Houston spearheaded the Indian Bureau reform programs.[23]

No American white of national reputation in the whole of the nineteenth century tried to do more for the cause of the Indian than Houston. That his attempts were ultimately to fail cannot reduce this distinction. He had more than repaid his debts to Oolooteka and Diana.

Nothing is known of Houston's farewell to Diana except that it occurred sometime in November, 1832. It has been written that Diana perished of grief shortly after Houston went away. The truth is that she married again, and died, four years later, of undetermined causes. All the same, their parting must have been painful, especially for her.

Houston owed her a great deal—perhaps even his life. He also owed her much for providing faithful and uncomplaining companionship. Yet he had been away so often that this leavetaking, however sorrowful because it seemed a final one, was merely one of many. Diana Gentry was not a woman to nourish feelings of self-pity. And as for Sam Houston, the great expanse of the Texas adventure lay before him.

9 2 1
5
46.05

X

TEXAS! EVEN in 1832, before its extent was known or its possibilities imagined, the name inspired feelings of awe. It was more than just another section of the continent to be opened by white settlers. It represented a final chance for many to get back on their feet. Because it was foreign soil, emigrants chose it as a place of exile to escape debts incurred as Americans. A family leaving home would tack a simple notice on the door of the abandoned dwelling: "Gone to Texas," or just, "G. T. T." Until it became part of the Union in 1846, Texas was to the United States what the United States had been to Europe—a refuge for those down on their luck. For others, the possibility of adventure rather than the reality of despair was the goad. And there was also the hope of wealth, to be gained through land speculation or even farming.

Conditions in Texas when Sam Houston prepared to cross the Red River were confused. Since 1821, when Stephen Austin had assumed his father's position as *empresario*, he had struggled with calm, intelligent resolution to regularize relations with Mexican administrations that changed mercurially from year to year. The first and most important of American *empresarios*, Austin was no demagogue. His virtues were tenacity, integrity, and utter dedication to those for whose lives he had assumed responsibility.

However, a lack of personal magnetism ultimately deprived Austin of the presidency of Texas, when independence was attained in 1836. He had maintained a posture of total propriety during his prolonged and convoluted dealings with the Mexicans, thus gaining their respect and sometimes their cooperation. However, his missions were more often failures than successes. Thus in the last month of 1832, Texas was in its usual state of political effervescence.

Several issues separated the Anglo-American Texans from the government in Mexico City. The main difference was over self-administration. In 1832 Texas was merely a province of the larger Mexican state of Coahuila. The majority of white residents wanted separate political identity, though they would continue loyal to Mexico. The Mexicans exasperated Texans by tactics of delay and contradiction. While these annoying methods had served more or less adequately for a decade or so, they resulted in the inception of a serious movement for total independence. Though he understood this goal and may have been personally sympathetic with it, Austin was in a difficult position. He did not believe that independence could be had without a bloody revolution. Revolution, in his view, could not succeed without assistance from the United States.

However, if Washington were suddenly to reverse its official position of recognizing Texas as a Mexican domain, the gesture might well invite hostilities with Great Britain. With the result of the War of 1812 still vivid in the memory of most American statesmen, especially the New Englanders, the prospect was not appealing. Therefore, Stephen Austin wisely discouraged talk of insurrection because he thought it would fail. Reason, however, rarely motivates a populace. A considerable proportion of the 20,000 whites in Texas then supported separation from Coahuila, if not from Mexico. The territory abounded in hotheads who asserted that freedom could be secured more readily than Austin supposed.

By the time Sam Houston set out for Texas, the Mexican government had officially prohibited all further Anglo-American immigration, a ban neatly circumvented by bribes. The stipulation that all settlers adhere to the Roman Catholic faith was grudgingly honored, though it was always an emotional point of contention. There was, on the other hand, considerable advantage for settlers in the form of tax exemptions for their first six years in Texas. In fact, immigrants encountered little official interference in their daily lives. Attempts to effect a ban against slavery had failed. An 1832 law prohibiting the importation of slaves was equally futile, for the land lent itself to the use of slaves and the majority of settlers were Southerners.

The municipal governments offered a minimal political continuity. Each of these, which comprised several small communities, was directed by an *ayuntamiento,* a civic unit presided over by the *alcalde* who embodied the powers of mayor, police chief, and magistrate. When Houston crossed the Red River, the number of *ayuntamientos* in what is now Texas could be counted on the fingers of two hands. By the end of 1834 there were only thirteen. White Texans could not complain of overgovernment. What they really objected to was the possibility that Mexican authority might become oppressive at some indefinite date in the future.

The duties of the *empresario* were considerable. He was obliged to survey all the land of his grant, to register transfers, to maintain public order, and to organize a militia for protection against marauding Indians. The Indians of the region presented the most serious problems. Though not all tribes were regularly hostile, certain nations were frequently troublesome—resentful of the land the whites had taken from them without recompense.

Austin's Indian policy was like his Mexican policy. It was better to placate them than fight them. Such was not the view of most other *empresarios,* who knew that dead Indians could neither maraud nor proliferate. Thus, many settlers, particularly those living on grants near the periphery of the vast Texas region, spent much of their time fighting Indians. Though the white man always insisted that he had come in peace and that initial hostilities had been undertaken by the natives, the Indians replied that the very first act of aggression was the arrival of the settlers, per se.

The economy of Texas was insignificant in 1832. No commercial manufacturing facilities existed. Trade was rendered nearly impossible by transport difficulties. Exchange was confined principally to barter, for there was little currency and not one bank in all of Texas. What attracted the very American statesmen who denied that they *were* attracted was the sheer vastness of Texas. Unwilling to admit their hunger for the land, they were even more unwilling to see it fall into the hands of a European power—least of all Great Britain.

But Texas was a domestic hot potato. The Abolitionist movement, just aborning, would oppose American annexation of Texas for obvious reasons. Its members were the same kind of people who had denounced the War of 1812. Wise leaders in Washington refused to grasp the nettle. Official attitudes, however, had little to do with the conduct or outlook of individuals. Texas represented for many of them, in one fashion or another, the last best hope of earth.

"I have arrived at [Fort Towson, Arkansas Territory] after a journey thro' the least inviting country . . . that I have ever seen. [It] is mountainous and Barren, with the exception of a few water courses upon which the Indians may form pleasant settlements." So wrote Houston on December 1, 1832, to Henry L. Ellsworth, Indian commissioner at Cantonment Gibson. He then described the ill will between red men and white that he found in the portion of the territory he had not previously visited, an unhappy reiteration of complaints he had stated two years before in the *Arkansas Gazette.*[1]

Also from Fort Towson he wrote his cousin John that he was about to enter Texas. "My health and spirits are both good, my habits sober, and my heart straight." Perhaps capriciously, he added, "It is reported that my friends have announced my name as a candidate for the next Governor of Tennessee. Shou'd I live, I must be back by the first of April . . . and see how the land lies for such business. My friends are sanguine of my success. I do not doubt it, if I should run! as I think I shall."[2] His name was not submitted, nor is there any serious suggestion that it was ever considered. The previous autumn, John Eaton had sought reelection to the Senate and failed, despite Jackson's influence. Houston's name in the state was even more sullied than Eaton's. The notion, therefore, was a delusion of grandeur if he seriously held it—yet it was just this positive quality that drove Houston to Texas.

He paused briefly at Nacogdoches, in the Redlands near the American frontier, before proceeding to San Felipe de Austin, where on December 24 he applied for a grant of land "with the understanding that I offer to settle and cultivate it within the provisions of the law."[3] Stephen Austin himself authorized the request. If the two men met, they did not make much of an impression on each other at this time. Houston spent Christmas at San Felipe with drinking companions, including Jim Bowie.

He was not long in Austin's town, and was probably not there in early January when a committee comprised of leading settlers called for a convention to take place at San Felipe April 1. In Bowie's company, Houston left for San Antonio de Bexar. There he established contact with several Indian tribes and without suggesting his military motives obtained the agreement of some chiefs to journey to Cantonment Gibson in April for a conference with American officials. He left the principal sachem a medal embossed with the features of Andrew Jackson, traditional symbol of Indian domestication. Reports to Washington were optimistic that when the time came, the tribes would side with the Texans.[4]

He certainly thought the land worthy of acquisition by the United States, as indicated by a passage in *The Only Authentic Memoir:* "[A] single glance at the resources of this new country, and the character and condition of its population, satisfied him that a great destiny awaited . . . and in imagination he already saw a new commonwealth rising into power. He was still in the morning of life—here was a new field for achievement, where all the bold elements of his character could find full play. Once embarked on the stream of a revolution, the world would learn, at last, the character of the man it had hunted from society, and history and time would pronounce his eulogy."[5]

Houston returned to Nacogdoches, where he paused long enough to make a strong impression on the residents, who obtained his permission to name him as a candidate for the April 1 convention. He called himself an advocate of separation from Mexico. He became a resident of Nacogdoches. He became a Texan, in love with that land. Later he would say, "You may escape the smallpox, but you can never escape the contagion of land loving."[6] But land loving was not powerful enough to induce him to settle down. It was the call of the people, (whether real or imagined) that stimulated him to work that would propel him toward his apotheosis.

In February he went to Natchitoches, Louisiana, and wrote Jackson his impressions of more than two months in Texas. He reported that Texans favored American annexation by a margin of 20 to 1, a figure he derived from conversations with such radicals as the Wharton brothers and Henry Smith of Brazoria. He accurately described the political disarray of Mexico, noting in particular the deteriorating economic conditions which "will render a transfer for Texas inevitable to some power, and if the United States . . . does not press for it, England will most assuredly obtain it by some means." He knew Jackson's views on the topic of annexation to be mixed—favorable, but not at any price. "I am compelled to assure you that your present minister [to Mexico], Col. [Anthony] Butler, does not desire the acquisition of Texas by the United States. . . . [He] has interests . . . which will be better served by absolute dependence . . . and attachment of Texas to Mexico." He thought Butler a tool of the British. "If Texas is desirable to the United States it is now in the most favorable attitude perhaps that it can be to obtain it on fair terms—England is *pressing* her *suit* for it, but its citizens will resist, if any transfer should be made . . . to any other power but the United States."[7]

Though Houston was accurate in his appraisal of British designs, his estimate of Texans' sympathy for annexation was wide of the mark. As many opposed total separation from Mexico as favored it. He failed to mention Austin, which is unpardonable, and his condemnation of Anthony Butler was too harsh, even though he was accurate in calling Butler a proponent of the status quo. But as time went on, it would be Mexican actions that persuaded a majority of Texans that revolution was the only acceptable course, a conviction ultimately shared by the conservative Stephen Austin.

Houston returned to Nacogdoches in March to find that in his absence he had been elected as one of five delegates to represent his new constituency at the San Felipe convention, which began April 1.[8] The election of William Wharton as chairman indicated that a majority of the representatives favored independence. However, Austin's moderates were not as small a minority as Houston had indicated. The topics raised were familiar—demand for repeal of the law against further immigration, and the question of separation of Texas from Coahuila. Houston chaired a committee to draft a state constitution, a document which drew heavily on the Anglo-American background of its framers. David G. Burnet, whom Houston had met years before in the North, was also a delegate; he composed a document to the United States Congress requesting recognition of this constitution. The Americans took no action on this plea, for it would have been tantamount to acknowledging Texan independence.

Stephen Austin was appointed ambassador to the newly installed Mexican government of Santa Anna—an ironic decision, for Austin was not the most enthusiastic supporter of the new constitution. Although his embassy was not entirely a failure, its principal aim was frustrated. Nevertheless, the fact that a duly elected convention had formulated a constitution seemed to support Houston's contention that some overt American gesture would be warmly received in Texas.

After the San Felipe convention, Houston returned to Nacogdoches where he remained long enough to make some friends and to establish himself as a member of the bar—Don Samuel Pablo Houston. But soon he was off again, back to Cantonment Gibson to confer with Indian commissioner Henry Ellsworth about the attitudes of the Texan Indians toward the United States. Then he went to Hot Springs, where he took the cure. Only in July, when he was once again in Nacogdoches, did he begin to leave a real mark on his fellow residents, and to understand the community which had elected him without knowing him.

The municipality of Ayish, of which Nacogdoches was the main town, numbered 1,272 whites (according to an 1833 census, which excluded slaves). About 80 percent of these were American immigrants, the rest Mexicans. The principal source of steady revenue was from smuggling across the nearby Arkansas border. Houston's talent for conviviality served him well. He soon struck up close relationships with some of the town's leaders—Adolphus Sterne, the local *alcalde,* and Henry Raguet, merchant and landowner. Sterne, a Rhinelander, invited Houston to reside in his comfortable house, an offer Houston eagerly accepted.[9] He was delighted with the comfort and hospitality extended by Sterne and his young wife, Eva, and he found himself strangely attracted to Anna Raguet, the teen-aged daughter of Pennsylvanian Henry Raguet. The cynosure of Nacogdoches and environs, Anna was quite attractive. She was an accomplished musician, something of a linguist, and of a very gentle disposition. Sam Houston was soon in love with her, though he must have realized from the beginning that in a field of eager young bachelors, his position was hardly favorable—especially since he was not merely forty, but married.

Even so, Anna was drawn to Houston, perhaps as Desdemona was drawn to Othello. How actively she encouraged him we do not know, since most of her letters to him have disappeared. However, for the next six years, she was the light of his life. And even after she married another man, Anna kept Houston as a friend. Their relationship was invariably above reproach.

Houston soon built a fairly remunerative law practice which took him frequently to the nearest large community, San Augustine, where Phil Sublett, whom he had known in Tennessee, had settled some years earlier and succeeded in land speculation. Sublett recorded an occasion when Houston arrived at his house drunk and eager to talk about himself. His host, thinking the moment suitable, questioned him about the separation from Eliza, a topic that fascinated all who knew the man. Houston sobered up at once, called for his horse, and departed. Wisely, Sublett never raised the subject again.[10]

During this same season of 1833, Mexican officials in Washington protested to the State Department that President Jackson and Sam Houston were conspiring to separate Texas from Mexico. The evidence for this claim is not clear. Perhaps Houston's correspondence from Natchitoches was monitored. In any case, the allegation was summarily dismissed.[11] The Mexican ambassador left the capital in an ugly frame of mind. Austin, in Mexico City, was distressed by this turn of events. His own mission had been thwarted by Mexican intransigence, procrastination, and suspicion. Immediately after the end of the year, he would be arrested and imprisoned, a precious hostage who would remain in custody until the middle of 1835. This proved the most shortsighted of Santa Anna's political moves, for Austin's inclination to moderation might have forestalled the uprising which his imprisonment helped to assure.

Before Austin's arrest, Houston was changing his mind about the desirability of Texan independence—or so he noted in *The Only Authentic Memoir*. He counseled his constituents against "unrestrained ebullition of feeling." Their enthusiasm for revolt "would be likely to plunge Texas into a bloody struggle . . . *before she was prepared for it.*" There seems no reason to doubt that Houston was representing his views accurately. Soon enough, he would be vigorously chastized for his growing conservatism, especially with respect to his conduct in the actual war with Mexico.

Ghost-writer C. Edwards Lester added a note on Houston's view of recent immigrants to Texas: "All new states are infested, more or less, by a class of noisy, second-rate men, who are always in favor of rash and extreme measures. But Texas was absolutely overrun by such men." Houston had decided to steer a middle course between the radicalism of the Whartons and Henry Smith and the conservatism of Stephen Austin. He would fill the role he thought Texas required, to be "brave enough for any trial, wise enough for any emergency, and cool enough for any crisis."[12]

As Houston seemed to be discovering patience, Austin was losing his. Disappointed by the temporizing of the Mexicans, he wrote a letter to the *alcalde* of San Antonio advising him to organize a separate government for Texas. This communication was intercepted and eventually served as the main reason for his arrest. By early November, however, discussions in Mexico City seemed headed for a satisfactory outcome. Santa Anna appeared amenable to many of Austin's requests—except the crucial one for separate statehood. More dickering was called for. But in a show of good intentions, the Mexicans repealed the immigration ban in December. Almost immediately, white settlers began to arrive in Texas in ever increasing numbers.

While negotiations teetered on in Mexico City, Sam Houston petitioned William McFarland, *alcalde* of the municipality of Ayish, for a divorce. The petition was granted and was probably one of the earliest Mexican divorces. Its legality was in question. So was its motivation. We may presume that Houston wanted it so that he might marry Anna Raguet.

By the year's end he had completed his obligations as a Texan by allowing himself to be baptized into the Catholic faith. Eva Sterne stood as his godmother. However cynical this gesture, it was essential if he meant to pursue a political and legal career in Texas. And he certainly planned to do both.[13]

In the year that followed Houston's hollow conversion to the Church of Rome, Mexico made a few further concessions to Texan requests. However, at least three major issues still divided moderates from their rulers in Mexico City—separate statehood, the location of the administrative center, and the promiscuous disposal of Texan land to speculators. The Texans saw these land deals as essential to attract the sort of men to Texas who were willing to serve in the militia. Some kind of armed force was needed for protection against the Indians who grew ever more restive as immigration increased. But the Mexicans realized that this militia might one day oppose the troops of the government that was authorizing the land grants.

Houston's public concerns during the early months of 1834 were aimed at mollifying Indians who found him sympathetic. The principal chief with whom he now dealt was The Bowl, a Cherokee whose friendship he is supposed to have won in 1818, by helping him to settle in East Texas. Now well established north of Nacogdoches, The Bowl became Houston's most powerful Indian ally in Texas, ready to provide armed aid whenever it was required. Despite their respect for Houston, white Texans were skeptical and even disdainful of his affection for the Indians.

In February he began a journey east, pausing for a meeting with Oolooteka and other Cherokees. The subject was Texas. Would these Indians and the Creeks come to the assistance of Texan whites? He appears to have received an equivocal answer. What would be offered in exchange? He had no dependable response. But matters were coming to a head. On January 3, just as he reached Saltillo on his way back from Mexico City, Stephen Austin had been arrested and returned to the Mexican capital, charged with treason for his letter to the *alcalde* of San Antonio. If the moderate leader of Texas could be so harassed, who was safe?[14]

For the eighteen months of Austin's detention, the conservative Texans were without an effective leader. Thus the field was left open for those who proposed violence.

By early March Houston was in Washington to confer with Jackson about the Texan crisis. He was also again in touch with James Prentiss, who wanted him to represent the Galveston Bay and Texas Land Company. Houston demanded a fee Prentiss could not raise. In Washington that April, the President pressed his friend about possible solutions to the Texan problem. Jackson was willing to buy the territory, but he was determined not to fight for it, for war would surely involve Great Britain. But there are many questions about this meeting. Did Jackson promise unofficial support for a "spontaneous" uprising of Texans? Or did he tell Houston, as he had written Anthony Butler earlier, that he would do all he could to prevent Americans from mounting an expedition against Mexico designed to "liberate" Texas? Or did he, rather, suggest that should such an event occur, he would try to look the other way? We just do not know. However their talks ended, Houston seemed undismayed by them.

In a letter to Prentiss from Washington on April 20, he wrote, "I do not think [Texas] will be acquired by the U. States. I do think within one year it will be a Sovreign State. . . . Within three years it will be separated from the Mexican Confederacy, and remain so forever. . . ."[15] This was pretty fair prophecy. Four days later he told Prentiss, "You need not hope for the acquisition (if ever) . . . of Texas during the Administration of Genl Jackson." He added a phrase that suggests he had been canvassing members of Congress. "If [Texas] were acquired by Treaty, that Treaty . . . would not be ratified by the present Senate—!!!" Therefore, Texans must act independently. Houston did not favor this course but thought it inevitable. The concluding paragraph of this letter shows his moderation: "Many suppose that such events will . . . be sought by us, but . . . the course that I may pursue . . . shall be for the true interests of Texas . . . as it ought to be; to preserve her integrity to . . . Mexico."[16] As events evolved, Houston found it necessary to change his mind.

He returned to Texas, where he discovered that Austin was still imprisoned (there had been a rumor in Washington of his release). Conditions were worsening. He felt it necessary to discuss the situation once more with Jackson in person, the mails being slow and not very private. Nothing but anecdotes survive from this journey, the most celebrated recounting a bibulous exchange with the British actor, Junius Brutus Booth, father of Lincoln's assassin. Booth said that Houston had boasted to him that he was "made to revel in the halls of the Montezumas." The incident was interpreted in Washington to mean that Houston planned to attack Mexico. It seems, instead, to have been drunken boasting—in keeping with earlier rantings about Texas and Oregon.

He made his way south again in late autumn of 1834. Near Christmastime, he was at Little Rock, where he met William F. Pope, who recorded the strong impression Houston made on him:

> Gen. Houston was one of the most magnificent specimens of physical manhood I have ever seen. . . . He was riding a splendid bay horse, and his saddle and Bridle were of the most excellent Mexican workmanship, and were elaborately ornamented. . . . He was enveloped in a Mexican "poncho" which was richly ornamented with . . . embroidery work. . . . [I]t was hard to believe that this elegantly appearing gentleman had voluntarily given up home and kindred and official preferment to join himself to a band of half-civilized Indians . . . and had adopted their dress . . . and habits of life.[17]

Not long after Pope saw him, G. W. Featherstonhaugh, an English traveler who found the frontier not at all congenial, met Houston at the hamlet of Washington, Arkansas Territory, about twenty miles from the Texas border. He said that Houston was "leading a mysterious sort of life, shut up in a small tavern, seeing nobody by day and sitting up all night. . . . I had seen too much passing before my eyes . . . to be ignorant that this little place was the rendezvous where a much deeper game than faro or *rouge et noir* was playing. There were persons . . . in the village from the States lying adjacent to the Mississippi, under the pretence of purchasing government lands, but whose real object was to encourage settlers in Texas to throw off their allegiance to the Mexican government."[18]

What was he up to? Featherstonhaugh's assumption is improbable. It is more likely that Houston was recruiting settlers willing to fight, if the need arose, rather than actually promoting rebellion. If so, his efforts were remarkably successful. In the first two months of 1835, 2,000 immigrants landed at the mouth of the Brazos. Others came by land. The rush to Texas was on.

XI

U PON HIS return to Nacogdoches early in 1835, Houston
resumed his law practice and continued to seek the hand of
Anna Raguet; she persisted in politely rejecting his suit.[1] Domestic
politics were colored by the publication of a letter that Stephen Austin
wrote late in August, 1834, to his brother-in-law James F. Perry. It
implied that Texan radicals were to blame for his continuing
imprisonment.[2] Specifically cited were William Wharton as leader of
the Separatists, and Sam Houston as one of his followers.[3] The stir that
followed the appearance of the letter caused a further fragmentation of
Texan opinion, which Austin certainly would not have desired. It
angered Houston, who wrote John Wharton, now practicing law at
Brazoria, noting that he had just been with his brother William and
seen the recriminating letter from Austin. "William shewed me his . . .
answer. . . . I think he has left the little Gentleman with very few
crumbs of comfort. . . . When I read his [Austin's] letter of August, I
must confess that it awakened no other emotion in my breast . . . than
pity mingled with contempt. He showed the disposition of the viper
without its fangs. . . . He aimed at me a few thrusts, but I will want an
interview with him before I make any public expose of his want of
understanding . . . or his political inconsistencies.[4]

The publication of Austin's letter had compromised whatever opportunity there might have been to achieve independence without a
war. That communication, so out of character for Austin, must have
been inspired by some extremely trying incident or circumstance.
Previously it was his poise and resolute adherence to the rules laid

133

down in Mexico City that had made him the enemy of the Separatists. Houston's reference to the "little Gentleman" is a reflection of the scorn felt for Austin among the extremists, for the "Father of Texas" had accomplished little more during his negotiations with Mexico than his own incarceration.

The Texan revolution, so long in the making, really began in May, 1835, when officials of the department of Texas met at Monclova, the provincial capital of Coahuila, to criticize Santa Anna. They were particularly incensed at his reimposition of tariffs. This may serve as the date that distinguishes "Texians" from Texans—"Texian" being those whose presence in Texas predated the war for independence, a distinction to which some modern Texans proudly refer. Upon learning of Texan objections, Santa Anna ordered his brother-in-law, General Martín Perfecto de Cos, to disperse the assembly at Monclova. As a countermove, Governor Agustín Viesca began to evacuate Monclova, sending delegates and civil servants to San Antonio and the protection of the Alamo. Viesca himself, however, was apprehended by General Cos and sent to Mexico City in custody.

On May 8 the citizens of Bastrop (then called Mina) instituted a committee of public safety and correspondence to maintain a regular flow of information about the movement of Mexico's men in Texas. By the summer's end, almost every municipality had a similar organization.

In late June, General Cos advised Santa Anna to reinforce the small Mexican garrison at the customs post of Anahuac. The message fell into Texan hands, and William B. Travis was ordered to assemble as many volunteers as he could muster to drive the Mexicans from Anahuac before the post could be reinforced. He set out with no more than thirty riders, besieged Anahuac and, on June 30, he and his men forced the garrison to surrender. Few casualties were suffered on either side. About forty-five prisoners were taken and immediately paroled to Mexico on condition that they never fight Texans again. Texan reaction was mixed. The *ayuntamiento* of Columbia protested Travis' action, fearing that serious violence would erupt. It is unusual for victors to apologize, but this is what occurred. Reaction against the siege of Anahuac was astonishingly strong in Texas, because conciliation with Mexico was thought the sanest policy, at least for the moment.

Sam Houston had taken no part in any of these dramatic events, apparently because hostilities were extremely unpopular in the East

Texan Redlands district of Ayish, where he lived. When Moseley Baker visited him at Nacogdoches in early August, in hopes of recruiting him to a more activist cause, Houston advised Baker to lie low as long as he was in the Redlands. However, on August 15 Houston did attend a meeting directed by William Wharton. It was proposed that all of Texas be consulted about future actions, for it was now certain that Santa Anna planned a large-scale military exercise to bring the department to heel. On the seventeenth General Cos wrote the *alcalde* of Nacogdoches who had replaced Houston's friend, Sterne: "The plans of the revolutionists are well known. . . . The constitution by which all Mexicans may be governed is the constitution which the colonists of Texas must obey." Meaning, quite simply, that Santa Anna was the law.[5]

The Nacogdoches committee of vigilance named Sam Houston commander in chief of the nonexistent army of the surrounding East Texan territory. On August 29 he issued this proclamation to all Texans:

> From reports which have reached me I am induced to believe that our situation is unsafe; some Cherokees . . . have returned . . . from Matamoros, and say that the Indians of the prairies and a Mexican force . . . are about to attack this portion of Texas; the counties of San Augustine, Sabine, Tenahaw, and Bevil, as well as Nacogdoches, will *forthwith* organize the MILITIA of each county. The following requisitions are made to sustain the United States forces until reinforcements can arrive at this place from General Gaines [commander of American troops garrisoned on the east bank of the Sabine]. . . . The troops will repair to this place with the least possible delay. . . .
>
> Let arms and ammunition be brought, at least one hundred rounds is requested. The commander-in-chief will be with the freemen of Texas if they have to meet an enemy; all the men of Texas must have their arms in order; to have liberty we must be watchful.[6]

This was the first of Houston's political manipulations in Texas. He knew very well there was no possibility that General Gaines would march American soldiers into Texas unless he had evidence of a clear and present Mexican threat to the Sabine border with the United States. However, by suggesting that the Americans' arrival was imminent, he hoped to obtain needed recruits and to calm the fears of the citizenry that they might be overwhelmed by Mexican troops. As it happened, East Texas was in no danger. But in early September an action by General Ugartechea, a subordinate of Cos', reinforced the conviction that Santa Anna was serious in his intent to subdue those who opposed his authority. Ugartechea sent five riders to Gonzales to retrieve a small cannon previously given to the residents there to ward off Indians. Andrew Ponton, *alcalde* of Gonzales, ordered the field piece hidden. He informed the Mexicans that he was not empowered to surrender it. In the meantime, he sent messages to settlers of the district requesting immediate military assistance. Meanwhile some of Houston's little force was preparing to meet an expected assault by 400 Mexicans whom General Cos had brought ashore at Copano; when Ponton's appeal reached them, they headed at once for Gonzales. So did 100 of Ugartechea's men. The town lost its cannon and was occupied, as was Goliad. The Texans saved themselves.

At about the same time, Stephen Austin was allowed to return to Texas. His compatriots looked to him hopefully for advice in this critical hour. He was surprisingly bellicose. Embittered by his long detention, disillusioned by broken Mexican promises, he announced that Texas must seek total independence, not merely the status of a separate political entity under Mexican aegis. Even Sam Houston, reputedly much more hot-tempered than Austin, believed that a successful outcome of war with Mexico depended on American aid. Austin's pronouncement convinced many Texan moderates that war probably could not be avoided, however unprepared their state was —and it was almost totally unprepared. By his change of position Austin had committed Texas to the new course. He lost no time in assuming the leadership he had forfeited during his long absence. He became president of the committee of safety of San Felipe, where, in mid-October, an assembly would convene representing all Texan municipalities. Less than a fortnight after his return, a proclamation urging full attendance at the San Felipe meeting made the general Texan position clear: "War is our only recourse.... We must defend ourselves by force of arms."

Sam Houston offered 4,000 acres of land on the Red River for sale, asking a price of $2,500, $1,000 in ready money. He needed funds to equip himself for his part in the coming war. From New Orleans he ordered the uniform of a general, with stars and a sash on which to wear the decorations he had earned at Horseshoe Bend and those to be gained in the coming struggle. In early October, as he and other delegates set out for San Felipe, Houston met an acquaintance who was bound east. He gave him a letter to be published in the United States:

> ... *War in defense of our rights, our oaths, and our constitutions* is inevitable ... in Texas!
>
> If *volunteers* from the United States will join their brethren in this section, they will receive liberal bounties of land. We have millions of acres of our best lands unchosen and unappropriated.
>
> Let each man come with a good rifle ... and one hundred rounds of ammunition, and ... soon.
>
> Our war cry is "Liberty or death."
>
> Our principles are to support the constitution, and *down with the Usurper!!!*

The letter was printed three weeks later in the *Arkansas Gazette.* Alongside it was a statement by General Cos that his army's intention was to "collect revenue, disarm the citizens, establish a military government, and confiscate the property of the rebellious." Such aims could only inflame the passion for independence which Santa Anna hoped to suppress.[7]

On October 6 Houston was named commander in chief of *all* troops mustered in East Texas, by a committee headed by his friend Phil Sublett.[8] He was not yet in field command of all Texan forces, such as they were. This assignment was given to Stephen Austin, a man even less qualified for it than Houston. When he had left Nacogdoches for the San Felipe meeting, Houston had placed young Thomas Rusk in charge of the gathering militiamen. Austin soon ordered these troops to proceed at once to the west, where a battle seemed inevitable. A minor battle had already taken place at Gonzales on October 2, when a zealous handful of Texans had driven the Mexicans toward refuge with their compatriots at San Antonio. It was at this juncture that Austin took the title of commander in chief of an "Army of the People," with a cry of "On to San Antonio!"[9] The Father of Texas was no more fortunate than Houston in rallying disciplined men.

At San Felipe, on October 11, a provisional government was born—a "Permanent Council" which lasted only three weeks. It performed admirably, given the size of the problem and the inexperience of its membership. Austin was not on hand for meetings, since he had gone to Gonzales to lead the "army" to San Antonio. He contributed little to strategy, his function being essentially that of morale builder. The best news received at San Felipe in that second October week was that Captain James Collinsworth had captured Goliad and with it important quantities of supplies and ammunition.

The Permanent Council, after issuing a call October 26 for volunteers from the United States and legitimizing privateering against Mexican shipping in the Gulf, gave way to a second provisional government called the "Consultation." This heterogeneous collection of Texans, mostly American immigrants, remained in session until mid-November. Sam Houston served on a committee dealing with Indian relations, whose aims must have seemed irrelevant when the immediate enemy was Mexico. However, Houston insisted that valuable Indian aid could be obtained if promises made were strictly kept, a notion just barely thinkable to Texan whites. In plenary sessions of the Consultation he did little of note, offering resolutions of thanks to Austin and others serving Texas.[10]

Stephen Austin was not present to hear his praises sung by Houston, who had, not long before, referred to him as the "little Gentleman." The two men had not met since 1832. There was little friendship between them, but personal feelings were suspended for the duration of the emergency. Feeling himself inadequate as an army commander, Austin sent a message to the provisional government November 3, urging that he be replaced. The same day Houston joined a committee whose task was to prepare a public declaration of the reasons that impelled Texas to rise against Mexico.[11]

Marquis James avers that Houston was the dominant personality of the Consultation. However, the composition of the government that resulted from its meetings suggests that he was far from the man of *that* hour. Henry Smith of Brazoria was named governor; James W. Robinson of Nacogdoches was lieutenant governor. A General Council, something like a cabinet, was established, of which Houston was not a member. The head of the Military Committee was Wyatt Hanks, a splenetic armchair strategist who became Sam Houston's principal bane during the difficult months to come. Hanks was one of many Texans who believed that the enemy would run from the merest offer of a fight. Therein lay the seeds of his differences with Houston, whose prudence never ceased to enrage Hanks. Stephen Austin, Branch T.

Archer, and William Wharton were delegated to travel to Washington, D.C., to seek official American aid.[12]

However, Houston was not invisible during the meetings of the Consultation. On November 5 Gail Borden, Jr., of Galveston wrote that the day before Houston had "made the best speech I ever heard; the whole tenour of it went to harmonize the feelings of the people and to produce unanimity of sentiment."[13] We have no record of what he said, but may infer that it was a plea for political caution. Before it broke up, the delegates defeated a resolution calling for an immediate declaration of independence from Mexico by a vote of 33 to 15. The purpose of war at that time was only to secure separate statehood in the Mexican confederation. To the Mexicans, however, this distinction was moot.

On November 12 Sam Houston was made commander in chief of the Texan army by a vote of the Consultation. The post was administrative; he was not to command the army in the field at this time. His election was not unanimous. Moseley Baker, writing Houston nine years later, noted that his nomination had surprised younger officers like himself. Mirabeau Buonaparte Lamar, who was to become one of Houston's major adversaries, believed that Austin would have received the post had it not been for Houston's opposition, which was offered on the ground that Austin had urged his own replacement.[14]

Among the final acts of the Consultation was a declaration that the Cherokees had legitimate claims of land against Mexico which would be made good by an independent Texan state. This was a cynical gesture of propitiation to Houston, whose committee had produced the resolution. Even Houston must have appreciated how slight the chances were that this resolution would ever be implemented. The Consultation adjourned November 14.

Houston's first communication as commander in chief was to James W. Fannin, then stationed at the gates of San Antonio. He offered Fannin the post of inspector general with the rank of colonel. Presuming that Fannin would accept, he went on to write of strategy. Since agents had been sent to New Orleans only two days earlier in quest of artillery with which to reduce the Alamo fortress, Houston thought it wise to pull the troops back to Goliad and Gonzales in order to protect the Rio Grande frontier. When artillery could be brought into play, the army would be called back to "march on the combat with sufficient force and at once reduce San Antonio!" To men like Wyatt Hanks this was a ludicrous and even a shameful proposal. But Houston's defense was actually quite sound. The army at the moment was inadequately armed and supplied. He had greater fear of epidemic than of enemy attack. Since he believed nothing could be accomplished at San Antonio without artillery, "and so long as there is subsistence in the neighborhood, the enemy will command it as well as you! So that by the time they are starved out, you will have nothing to subsist the Troops or the people."

He asked Fannin to convey Godspeed to "Col. Bowie," who was at the head of the small force outside of San Antonio, and urged on both men a recollection of the maxim: "[I]t is better to do well ... *late* ... than *never!*"

Houston's first letter to Fannin is of central importance to an understanding of his strategy in the war he was charged with waging. He was endlessly criticized at the time, and long afterwards, for "cowardly" retreat. His detractors alleged that he won the decisive battle of San Jacinto, five months later, by accident, because he found his troops in a position where, at last, they had no choice but to fight. Despite his detractors, he had a policy from the beginning that was ultimately successful. But between November and late April Houston would need patience to endure the criticism of those to whom he was answerable, particularly the irascible Wyatt Hanks.

The Consultation was to reassemble March 1. In the interim, Texas was to be administered by Henry Smith and members of the General Council. For perhaps a month there was substantial agreement about immediate needs. An effective political structure was essential for the new state. The government also did what little it could to establish a navy and to support Sam Houston's scattered and minuscule army. Furthermore, the condition of communications was extremely poor. Houston's express letter to James Fannin November 13 finally received an answer ten days later. Yet the distance between San Felipe and San Antonio was less than 100 miles.

Fannin's first letter offered an ambivalent reaction to Houston's plan to move the army back to Goliad and Gonzales. While conceding its prudence, he was "fully convinced that with 250 men, well chosen & properly drilled ... [San Antonio] can be taken by storm." As for the offer to be inspector general, he was less than enchanted. He wanted the rank of general, preferring a "post of danger ... where I may seek the enemy & beat him."[15] Houston ignored Fannin's request for active duty, naming him inspector general. Instead of replying directly to Fannin with respect to strategy, he wrote Captain Wyly Martin, commander of a company then standing before San Antonio and a known opponent of total independence from Mexico. He informed Martin that should withdrawal from the present position be deemed necessary he hoped the army would split into two groups, one proceeding to Goliad, the other to Gonzales.[16] Although he knew Jim Bowie was in command Houston probably wrote this proposal to Martin because he knew Bowie would disobey his orders. Proper respect for the military chain of command was lacking during the war for independence.

On November 24, Edward Burleson, a former Indian fighter, was named to replace Stephen Austin as commander of the Texan army in the field.[17] Austin was now officially free to accompany Wharton and Archer on the vital mission to Washington. Ed Burleson was obviously more qualified than Austin, who is not known to have ever fired a gun at another human.

Increasingly frustrated by appalling communications and persistently inadequate obedience to the few orders he managed to transmit, Houston did his best to organize a proper headquarters at San Felipe. At the end of November he wrote an American acquaintance that by March 1 Texas would require 500 volunteers to meet the thousand Mexicans he expected Santa Anna to put into the field against him in a spring offensive. While Houston issued futile orders and shuffled papers at San Felipe, and while Santa Anna made preparations for a major spring campaign in 1836, the soldiers in the field grew restless. Finally, weary of apparent indecision at higher levels of command, a body of volunteers, recklessly but bravely led by Ben Milam, stormed San Antonio on December 5. After five days of bitter combat, in which 300 Texans without artillery engaged the far larger Alamo garrison, General Cos surrendered. Pledging not to fight in Texas again, 1,400 enemy soldiers were paroled to their homes.[18] Thus, on December 10, there were no more enemy troops on territory that is now Texas. Ben Milam's death was the major price for this stunning victory.

According to Edward Burleson the war had ended. He resigned his commission and was succeeded by Francis (Frank) Johnson. Burleson's opinion was shared by many Texans who received the news of San Antonio's fall with rejoicing. Houston, however, was certain that Santa Anna would wage a much more serious campaign. In his view the war had just begun. He issued a call for more volunteers. It was a failure. Furthermore, his reputation as commander was tarnished because of his counsel against the action at San Antonio which had produced so brilliant a victory. There were calls for his resignation. One of the loudest was Dr. James Grant, an ambitious Scot, who persuasively argued for immediate pursuit into Mexico. He wanted to march to Matamoros and confront the enemy on home ground.[19]

Houston had moved to new quarters at Washington-on-the-Brazos, where on December 12 he issued a second call for volunteers. One sentence struck Texans as incredible: "By the first of March next, we must meet the enemy with an army worthy of our cause."[20] Hardly anyone believed there would be another significant battle. To the soldiers who had captured San Antonio, there seemed two possibilities—to pursue the enemy into Mexico, or to go home. Like the army, the General Council was in danger of collapse for want of firm leadership. When Governor Henry Smith learned of the Matamoros plan, he opposed it. So did Houston, who considered it frivolous, detrimental to the discipline of the army, and irrelevant to the cause of Texan independence.[21]

Despite the views of Houston and Smith, Grant's scheme was being implemented. By mid-December Jim Bowie was to lead a force that would seize Matamoros and then secure the port town of Copano to allow volunteers arriving from New Orleans to land there. Governor Smith was informed that Texan troops had almost completely abandoned San Antonio, taking with them most of the supplies necessary to sustain that essential garrison. This action had the consent of the General Council. Wyatt Hanks' views had prevailed. Smith was unable to contravene the orders and his position was now untenable. Although Houston resented Hanks' allegation that he had neglected his duties, he played the good soldier. On December 17 he ordered Jim Bowie to proceed against Matamoros and Copano, thus sanctioning the Council's will.

By the end of 1835 Sam Houston was, in effect, a commander without a command.

XII

DURING THE first fortnight of 1836, Mexican troops moved to offset Texan successes at San Antonio and Gonzales. Santa Anna recruited an army large enough to overwhelm the undermanned, poorly organized, ill-equipped rebels. A force led by General Joaquin Ramírez y Sesma was sent to the west bank of the Rio Grande. Another, under General José Urrea, marched to Matamoros with orders to secure the right flank of the main army which Santa Anna himself would lead.

There were complications on the Texan side. Jim Bowie did not receive Houston's order to lead the disputed expedition against Matamoros, and the operation was never undertaken with the enthusiasm or diligence its supporters had shown in advocating it. Mercifully, communications among Mexican commanders were equally poor.

Aware at last that Bowie was not going to move toward Matamoros, the General Council ordered Frank Johnson to lead the expedition, with Dr. James Grant as his second-in-command. On January 3 Johnson declined the assignment. When he learned this, Wyatt Hanks, the headstrong leader of the Council's military committee, gave the task to James Fannin. In the interim, however, Johnson wrote Hanks that he would take the command after all. The committee reaffirmed Johnson's orders without countermanding those sent to Fannin. In theory, then, the mission had two leaders.

Soon it had a third. On January 8 Houston acknowledged an order from Governor Smith to proceed to the army, where *he* should take charge of the Matamoros force. Houston noted the confusion involving

143

Johnson and Fannin and spoke bitterly of Wyatt Hanks, whom he described on January 11 as "the *basest* of all mankind."[1]

By January 15 Houston was at Goliad, thinking to find the main body of the Texan army there. He was not encouraged by what he discovered. He tried at once to organize the ranks and clarify the lines of command. He decried the failure of many Mexicans living within Texan boundaries to rally to the rebel cause. "[H]e who is not for us is against us," he said. Since this was the case, he called for the severance of all ties with Mexico: "[L]et us break off the live slab from the dying cactus that [Texas] may not dry up with the remainder; let us plant it anew that it may spring luxuriantly out of the fruitful savannah. Nor will the vigor of the descendants of the sturdy north ever mix with the phlegm of the indolent Mexicans, no matter how long we may live among them. Two different tribes on the same hunting ground will never get along together. . . . All of Texas is for separation. . . . 'Texas must be a free and independent state,' is the general word." He concluded: "A general convention of the representatives of the People will be held at Washington [on-the-Brazos] on the first of March of this year. It is the duty of the army to send several representatives; and I hope that my comrades will elect only men who will vote for our independence. . . ."[2]

This was, of course, an election campaign speech, and a successful one. Although Houston planned to run for a convention seat from his residence at Nacogdoches, he meant to take no chances; should he fail there, he intended to be sent as a delegate from the army. There are distinctly racist notes in this address which permeated Texan thinking long after. It is ironic to hear disdainful references to "half-Indians" from the mouth of a man who had long lived with Indians.

However, having swayed the soldiers as voters, Houston now was able to sway them as soldiers. His presence at Goliad had the effect of discouraging them from joining Johnson on the Matamoros mission. Despite his orders, he rightly thought the action ill conceived. On January 17 he wrote Henry Smith that he was leaving at once for Refugio, twenty-five miles away, with about 200 able men. Then he added lines that were the first of record in the saga of the Alamo: "Colonel Bowie will leave here in a few hours for [San Antonio] with a detachment of from thirty to fifty men. . . . I have ordered the fortifications [the Alamo] to be demolished, and, if you should think well of it, I will remove all the cannon and other munitions . . . to Gonzales and Copano, blow up the Alamo and abandon the place, as it will be impossible to keep up the station with volunteers...." He was still convinced that "the army should not advance with a small force upon Matamoros with the hope or belief that the Mexicans will cooperate with us."[3]

So began the story of the Alamo. Governor Smith confirmed Houston's orders to Jim Bowie to destroy the Alamo and abandon the town. It is not certain that Smith was empowered to take this action since he had been dismissed by the General Council, because of his refusal to follow its reckless dictates. On the other hand it is equally doubtful that the Council had the authority to depose Smith and replace him with James Robinson. In any case, Houston's orders to Bowie were never obeyed.

There is a final irony in Houston's letter to Henry Smith: "I would myself have marched to [San Antonio] but the Matamoros rage is up so high...." that he must stay and cool that passion. Had *he* gone to San Antonio instead of Bowie, the town would have been abandoned, as he commanded, and the senseless carnage that took place, militarily irrelevant to the Texan war for independence, would not have occurred.[4]

At Refugio, on January 20, Houston found himself in a position he thought untenable. On the evening of his arrival, Frank Johnson appeared, "and it was understood that he was empowered, by the general council of Texas, to interfere with my command." Added to this was word of Governor Smith's ouster. Houston immediately returned to Washington-on-the-Brazos and on January 30 reported to the deposed Smith. He would not allow the Council to have "the pleasure of ascribing to me the evils which their own conduct ... will, in all probability, produce." He was convinced that the Matamoros scheme would "protract the war for years to come ... and the field which they have opened to insubordination ... will cost the country more useless expenditure...." Failure to capture Matamoros would imperil the entire frontier of the southern tip of Texas. The Goliad garrison could not long sustain itself without supplies arriving from Copano. The Council's madness, he told Smith, had placed the resources of Texas in the hands of reckless adventurers.

In a long letter of self-justification to Smith, Houston sharply criticized James Grant, author of the Matamoros plan, whom he accused of jeopardizing the whole Texan cause for hope of personal gain. He said some hard things about Fannin, too, whom he charged with seeking to subvert the power of the commander in chief. But he laid principal blame for the present confusion at the door of the General Council, well knowing that this would evoke a sympathetic response from Smith.[5]

The deposed governor furloughed Houston at his own request until March 1, when the convention was to meet. The frustrated commander in chief left at once for Nacogdoches, wanting no part of military adventures in which he had little confidence. His purported reason for going to East Texas was to solicit military assistance from the Cherokees. He would also campaign for a seat at the convention. From New Orleans Stephen Austin wrote Houston, "I can only say that, with the information now before me, I am in favor of an immediate declaration of independence."[6]

While a disillusioned and disheartened Houston moved east, a number of ill-starred figures were gathering at San Antonio. First of these was Jim Bowie, with about twenty-five men, who decided that the town, with its impressive fortress, should be held at all costs for Texas. David Crockett, with another handful of volunteers, reached San Antonio in early February. William B. Travis, on orders from Henry Smith, mustered approximately thirty militiamen to go there to help save the town from capture. Meanwhile Mexican forces were collecting outside the walls to begin the most celebrated siege of American history.[7] By the middle of the month, between 150 and 200 Texans and Americans were prepared to defend the town.

By the middle of February, Santa Anna had amassed as many as 6,000 men on the Mexican side of the Rio Grande at Laredo. On the twenty-third the first of his troops began to assail San Antonio. This is customarily used as the beginning of the siege, for it was then that the defenders took refuge within the Alamo itself. Jim Bowie took to his bed with typhoid and pneumonia the next day. William B. Travis assumed command and at once composed a message that has been committed to memory by loyal Texans ever since:

To the People of Texas & all Americans in the world: . . . am besieged by a thousand or more Mexicans under Santa Anna. I have sustained a continual Bombardment & cannonade for 24 hours & have not lost a man. The enemy has demanded a surrender at discretion [meaning that survivors need not be treated as prisoners of war], otherwise, the garrison

146

are to be put to the sword . . . if the fort is taken—I have answered the demand with a cannon shot & our flag still waves proudly from the wall. *I shall never surrender or retreat. Then,* I call on you in the name of liberty, of patriotism & everything dear to the American character, to come to our aid with all dispatch. The enemy is receiving reinforcements daily & will no doubt increase to three or four thousand in four or five days. If this is neglected, I am determined to sustain myself as long as possible. . . . VICTORY OR DEATH.[8]

Meanwhile matters were becoming even more serious south of San Antonio. With a force of no more than 150 men, Frank Johnson —originally determined to capture Matamoros—had been wandering ineffectively near San Patricio, 100 miles north of Matamoros. On February 27 his detachment met a force under General Urrea and was wiped out. Inexplicably, James Grant was in the same neighborhood with another small group. On February 28 a messenger arrived at Washington-on-the-Brazos with Travis' message of proud despair. To whom should it be handed? The General Council, having moved there from San Felipe, was presided over by James Robinson who, according to the journal of Virginian Colonel William F. Gray, was "treated coldly and really seems of little consequence." Houston arrived February 29.

Although he had been defeated in the Nacogdoches vote for delegates, he was elected by the voters of Refugio. His speech had served him well. Gray's journal set the scene: "Gen. Houston's arrival has created more sensation than that of any other man. He is evidently the people's man, and seems to take pains to ingratiate himself with everybody. He is much broken in appearance, but has still a fine person and courtly manner."[9] Houston's first action was to report to Henry Smith, who, so far as he was concerned, remained the governor. For most arriving delegates, the principal topic of conversation was the desperate state of Texans besieged at San Antonio.

The only hope of relieving them lay in the hands of James Fannin, who had about 450 men at Goliad and Refugio. Houston ordered him to proceed immediately to the relief of the Alamo. Fannin's excuse for failing to do this was that the muddy roads were impassable for his supply wagons. Houston later asserted that the breakdown of a single wagon caused Fannin to call off the mission. However, thirty-two volunteers from Gonzales reached San Antonio on March 1. It was a false moment of hope. Five days later the last of the insubordinate heroes perished. All that remained was the rallying cry: "Remember the Alamo!"

As Houston had understood, the fate of San Antonio had been incidental to the essential course of the war for Texan independence. The situation on March 1 when the convention met in Washington-on-the-Brazos was desperate. Some of Urrea's troops were moving toward Goliad to confront Fannin's little force. Houston had almost no organized troops. On the other side, as Travis' last message had indicated, Santa Anna had legions.

The first major act of the convention was to draft a declaration of independence. Because they were away on duty when it was published, Sam Houston and Stephen Austin were not signatories. Those who did sign the document were men of little renown outside Texas, though their service to the new nation would be considerable. Best known, perhaps, were Thomas J. Rusk of Nacogdoches and Lorenzo de Zavala, the most distinguished Mexican to sign the document.

Yet it is evident even from the most grudging record that Sam Houston emerged from the convention as the leader of Texas. He seemed to know how to command and to inspire confidence. The first draft of the Declaration was completed March 2, Houston's forty-second birthday. That day, though he had as yet no official status, except as delegate, he issued a proclamation on the state of affairs:

War is raging on the frontiers. [San Antonio] is besieged by two thousand of the enemy. . . . Reinforcements are on the march to unite with the besieging army. By the last report, our force at [San Antonio] was only one hundred and fifty men. The citizens of Texas must rally to the aid of our army, or it will perish. Let the citizens of the east march to the combat. The enemy must be driven from our soil, or desolution will accompany their march upon us. *Independence is declared;* it must be maintained. Immediate action united with valor . . . can alone achieve great work. The services of all are forthwith required in the field.

Sam Houston Commander-in-Chief of the Army

P.S. It is rumored that the enemy are on the march to Gonzales, and that they have entered the [Texan] colonies. The fate of [San Antonio] is

148

unknown. The country must and shall be defended. The patriots of Texas are *appealed to in behalf of their bleeding country.*[10]

Houston realized that his problem was not merely the need for troops. He required supplies, which could only come from the United States. This was the main mission of Austin, Archer, and Wharton to the American capital. They still had not arrived there. Austin's absence from Texas at this time was decisive to his future from a political point of view. Had he been present, there is no reason to doubt that he would have assumed the mantle of leadership that ultimately fell on Houston's shoulders. Yet Houston performed the task more effectively than Austin would have done, for he had a natural authority.

Time was of the essence. Even as Houston wrote out his March 2 proclamation, Urrea was on the trail of Grant and his men, whose only object now was to save their skins.[11] The end of the Alamo siege was in sight. It seemed possible that Texas would be wholly restored to Mexico before an army could be raised to offer more than symbolic resistance. On March 4 Houston was renamed commander in chief. His task was to organize and direct an army. He left two days later for San Antonio, still ignorant that the siege had ended.

His journey took him to Gonzales. He sent a messenger ahead ordering Fannin to join him there.[12] His only thought now was to put together a force which, at a time *he* deemed judicious, could inflict a decisive defeat on the invading Mexicans. The deeper the enemy penetrated into Texas the more difficult it would be for the invaders to maintain their lines of supply and communication. So vast was the territory that Houston could afford to yield great portions of it without incurring substantial loss of anything but land; there was little property of real value for an enemy army to capture. When the Mexicans were overextended, Houston planned to strike. In the meantime he wanted very much to avoid battles in which Texans would be at a disadvantage.

As his policy became clearer during the next six weeks, his reputation plummeted. Retreat, it was argued, was not the way wars were won. But there was no alternative strategy and no one else stepped forward to assume command. On March 7 Urrea finished off James Grant's detachment at Aqua Dulce. On the sixteenth the Texan defenders of Refugio were defeated. Fannin surrendered his force at

Goliad on the twentieth, and a week later, he and the other Goliad survivors were executed by Urrea's order. With this Santa Anna thought to intimidate Texans who presumed to proclaim their independence from Mexico.

From the day of Fannin's defeat at Goliad until the second week of April, there were no other major engagements. Three Mexican armies marched north and east across the Texan river systems. Defeat seemed inevitable. Meanwhile Houston's little army retreated along a generally parallel course. He was watching and waiting for the moment when it would seem propitious for him to risk all.

After Houston left the provisional capital of Washington-on-the-Brazos, the convention organized a government and drafted a constitution for submission to the voters. David G. Burnet was named provisional president, Zavala vice-president. Rusk was named secretary of war—a fortunate appointment, for he admired Houston.[13] The news of the Alamo's fall reached the convention on March 11, causing consternation, but faith in Houston remained strong.

At Gonzales, Houston was still unaware of the fate of the Alamo. He daily expected Fannin's force to join him, also unaware that his fate was sealed. He was joined by Captain Moseley Baker, with a company, and Erastus "Deaf" Smith, a scout whose services to the Texan cause during the next week would be of capital importance. On March 13 three survivors of the Alamo, all black slaves released by the Mexicans, arrived in Gonzales. Their account of events at San Antonio was harrowing.

Houston sent Deaf Smith and another invaluable scout, Henry W. Karnes, to confirm the fate of the Alamo.[15] He also wrote Henry Raguet that day of his perilous condition, noting, all the same, that he had 700 men at his disposal. He asked his friend to alert the residents of the Nacogdoches region and the Texan Redlands to the need "*to awaken and aid in the struggle!*"[14] In the meantime he moved his force eastward.

On March 15 he learned from Smith and Karnes that initial reports about the Alamo were accurate. Still unaware of Fannin's condition, he wrote James Collinsworth that he now feared for Fannin at Goliad. He had ordered the destruction of the fortifications there, but now wondered if the colonel had received the instructions. "Our forces must not be shut up in forts, where they can neither be supplied with men or provisions." That, he observed, had been his reason for ordering Bowie to blow up the Alamo, an action "prevented by the expedition upon Matamoras, the author of all our misfortunes." He concluded his letter with the news that he had destroyed fortifications at Gonzales.[16]

By March 17, Houston's army, which he now estimated at only 600 men, was on the banks of the Colorado River, near La Grange. Soldiers from East Texas were on their way.[17] Houston's scouts reported the movements of the main Mexican army, led by Santa Anna himself, making it possible for the Texans to move eastward without engagements of significance. The new government began to be alarmed at the speed of the enemy's unimpaired advance. On the eighteenth President Burnet ordered the evacuation of the capital to Harrisburg, on Buffalo Bayou. This act marked the beginning of what was known in Texas as the "Runaway Scrape." Every Texan with a means of transportation fled in the face of Santa Anna's army. By the twentieth it seemed that the whole of southwest Texas was in flight.

Though increasing numbers of volunteers joined Houston's forces, bringing their ranks to a maximum of 1,400, they were still poorly armed, lacking in artillery, and in very volatile emotional state. Hearing that the Mexican General Sesma was approaching the Colorado with about 700 men, Houston crossed the river and moved a few miles downstream. He was still determined not to fight despite entreaties from his junior officers and from President Burnet, who wrote that the salvation of the country depended on stubborn and immediate resistance to the enemy.[18] For the better part of five days, the two forces confronted each other with only the swollen Colorado between them. Nothing more serious than a few inconclusive exchanges occurred.

By March 21, the hysteria induced by the government's removal from Washington-on-the-Brazos had infected Houston's army. He ordered that all deserters be arrested and attempted to convince his men that panic was not in order.[19]

On the twenty-fourth Houston's aide, Major George W. Hockley, wrote Secretary of War Rusk that Santa Anna was reported to have left San Antonio for Mexico and that the Texan army was in good heart, with spies "active and vigilant."[20] Two days later, however, Houston wrote Rusk that things did not look promising. "You know I am not easily depressed, but . . . before God, since we parted, I have found the darkest hours of my . . . life! My excitement has been so great . . . that . . . for forty-eight hours, I have not eaten an ounce, nor have I slept. I was in constant apprehension of a rout; a constant panic existed in the lines; yet I managed so well, or such was my good luck, that not a gun was fired in or near the camp, or on the march (except to kill beef), from the Guadalupe to the Colorado. All would have been well . . . and all peace on this side of the Colorado, if I could only have had a moment to start an express [proclamation] in advance of the deserters; but they went first, and, being panic struck, it was contagious, and all who saw them breathed the poison and fled."

Houston was annoyed by the precipitous flight of the government from Washington-on-the-Brazos. The retreat of the administration and the ensuing panic of the populace "pained me infinitely . . . weigh upon me to an agonizing extent." Still, although he now knew of Fannin's surrender, he remained hopeful, and urged Rusk to do all he could to rally volunteers to the Texan army.[21]

News of Fannin's defeat spread through Houston's anxious camp. Officers demanded an immediate attack on the Mexicans across the river. The commander in chief sadly refused. This reluctance was wise, for during the night that followed, Sesma's forces were nearly doubled. Houston enraged his best young officers by ordering the army to start falling back from the Colorado on March 26. On Palm Sunday, the twenty-seventh, the day when Fannin and his men were executed, Houston had put nearly thirty miles between his army and Sesma.[22] The next river was the Brazos.

Word of Fannin's fate, when it reached the United States, served even more than the Alamo tragedy to rally men and arms for Texas. Most, however, would arrive too late to be of service in the crucial battle which Sam Houston seemed to be doing his best to avoid. President Burnet sent his secretary of state, Samuel Carson, to Louisiana to persuade General Edmund Gaines to send American troops into Texas. But Gaines had orders from Andrew Jackson not to cross the Sabine unless the American frontier were directly threatened.

By March 28, Houston's army stood on the west bank of the Brazos. It began to rain. Colonel Sidney Sherman and Captains Moseley Baker and Wyly Martin, three of his best officers, sent him a message refusing to retreat another foot. Responding in Houston's name, George Hockley ordered Baker to take up a position defending the river crossing that gave access to San Felipe. Martin was to perform a similar task downstream at Fort Bend. Then Houston turned the main body of his little army northward, still following the west side of the Brazos, in the direction of the deserted capital.

During three days of appalling rain, he was able to cover only twenty miles. On the day of the abortive revolt of the three young officers he alluded to the incident in a letter to Rusk: "[H]ad I consulted the wishes of all, I should have been like the ass between two stacks of hay. Many wished me to go below, others above. I consulted no one—I held no councils of war. If I err, the blame is mine." He expected fresh troops, and believed that the Mexicans would move along a more southerly path (as was the case). He concluded: "For Heaven's sake, do not drop back again with the seat of the government! Your removal to Harrisburg has done more to increase the panic in the country than anything else that has occurred in Texas, except the fall of the Alamo."[23]

On March 31 Houston set up camp on the west bank of the Brazos and wrote Rusk again, pleading once more for calm. "For Heaven's sake do allay the fever and chill which prevails in the country, and let the people from the east march to the camp!" His men, he said, "have suffered much from heavy rains and dreadful roads."[24] His numbers were declining. Hopes for substantial American assistance seemed vain, for it was only on this last day of March that the three-man Texan delegation reached Washington, D.C. Houston would have been even more discouraged had he known this. Austin, Archer, and Wharton had been en route for more than three months.

Houston's position was just about due west of Harrisburg. He had his best scouts out and still had no reliable information of Santa Anna's army. He needed supplies. "I must let the camp know something," he wrote Rusk, "and I want everything promised to be realized by them; I hope I can keep them together; I have, so far, succeeded beyond my hopes."[25] He remained at this camp, called Groce's Point, for twelve days, awaiting supplies, reinforcements, and definite news of the enemy's movements.

The difficulties confronting him and Texas mounted during this excruciating period. The "Runaway Scrape" continued. One of Moseley Baker's subalterns arrived at the main camp to announce that Colonel Sidney Sherman had been named commander to replace Houston. Few took this news seriously. A friend of President Burnet's in the commander's entourage wrote him that Houston had renounced drink during the campaign in favor of opium. Nothing supports the charge. To rally the spirits of East Texans, Houston published a communiqué denying his intention to cross the Brazos and condemning the action of residents of San Felipe who, on hearing of the enemy's approach, had burned the town to the ground.[26]

Rusk arrived at Houston's camp on April 5 to see for himself how matters progressed. He, at least, was satisfied with the commander's performance.

Houston wrote that day that Santa Anna's troops were suffering "miserable conditions . . . much dissatisfaction prevails in their ranks, from the severity of treatment and deprivation of the necessaries of life."[27] He was still convinced that his policy of causing the Mexican to overextend his supply lines would produce victory.

On April 7 an enemy contingent reached the Brazos at the point defended by Moseley Baker. Houston made haste to reinforce that position and, for three days, the Mexicans were prevented from crossing there.[28] President Burnet, in the meantime, had lost faith in Houston and his conduct of the war. He wrote: "Sir: The enemy are laughing you to scorn. You must fight them. You must retreat no farther. The country expects you to fight. The salvation of the country depends on you doing so."[29] Given Houston's temperament, it must have required a herculean effort of self-restraint to keep his calm in the face of Burnet's disdainful provocation. He felt he had no choice but to pursue the course he had set. However, there was no doubt that the men in his command were eager to do *something*.

Thwarted in their efforts to cross the Brazos where Moseley Baker had taken his stand, the combined armies of Sesma and Santa Anna turned south on April 10, following the river to Fort Bend. There, in spite of Captain Wyly Martin's dedicated resistance, they were able to cross. Hearing that the enemy approached, President Burnet ordered the evacuation of Harrisburg on April 17, taking the government to Morgan's Point on San Jacinto Bay, a cove of Galveston Bay. Santa Anna reached the deserted Harrisburg hours after the administration had left. He demolished it.[30]

Meanwhile Houston had learned that Santa Anna was moving downriver on April 11. He ordered the main Texan army to cross the river at Groce's Point. The operation was completed on April 13. Once his entire ragtag army had crossed the Brazos, Houston led it at forced-march speed in the direction of Harrisburg, some sixty miles off, a distance he covered in less than three days, something of a miracle in such difficult terrain. During this march Moseley Baker requested an assurance from Houston that if he caught up with Santa Anna he would fight him. Houston refused to reply.[31] With frustration and rage in their hearts, 300 or more soldiers deserted Houston's ranks to serve with the rebellious Wyly Martin. When Houston left Groce's Point, he had a force of 1,400. By the time he got to Harrisburg on the morning of April 18 the number was perhaps 1,000.

Houston camped on the opposite side of Buffalo Bayou from the razed provisional capital. Deaf Smith swam across the stream and returned at dusk with news that greatly cheered the commander. In his effort to capture President Burnet and the fleeing government (thinking thus to snuff out all further resistance), Santa Anna had brought only 800 men with him to Harrisburg. The remainder of his army, under General Cos, was following at a more leisurely pace. The Mexican dictator was on his way to Morgan's Point, entering the estuary of the San Jacinto River with its bayous and marshes. Burnet and his attendants had left the mainland for the security of Galveston Island before Santa Anna could apprehend him.

Sam Houston consulted his maps and his guides. By the morning of April 19, he knew that he finally had the enemy in a predicament. Santa Anna had cornered himself.

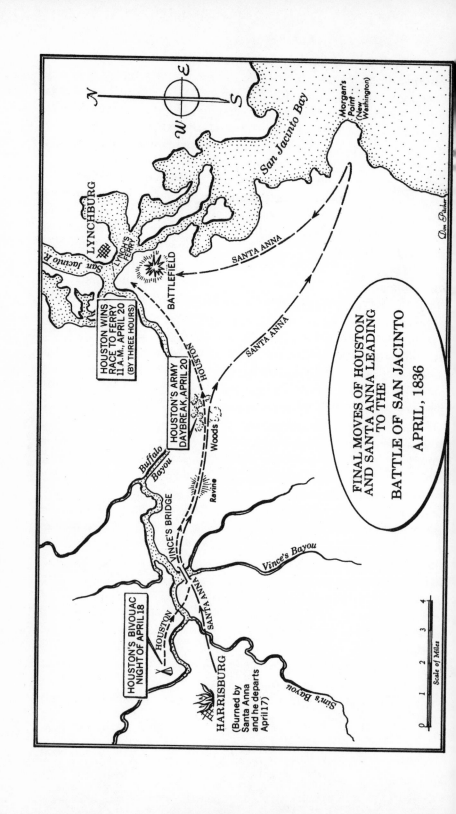

FINAL MOVES OF HOUSTON
AND SANTA ANNA LEADING
TO THE
BATTLE OF SAN JACINTO
APRIL, 1836

San Jacinto Bay

Morgan's Point
(New Washington)

Don Parker

LYNCHBURG

San Jacinto R.

LYNCH'S FERRY

SANTA ANNA

BATTLEFIELD

SANTA ANNA

HOUSTON WINS
RACE TO FERRY
11 A.M. APRIL 20
(BY THREE HOURS)

HOUSTON

HOUSTON'S ARMY
DAYBREAK, APRIL 20

Buffalo Bayou

Woods

HOUSTON

Ravine

VINCE'S BRIDGE

Vince's Bayou

HOUSTON'S BIVOUAC
NIGHT OF APRIL 18

HOUSTON

SANTA ANNA

HARRISBURG

(Burned by
Santa Anna
and he departs
April 17)

Sim's Bayou

0   1   2   3   4

Scale of Miles

XIII

"C APTAIN [HENRY W.] Karnes, with his detachment . . . , will remain on the east side of . . . [Buffalo B]ayou if he can in safety while the army will pass below, and he will then unite with the main army so as to cooperate. Great caution must be observed to conceal our movements from the enemy." This order of Houston's to one of his two best scouts was the first communication of April 19, 1836, the day on which the general plotted the Battle of San Jacinto.

Houston's maneuvers during the next two days were dictated by those of the enemy. Santa Anna took his troops over a bridge that crossed Vince's Bayou, a tributary of Buffalo Bayou. Houston ordered his men over the same bridge. For the first time in this phase of the revolutionary war, there was no river between Houston and his enemy. He was in close but stealthy pursuit of the hostile forces throughout the nineteenth and into the earliest hours of the twentieth. About four miles beyond Vince's Bridge, Houston rested his men. They were not allowed to stand down for long. Scouts reported that having marched his men all the way to Morgan's Point, Santa Anna was now moving them in the direction of Lynch's Ferry, about eight miles northeast of the Point. With the exception of Vince's Bridge, which Houston commanded, the Ferry was the only spot from which it would be possible for the Mexican to take his army of 800 across Buffalo Bayou. If Houston could reach the Ferry before the enemy, Santa Anna would have two alternatives: fight, or turn his force due west, leading them over the marshes of the estuary. This was a strategy determined by the terrain.

Houston meant to force a fight before Santa Anna received reinforcements. The odds would still be against Houston, for he was outmanned and outgunned. However, the Texans had the advantage of a greater familiarity with the terrain. Houston aroused his troops and set them off at top speed toward Lynch's Ferry. The Point was secured late in the morning of the twentieth. By nightfall, Houston had complete control of the vital crossing and the ground adjacent to it. He arranged his men in the order of battle for the next day. He had no doubt that this encounter would occur, and he meant to choose the ground. He hid his soldiers in a grove of oaks, festooned with Spanish moss. Behind this encampment lay a bayou. Just to the south was an alluvial prairie which the enemy must enter in order to reach the Ferry. Meanwhile the main body of Santa Anna's troops was encamped a few miles north of Morgan's Point.

Early that afternoon scouts reported that a force of Mexican infantry and cavalry, protecting a single cannon, had taken an offensive position on a slope at the edge of the prairie. The Texans, with two smaller fieldpieces as their only artillery, quickly took a defensive position. There followed an engagement. So fierce was Texan resistance that the enemy broke it off after a few minutes, withdrawing in good order—but not before Colonel Sidney Sherman made a bold attempt to capture the precious Mexican cannon. In this sortie, Mirabeau Buonaparte Lamar so distinguished himself in the eyes of General Sam Houston that he was promoted on the spot to command a "regiment" of Texan cavalry—perhaps fifty horsemen.

Following a restless night, Houston rose at sunup on April 21, and, according to *The Only Authentic Memoir,* said to George Hockley, "The sun of Austerlitz has risen again." He had little time to contemplate the Napoleonic parallel. Deaf Smith galloped into camp with news that General Cos was arriving with more than 500 reinforcements—a number that would give Santa Anna an advantage of two to one. Houston ordered the destruction of Vince's Bridge to prevent the advance of Cos. He had left it standing as a means of retreat for his own army. Soon afterward, there was further distressing intelligence: General Filisola was also advancing toward Buffalo Bayou with as many as 3,000 troops. Vince's Bridge was burned.

Throughout the morning and early afternoon of April 21, Houston's officers whipped their men into a frenzy for the fight which had to take place that day. At 3:30, the commander mustered them into the ranks he had laid out the evening before. At 4:00, he began to dispatch them along the edges of the clearing through which the Mexicans would have to march. At about 4:10, the enemy fired an initial volley. Houston ordered his troops to hold their fire until the enemy was within effective range of their musketry. He had no ammunition to squander. Finally he gave the command to open fire with his two little cannons. The Battle of San Jacinto was joined.

Houston's official account states that the battle proper lasted eighteen minutes.[1] The rounding up of the prisoners and the reduction of minor pockets of resistance was not completed until the following day. Although the engagement was surprisingly brief, Houston was on his third horse when it ended, and he had sustained a serious wound between knee and ankle of his right leg. But he had his victory.

When he saw that the battle was over, he passed out in the arms of George Hockley. While he remained in a state of shock from his wound, his troops pursued the fleeing enemy, taking in stragglers, and accepting the surrender of 400 of the enemy in a group.[2] Houston's report indicated 730 Mexican casualties and an equal number of prisoners. The triumph was complete—except that Santa Anna appeared to have eluded capture. Had he managed to get away, the victory of San Jacinto would have been a hollow one, for he could surely have rallied the thousands of Mexican soldiers in Texas—far more numerous and better equipped than Houston's rabble—and perhaps eventually succeeded in bringing Texas to her knees. Fortunately, however, the dictator was caught the next day and brought to the tent of the Texan commander in chief who had so dazzlingly turned the war about, completely vindicating a policy which almost every other Texan had condemned.

On the day after the battle which made Texan independence a reality, Sam Houston sent Anna Raguet this note: "These are the laurels from the battlefield of San Jacinto."[3] However touched she was by the gesture, she would not be his wife. This was not the last time Houston would be lonely in a moment of triumph.

As soon as he was presented to the victorious general, Santa Anna proposed an immediate armistice. Terms were tentatively agreed on. They called for withdrawal of all Mexican forces to the Guadalupe and San Antonio.[4] Pending the acceptance of more definite conditions by

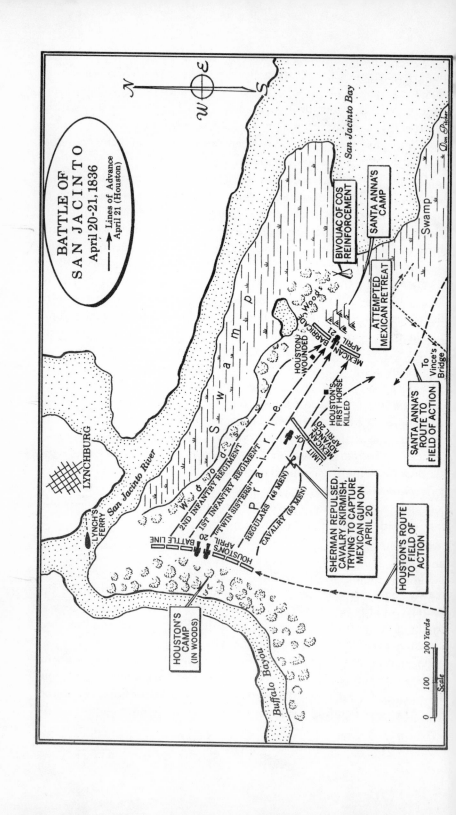

BATTLE OF
SAN JACINTO
April 20-21, 1836

Lines of Advance
April 21 (Houston)

N
W E S

San Jacinto Bay

Don Picher

BIVOUAC OF COS
REINFORCEMENT

SANTA ANNA'S
CAMP

S w a m p

Swamp

ATTEMPTED
MEXICAN RETREAT

To
Vince's
Bridge

MEXICAN BARRICADE

Woods

HOUSTON
WOUNDED
APRIL 21

HOUSTON'S
FIRST HORSE
KILLED

SANTA ANNA'S
ROUTE TO
FIELD OF ACTION

LYNCHBURG

San Jacinto River

LYNCH'S
FERRY

W o o d s

2ND INFANTRY REGIMENT

1ST INFANTRY REGIMENT

"TWIN SISTERS"

P r a i r i e

MEXICAN
ADVANCE
APRIL 20

LIMIT OF

BATTLE LINE

20

HOUSTON'S
APRIL 20

REGULARS (46 MEN)

CAVALRY (53 MEN)

SHERMAN REPULSED,
CAVALRY SKIRMISH,
TRYING TO CAPTURE
MEXICAN GUN ON
APRIL 20

HOUSTON'S ROUTE
TO FIELD OF
ACTION

HOUSTON'S CAMP
(IN WOODS)

Buffalo Bayou

200 Yards

0   100

Scale

the Texan Republic and Mexico, Santa Anna was to remain hostage as a guarantee.

Only on April 25 was Houston strong enough to compose a formal report to President Burnet on the battle.[5] The Texan government was still in hiding on Galveston Island. News of the victory traveled swiftly in all directions. Burnet soon transferred the administration to Velasco, a Gulf port on the mainland. Praise came to the victor from many quarters.

An interesting note came to Houston from General Gaines: "[Andrew Jackson] has often taken occasion to say to young officers who were liable to be rendered inefficient by the natural exultation which usually follows the achievement of signal victory—*be vigilant*—be magnanimous, be just, be generous to the vanquished—but above all be vigilant!"[6]

By the time Houston received that message on May 2, he had already taken the precautions the American commander suggested. Indeed, it was thought by many Texans that the commander in chief had been far too generous in his treatment of the vanquished Santa Anna, on whose hands lay the blood of hundreds butchered at his order. However, Houston felt that Santa Anna alive was worth much more to Texas than the brief ecstasy which might attend his summary execution.

President Burnet proved a hard man to please. He grumbled ungraciously when he arrived at the San Jacinto camp, shortly before the wounded hero turned command of the army over to Thomas Rusk. Houston was leaving to get medical attention at New Orleans. Having no reason now to fear Houston's failure, the president was apprehensive over the implications of his success. With the war evidently won, Texas faced a flurry of political activity. Burnet must now administer the nation Houston had saved. Sooner or later there would be an election in which the chief executive was chosen by the people. Burnet wanted to succeed himself but the wave of adulation which now broke over Houston might easily erase Burnet's chances.

Houston was not thinking as far ahead as that. On May 3 he conveyed to Thomas Rusk his views on the treaty to be negotiated with Mexico while he was away in Louisiana:

I have not the pleasure to know on what basis the Executive Government contemplate the arrangements with Gen. Santa Anna, but I would

161

respectfully suggest that so far as I have been enabled to give my attention to the subject, the following points should have some weight. The recognition of the Independence of Texas should be a sine qua non. The limits of Texas should extend to the Rio Grande, from the north, pursuing the stream to its most north western source, and from thence northeast to the line of the United States. Indemnity for all losses sustained by Texas during the war. Commissioners to be appointed for ascertaining the fact. One Mexican, one Texian, and one American. The guarantee to be obtained from the United States. . . . Gen. Santa Anna to be retained as a hostage, until [the terms of the treaty] are recognized or ratified by the Mexican government. Immediate restoration of Texian or Mexican citizens, or those friendly to the cause of Texas, who have been retained with their property. Instantaneous withdrawal of Mexican troops from the limits of Texas. All property in Texas to be restored, and not molested by the troops or marauders in falling back. Cessation of all hostilities by sea and land. A guarantee for the safety and restoration of Mexican prisoners, so soon as the conditions shall be complied with. Agents to be sent to the United States to obtain the mediation of the government . . . in the affairs of Mexico and Texas.[7]

In broad outline, these were the terms demanded, and though Mexico never ratified the treaty, the armistice with Santa Anna was in complete harmony with these stipulations. Consequently, it is fair to say that Sam Houston won the war and dictated the settlement which followed it.

On May 5 Houston was carried away from his San Jacinto camp. He took Santa Anna with him as he hoped to keep him in safe custody on Galveston Island. John A. Quitman, a young soldier who had served with Houston in those stirring April days, wrote of the boat ride across Galveston Bay. Of greatest interest are quotations from the Mexican general: "[H]e remarked that he was persuaded that Texas, if reconquered by the power of Mexico, could never be retained—that the cost of such an attempt to Mexico would greatly exceed the value of the acquisition—that it would be policy in Mexico to suffer an independent nation to grow up between her and the great grasping power of the United States, and that, should his influence prevail in Mexico, he would urge the recognition of the independence of Texas; that all must be sensible that such was the true policy of Mexico, and that no obstacle could be thrown in the way but what might grow out of national pride."[8]

The point is that Santa Anna, during his captivity, agreed to terms he later rejected once he had been liberated. Thus, Houston's advice to Rusk was surely to the point: Guarantees must be obtained from the United States that Texan independence would be inviolable.

The author of Texan independence could not gain passage to New Orleans on a Texan naval vessel. No explanation for this snub has been offered, beyond the ugly one that Burnet had no interest in Houston's recovery. Finally on May 11 he sailed from Galveston aboard a commercial ship. It was not in his character to do anything public without some flourish. This time he wrote a farewell message to his troops—of which he remained nominal commander in chief. He praised their bravery and urged that they "render obedience to the commands of their officers, and that the strictest order and subordination . . . be maintained. . . . Texas has gained imperishable renown—union will secure the present advantages . . . and open the way to higher achievements."[9]

Three days after Houston sailed to New Orleans, Santa Anna was brought from Galveston to Velasco to sign two protocols. A public document ended armed conflict, called for the restoration of property confiscated by Mexican troops, return of prisoners by both sides, and the withdrawal of the enemy army beyond the Rio Grande. A secret treaty provided that Santa Anna, if allowed to return to Mexico, would use his influence to obtain assent to the other proposals which Houston had recommended to Thomas Rusk.[10] The details of the public treaty were forwarded to Mexico City, where, on May 20, they were rejected by a Congress which vowed to bring the rebellious Texans to heel. But without leadership, the danger was minimal.

Reaction to Texan success in Washington, D.C., was mainly surprise. At issue, so far as the United States was concerned, was the possible annexation of Texas, though formal application had not yet been made.[11] At that time an international power game that would be played for more than a decade was initiated. The British minister to Mexico perceived the possibility of driving two wedges—one between Texas and Mexico, the other between Texas and the United States—for the benefit of Great Britain, still Mexico's prime creditor. If he could neutralize Texas by befriending her, the emissary might salvage his country's investment and cause distress in Washington.

Houston arrived in New Orleans to a warm reception which, because of his injury, he was unable to enjoy. Marquis James tells us that in the welcoming crowd was Margaret Lea of Alabama, aged seventeen, who became his wife almost exactly four years later. If so, the general was in no condition to notice the lovely girl. His wound was infected. Doctors attending him were apprehensive; amputation might be necessary. Fortunately, the limb was spared.

After surgery, Houston was a guest in the house of William Christy. An important friend to Texas during her darkest hours, he had sent funds and recruited troops for the Texan cause. So grateful was Houston that he had sent Christy the handsomely wrought saddle of General Cos as a token of the nation's appreciation. Now the obligation was compounded by the banker's hospitality.

Houston's role in the future of Texas was a major preoccupation of William Wharton, who had just returned from Washington. In late May he wrote Stephen Austin urging him to return from the American capital, and noting that he had been told that Houston was opposed to the annexation of Texas by the United States. "If this is so it is truly and deeply to be deplored. Like all triumphant conquerors he will be omnipotent for a time at least. . . . Knowing . . . that I have some influence with Houston I shall be in misery until I see him. . . ."[12] For some years, as a matter of fact, Houston supported the idea of annexation. To become an American state would help to solve difficult problems, economic and military. His opposition developed only later, after efforts to attain that end proved futile, and even then his reluctance was more apparent than genuine.

At the time Wharton wrote Austin, however, Houston was much more concerned about resolution of peace terms with Mexico. He suffered from a lack of accurate news about the state of negotiations. It was probably as well that the convalescent did not know what was happening at home. Preparations were set for Texas Vice President Lorenzo de Zavala and an aide to leave Velasco for Vera Cruz to represent Texas in the drafting of a final agreement with Mexico. Aboard the ship to carry them across the Gulf was Santa Anna, who had promised to cooperate. The departure did not take place.

Since the signing of the two treaties on May 14, there had been mounting opposition to their terms both in Mexico and Texas. Texans were especially loath to lose the precious prisoner until agreement was

164

ratified. The loudest protest was offered by Thomas J. Green, a recently arrived soldier of fortune and self-styled general, who was boldly importunate. President Burnet, yielding to this pressure, ordered the removal of Santa Anna from the ship. He was imprisoned at Quintana. It seemed possible that there would be more fighting, the only advantage for Texas now being that she had more troops and supplies than before.

Houston began to receive callers at William Christy's house, but the strain was too great. He fainted dead away during one audience.[13] Although the state of his health appeared precarious, he was already thinking of the expense of his stay in New Orleans, and worried about his usual want of ready money. Through John T. Mason, who represented the Galveston Bay and Texas Land Company, he made an agreement to undertake legal matters for the firm and accepted a retainer of $2,000 which would tide him over his present financial crisis. In 1836, "conflict of interest" was a topic not often raised.

In response to an inquiry from M. B. Lamar, Houston wrote in early June, "My wound has improved. Some twenty or more pieces of bone have been taken out of it. My general health has improved slowly. It is only within the last four or five days that I have been able to sit up any portion of the day."[14] At the time Houston was unaware of Lamar's increasing involvement in Texan politics. As the month progressed, the general's condition improved and that of Texas worsened.

The Mexican government repudiated the Velasco treaty and arrested three Texan agents who had proceeded innocently to Matamoros with passports authorized by General Filisola. Mexican garrisons in Texas were resupplied. The opportunistic "General" Green now called for the execution of Santa Anna, a demand in which he was joined by many Texans who had fought and Americans who had come to fight. Sam Houston left New Orleans for home in the middle of June, even though his wound was not completely healed. The news was too alarming to permit him to languish in a sickroom. He was certain that he alone could preserve Texan independence and restore a measure of domestic order. He chose an overland route to Nacogdoches. His progress was slow because he still tired easily. On June 26 he was at Natchitoches, where he conferred with the American, General Gaines. There he also met young Robert Irion, an adventurous physician bound for Texas, who dressed his wound and became his friend.[15]

By the time he reached the west bank of the Sabine, early in July, there was widespread chaos in Texas. Since Thomas Rusk had seemed unable to control the army, President Burnet had briefly replaced him with Lamar, who proved even less effective. Rusk was reinstated and Burnet wrote Texan agents in New Orleans to accept no more short-term volunteers. These men were the most intractable elements of the army. Unaware of this, Houston wrote a friend at Nashville to send more guns and men.[16]

With Irion as his traveling companion, Houston reached Nacogdoches about July 2, and introduced his new friend to Henry Raguet and his beautiful daughter, Anna. Whether or not it was love at first sight, the bond established that day resulted in marriage a few years later. Meanwhile, army officers were now threatening not only to execute Santa Anna but to try David Burnet for treason because of his resistance to the idea.[17] Thomas Rusk wrote Houston that he must return to his post as commander in chief. The general received the letter about July 9.[18]

Even before he read Rusk's message, Houston knew he was needed. He left Nacogdoches hurriedly, passing July 4 at San Augustine with Phil Sublett, Irion still his companion. His wound was giving him trouble, but he refused to stop. Stephen Austin was now at Columbia, where Santa Anna was being held. He wrote Houston that he must try to persuade Gaines to send a detachment of American troops to Nacogdoches and come in person to Columbia to "give the people here assurances of the good faith of . . . Santa Anna in these treaties he has made with you and with this Government."[19] Houston sent the message on to Gaines with a laconic addendum: "General, I refer this letter to you and can only add that such a step as your taking post at Nacogdoches will SAVE Texas."[20]

To Houston's astonishment, Gaines received Andrew Jackson's permission to send American soldiers to Nacogdoches on the pretext of protecting the frontier against possible Indian attack. The effect of the action was salutary. Volunteers flocked to Texas in ever greater numbers.[21] Jackson's intervention at this critical moment caused second thoughts in Mexico City. The Mexicans continued to sound bellicose, but the threat of war diminished markedly.

Houston feared for Santa Anna's safety, for which he felt personally responsible. The Mexican was aware of his captor's solicitude. On July 22 he wrote Houston, "Your return has appeared to be very apropos

. . . because it seems to me that your voice will be heard and properly respected." Houston could "easily remove" the difficulties preventing Santa Anna's release and bring to Texas "complete happiness. . . . Hurry yourself then to come among your friends. Take advantage of the favorable time that presents itself."[22] Santa Anna's suggestion that Houston assume leadership of the Texan government was the first of a series of propositions which, before very long, constituted an offer he was unable to refuse.

Undoubtedly the wisest move of Burnet's administration was a call he issued on July 23 for a general election to be held on September 5. The voters were to elect a president, a vice president, and members of a bicameral legislature. Also, they were to vote on the draft constitution and annexation by the United States. Thus the energies of many partisans of war were diverted into the arena of politics. But the hotheaded Thomas J. Green made one final attempt on Santa Anna's life. Fortunately it failed. The embittered Green rallied two equally emotional colonels and absurdly proclaimed his intention to overthrow the Texan regime. Had communications been more rapid, the announcement might have been more serious than theatrical, for there was ample exasperation with the ineffectual Burnet.

News of the impending election did not draw Sam Houston into the contest. Indeed, one of his first utterances on the topic was a sort of endorsement of his friend, Thomas Rusk, for the presidency. Stephen Austin allowed his name to be placed before the electorate, as did Henry Smith. For more than three weeks of the six-week campaign, these three were the only candidates. In early August Gail Borden produced the first edition of the *Texas Telegraph and Register* at Columbia. The voters now had a newspaper again to advise and inform them.

Houston did nothing that could be construed as political. He was in Nacogdoches on August 8, where he wrote Rusk that another scheme to pillage Matamoros was as wrongheaded as its predecessor. He regretted that his health prevented him from returning to command of the army. "Let us act on the defensive. If the Enemy chooses let them run the risk. A wise man will wait for the harvest, and prepare the reapers for when it comes." It was the policy which had brought Texas the victory of San Jacinto. One could quarrel with it, and many aggressive officers did, but with Rusk in basic agreement with Houston, men like Thomas Green were powerless to act.[23]

Rusk had been flattered that Houston thought him worthy of high office. He claimed that his age (he was only thirty) precluded him from running. He wanted to see Houston become a candidate, but also felt that the head of the armed forces could not be spared. Consequently, he would support any man for the presidency who vowed to back Houston's military policy.

Except for a brief visit to San Augustine in the middle of the month, Houston spent all of August at Nacogdoches, concerned mainly with army paperwork. Rusk noted in the third week of August that Henry Smith appeared to be leading Stephen Austin in the two-man presidential contest.

At approximately the time Rusk was writing Houston about the campaign, there was a hastily gathered meeting of citizens at the Mansion House of San Augustine. To this crowd Phil Sublett offered the names of Sam Houston and Thomas Rusk for president and vice president. Houston's only reaction is contained in an undated note, published August 30 by the *Telegraph:* "You will learn that I have yielded to the wishes of my friends in allowing my name to be run for President. The crisis requires it or I would not have yielded. Duty, I hope, will not always require this sacrifice of my repose and quiet."

He did practically no campaigning because there was little time for it, and he did not feel strong. However, word of mouth and press commentary were apparently enough. "Old Sam Jacinto" was a household name in Texas. The *Telegraph*, sympathetic to his candidacy, published in the August 30 issue the observation: "No man in Texas stands so high in the United States and Europe." When Henry Smith learned of Houston's candidacy, he sought to have his own name removed from the ballot. This was impossible. As for Austin, he waged a desultory campaign.[24]

Houston was not without critics, especially those who insisted that his conduct of the war had been cowardly and who insisted now on a war of aggression against Mexico, but it was impossible to dispute Houston's success. San Jacinto was his monument. Another accusation was that he drank too much, which was probably true. There is no record of any response from Houston.

Whether or not Houston knew his election was a foregone conclusion, Austin knew it. On September 2, three days before the vote was cast, he wrote James Perry, his brother-in-law, to see to the construction of a house for his occupancy. "These arrangements are made on the supposition that I shall not be elected—Houston will, I am told, get all the east, and Red River now—Many of the old settlers who are too blind to see or understand their interest will vote for him, and the army I believe will go for him. . . . So that I have a good prospect of some rest this year." Austin was entitled to his feeling of dry bitterness.[25]

The election took place on the appointed day. The constitution and the annexation referendum were adopted almost unanimously. In the race for the presidency, the result was not quite so lopsided. Austin polled only 587 votes, Henry Smith 743, Sam Houston 5,119. Since Rusk had refused to accept the vice-presidential nomination, Mirabeau Lamar, also a hero at San Jacinto, was the popular choice.[26]

So Sam Houston had his apotheosis. He could fairly state that he had attained it without lifting a finger. The honor had been thrust upon him.

XIV

T HE NEWS of his triumphs traveled to Tennessee. Several weeks before his inauguration as president, Houston received a letter from an acquaintance with news of Eliza. "About the time the news [arrived] that you had gained the victory over Santa Anna . . . [Eliza] showed great pleasure at your success and fairly exulted. . . . No subject . . . was so interesting to her as when you were the subject of conversation; and she shew[ed] evident remarks of displeasure and mortification if some person was to say anything unfavorable to you. . . . Some of her friends wanted her to git a divorce; and she positively refused; and said she was not displeased with her present name; therefore she would not change it on this earth; but would take it to the grave with her. . . ."[1] If Houston felt the slightest tremor of emotion at the news that Eliza was once again proud of the name she bore, he left no record. He had apparently not informed her of his Mexican divorce. As it turned out she eventually did remarry.

Houston's preoccupations were with the state of the infant republic, which was untidy and not very promising. The first Congress of Texas met at Columbia on October 3, 1836.[2] Houston arrived six days later. Technically, he was to take office on the second Monday of December. Vice President Lamar accused him afterward of having been so impatient to assume the responsibility that David Burnet resigned in order to make way for him. "That little month," Lamar wrote, "Houston could not wait; nor could the hungry expectants brook delay, who were looking forward to presidential favors."[3]

The question of annexation was the most pressing international

171

issue. Acquisition by the United States would go a long way toward resolving many problems—especially those that were economic and military. During the year before independence, the provisional republic had run up a debt of more than $1,500,000. The army was inadequate and the navy was nearly a fiction.

Houston took the oath of office October 22. His inaugural address followed a variety of turns, many of them perfunctory. The struggle for liberty had merely begun, but in "the attainment of this object, we must regard our relative situation to other countries." Since the Mexican attitude was well known, he was apparently trying to attract the attention of Andrew Jackson. Peace must be reached and maintained with the Indians. The "maintenance of good faith" with them was preferable to more bloodshed. "Let us abstain on our part from aggressions, establish commerce with the different tribes, supply their useful and necessary wants, maintain even-handed justice with them, and natural reason will teach them the utility of our friendship."

The final paragraph merits citation because of the asides provided by the official reporter:

[Here the President paused for a few seconds and disengaged his sword.]

It now, Sir, becomes my duty to make a presentation of this sword—this emblem of my past office! [The President was unable to proceed further; but having firmly clinched it with both hands, as with a farewell grasp, a tide of varied associations of ideas rushed upon him in the moment; his countenance bespoke the workings of the strongest emotions, his soul seemed to have swerved from the hypostatic union of the body, and to dwell momentarily on the glistening blade; and the greatest part of the auditory gave outward proof of their congeniality of feeling! It was in reality a moment of deep and exciting interest. After this pause, more eloquently impressive than the deepest pathos conveyed in language, the President proceeded]: I have worn it with some humble pretension in defence of my country; and should the danger of my country again call for my services, I expect to resume it, and respond to the call, if needful, with my blood and life.[4]

Shortly after his inauguration, Houston was convinced by Santa Anna of the wisdom of allowing him to go to Washington. He planned to discuss with Jackson the possibility of transferring possession of

Texas to the United States in exchange for some cash that would expunge the Mexican debt to Britain. This would minimize the significance of the British presence in the Gulf and Caribbean areas. Whether these negotiations proved successful or not, Santa Anna was then to be permitted to return to Mexico. Houston realized that if he failed to get Santa Anna off his hands he would face the same cries for blood that had so upset the last days of Burnet's administration.[5]

Meanwhile there were mundane matters to attend to, especially the nomination of a cabinet and the creation of a government bureaucracy. This took several weeks. Also there was need to furbish the capital. Conditions in Columbia were practically primitive. Congress had to meet in two barren rooms of an unfinished house. Members of the legislature, the cabinet, and the administration were lodged with local householders. The president was provided with an unfurnished two-room dwelling, one of whose chambers served as the executive office. When he entertained a guest for the night, it was Houston's custom to sleep on the floor, offering his visitor the solitary bed.[6]

The membership of the first Houston government reflected favorably on the man who had named them: Henry Smith became secretary of the empty treasury, Thomas Rusk secretary of war, S. Rhoads Fisher secretary of the two-ship navy, and J. Pinckney Henderson attorney general—after this office had been rejected by James Collinsworth, who later became chief justice.[7] Symbolically, the most important cabinet appointment was secretary of state. Houston named Stephen Austin. Although he was dying, he accepted the appointment on condition that his health might require his resignation at any time. Another kind of man would have elected to expire in peace. But Austin wrote, "The prosperity of Texas has assumed the character of a *religion* for the guidance of my thoughts." He did not live to see the new year in.

Two of the problems of these early months were ones Burnet had previously found intractable—an insubordinate army and a congress insistent on creating a land-grant policy which made it difficult, if not impossible, to sell much of the 180 million acres of public lands for the benefit of empty Texan coffers. The population of Texas at this time was about 30,000 whites.

While questions of international recognition and possible annexation by the United States disturbed Houston and Austin, the deplorable financial conditions of Texas chiefly concerned Henry Smith. The secretary of the treasury persuaded Houston to authorize Thomas Toby and Brother of New Orleans—provisioners, freight forwarders, bankers, and underwriters—to send guns, file cabinets, stationery, wafers, and wax for the Great Seal of the Republic, and to sell Texan bonds at a rate of interest as high as 12.5 percent.

There was also the matter of an acceptable Texan currency. The nation adopted a dollar which, on issuance, stood nominally at par with that of the United States. Systematic devaluation during the life of the republic made it worth no more than fifteen cents when Texas finally joined the Union. Despite all measures of austerity, the Houston administration saw an increase of the Texan national debt by $2,000,000.

It took some time to make the necessary arrangements for Santa Anna to travel to the American capital—in part because the Texan senate demanded a voice in the decision. William B. Lewis, Jackson's secretary, wrote Houston from Washington that Old Hickory thought the eventual return of Santa Anna to Mexico a prudent move, since his apparent acquiescence to Texan peace terms would cause controversy in Mexico City. This would make it more difficult for Mexicans to "war against their neighbors."

On November 26, to the consternation of many Texans, Santa Anna rode out of Columbia on a fine horse, wearing an impressive costume purchased with funds he had borrowed from Colonel Bernard E. Bee, the officer who escorted him. Another member of the party was William Wharton, charged with seeking to persuade the United States government to recognize Texan independence, and possibly to negotiate annexation.

Though still not disposed to admire Sam Houston, Stephen Austin was sufficiently impressed by the first weeks of the administration to write, "[E]verything is going well. All the temporary excitements of the past have entirely subsided—Houston goes into office under favorable auspices and harmony and union is the order of the day."[8] Though there is no record of a meeting between the two great men of Texas at which their differences were reconciled, they certainly met on many occasions. Whatever Austin may have felt about taking so terrible a beating at Houston's hands in the election, he had come to terms with the current realities—"harmony and union."

In Washington, Wharton encountered surprising resistance to his mission from Andrew Jackson. The President urged Congress to defer any action either to annex Texas or even recognize its independence. To extend recognition was but a short step from annexation in the public mind. Annexation could be accomplished in one of two ways—by purchase or by war. Though Santa Anna believed the sale could be arranged, there was much skepticism in the American capital that the Mexican president's compatriots would yield readily to his views. That left war as the alternative. To acquire Texas by involving the United States in war would evoke powerful opposition among the Whig Abolitionists and even on the part of some northern Democrats who feared that the admission of the new nation to the Union would upset the delicate balance established in 1820 by the Missouri Compromise, whereby slavery would be permitted in no new state west of the Mississippi or south of the Missouri border.

Sam Houston was unaware of these impending complications. On November 16 he wrote Jackson a letter in which he announced: "My great desire is that our country . . . shall be annexed to the United States. . . . It is policy to hold out the idea . . . that we are very able to sustain ourselves against any power . . . yet I am free to say to *you* that we cannot do it."

He had released Santa Anna for the journey north only because he believed it to be Jackson's wish. To the President he confided: "I look to you as the friend and patron of my youth and the benefactor of mankind to interpose in our behalf and save us."[9]

With Santa Anna on his way, Houston tried to cope with pressing domestic problems and predicaments—finances, Indian relations, and the establishment of a proper capital city. A bond issue of $5,000,000 was a calamitous failure. The refusal of the Texan congress to ratify Indian agreements annoyed the red men, who had been promised fair treatment. However, Houston was successful in preventing serious clashes between whites and Indians during his first presidential term.

Houston was able to pay a little attention to his personal life. "By the month of *May*," he wrote Anna Raguet, "war or no war, I hope we will meet . . . at the new city, and that its improvements will invite the visits of many Ladies."[10] It was to be called Houston City, but the president's hope that Texas finally settle on it as the permanent capital was vain. At this time Houston received from his Nashville cousin, Robert McEwen, word that Eliza was allowing it to be known that she would welcome a reconciliation, an event that would bring joy to Tennessee.

"You occupy the position of a second Washington," McEwen wrote, and added that he was "gratified to learn that you have become a sober man." No reply survives.[11]

With hopes for Texas' immediate and long-term future depending principally on decisions made in Washington, Houston impatiently awaited a report from William Wharton. When it came, it proved disappointing. Santa Anna's plan of selling Texas was coolly received. The question of annexation was to be left for the Van Buren administration, which was known to oppose it because of its implications among Abolitionists. The most that Jackson would promise was to leave the issue of recognition in the hands of Congress.[12]

If annexation depended on the abolition of slavery in Texas, the new nation would have no choice but to remain independent. Its economy, frail as it was, could not function without slaves. The only action against the slave traffic during Houston's first administration was a ban against the importation of blacks from Africa or Cuba. However, they could be freely introduced from the United States—and were. Also, a brisk commerce in smuggled slaves flourished. On December 19, the president pointed out in a proclamation that this practice was illegal, but it was a futile gesture.

On Christmas Eve 1836, Stephen F. Austin took to his bed with a chill. Three days later he was dead. Houston published a general order to the army about the honors to attend this sorrowful event—a salute of twenty-three guns (one for each Texan county). "The Father of Texas is no more!" he lamented. "The first pioneer of the wilderness has departed!"[13]

In only one major sense could Houston's first presidential term be considered a success. By the main force of his personality, he held the republic together. The single significant triumph occurred on March 4, 1837, when Andrew Jackson, in his final act as President, signed a measure which had the effect of according recognition of Texan independence. Old Hickory left office in the middle of the first major financial panic the United States had known. The effect of America's monetary problem on Texan finances was direct and equally catastrophic; when the United States sneezed, Texas came down with pneumonia. No one was willing to speculate in Texan bonds. The local currency rapidly lost whatever real value it had originally possessed.

176

For this Sam Houston was not to blame, but since responsibility had to be placed on someone, he got it. Because money was increasingly tight, the Texan president ordered the printing of more currency.

Meanwhile he assisted his new minister to Washington, Memucan Hunt, in the drafting of a proposal advocating annexation, which they hoped the Van Buren administration would present to Congress. Annexation was the only rational solution of the Texan question in the long run.

Because his country's credit could scarcely get worse, Houston saw no harm in contracting a New York shipyard to construct a seven-vessel navy to replace the two ships that had been lost in the Gulf while attempting to interfere with Mexican commerce. To ease the financial burden of maintaining a large army in the field and to reduce the possibility of a potentially disastrous filibuster against Mexico, he furloughed about three-quarters of the troops. Texan soldiers could return to their homes. Americans in the service of Texas were not so fortunate. Wherever they turned, they encountered local hostility. Penniless, they drifted in and out of the towns where they divided their time between saloons and the revival meetings that had become epidemic in Texas as Baptist missionaries spread over the new nation like locusts. Often drunk and disorderly, the soldiers disrupted the religious gatherings. The atmosphere of the average Texan community during 1837 was not happy, though Francis Lubbock (soon to be secretary of the treasury, but not always an admirer of Houston's) described the furloughing of the army as "one of the most marked evidences of statecraft I have ever known."[14]

The first anniversary of Texan independence, March 2, 1837, Houston's forty-fourth birthday, was wildly celebrated throughout the country. A fortnight later word was received that Jackson had signed the bill recognizing Texan nationhood and naming a chargé d'affaires to establish himself at Galveston. The principal celebration of this event took place at Washington-on-the-Brazos, where the declaration of independence had been promulgated. A dinner and ball were offered in the former capital, where the name of Houston was toasted, though he was not present to hear it. One of these proposed the health of "Sam Houston, the man who is contented to be called Sam, and who has proved a Sam's-son to the enemies of Texas."[15]

A letter written to Irion on the nineteenth reflected the President's state of mind soon after he knew of recognition by the United States.

[Recognition] alone is a cause for joy, but annexation wou'd have rendered me truly happy, and secured all that we contended for. My only wish is to see the country happy—at peace and retire to the Red Land [of Nacogdoches], get a fair, sweet "wee wifie," as [Robert] Burns says, and pass the balance of my sinful life in ease and comfort, (if I can).

Your advice will not be neglected about my health. The moment that I can possibly, I will repair to "Houston" and hope to be a comfortable Houston! My health, under your Esculapian auspices, thank God, is restored, and my habits good. I am informed that many ladies are going to Houston and that society will be fine. We will not have the fair Miss Anna there—for she has a great aversion to "Houston," and I dare not invite her, or I would wait upon her and ask her to a "levee" of the President. How sad the scenes must be at my Leevees [sic], no Mrs. H—— there, and how many who will attend can claim fair Dames as theirs!!! You know the adage, "every dog," etc. My day will come!

Not renowned for his capacity to laugh at himself, he did on this occasion chuckle, if ruefully, over his unmarried state. However, he had little time for such thoughts. He wrote almost daily to Colonel Albert Sidney Johnston, field commander of the army, about reports of ferment in the ranks. At all costs, he ordered, no filibustering expeditions were to be permitted. He instructed Secretary of War Rusk, then at Nacogdoches, to try to placate the restive Indians, impressing on them "that they must not invade our frontier, or I will make a serious matter of it."[16] The removal of the capital from Columbia to Houston City was begun in mid-April. The President himself arrived there on the twenty-first, San Jacinto Day. A week later, he described for Irion the town that bore his name: "It combines more advantages and is far superior in every point of view to any situation I have yet seen in Texas for the seat of Government, and commercial and mercantile enterprises." He marveled at the speed with which it had been built: "On the 20th of January, a small log cabin & 12 persons were all that distinguished it from the adjacent forests, and now there are upwards of 100 houses finished and going up rapidly (some of them fine frame buildings) and 1500 people, all actively engaged in their respective pursuits. It is remarkable to observe the sobriety and industry like we see in the north—I have not seen a drunken man since my arrival." He concluded his assessment of the town's virtues thus:

As regards the health of the place, I can perceive no local cause of insalubrity. A fresh breeze, which is generally prevalent, renders the temperature comfortable. The citizens propose, during the sickly season [yellow fever was endemic], should it become necessary to preserve health, passing that period on [Galveston] Bay, in bathing, fowling, fishing, and other amusements. These views . . . I believe are practical —and that in a few years it will be an important commercial city; and will continue the permanent seat of Government. The members [of Congress] who have arrived here are well pleased, even those that opposed the location. . . . There are more than 100 ladies resident in town; and at a ball given on the 21st, 73 [women] attended!! They are arriving daily. You can have no conception of the reality— It seems like magic.[17]

In the unfinished capitol building, Houston delivered a state of the union speech May 5. He had little of comfort to recount. He concluded, nonetheless, on a salutary note: "While reflecting upon the dispensations of an Almighty Being, who has conducted our country through scenes of unparalleled privation, massacre and suffering it is but gratitude and sensibility . . . to render to him our most devout thanks, and invoke his kind benignity and future providence, that he will preserve and govern us as a *chosen people.*"[18]

As Texas seemed to become increasingly safe, people arrived in ever greater numbers. "Crowds of enterprising emigrants are arriving on every vessel," the *Telegraph* reported in the middle of May, "and so numerous have our citizens already become . . . that we confidently believe Houston [City] alone could, in case of a second invasion, furnish an army of able-bodied men, nearly equal to that now encamped on the banks of the La Baca." While Vice President Lamar was visiting his native Georgia, a friend wrote him of events in the Texan capital and left us a negative portrait of Sam Houston during his first administration. The president was seldom out of his quarters before eleven, was dressed in the gaudy style that was "self peculiar," admired himself in a glass, adjusted his hat, and finally took "the inebriating sip" that made him once more the hero of San Jacinto. Then "with a tread of dominion in his aroganic [*sic*] step strides . . . across his own nominated metropolis . . . to the bar keeper."[19] In this same month, another of Lamar's informants urged him to return to Texas at once, for Houston's health, he wrote gleefully, was being

179

destroyed by his debauchery. Apparently this man knew little about Houston's capacity to live with his drinking.

In June, J. Pinckney Henderson was confirmed by the Senate as "agent commissioner" to Britain and France. So began a second chapter in the history of the republic.[20] Though he had only recently sent Memucan Hunt to Washington to promote annexation, Houston thought it wise to add another string to his bow by seeking simultaneously to establish Texas as an authentic political entity in the eyes of the two most important countries of Western Europe. That Great Britain should be the first foreign nation approached was no coincidence. The president hoped that negotiations in London would goad members of Congress in Washington toward annexation. If the United States failed, Texas required other choices. Britain and France were already financially and politically committed in Mexico; it was logical that they should have an interest in the fate of Texas.

A picture of Houston's manner of living at this time has been provided by John James Audubon: "We approached the President's mansion wading in water above our ankles." It was "a small log house, consisting of two rooms and a passage through. . . . We found ourselves ushered into . . . the ante-chamber; the ground-floor . . . was muddy and filthy, a large fire was burning, and a small table, covered with papers and writing materials, was in the centre; camp-beds, trunks, and different materials were strewed around the room." The great artist-naturalist was presented to members of Houston's entourage, notably to the surgeon-general of the army, Ashbel Smith, a Connecticut man who had come to Texas at the urging of J. Pinckney Henderson, ostensibly to recover from a luckless love affair. He now shared the cramped quarters of the president.

We do not know when this friendship began. Perhaps Dr. Smith made an appearance when Houston needed a physician. Given the roisterous habits of the president, the moderate, temperate, moody Ashbel Smith seems to have been an ideal companion. He was to prove an intimate and lifelong friend—perhaps the closest Houston ever had.[21]

After a trip to Nacogdoches at the end of June, followed by some negotiations with Creeks and Cherokees that finally led nowhere, Houston was back in the capital in late July. A visitor during this broiling summer season was Erasmus Manford. He called the place "a moral desert—a hell on earth." He found that "vice of most every name and grade reigned triumphantly" there. He described the president of the republic, with whom he dined, as "a good talker but an awful swearer."[22]

In early August, at Washington, Memucan Hunt asked Secretary of State John Forsyth to recommend legislation for the annexation of Texas. Hunt put as favorable a light on the proposal as he could, not alluding to a renewed threat of invasion by Mexico. Three weeks later, Forsyth politely refused. The official reasons were constitutional—it was not clear whether the United States could legitimately annex an independent nation. Unmentioned was the common sense explanation: It was impolitic to provoke Mexico, which was still officially at war with Texas. Also, beneath the surface remained the much touchier issue of slavery. So, for the moment, nothing was to be accomplished in Washington. Texas must seek salvation elsewhere.[23]

This was not to be easy. When Henderson presented himself to Foreign Secretary Lord Palmerston, in London, he was received with cool correctness; his mission of recognition and commerce was not accorded much interest. Like France, Britain's investments in Mexico were too substantial to allow the risk of a breach of relations merely to gratify a state which, sooner or later, must logically become part of the United States.

In October the president fell ill. The nature of his malady is not known, but it was thought serious enough to warrant a summons to bring Lamar back from Georgia. It seems probable that his affliction was a recurrence of malaria. He was well enough on November 1 to write an apology to Congress for having failed as yet to deliver a message on the state of the nation, and he maintained a steady stream of correspondence with department heads.[24] Lamar reached Houston City November 9 and immediately made a speech calling for calm.[25] It was the address of a man who hoped, one way or another, to succeed to the presidency. However, Houston recovered completely, to Lamar's chagrin. To Henry Raguet, Houston wrote on November 16: "There is a systematic opposition to the President, and . . . it grows out of the very *laudable* feeling . . . of envy, and a disposition . . . to put him down that they may have it in their power to establish all the fraudulent land claims which *corruption* . . . has originated—but in *this* . . . I trust they will fail."[26]

The major controversy of the session of the Texas Congress which sat in the autumn of 1837 was a measure to provide immediate grants to established settlers and volunteers who had fought in the war for independence. For all other petitioners, grants would be offered six months later. Houston vetoed the act because he thought it premature; much of the land to be distributed had yet to be surveyed. His veto was overridden. There ensued another mad scramble for land, and another Texan bonanza for speculators.

The final year of Houston's administration was, in the main, a replica of the first. Patterns established in 1837 continued through 1838. One development was the outbreak of the so-called Pastry War, a French effort to collect claims against Mexico by blockading Gulf ports and sporadic raids on Mexican shores. These hostilities served Texan interests, at least to the extent of causing France and Britain to reconsider their views on recognition and trade agreements. Henderson's negotiations began to enjoy promise of success.

Though wounded by the rejection of her original application for annexation by the United States, Texas presented the request again early in 1838. This time a bill for annexation was introduced in Congress. Legislative opposition was more vigorous than it had been the year before. The most outspoken critic was Congressman John Quincy Adams. He made a whole session's career of the issue—using it as a springboard to attack Houston's integrity and, through him, to strike at the real enemy, Andrew Jackson. Adams' performances in debates on this question were perhaps the most brilliant of his political life. Since he was both an Abolitionist and an anti-Jacksonian, he succeeded in linking his two manias. Making use of questionable documents, he argued that the effort to incorporate slaveholding Texas into the Union had been part of a conspiracy conceived by Jackson and executed by Houston. He accused Old Hickory of having occasioned the war for Texan independence in order to acquire that territory for the United States. Since President Van Buren had acquiesced in recognizing Texan independence, the present administration was almost as guilty as Jackson's. The underlying purpose of Adams' attack, however, was to use the Texan question as a means of circumventing the gag rule imposed on the slavery subject in the House of Representatives.[27] Annexation was lost again. Houston instructed Memucan Hunt to announce that Texas no longer sought affiliation with the United States.

The reputation of a public personality, once firmly established in the minds of the electorate, is difficult to alter significantly. Almost every report about Sam Houston surviving from these middle years of his life mentions his gaudy dress and his strong predilection for drink. In a sense the colorful attire which he affected for public appearance became a trademark. He also drank heavily, but whether or not his drinking was a problem that affected his ability to effectively carry out his responsibilities during his first administration as president is another matter. His achievements suggest that he had control of his habit whenever he needed to. There was no repetition of the sordid incidents that marked his life in the Arkansas Territory. Yet he was still frequently referred to as "Big Drunk."

Recognition that drink was a problem is verified by the terms of a formal wager he made January 7, 1838, with Augustus Chapman Allen, a mathematician and accountant from Nacogdoches who had been instrumental in gathering funds for the Texan cause:

> AGREEMENT.—The conditions are these: A. C. Allen alleges that Sam Houston will not abstain from the use of ardent spirits, wines and cordials; and should said Houston do so, then Allen is to pay said Houston . . . a suit of clothes . . . which shall cost and be worth $500.00; said Houston alleges that he is not to use any ardent spirits, wines or cordials, and is only to use malt liquours, and should he violate this agreement, then . . . he is to pay the said Allen a suit of clothes worth $500.00. This agreement is to expire on the 31st day of December, 1838. The clothes are to be paid immediately thereafter.[28]

Houston did his best. A couple of weeks later confirmation that he was sticking to the terms is offered in a letter from W. T. Brent of Virginia, who wrote: "Whilst I remained in Houston I called on the President, found him in good health, and perfectly sober. He told me [he] had resolved and was determined to stand to it: not to 'touch, taste, or handle the unclean thing,' until the first of January next. I am in hopes he will refrain from intoxication for the short term of one year, which will do credit to himself, and be a fine thing for the Republic of Texas."[29]

Houston was looking to the future in another respect. Though he had bought and sold many tracts of land, he had so far never acquired one on which he planned to live. Late in 1837 or early the following year, he purchased some acreage on a small peninsula on Galveston Island, called Cedar Point. He made the investment sight unseen, relying on information provided by Robert Irion, who described the spot as "the only Eden on Earth!" It was one of the few pieces of land he did not later dispose of.

Houston City had been national capital for nine months, but the presidential mansion was still unfinished. "It is late at night," he wrote, "and I am freezing in a miserable open house . . . no ceiling and the floor loose laid. Is this not a 'White House' with a plague to it? The Palace is not finished, but it is said to be in progress and will soon be completed. I have sent to New York for magnificent furniture, and when it arrives, what a beautiful contrast I shall enjoy!"[30] The president seemed to bear up well under the combined strains of roughing it in an ill-made shanty and abstaining from the use of ardent spirits. A friend wrote Ashbel Smith, who was on a mission in the north, "The President is in fine health and has not tasted strong drink since you left."[31]

As winter gave way to spring, Houston City matured sufficiently to provide a number of galas—to commemorate the birth of George Washington, to mark the second anniversary of Texan independence (Houston's forty-fifth birthday), and the grandest occasion of the Texan year: San Jacinto Day, April 21. The president must have been gratified to read in the *Telegraph* of February 24 a letter by Ashbel Smith, written originally for a New Orleans paper. For once, a friend sprang to Sam Houston's defense:

[Houston] has been represented as an imbecile in body and in-tellect:—a moral and physical wreck. Never was calumny more false. His health has certainly been impaired by privations and exposures; but he possesses at this moment more physical force—despite his severe attack of congestive fever last summer—than ninety-nine able bodied men out of one hundred; and he is still capable of enduring fatigue, privations, and watching in a most extraordinary degree. As regards his mind, he is still in the prime of his intellect. . . . His bearing is that of the most lofty and princely courtesy; and he is singularly endeared to his personal friends; and despite all that has been said to the contrary, I believe him the most popular man in Texas. The statements of his being a madman and cutting tall antics before High Heaven and man ... are utterly and gratuitously false.[32]

He needed all the energy and talent Smith ascribed to him to confront the problems that beset Texas. Having ordered Memucan Hunt to retract the request for annexation, the new country must become a genuinely separate and viable political entity. Then Texas could gain admission to the Union—for only under such conditions would the issue of slavery be subordinated. The Abolitionists might mellow if Texas were a true power with important commercial advantages to offer the United States. At the moment Texas was hardly in a position to present herself as anything more than a potentially great land. To create a strong economy demanded peace and security, conditions difficult to attain while Mexico continued to menace the disputed Rio Grande frontier.

At least one source of disagreement between Texas and the United States was eliminated in the spring of 1838 when a joint commission settled the boundary lines that separated them.[33] In late May, Anson Jones, a Texas senator who favored withdrawal of the annexation petition, was named to replace Memucan Hunt in Washington. Jones, like Houston, saw that he was bargaining from a posture of weakness, and must necessarily fail to secure terms that were agreeable, should annexation occur. Because of their agreement on this key matter, Houston thought him the right man for the delicate diplomatic task in Washington.

There were some military stirrings in Texas during the summer. A Mexican from Nacogdoches, Vicente Córdova, led a mixed group of disgruntled Indians and Mexican loyalists on a series of raids in the East Texan region of the Angelinos River, causing some bloodshed and much alarm. Houston saw these maneuvers as essentially frivolous, hardly threats to the territorial integrity of Texas.

Meanwhile the season was open for heightened political activity. Under the terms of the Texan constitution, Houston could not succeed himself as president. His preferences were for Peter Grayson and James Collinsworth, in that order. His influence would have been sufficient to secure the election of either. Fate blocked the path. Grayson committed suicide and Collinsworth drowned in Galveston Bay. Collinsworth's death occurred so late in the campaign that it left the field open for the election of Mirabeau Lamar on September 3. His running mate was David Burnet. Both men were bitter enemies of Houston. It is easy to understand Burnet's feeling. As for Lamar, he could not have been temperamentally or culturally more different from Houston. Lamar considered himself a scholar-patriot. The fact that Houston had awarded him a battlefield commission at San Jacinto could not offset what Lamar regarded as the president's deplorable persona: "Big Drunk," the man who had lived openly with an Indian woman, who had hardly attended school, who had risen to fame on the strength of an honorary title of general. The difference between the two men is best indicated by their respective administrations of the country. Lamar's was ruinous, save only for his contributions to public education; Houston's two terms were marked by guile and caution, Lamar's by political and economic profligacy.

In the meantime, the Congress of the United States adjourned without taking any action on the annexation application which Memucan Hunt had not seen fit to withdraw before he left office. Anson Jones was delighted. *"If the next administration pursues a proper course* not many in Texas will wish for it [annexation]. How *glorious* will Texas be standing alone, and relying upon her own strength."[34]

As Houston prepared to relinquish his office to Lamar, he summarized his apprehensions for Texas in a letter to Andrew Jackson. Texas was in a more tumultuous condition than prior to the Battle of San Jacinto. Other politicians, he suggested, were unable to understand the nature of the problems besetting the young nation. He said he might resume command of the army, to "see what has to be done."

The main embarrassment of Houston's last months in office was the Córdova scrape, which seemed more dangerous because of Indian participation. The president wrote The Bowl and other chiefs reminding them of their vows not to attack whites except in self-defense. The Indians felt bound by no promises since the Texan legislature had not ratified treaties negotiated before the creation of the republic. Moreover, they could claim with some justification that they *were* acting in self-defense; their lands were constantly violated by whites. The Bowl, in particular, was offended by these breaches of faith.

The Córdova scrape provided powerful political fodder. One of the most popular aspects of Lamar's campaign was the irresponsible promise to resolve the Indian question, once and for all, by force. This was language that Texans perfectly understood. The most serious charge against Sam Houston's administration was that he had been soft on the Indians.[35]

Commander of the troops marching against Córdova was Thomas Rusk. Houston was in constant touch with him, advising Rusk to avoid direct engagement with the renegade leader if that was possible. It was not an easy path to follow nor to advocate. The president's feeling of impotence is disclosed in every letter he wrote to Rusk and to the Indian chiefs. Córdova became exactly what Houston had been to Santa Anna: a gadfly.

When Congress reconvened after the September 3 election, in early November, it resolved that the outgoing president could communicate with it only in writing. Taking this, rightly, as a manifestation of disdain, Houston pettishly refused to do more than transmit to the legislature reports from the various executive departments. "Had no restrictions been placed ... on the right of the President to select the mode [of communication]... he had important information to lay before the honorable body, and would have rendered it with pleasure. ... But for reasons ... which to his mind ... are unsatisfactory, he declines ... any further communications. ..."[36]

One might reasonably observe that Houston's behavior during the ten weeks between the election and the inauguration of Lamar was characterized by a degree of capriciousness unmatched since the first months of his stay in the Arkansas Territory in 1829. He surely was drinking heavily again. He became involved in a shouting match with vice president-elect Burnet—the latter describing the outgoing president as a half-Indian, Houston calling Burnet a hog thief. Using Branch T. Archer as intermediary, Burnet challenged Houston to a duel, an offer the president wisely rejected, saying with unwonted humility that the citizens of Texas "are equally disgusted with both of us."

He had so violent a quarrel with his erstwhile intimate, William Wharton, that the latter reached for his Bowie knife. Houston is supposed to have dared him to draw, an invitation Wharton refused. At about this time Samuel Colt arrived in Texas and made his name known for his invention of the revolving pistol—the "gun that won the West." A new era of violence was at hand, and Sam Houston had to assume responsibility for some of it.[37]

December 13 was Inauguration Day. Houston made a brief but impassioned farewell speech. Lamar presented his message in writing because of an "indisposition." Some said he was reluctant to appear on the same platform with his predecessor.[38]

XV

DURING THE early months of the Lamar administration, Houston remained detached, though he was quite concerned about many of his successor's policies, especially his intention to dispose of the Indian problem by force. The Córdova uprising, initially subdued by Thomas Rusk in the autumn of 1838, had a resurgence the following winter. The Mexican leader reappeared and persuaded several Indian tribes to join him in a struggle to expel white Anglo-American Texans from their ranches in the Redlands. Ironically, though The Bowl and his Cherokees had refused to join Córdova, they bore the brunt of official Texan retaliation. On Lamar's order, The Bowl was murdered and his nation driven from Texan soil. This total disregard for promises made by other Texans served to increase Indian resentment. Violence begot violence. Once embarked on a campaign of expulsion and/or extermination, the government of the republic found itself committed to perpetual warfare against the Indians in most border areas. The attitudes of whites and Indians hardened to the point where reconciliation became impossible.

The first session of the Texan Congress of 1839 decided to move the national capital from Houston City to San Felipe de Austin, recently renamed Waterloo and soon to become, simply, Austin. The ex-president saw this as another gesture of scorn toward him, though the avowed intent was to locate the administration nearer the center of the country. This conflict provided sorely needed comic respite for the next three years.

During Lamar's first year as president, Texas was recognized by

France and a commercial treaty was concluded by the two countries. Credit for this really should go to Houston. However, Lamar's major lasting achievement was support for the creation of a system of public education funded by grants of land—hardly a controversial measure in a nation that enjoyed a glut of unused land.[1]

By early February, Houston was preparing for a trip to the United States. According to a letter he wrote to Anna Raguet, he was planning to settle at Nacogdoches and had just paid for the construction of a house there which was to be ready by midsummer. One statement in this letter is startling: "Were it not that I am anxious to see my sisters . . . , I wou'd pass the Spring and Summer at home with my Texas friends." This is the first reference to his immediate family since the death of his mother in 1831. He also mentioned his involvement with the development of a new town, to be called Sabine City. This was the principal reason for his journey east. He had been joined in this project by a number of prominent Texans including his friends Phil Sublett and George Hockley.[2]

Prior to his departure he spoke at the first meeting of a temperance society formed at Houston City, where he offered "a resolution favorable to the cause." Evidently, after his lapses of the autumn, he had sworn off once again. However, moderation did not seem to have impaired his social life. There were more invitations than he could accept—though he did take part in a "frolic" aboard the British ship *Ambassador* toward the end of February.[3]

He finally left for New Orleans in mid-March, arriving there about April 1. His principal concern was the sale of scrip for the construction of Sabine City. Business went well. As a major public figure of the Southwest, he was an ideal salesman. The hero of San Jacinto was warmly received. He accepted all the honors which his wounds had prevented him from acknowledging during his previous visit there in 1836.

In early May he went to Mobile, where he made the acquaintance of the ailing William Bledsoe, a planter and land speculator, who invited him to visit Spring Hill, his home just outside the town. Bledsoe's wife, Antoinette, had a lovely young sister, Margaret Lea. A meeting between Houston and Miss Lea took place at a garden party given by the Bledsoes for Nancy Lea, Margaret's widowed mother.

Houston's presence at this gathering was due to Nancy Lea's interest in investing in Sabine City. Although he certainly did not fail to cultivate Mrs. Lea, the ex-president's eye from the beginning was drawn to her daughter Margaret, a dark-haired, violet-eyed, pale-featured, diminutive girl who had just turned twenty. Margaret Lea had been raised and educated in strict Baptist surroundings. In a sense she could be characterized as very nearly a religious fanatic. It seems doubtful that this aspect of her temperament emerged too clearly during this initial encounter. Margaret and Sam walked in the lush, perfumed gardens of Spring Hill. He was surely a model of courtliness, for he had a hand with women, and a taste for them, too—especially younger women.

Nancy Lea had heard a good deal about Sam Houston. Although she was not enthusiastic over the idea that he was courting her younger daughter, she did not allow this to interfere with business. She also did nothing to discourage his attentions to Margaret. As the days slipped by, Mrs. Lea became so interested in Sabine City that she sent her frail son-in-law, William Bledsoe, to view the location in person. He had instructions to commit himself in her name to a substantial investment if he was satisfied with what he found.

While Bledsoe was on his way to the mouth of the Sabine, Houston remained at Mobile, completely enthralled by the beautiful Margaret. Nancy Lea, as if suddenly aware of the great man's somewhat sullied reputation, sought a means of preventing the continuation of what was plainly a very serious courtship. She did not know which of the tales about him most alarmed her—those of his womanizing or the ones about his drinking. It was his drinking that brought itself to her attention.

After Bledsoe left for Texas, Houston managed to drink himself into a near stupor, and retired to his room. Nancy Lea visited his bedside and, while he lay in a state of semiconsciousness, read him some lines from Holy Writ which she thought appropriate to his condition. She was not however the woman destined to steer him onto the comfortless path of virtue. By early June it was clear to her that her daughter was actively considering Houston's proposal of marriage. It should have been evident to a wise parent that in seeking to interpose herself as forcefully as she did between the two, she merely assured the result she hoped to prevent.

She decided to take Margaret home to Marion, unaware that the girl had already accepted Houston's offer. To his suggestion that they marry at once, however, Margaret demurred.[4] She was too dutiful a

191

daughter for that, and felt an obligation to prepare her family for this great change in her life. She insisted that Houston pay a visit to Marion, meet all her relatives and friends, before even announcing their engagement. He would do anything she asked.

While we can have little difficulty in appreciating the attraction of Margaret Lea for Sam Houston, we have to be surprised at his attraction for her. The aura of romantic glamor that he carried about with him was surely a factor at first. But given his deportment while a guest of the Bledsoes, we have to infer that some of this appeal was offset by his drunkenness. In addition, he was no longer, at forty-six, exactly in his prime—though he liked to think he was, and was pleased when flatterers said so. He had been too much punished by reckless living to be any longer the heroic specimen he had seemed, perhaps, to Eliza Allen a decade before.

Why, then, did Margaret agree to marry him? And why did she cling to her decision against the advice of her mother and brothers? An answer is provided by the pattern their marriage assumed during the twenty-three years of its duration. Like other religious fanatics, she had in her nature important elements of masochism. Martyrdom is the surest road to heaven. She was, as well, something of a missionary. In Houston she discovered a great man who stood sorely in need of just the kind of salvation to which she, as God's earthly agent, believed she had the key. She loved him in her fashion, and his was a soul worth saving. She could have no realistic idea of what it meant to be the bride of a prominent politician—and when she learned, she found the life abhorrent. She refused, because of ill health and pregnancy, to share much of his public career. This is far from saying that Margaret was insensible to the compliment of being the object of a great man's love, but his appeal to her cannot have been that alone.

Had he been, on the other hand, merely a man in his forties with a drinking problem, a record of inconstancy, and imbued with no serious thought about formal religion, she would doubtless have been repelled by his proposal. It was in her character to wish to suffer hardships in order to bring a hero into personal contact with his Saviour. Margaret was an evangelist; she would open to Houston the gates of heaven and, in the process, gain admission for herself as well.

She was never reluctant to express her views of his conduct before their marriage. She made it clear that she planned to change his ways. It is an important measure of Houston's infatuation and perhaps an indication of his awareness that he needed saving—whatever form salvation might take—that he so eagerly pursued a girl who, he must have sensed, would change his style of life and would at last domesticate him. We have to conclude that he wanted all this.

When they parted that June, all was understood between them. Houston would still have to convince Nancy Lea and her eldest son, Henry, that he was a suitable mate for Margaret—a task that was perplexing. He promised to visit her at Marion before returning to Texas. Then he journeyed to Tennessee to sell more scrip in the Sabine City project and, perhaps, to see his sisters. He bartered some of the shares for a number of bloodstock horses at Nashville.[5]

Despite the heat of his pursuit of the desirable Margaret and although he had promised to go to Marion in the middle of July, he allowed himself to be detained long in Tennessee.[6] He conferred several times with Andrew Jackson about the future of Texas, his own role in the nation's growth, and perhaps about possible annexation at some later date—for the two ex-presidents were equally certain that this must eventually occur. Naturally, he mentioned his plans for remarriage and was able to send Old Hickory's greetings to his fiancée.

Houston had not gone directly to Nashville from Mobile. Memucan Hunt wrote Lamar in July from Jackson, Mississippi, that after having delivered a temperance lecture at Columbus, in that state, the Texan hero had got drunk.[7] This event merely emphasized his need for Margaret, who wrote him, on July 17, the first letter of their intermittent correspondence. "My heart . . . is like a caged bird whose weary pinions have been fold[ed] for weeks and months—at length it wakes from its stupor, spreads its wings and longs to escape. . . . Last night I gazed long upon our beauteous emblem, the *Star of Destiny,* and my thoughts took the form of verse, but I will not inscribe them here, for then you might call me a romantic, star-struck young lady." Star-struck she was, but in the same letter she wrote of her faith, her prose purple with fervor.[8] Then, on a more practical note, she told him that her brother Henry and her mother planned to visit Texas in October, to view the site of Sabine City for themselves, but that they would not allow her to go with them unless Houston first visited Marion. She urged him to make haste.[9]

A fortnight later she wrote him again, her tone a little firmer: "I stated to you . . . that it was the wish of myself and relations that you should visit Marion. I have never yet taken sides in any affair of moment without being guided in great measure by my relations. . . . In this case . . . I shall rely entirely on their discretion." He took the warning, but not hastily. He visited Marion early in September. His reception seems to have been mixed. He made a good impression on Martin Lea, the younger of Margaret's brothers living in Marion, but on Henry and their mother the vaunted Houston charm was not altogether effective. Nancy Lea eventually accepted him; Henry never did. Though Houston again proposed an immediate marriage, the Leas insisted on further delay—hopeful that the impetuous girl would change her mind.

He proceeded to Nacogdoches, where he learned that in his absence he had been elected Congressman from this district. He was enraged to hear of the death of his friend, The Bowl. He delivered a blistering speech on the topic of Lamar's Indian policy in which he noted that The Bowl had been by far a finer man than those responsible for his murder. The address was not calculated to win him friends in East Texas. Even such stalwarts as Thomas Rusk, Adolphus Sterne, and Henry Raguet were dismayed by it.[10] However, Lamar was even less popular in East Texas. A misinformed friend had written Lamar before Houston's return to Texas that he had "nothing to fear from old Sam—he will drink too much of the ardent to injure you— He will kill himself."[11]

Others were convinced that if Lamar could make his genocidal Indian policy appear a success, he might control the succession to the Texan presidency in 1841. These men saw the appalling death of The Bowl as a political asset. The Congressional election that fall proved the fallacy of this reasoning. Of the representatives who had been sent to Houston City with Lamar the previous year, only ten of nearly seventy were reelected in 1839. There were, all the same, experts who thought Houston's name had lost its currency in Texas. Among these was Memucan Hunt. He wrote Ashbel Smith that he had heard that Houston had been drunk virtually every day of his visit to Nashville. Why Hunt should have thought this would be detrimental to Houston's political prospects in Texas is bewildering. He had long been called "Big Drunk." The nickname was something of an endearment.[12]

In November Houston went to Galveston to greet the Leas. Their arrival proved a disappointment, for Margaret was not with Nancy and Henry. According to Marquis James, Mrs. Lea huffed when he inquired after Margaret: "General Houston, my daughter is in Alabama. She goes forth in the world to marry no man. The one who receives her hand will receive it in my home and not elsewhere." He would have to go back to Marion to marry Margaret.[13]

But before this, the Leas wanted to look at the site for Sabine City, and Houston had his constituents to look after. In Austin, on the evening before Congress had convened there for the first time, Anson Jones chaired a dinner in Houston's honor. Of the numerous toasts offered, the one that most moved the ex-president was to "The soldier and the statesman: we have tried him once and we will try him again."[14] By early December Houston was convinced that Austin, whatever its geographic advantages, was not a suitable capital. He wrote Anna Raguet that it was "the most unfortunate site upon earth for the Seat of Government."[15] On Christmas Eve Anson Jones wrote in his diary: "I fear that Gen Houston does not care how complete[ly] L[amar] ruins the country, so that he can say, 'I told you so; there is nobody but old Sam after all.'" Jones had only recently proposed Houston as Lamar's successor in the 1841 election.[16]

In one way, 1840 was the most significant year of Houston's life, for it saw his marriage to Margaret Lea. It was an important year for Texas, also, bringing the recognition of Belgium and the Netherlands and additional agreements with Britain. There was no progress, however, on the annexation of the country by the United States, but then no one was pressing for it.[17]

The wedding was originally set for February, then for April, but the pressure of affairs prevented the bridegroom from being present on either date. A day in May was finally agreed on. Anson Jones's diary noted that Texas was "going to the [devil] as fast as General H. can possibly wish." Houston was dividing the country by the strong stand he took on the Indian question. The *Telegraph*, under new ownership that was not sympathetic to him, observed in early February that his behavior had "excited the grief and shame of his friends, and the just reproach and scorn of his enemies." There was no doubt about what Houston was up to. Lamar's friend Henry Thompson wrote the president that "Genl. Houston is the whole talk for your successor [in Houston City] and in Galveston." Although it was fully eighteen months before the presidential campaign got underway, Houston was tacitly declaring his availability. He used every issue possible to distinguish his position from Lamar's. As insurance, he would seek reelection to the Congress in the summer of 1840.

The *Telegraph* chided him for his ambition, expressing owlish incredulity that after vowing never again to seek high office he should be the candidate he so clearly was. "We cannot believe . . . that he will be so regardless of his reputation and *personal quiet* . . . as to consent again to engage in a political race, where every step will but plunge him deeper and deeper in the mire of political disgrace."

The political divisions that would dominate Texan affairs for the next decade were now arranging themselves. Although specific issues would change, the faces would remain the same. Houston could not persuade many voters to his point of view on the Indians and on land policy, but he was "Old Sam Jacinto," and for that reason alone he would always be a potent candidate. At a Washington's Birthday celebration, George Hockley proposed this toast: "Houston—He whose very battle field is holy ground which breathes of Nations saved not worlds undone."

Houston's views were given poignancy in March. A Comanche delegation, summoned to San Antonio for a parley, was unpardonably slaughtered to the last man. Their fellow tribesmen decided that the only satisfactory reprisal was the murder of white hostages. The Indian conflict was thus senselessly escalated; mutual hatreds were intensified. At the time of the San Antonio massacre, Houston was in Galveston, getting ready to go to Marion for his wedding. He ought to have gone to Nacogdoches to campaign for reelection to the House, but he dallied at Galveston, currying favor with Margaret's mother, Nancy Lea, who had bought a house there and planned to settle permanently in Texas.[18]

While he waited, there seemed to be a slight softening of Mexico's attitude about Texan independence. This could be ascribed to a combination of circumstances—the intercession of the British, the appearance in the Gulf of the new Texas navy, and the continuing "Pastry War" with France. As the end of April neared, Margaret Lea wrote her mother that she had been preparing her trousseau, which she described in detail. There had been nothing less maddening to relieve the monotony of life at Marion than the marriages of other couples. Whether Houston and the Leas voyaged to New Orleans together is uncertain. Nancy Lea proceeded with Henry directly to Marion, while Houston languished in Louisiana, suffering financial embarrassment.

On May 3 he had to borrow $250. Finally, on the seventh, he arrived in Marion for a wedding to occur two days later.[19]

May 9 was a Saturday. The ceremony took place in the parlor of Nancy Lea's house, performed by the Reverend Peter Crawford.[20] Best man was Margaret's brother Martin, who stood in for Ashbel Smith—the latter being unable to finance the trip from his home in Galveston. Henry Lea gave his sister away, though he was still skeptical about the wisdom of the match. None of the bride's relations was wildly enthusiastic about the marriage. Too many clouds hung over the past of the groom, drink the darkest.

Ashbel Smith believed that alcohol was at least as responsible for Houston's periodic ill health as his old wounds. He noted, too, that during the weeks of waiting at Galveston, Houston had been drinking alone in his room—a sure sign, the doctor thought, that liquor had got the better of him. Margaret was undismayed, indeed, she appears to have relished her husband's problems. She could eliminate them.[21]

After a wedding breakfast, the Houstons retired to the Lafayette Hotel in Marion, where they remained for a week, while all of Margaret's possessions were packed and crated. Besides, now that the marriage had occurred, the townspeople wanted a chance to fete the couple. There were several celebrations in their honor. The great man spoke informally to the citizens. At a barbecue in a grove adjoining the Baptist graveyard, a gentleman proposed the health of "The Conqueress of the Conqueror."

When Margaret and Sam left Marion, they were accompanied by Eliza, the bride's black servant. Her three other slaves would proceed to Texas with Martin Lea and the luggage. They were greeted at Galveston by Ashbel Smith, who had misgivings about the propriety of the marriage. There was so great a difference in their ages.[22] Nor was he alone among Houston's friends who thought it rash. George Hockley wrote Smith in early June, still unaware that the affair had been consummated: "This marriage I fear is [Houston's] death warrant —i.e., *if it ever occurs*. Even so far as it has now progressed I shall only believe it when I hear that it has been perfected."[23]

"The Conqueress of the Conqueror" set about her task of mastering her husband with dispatch. Whether guided by God or instinct, she discovered early in their marriage the secret of controlling her husband—illness. She appeared frail, though she bore him eight children.

She would play the part of the fragile bride. She probably *was* delicate. She certainly detested everything "public" about his life; and from the outset she took as small a part in that as she could. It was not to bask in the sunshine of his greatness that she had married him.

Margaret preferred tranquillity. She was a nest maker, a homebody—everything, then, that Houston claimed to desire in a wife. She was also lovely, in a pale, demure, somewhat ethereal way, acutely sensitive, extremely affectionate—but above all, a private person. She saved her husband from himself by compelling him to save *her* from the sort of life he had previously led. Whether contrived or natural, her policy was brilliantly effective. Within months of their wedding, all were agreed that he seemed a new man. He was deliriously fond of Margaret. The difference of twenty-six years in their ages must have been an important part of her power over him, for she knew he found her physically irresistible.

Their relationship was, in the main, a happy one of mutual dependence and affection and obligation. Margaret made Sam Houston a respectable, sober, and finally a Godfearing man. Those were spectacular accomplishments. Her secret weapon was poor health, and she deployed it in a way we *have* to think cynical—though no such interpretation is mentioned in any document of the day. She caused him to worry about her constantly. Since he had a powerful conscience, all Margaret did was prod it judiciously. She knew just what she expected of him, and she meant to have it—peace, probity, children, financial security, and a home of her own. If she was not completely successful, her failures were minor when set against her triumphs.

They had too many homes and moved too often. Also, Houston did continue to be a prominent politician. In this his nature was as firmly fixed as her own. She wounded him with her obdurate refusal to share this aspect of his life, and she surely helped to prevent him from taking the ultimate political step—to the Presidency of the United States. But if he blamed her for this—or, indeed, for anything—he never said so. His adoration for Margaret was touching, his attention steady, his obedience to her dictates almost absolute. The world had to count it a great marriage, and it did.

XVI

THE HOUSTONS lodged temporarily in Nancy Lea's Galveston house while the small residence which Sam had contracted for at Cedar Point was completed. Margaret was anxious to move her husband to the remoteness of Galveston Island. He had described to her the healthful effects of sea air and she foresaw in their establishment there a chance to restore him totally. Another reason for quitting Galveston at the earliest opportunity was the outbreak of yellow fever.

While the Houstons were enjoying their first weeks of marriage, others were disturbed. A letter from Bernard E. Bee to Ashbel Smith suggested that a second divorce which Houston had obtained in 1838 was defective because it had been procured almost in secret. He said he had begged the ex-president not to remarry until the legal point had been clarified. In any case, Bee was not reconciled to the marriage, legal or not. "I see with great pain the marriage of Genl. Houston to Miss Lea! I had hoped it would never be consummated—in all my intercourse with life I have never met with an individual more totally disqualified for domestic happiness—he will not live with her 6 months. I suppose his chance for the Presidency is good—no matter what occurs."[1]

The Houstons did not enjoy much of a honeymoon. By the end of June, Sam left his bride with her mother and took a steamer to Houston City to give a speech. He was not away for long, but on his return he announced his intention to go to the Redlands to campaign for his House seat. As a result, he was gone for most of the summer. Margaret remained at Galveston for some weeks, then went to Cedar Point when the cabin there was ready for occupancy. With her slaves and a few pieces of the furniture she had brought from Marion, she waited (but not too patiently) for her husband's arrival. She thought Cedar Point not an attractive piece of land, nor was the house luxurious—a typical two-room log-and-pitch building, with a center hall whose two outside doors were left open to the winds of the Gulf and bay, though neither body of water was visible from the house. She called the place Ben Lomond.

Not one to harbor feelings of loneliness, except for Sam, Margaret was doubtless comforted to know that two of his closest friends, George Hockley and Ashbel Smith, had summer houses nearby. She probably surprised these gentlemen by her assertion that Houston had promised to abandon public life.[2] Whatever they made of it, the *Telegraph* of July 1 was certain that Houston would enter the presidential campaign of 1841. The paper was not sympathetic to the possibility.[3]

Having returned briefly to Cedar Point in mid-July, Houston persuaded his wife to go with him to Houston City. On the twenty-seventh, the ex-president introduced Margaret to his friends in the former capital. Ashbel Smith was there. He wrote Bee of the changes in Houston since the marriage: "His health is excellent, as good or better than I have ever seen it. He indulges in no conviviality with his friends—but strange to say is a model of conjugal propriety. I had dreadful misgivings as to the propriety of his taking this step—thus far I have been most agreeably disappointed. His health and ways are infinitely mended. Will it last? I always hope for the best."

From Houston City they traveled to the Redlands. At San Augustine, Margaret met Phil Sublett and his wife. Mrs. Sublett was not immediately taken by the young woman. At Nacogdoches, she was introduced to Jesse Walling, a frontier character who was a strong Houston backer. He asked her, according to John Salmon Ford, "Mrs. Houston, have you ever been in Shelby County?" Her reply was negative.

They went from Nacogdoches to Grand Cane, where Margaret came down with the first illness of their marriage. If she was testing Houston, she could only have been gratified by his tenderness and solicitude. However, he left her with the Bledsoes to make some more speeches. In late August, he wrote her from Crockett that he had been ill. "Sickness has been universal in Texas. I am more lonely each day. . . ." When he came back to Grand Cane, his wife's condition had not improved. He sent at once to Houston City, where Ashbel Smith was visiting, and had him brought to Margaret's bedside. The doctor prescribed rest. Instead of pursuing his political adventures, Houston remained with her. Smith was amazed. He described Houston as "a model of domestic propriety and kindness." In any event, his seat in the House was secure.

By mid-September, Margaret was well enough to return to Cedar Point.[5] Her husband did not stay with her long. By the twenty-third, he was in San Augustine, attending to his law practice, which was prosperous whenever he found time for it. One paragraph of a letter to his wife reflects her reaction to the rough-and-tumble of Texan politics: "My Love, I do sincerely hope that you will hear no more slanders of me. It is the malice of the world to abuse me, and really were it not that they reach my beloved Margaret, I would not care one picayune—but that you should be distressed is inexpressible wretchedness to me!" He swore he was staying away from alcohol.[6]

In late November the Houstons moved to Houston City for the winter. Margaret, prepared to find the town disreputable, was pleasantly surprised at first. She entertained dutifully in the house they rented and furnished the place with some elaborate pieces, notably a rosewood piano that contrasted with the crude, unplastered rooms. Soon, however, life at Houston City palled; there was too much of a good thing—too many callers, too much bustle, and little of it to her liking. She longed for the calm of Cedar Point.[7]

With his wife settled at Houston City, Sam went to Austin for the convening of Congress. The state of the nation was terrible. Almost everything to which President Lamar had put his hand proved a failure. The value of Texan currency was now only 20 percent of its worth at issuance in 1837. Since he was ailing, Lamar allowed day-to-day affairs to be run by Vice President David Burnet, who, he hoped, would succeed him. Lamar's chief interest now was in a scheme to exploit disputed territories in the west, at the end of the Santa Fe Trail. Another grand plan, to which he was opposed, was a measure called the Franco-Texienne bill. This would have allowed 8,000 French families to settle on a tract in West Texas, giving them virtual autonomy and using them as a buffer against Mexico.

Houston opposed Lamar's position on both items. His support of the Franco-Texienne proposal requires some explanation. One can understand his desire to place an important colony between Mexico and the Texans, but the matter of autonomy is puzzling. One possible explanation places Houston's motives in doubt. The Franco-Texienne scheme was in part the brainchild of New York speculator Samuel Swartwout, with whom Houston had had friendly dealings before coming to Texas in 1832. Swartwout made it obvious that Houston's support of the measure would be to his substantial financial advantage. Whether because he thought it to Texas' interest or his own (or both), Houston actively promoted the measure in the House of Representatives. It died in the Senate owing to Lamar's opposition.[8]

Margaret stayed in Houston City no more than a week after her husband left for Austin. She went at first to stay with her mother at Galveston, but found little pleasure there. Her letters to Sam made no effort to conceal her feelings. She was sick as well as lonely. With Nancy Lea and a faithful servant to care for her, she took to her bed for the better part of each day, ostensibly to relieve her asthma. A letter of December 7 was especially mawkish: "My mind . . . fixes itself on the bright hour in which we first *met* and *loved*. Ah how sweetly the lone evening star shone upon our village home! I trembled to think there was one dearer to me than all the hallowed ties of kindred . . . yet there was a strange joy in my heart. . . . I felt the majestic being who sought my hand haunted the visions of my youth. I thought not of disappointment except to know and feel that I would rather suffer misfortune with *him* than enjoy prosperity with another."

She racked him with such letters. It is remarkable that politics should have had so powerful a hold on him that he could resist this kind of blackmail. However, despite this pressure he stayed at Austin and attended to business. It was an important time for him to be active. Lamar had all but abdicated in favor of Burnet. Houston was not a man to forgive old injuries. Moreover, it was generally agreed that these two men would oppose each other in the September presidential election.

While the legislative session droned on into the new year, Margaret went to Cedar Point to see what had been done to increase the size of the house there. She then went with her youngest brother, Vernal, for a visit to Houston City. Near the end of January she wrote her husband that she had heard a report that he intended to run for the presidency. She was not pleased. Houston turned her asperity aside with an evasive answer that can scarcely have mollified or even deceived her.[9]

At about this time, Felix Huston, an officer who had been

disillusioned when Houston had furloughed the army, was presented with an opportunity for gold and glory. He received an invitation from adventurer William Fisher, who had served as an officer in the Mexican army, to take part in an expedition on the Mexican side of the Rio Grande. This could be accomplished by a few hundred volunteers operating outside the Texan law. The incentive was wealth and power. Fisher had been assured that Felix Huston was "the person . . . who . . . must necessarily conquer Mexico."[10] So began a lunatic foray that was to prove embarrassing to Texas and the United States. For those involved it became a catastrophe of long duration. It would be called the Mier Expedition. If Sam Houston had been aware of this plan, he would have been appalled.

He was preoccupied, however, with Margaret's health, which, according to her account, was not improving in his absence.[11] He left Austin before the Franco-Texienne bill had been defeated. Before he reached his wife at Houston City, he wrote a letter to Anthony Butler (the former American minister to Mexico, now living in Texas), in which he expressed his feelings about his probable opponent, David Burnet: "The truth is that useless extravagance and the most unprincipled profligacy have characterized the present administration. Recklessness, the most palpable and barefaced, has been practiced to such an extent that they can neither blush for their crime, nor relent at the calamities which they have inflicted upon a generous, poor, and confiding people." Though still not overtly announcing his candidacy, the conclusion was plain. "I cannot see how we could . . . be in a worse condition."[12]

The next day, February 3, he was still at Austin. By this time his intention to seek the presidency was becoming quite obvious. He wrote his wife: "By the enclosed News Paper, my *Beloved* will see . . . that I have *not consented to be a Candidate for the Presidency!* The affections and happiness of my endeared Margaret are more to me than all the Gewgaws of ambition or the pageantry of Royalty." Then he gave the knife one twist. "Should she desire me to do so, I will consent but not otherwise! . . . The determination of my Love I will abide by." He proffered a second twist. "Thy people shall be my People; and thy God shall be my God! . . ." He knew her well enough by now to be sure that she could not deny what he wanted almost as much as he wanted her, but she would exact her toll by complaints of ill health—real and imaginary.

Toward the end of February, the Houstons returned to Cedar Point, where they stayed a little more than a month, though Houston made several trips off the island to fill speaking engagements. On leaving, he deposited Margaret with her mother at Galveston. By this time she must have known he was an active candidate. He officially declared his candidacy in early spring. Though David Burnet was to be his opponent, Houston campaigned mainly against Lamar.[13] When Congress had defeated the proposal to send a commercial expedition westward on the Santa Fe Trail, Lamar had circumvented the legislature by printing $500,000 in currency with which to finance the adventure. It attracted interest among American speculators, but ultimately added to the difficulties Houston would have to deal with in seeking annexation—for the purpose of the venture, in the view of Abolitionists, was to extend the slaveholding areas of Texas.[14]

While Houston campaigned, the entire Lea family gathered at Grand Cane, where Nancy Lea assumed management of the plantation, for Bledsoe's health had worsened appreciably. Not until May did he arrive there and take Margaret to Cedar Point.[15] She tried to content him with music. He tried to shield her from the more virulent attacks upon him as the campaign warmed with the season. One of the milder assaults appeared in the *Telegraph* of May 19, which came out for Burnet. The editor described Houston as "a noble wreck of humanity—great even in ruins." Other Texan papers were less generous. Houston retaliated by writing many articles vilifying the opposition. Despite all this, the political reality was simple: There was no Texan in the summer of 1841 who could beat Sam Houston in an election.

In June the great news was the departure of Lamar's extraconstitutional Santa Fe expedition from Austin. It was headed by Colonel Hugh McLeod, who led 270 mounted soldiers, a handful of merchants, and a reporter from the New Orleans *Picayune.* In bidding the mission farewell, Lamar pointedly remarked that it was a pity its outcome would not be known before the September election.

Throughout the balance of the campaign, Houston spent more time at Cedar Point than on the hustings. In July he was told that his popularity in the Redlands, the area of his greatest strength, seemed to be fading. Some of his statements about land and Indian policy were coming back to haunt him. He proposed a brief visit to Nacogdoches and San Augustine, and wanted Margaret to accompany him. She pleaded frailty. He reluctantly agreed to make the trip alone. However, as he was about to leave, her illness worsened. He postponed his departure. He was still at Cedar Point on July 28, when he wrote, "Things move on with me pretty coolly, and very dryly—*drily* because we have had no rain for the last nine weeks, *drily* . . . because we have no *liquor,* and I do not taste one drop of it, nor will I do it! My health is pretty fine, but Mrs. Houston's is not good, but better than it has been."[16]

Margaret's illness kept him from campaigning for at least a month. Another month would elapse before he got away—this time under circumstances that seem to substantiate the suggestion that Margaret was playing games. On August 31 he informed her that he could not afford to delay his departure for East Texas any longer. When she realized that he was in earnest this time, she found the strength to go along with him. To be alone was worse than having to travel through the heat of the Texan summer. He was grateful for her company, knowing her presence would attract some votes, especially among those who remained skeptical about his purported reform. He engaged the services of a Dr. Fosgate, whom he described as an "eminent physician," to go along with them and watch over Margaret's health.

They traveled in a hardsprung wagon drawn by mules and driven by their slave, Joshua, over dreadful roads. Whenever they reached a town (sometimes after having camped out overnight), there was a festivity to mark their arrival. There were camp meetings, weddings, dances, and barbecues. Houston, who was so obviously in his element, evinced pleasure that Margaret seemed to be accepting with grace what she had been unable to forestall.[17]

The election was a runaway for Houston. He defeated Burnet by a margin of better than 2 to 1. Edward Burleson, not his favorite politician, was chosen over Memucan Hunt as vice president. Since everyone loved a winner, there was more celebration. At Washington-on-the-Brazos there was a barbecue at which thirteen hogs and two great steers were roasted. "Strange to say," wrote a friend to Ashbel Smith, "it was cold water *doins,*" since Houston did not imbibe "the smallest drop of the ardent. . . ." Texans still had trouble adjusting themselves to the idea that he was really not drinking anymore. Some would never get used to it.[18]

Dr. Fosgate announced that he was unable to sustain the pace any longer and returned to Houston City. For the next few weeks the

Houstons were on the road constantly. Margaret made it clear that she hated political life, but she must have been pleased by her husband's complete abstinence from drink. Almost never again was alcohol to prove a problem for him. Margaret could pride herself on an accomplishment which no one familiar with Houston would have thought possible. He surrendered to her strictures because he loved her and wanted to keep her love at any cost save that of abjuring politics. Also, he must have realized, at forty-eight, that his life depended on it.

The Houstons spent almost two months traveling about East Texas, pausing nowhere for more than a few days. Margaret was introduced to many of her husband's old friends. She met Robert Irion and his bride, the former Anna Raguet. The two young women did not become intimates. But when Anna gave birth to a son, she and Robert named him for Sam Houston, and Margaret presented the infant with a blanket on which she had embroidered initials.

As the hard weather of November set in, the couple traveled to Houston City. By then, Margaret was so depleted by her ordeal that she took to her bed at once. As soon as she was somewhat restored, Sam went with her to Cedar Point, where she could get the prolonged rest she required. By the fourth week of November he was back at Houston City making plans for his cabinet. His first concern was to fill the post of secretary of state, which he offered to Anson Jones, adjuring him not to refuse on grounds of poverty. "Don't say you are 'poor.' I am—all are so! The officers shall have salaries, and in good money. It can be done—and shall be done!!!"[19]

On November 25 he addressed the people of Houston City at a farewell gathering. His speech, as usual, was warmly received. After expressing his respect for womanhood at effusive length ("Oh! it is woman who makes the hero"), he got down to cases. He spoke of taxation, the nation's overextended credit, the Santa Fe expedition (of which nothing had been heard), and the hiring out of the Texan navy to rebels of the Mexican province of Yucatán. He reserved several paragraphs of invective for Lamar. He concluded by promising to do his best to right all wrongs and effect a prosperous peace.[20]

Margaret had insisted on accompanying him as far as Houston City. He left her there December 1 to go to Austin. Her excuse for staying behind was that her presence would slow the trip, and that it was costly. While the Houstons enjoyed practically unlimited credit, as do most important political families, they did not abuse the privilege. Consequently, Margaret was not on hand to see her husband sworn in as president of Texas for the second time. Her heart, in any case, would not have been in it, for it was not an event that pleased her. Texas' gain was her loss.[21]

XVII

FOR HIS second inauguration Houston chose bizarre attire—a hunting shirt, buckskins, and the widebrimmed beaver hat for which he was known. Some who attended were scandalized. A witness thought the president had evinced more *hubris* than if he had worn "an ordinary cloth suit." When he attended a ball that evening in the Senate chamber with Vice President Burleson, he was more soberly attired.

Since Margaret was not with him, he elected not to occupy the executive mansion, but chose cramped quarters in the best Austin hotel, Eberly House. Like his inaugural costume, the gesture was intended to emphasize Texan poverty. Another was to halve his salary to $5,000, hoping thus to set an example for other members of his administration. He worked in a one-room building which afforded just enough space for himself and W. D. Miller, his intimate and secretary—again to stress the penury of the nation and the need for economy.[1]

In his first message to Congress, he did not please his hearers greatly. "Aware of the Mexican character, and believing as I always have that Mexico is and will remain unable to invade us with any hope of success, I would recommend the kindest treatment of her citizens." The wisest policy with respect to Mexico was one of watchful waiting. There was dismay among legislators when the president asserted that the Indian question could be satisfactorily resolved for one-fourth the amount expended by Lamar—simply by making and then adhering to treaties. He complained that his predecessor had left finances in such a confused state that a week after taking office, he was unable to determine just how grave the situation was. Since Texas could not now honor its debts, he requested a moratorium on all public obligations. He proposed other resolutions to the economic problem, including the issuance of new specie to be backed by the sale or mortgage of land in East Texas expropriated by Lamar from the Cherokees. Although Houston had deplored Lamar's actions against The Bowl, he sought to take advantage of their result. The predominating tone of this message indicated the need for caution and retrenchment.[2]

By the second week of 1842, Margaret wrote her husband from Houston City. She had heard that the Mexican threat was more serious than he had stated in his Congressional message: "I am told that [the United States] only await your permission to send an army through Texas into Mexico."[3] The report was false. However, another report arrived with news of the fate of Lamar's illicit Santa Fe expedition. Almost every man who had taken part had been captured and imprisoned at Castillo Perote, an uncomfortable fortress in Mexico. As word spread, so did a fever for vengeance. But short of war, which most Texan legislators knew to be impossible without American intercession, little could be done. Houston expressed a polite concern for the captives that failed to hide his indifference to their plight.[4]

He was much more interested in the location of the national capital and was determined to move it back to Houston City. Other cities wanted the honor of being the capital. The authorities of Washington-on-the-Brazos made a proposal to pay for the removal of all government employees and legislators and to erect suitable buildings for the seat of government.[5] Unfortunately for Houston, the citizens of Houston City refused to make a comparable offer.[6]

Relations with the United States were flawed. James Reily was sent to Washington to try to persuade the Tyler administration to control attacks against Texans by Indians living on American soil. Reily was also to let it be known discreetly that the door which Texas had closed against annexation could be reopened.[7] Meanwhile, in early February Houston vetoed a bill declaring all Mexican land as far west as the Pacific to be Texan. Congress overrode his veto and adjourned almost immediately afterward. No effort was made to implement the measure until the Mexican War.

On February 5 the president left Austin to join his wife at Houston City. While he was en route (four days in all), Adolphus Sterne heard that Houston was dead. "[H]ope it is not so as we would surely be in a worse fix than we are now (as far as a *President* is concerned)." This was the second time that a friend had prematurely recorded Houston's demise. Margaret welcomed her husband at the door of their rented house. Since her mother and other relations were at Grand Cane, near Liberty, the couple was afforded the luxury of privacy. But the president remained president. He communicated almost daily with Miller at Austin. In a letter of February 15 Houston appraised Santa Anna's capacity to make war against Texas. He thought the enemy whose life he had saved would harass frontier communities, but that domestic strife and the problems with foreign creditors would prevent a large-scale conflict.[8] Although his evaluation was accurate, he failed to consider the emotion that Mexican raids would generate in Texas.

He and Margaret left by boat for Galveston February 22. Following a luncheon offered there by Ashbel Smith, soon to leave for Europe as minister to France and England, the president's wife fell ill, necessitating a longer stay at the Gulf town than she had wished. In early March they were at Galveston when the Mexicans attacked some border communities. Though comparatively little harm was done, the citizens of West Texas began a hasty emigration eastward, causing much panic. It was the most serious threat to Texan morale since the "Runaway Scrape" of 1836.[9]

Houston responded with calm and cynicism. He told those who demanded war that war would doom them. "The true interest of Texas is to maintain peace . . . and cultivate her soil. . . . [T]he President . . . has no power to lend the flag to any nation, association, or enterprise not recognized by the constitution . . . nor will he violate his oath, the laws or the constitution.[10] Nevertheless he made efforts through diplomatic channels to secure the intervention of the United States, Britain, or France in persuading Mexico to recognize Texan independence. Furthermore, if Mexico must prosecute a war, it should be according to the rules.[11] Nothing helped.

On March 10 Houston ordered preparations of the militia "for defensive war." Volunteers flocked toward San Antonio. He was almost more apprehensive about Texans taking matters into their own hands than about the Mexican threat. In a letter of that day to Edwin Morehouse, a militia officer, he wrote: "System and order must be preserved, or we will again have the scenes of the Alamo, Goliad, and

Santa Fe renewed. . . . Without these prerequisites to defence, we may anticipate every disaster."[12]

He ordered the evacuation of Austin as the capital, requesting that a provisional establishment be made at Houston City. He expressed a special anxiety that the national archives should not fall into enemy hands in the event that the danger of invasion proved genuine. He did not really believe it was, but in this way he used the apparent emergency to gain an end which had nothing to do with the current crisis.[13] In fact, the archives were safer in Austin than in Houston City, but Houston wanted the capital back in the city named for him.

Thus began an entertaining chapter of Texan history called the Archives War. Sensing that the removal of state papers would bring about the relocation of the capital, enterprising Austin residents hid them and kept them throughout Houston's administration. Fortunately, W. D. Miller had sent Houston's personal and public papers to Houston City before the presidential order was received. Thus, at least his office could function normally during the Archives War.

As it became clear that West Texans were still alarmed by reports of invasion, Houston issued a second edict on March 14 urging calm and confidence.[14] He knew that the Mexicans were no more eager for a major war than he was. But news traveled slowly and inaccurately in those last years before the proliferation of the telegraph, and it was often obfuscated by journalists who thought to further their views by misrepresentation or omission. Also, while not so dangerous as those who promoted filibusters, there were political freebooters like James Hamilton and Bernard Bee who got word to Santa Anna in early March that they were prepared to bargain with him for recognition of Texan independence in exchange for $5,000,000, not including the lagniappe for bribes to key Mexican officials. Santa Anna's response to this fanciful proposal was chilly.[15] Another annoyance with which Houston had to deal was the propensity of militiamen to pillage the households of their fellow citizens. In every message to commanding officers, he emphasized the illegality of such actions.

With probably a majority of Texans wanting war, the president's restraint was not popular. He wrote Miller on March 17, "War does not press upon us. . . . We will be in no hurry, and one thing is true, that few *wise men* are hasty *in great business!* . . . The people of Texas may rest assured that *I will never cease to war upon Mexico, until Independence is secured, or the nation is conquered!* No time until the present . . . has justified the resolution of carrying the war into Mexico. I will now press the figure and trust to a brave people. Our cause is holy, and all we have to do now . . . is to act with wisdom, direction, and valor!"[16] There was more poetry than truth in this letter, for Houston did everything to prevent an offensive war, while seeming to advocate one. He thus found himself in the classic political posture of sitting on the fence with both ears to the ground. Those who favored or opposed a war despised him equally. Not since the terrible spring of 1829 had he been the object of such unmitigated obloquy. Now, however, his hide was a bit tougher.

Perhaps the most extraordinary of Houston's letters in this tumultuous time was addressed to Santa Anna. The Mexican was so pleased with the exchange of letters with Hamilton and Bee, which portrayed him in what he thought a favorable light, that he released the correspondence to the press of Mexico and the United States. For he had spurned the offer. Houston, who was apprised of it only in March, responded with exceptional emotion. The tone of his communication may be inferred from its conclusion:

> In the war which will be conducted by Texas against Mexico, our incentive will not be love of conquest; it will be to disarm tyranny of its power. We will make no war upon Mexicans or their religion. Our efforts shall be made in behalf of the liberties of the people; and directed against the authorities of the country, and against your principles. We will exalt the condition of the people to representative freedom. They shall choose their own rulers—they shall possess their property in peace; and it shall not be taken from them to support an armed soldiery for the purpose of oppression. With these principles we will march across the Rio Grande, and, believe me, Sir, ere the banner of Mexico shall triumphantly float upon the banks of the Sabine, the Texian standard of the single star, borne by the Anglo-Saxon race, shall display its bright folds in Liberty's triumph, on the isthmus of Darien.[17]

Had there been ground to hope for reasonable negotiation with Mexicans, Houston dashed it with this petulant and racist outburst. Yet both leaders knew that neither could bring the other down without foreign approval and aid. The war continued to be mainly one of words, now and then interrupted by rash deeds.

The most bellicose act of Texas that season was Houston's order to blockade Mexican ports, issued March 26. This had to be deliberately handled so as not to offend Britain and France, who traded regularly with Mexico.[18] By early April the president had achieved a few fundamental goals: The capital had been removed from Austin and the Mexicans had been deterred if not wholly cowed.[19] Although the Santa Fe prisoners were still in custody, Houston was not greatly disturbed. But there was deep dissatisfaction. Albert Sidney Johnston, no longer on active military service, was so enraged by the president's reluctance to call for a serious advance into Mexico that he sent a challenge. Houston is supposed to have told his secretary to file it with others he had received: "Angry gentlemen must wait their turn."[20]

A number of militiamen under the command of Vice President Burleson were restive. On April 6 Burleson complained to the people of Texas that Houston had placed shackles on his movements.[21] The president learned of Burleson's insubordination five days later. "To oppose the orders of the Executive," he wrote him, "when he is in the exercise of his constitutional functions, is insurrection."[22] Burleson made no effort to cross the Rio Grande. Yet the president was aware that his constituents wanted action. Instead he gave them more words, in the form of another lengthy proclamation. Its conclusion was probably all that most Texans bothered with, if they read it at all:

> Thus far the course of Texas has been one which has left no stain upon our national escutcheon. If our enemies degrade themselves by acts of inhumanity, cruelty and oppression, let us exhibit the beautiful contrast of mercy, magnanimity and justice. If they conduct war by artifice, duplicity and meanness, we will meet them with frankness, boldness and chivalry. The Mexican despot should be admonished by the truth that we have sprung from a race who, since their landing at Jamestown and upon the rock of Plymouth, have never quailed or been appalled by dangers. Our march to greatness cannot be impeded. The puny efforts of Mexico will be harmless. Our triumph will be that of reason, intelligence and civil liberty. We must sustain our past character, maintain the present and illustrate the future. And while commending ourselves to the approbation of men, let our courage be always such as to merit the wise direction of the God of battle, who pulleth down and buildeth up nations.[23]

Meanwhile American President John Tyler was reported by the

Texan chargé d'affaires in Washington, James Reily, to favor annexation. Reily informed Houston of this change of position on April 15. Houston's view of the situation was mixed. He could see the virtues of the young nation's coming under the protective wing of the American eagle, but as he had indicated to his emissary in Washington, the initiative must seem American, not Texan. It was a position to which he clung stubbornly throughout his term. He would not be responsible for a second rejection.

Margaret Houston, though still her husband's darling, had been thrust into the background of his life since he had become president. Now she feared he might "take a fancy for the Rio Grande and 'dodge' her until the war with Mexico [was] ended." In a letter to Treasury Secretary William H. Daingerfield, Houston called his wife's fears "groundless." However, he stimulated her apprehensions by planning to send her back to Alabama to recover from the most recent of her illnesses and, she presumed, to be out of danger if Santa Anna decided for war in earnest.[24] After putting her on a boat for New Orleans, he returned to Houston City.

His main preoccupation during the first fortnight of May was military preparedness. He sent a veiled rebuke to Edward Burleson on May 12, and at the same time promised that in due course Texas would move over to the offensive. However, the hour for invasion would be Houston's decision alone. "Until such orders are given ... I would regard all attempts without authority as injurious to success, and ruinous to our character abroad."[25]

Indians on the Texan frontiers, aware that the country was beset by the Mexicans, were harassing residents at will. The president had dispatched agents to attempt to placate the tribes whenever possible. These efforts were partially successful, but in the long run, because the Indians had "taken advantage" of the nation's discomfiture, they paid a terrible price. Financial difficulties were also pressing. On May 17 Houston sent Daingerfield to the United States to negotiate a loan. As always, the collateral was land.[26] On May 24, with Indian, Mexican, and money crises mounting, Houston summoned the Congress to a special session at Houston City to open June 27.[27] Whether he acted on impulse or after due consideration, the call was an error.

Before Congress met, the president had word from Ashbel Smith in London that Britain had recognized the Texan republic and was sending Captain Charles Elliot as its representative. From Washington, James Reily wrote Texan secretary of state Anson Jones that American friends of Texas had misgivings about the impending session of the legislature.[28] Jones, not always an admirer of Houston's, received this news with some pleasure. American doubt had increased with Britain's recognition, which reinforced Houston's expressed desire that Texas be regarded as a viable independent state. When Congress convened on June 27, however, the president sent the members a message in which he seemed to suggest that he had some second thoughts himself about the wisdom of having summoned them. Initially, he denigrated Santa Anna, "the self-created potentate." But he backed away from suggesting a direct confrontation with Santa Anna. He appeared to leave the decision of war or peace with the Congress. It was one of the most equivocal and confusing of his messages, because the implication of his calling them to a special session was that he had made a decision.[29]

Immediately after submitting his message, Houston left for Galveston to greet Margaret on her return from Alabama. Word awaited him there that she had been too ill to make the journey.[30] He went on to Sabine, and on July 2 he issued a proclamation on the need to regain the few Texan communities still in Mexican hands.[31] Two days later he was back at Houston City and spent the ensuing three weeks exhorting the army and navy to behave bravely but not foolishly while he awaited Congressional action on a state of war.

While the Texan Congress debated Houston's proposal about the sort of war to be fought, James Reily wrote Anson Jones in early July that President Tyler wanted to settle the annexation question at once. Tyler hoped to restore peace with Mexico and prevent British intervention in the matter.[32] Reily then resigned, to be replaced by Isaac Van Zandt, who remained in Washington for the balance of Houston's term.[33]

By the time Reily's last letter reached Houston City, the Texan legislature had reached a conclusion that appeared to preclude annexation. On July 21 it voted to give the president more than he had requested—a declaration of full offensive war and the powers of a dictator. Memucan Hunt wrote him urgently not to veto the measure, for the rumor was rife that such was Houston's plan. It was correct. The day after its passage, the president composed a long veto message setting forth his many objections to the bill. The proposal to grant him dictatorial powers set a dangerous precedent. "I can never sanction the adoption of a principle at war with the convictions of my mind, the practice of my life, and the liberties of my fellow men."[34] If he had been half so forthright in his introductory message to the Congress, or had not summoned it at all, he would not have needed to write such a comprehensive veto.

On August 2 Houston wrote a letter to Anson Jones which is one of the most revealing documents he composed during this hectic period.

[Members of Congress] are gone ... and no war [has been declared], nolens volens, but as much as can be had of the willing kind. ... It is the only kind of war that the country can sustain. Had I sanctioned the war bill, I could not have commanded any means within twelve months, and the ardour of our people[,] while it is restrained, is most impetuous. I would have been in a state of constant vexation, and threats of revolution would have been constant. As things now stand, there can be no censure upon the Executive. ... ... for my country's sake, and for the credit of those who have been so anxious, I sincerely hope there will be volunteers enough to answer the design of a visit to the Rio Grande. We will see!

This moment I have learned that our Santa Fe prisoners have been released, and will soon return to Texas. ... We have one cause less of irritation, and so much the less food for demagogues and agitators. When the matter is understood of their release, it may give us a squint into the affairs of Mexico which we have not before enjoyed.[35]

Although Anson Jones could not know it, the allusion to "a visit to the Rio Grande" was the first mention by Houston of the embarrassing Mier Expedition, a disaster to evolve before the year 1842 was out. As for the release of the Santa Fe prisoners, the cause was evidently a strong letter from American Secretary of State Daniel Webster to Santa Anna urging peace and the elimination of causes of friction between Texas and Mexico. Direct negotiations on this matter had been carried out by Waddy Thompson, American minister in Mexico City.[36]

In his efforts to keep Texan options open, Houston had increased his unpopularity, especially among those who wanted full-scale war. But there was support for his action. From the Hermitage, Andrew Jackson wrote him on August 17 to praise his veto of the war bill. "You have saved [Texas] ... and yourself from disgrace."[37] At about this time, a friend in Texas wrote the absent Ashbel Smith that anger over the veto has "pretty much died away, and 'Old Sam' is more popular than even I believe."[38] He temporarily lost the services and the friendship of George Hockley, secretary of war and marine, who resigned in a huff September 1 over a trivial matter.[39] Llerena Friend cites from the papers of Ashbel Smith this comment about Houston's treatment of those closest to him: "He exhibited a propensity which to his friends seemed unaccountable and injudicious—it was to make enemies of persons who were desirous of friendly relations with him. He acted on one of Talleyrand's strange maxims, 'Would you rise, make enemies.' "

On September 11 Mexican General Adrian Woll captured San Antonio with little loss of life and held the town for nine days. When he withdrew, he took all portable property of value and fifty prisoners, including the personnel of a court which had been in session when he arrived. It was some time before Sam Houston learned of this provocative event.

On the twelfth, ignorant of Woll's action, and at the urging of Charles Elliot, the British emissary, he lifted the blockade against Mexican shipping.

As late as the fifteenth, Houston was still in the dark about Woll's occupation of San Antonio. He was in such pain from his old wounds that W. D. Miller was taking his dictation.[40] Margaret ascribed his condition to the humidity of Houston City and urged her husband to go with her to Cedar Point. With plans pending to move the capital to Washington-on-the-Brazos for the reconvention of Congress in December, the president refused. The news from San Antonio came the next day.[41]

About 1,200 men were quickly mustered to relieve the Alamo town. A vanguard of 200, led by Captain Matthew Caldwell, was met at the outskirts of San Antonio by a much larger Mexican contingent. The Texans won a stunning victory. By the time they entered the town itself, the enemy forces had left.[42]

Houston remained in ignorance of this success for some days. The urgency of the moment prompted him to ask Anson Jones, who had been ill, to return to his duties as secretary of state to help negotiate with British and French representatives.[43]

At the end of September Houston departed for the new capital at Washington-on-the-Brazos. By then he knew of Caldwell's victory at

San Antonio. The Houstons reached Washington-on-the-Brazos October 3. The journey had taken four tedious, rainy days over muddy roads in a hardsprung covered wagon. They had had to camp out at night, as they had done the year before when he was campaigning for the presidency. Margaret complained little, for she had a few days alone with her husband. They took with them only the least cumbersome of their possessions, sending the remainder to Cedar Point. There were few amenities for Margaret in the new capital. Her only consolation was Sam's presence. She continued to loathe the public aspect of his life and always would. The only lodging they could find and afford was in the home of Mr. and Mrs. John Lockhart, acquaintances of Houston's. Mrs. Lockhart generously provided the president and his wife a room which she furnished with her prized possessions, including a mahogany four-poster bed of which she was very fond. Margaret was not pleased; indeed, she seemed especially querulous now. Though she had been frequently ill during their thirty months of marriage, Houston had rarely known her to be so disagreeable. By the end of their second week at Washington-on-the-Brazos, he had an explanation: She was pregnant. His cup of joy ran over.[44]

There were serious matters to cloud his pleasure. He immediately ordered General Alexander Somervell to take as large a force as he could muster and proceed to the southwestern frontier "and if you can advance with a prospect of success into the enemy's territory, you will do so forthwith." The object was to retaliate for Woll's action at San Antonio.[45] By the time the capital had been shifted to its present location, the national archives had been buried in trunks by the citizens of Austin. On October 8 the president made another demand to have them transferred; it was ignored.[46]

While Texan preparations for war continued along with efforts to placate the Indians, representatives of the United States, Britain, and France tried to persuade Santa Anna to come to satisfactory terms with Texas. On November 5 Houston authorized Charles Elliot to represent Texas in any negotiations with Mexico that might lead to peace.[47] By mid-November, however, General Somervell had about 750 volunteers ready to march for a Rio Grande crossing point. Meanwhile the seventh Texan Congress gathered at Washington-on-the-Brazos. Representatives refused to acknowledge the presence of a quorum and demanded that Houston issue a second call for a session to begin December 5.[48] He complied November 22.

The next day he wrote an equivocal letter to Somervell, at once urging action and caution. He complained that the general had not kept him well enough informed about his plans and that the chance of success had been compromised by the length of time required for preparations and the likelihood of enemy spies in his ranks. He also criticized Somervell's plan to attack the Presidio, which he thought too well defended to succumb to easy capture.[49] Careful reading of this letter leads one to think that while he hoped for the best for the mission, Houston feared the worst and wanted his apprehensions on the record.

Congress mustered a quorum December 1. Houston submitted a long message in which he outlined the events which had occurred since the special session had ended in July and the problems the country now faced. His only request for specific legislation was for more money to finance current operations. He avoided asking for a declaration of war. Instead, he detailed the negotiations currently under way to secure reliable terms of peace.[50]

The first days of December passed without great stir. Nancy Lea arrived at the capital to help look after Margaret during her pregnancy. The living arrangements with the Lockharts were strained, but they managed. With Congress in session and Somervell on the march, the president welcomed the presence of his mother-in-law to relieve him of pressure at home.

Houston's fears for the fate of Somervell's men turned out to be ill founded. On December 3 the general ordered his troops across the Rio Grande and moved them toward Laredo, which they captured on the eighth without many casualties on either side. Apparently having read the president's last letter with care, Somervell brought his little force back to Texan soil and disbanded it. It was his impression that no more serious venture should be undertaken without a much larger army. However, William S. Fisher, who had been Lamar's secretary of war, gathered 300 of these men and led them back across the Rio Grande in quest of gold and glory.[51] Fisher and his rabble set off December 19, reaching the Mexican town of Mier the day before Christmas. There they were rudely met by General Pedro Ampudia and decisively thrashed. The survivors were marched to Castillo Perote, the prison which had long held the Santa Fe captives and now contained those taken by Woll at San Antonio. By lottery, 10 percent of Fisher's volunteers were executed at Ampudia's order. News of the Mier calamity was some time in reaching the capital. When it did, Houston would be blamed for having allowed it to occur—though he could truthfully claim innocence of responsibility. Fisher's expedition was just the sort of filibuster he had consistently opposed. Yet even Anson Jones, who had access to all the facts, felt Houston guilty by reason of having authorized the Somervell sortie, which had proved little, if anything. It was hardly less a filibuster than Fisher's. One is constrained to agree with Jones's estimate.

The tumultuous year of 1842 ended on a grotesque note. After months of hugger-mugger, the archives were at last dug up by Texan soldiers in Austin and loaded onto wagons. Angelina Eberly, owner of the town's best hotel, fired a warning shot which brought many residents in pursuit. Without the state papers, the residents of Austin had no lever to bring the capital back to its constitutional location. The papers party was apprehended a little distance out of town. On the last day of the year, the cargo was returned to Austin. The Archives War was over; Houston had to concede or risk the destruction of the documents.

XVIII

THE HOUSTON administration grew increasingly unpopular as he steered it on a course that pleased fewer and fewer of his constituents. The president knew better than most that he was playing poker with a very cold deck of cards. The best that could be said was that Texas still existed as a nation. Houston understood that this was so because Texas was a useful pawn in the game being played against Mexico by the United States, Britain, and France. Difficulties increased. The persistent Mexican menace, managed more cannily by Santa Anna now than in earlier years, discouraged foreign investment. Immigration, though it had continued, had failed to attract the rich entrepreneur who would bring capital and therefore commerce. Those who came brought ragged clothes, old rifles, and ball ammunition in inadequate quantities. For some of the domestic difficulties Houston was himself to blame. His speeches about civil liberties and the rights of Congress bore only occasional relevance to the way he exercised the power of his office. Since Texas was, after all, a constitutional replica of the United States, a comparison is interesting. Historically, even by 1843, strong American Presidents had occluded the arteries by which much governmental business was normally transacted. Since Houston's model was Andrew Jackson, certainly the strongest President the United States had seen yet, it is easier to understand the role Houston had created for himself.

In a letter of January, 1843, a friend wrote Ashbel Smith that the present Texan Congress was "one of the weakest that was ever assembled in any nation," because "they are continually sparring at they know not what themselves."[1] Sam Houston had caused the divisions in Congressional ranks; if he kept the members quarreling, he could more easily have his own way. The fundamental question, then, was what he wanted for Texas. Did he genuinely desire American annexation? His reply at this time would have been an Irish one: He did, and he did not. A letter of the previous December from James Reily had indicated that while President Tyler favored the action, it was doubtful that the Senate would ratify the required treaty. Instead of publicly supporting an effort to persuade reluctant Senators, Houston played a double game—on the one hand acknowledging that annexation would solve the most urgent of Texan difficulties, but at the same time reluctant to sacrifice national sovereignty to the will of Washington. So he seemed to be listening seriously to the arguments of England's Charles Elliot, who wanted to prevent an affiliation of Texas and the United States, since it would strengthen the American hand in an area that had previously been subject to European control—Mexico and the Caribbean.

It was argued at the time that Houston's vacillation was intended to secure the best terms for annexation. This was probably so. It was also said that he did not know his own mind. At times this too seemed so. Had Texas been able to locate a private underwriter with sufficient wealth, Houston would have kept his country out of the Union. Eighteen years later, when the political climate had altered dramatically, he did his best to keep Texas out of the Confederacy.

The safest analysis of Houston's view as president is to characterize it as opportunistic. While this has pejorative connotations, it is a simple fact that few successful politicians have not been opportunists—and the career of no political figure better demonstrates the accuracy of that statement than Houston's later one. When he refused to bend, when he stood resolutely on his principles, he was broken.

On January 10, 1843, the president estimated for Congress the likelihood of a Mexican invasion. Basing his prediction on intelligence two months old, he observed that Santa Anna would attack Texas only if he were successful in putting down a rebellion in the Yucatán. This was unlikely before the coming spring. Was Texas prepared to repel a serious invasion? He was confident that it could be, provided that the army maintained discipline. A surprising conclusion was that the main

Texan force should consist of infantry. "Comparatively few mounted gunmen or cavalry, with some companies of scouts, and spies will be necessary. Our men are without discipline; and when they are once called into camp, to remedy that evil should be the unceasing duty of the officer in command. If individuals are permitted to repair to the camp mounted, their attention will necessarily be called to the care of their horses." That is probably the most astonishing argument ever advanced against the deployment of cavalry. Houston concluded the message with the suggestion that he might, in the event of emergency, assume personal command, thus to rally the veterans of 1836 and inspire discipline.[2]

Toward the middle of the month, Margaret Houston and Nancy Lea reached Grand Cane. With his wife away and Congress adjourned, Houston had some free hours, and he fell once more from grace. On one occasion he returned home to his room in the Lockhart house very late at night and, while reclined on the splendid mahogany bed, concluded that one of the posts obstructed his vision. He called for his slave, Joshua, and ordered him to cut the offending column off with an ax. The sound of chopping aroused the owners of the house, who entered the president's room to find the treasured bed atrociously mutilated. The story circulated through the capital village. Once again, Sam Houston was "Big Drunk." His greatest humiliation, however, was that his pregnant wife would hear of the incident. But he must have sensed that her dismay would be mixed with perverse pleasure; so long as he was subject to such lapses, he needed her stabilizing influence.[3] A biographer has it that his immediate reaction was to go at once to Grand Cane and confess to his wife. This is not borne out by ascertainable facts. What he did was to dispatch to her an enormous order of all sorts of special foods, fine fabrics (including diaper material), china, harness, and a "Good Dearborn waggon" to be sent by a provisioner in New Orleans.[4]

That same day, January 24, he learned the ultimate fate of the Mier prisoners and wrote at once to Charles Elliot to seek the release of those who had been spared. In this same letter he discussed the annexation matter at length, implying that he opposed it.[5] Yet the week after, W. D. Miller wrote President Tyler, surely at Houston's behest, to deplore the close ties developing between Texas and Britain. He urged swift action in Washington to secure annexation. Miller's conclusion is a masterpiece:

General Houston, *I am sure,* entertains for [annexation] the liveliest wishes; and for yourself the best good feelings. He has heard through various channels of your many partial inquiries & friendly expressions concerning him; and he reciprocates them freely. The time is favorable for the consummation of the work—none in the future can ever be more so. I pray you, therefore, let it be done. Let it be done before peace with Mexico is obtained. That is important. If you fail with the Senate, the fault will not be yours, and the loss of [the] country will be chargeable *alone* to that body.[6]

Houston was not in a position to compose that letter, with its bold implication that once peace with Mexico had been secured, Texas might remain forever beyond America's grasp. The Texan president wrote Andrew Jackson a long letter on January 31. There was no statement of Houston's position about annexation—the topic of greatest interest to Old Hickory. The single reference to current affairs is in the concluding paragraph: "I will not close . . . without assuring you that I entertain confidence in the speedy success of Texas, if I am sustained in carrying out a wise policy, to live within our means, act defensively, cultivate our rich land, raise a revenue from import duties, make and keep peace with the Indians, and, if possible, get peace with Mexico, in the meantime watch her, be prepared, and if an army invades us, never to let them return."[7]

When Margaret Houston and her mother returned to Washington-on-the-Brazos in the middle of February, they rented a cottage on the edge of town, so that the few hours the president spent there might be ones of privacy. Although he was importuned even at home, he did have more moments with Margaret than he had expected at the beginning of the year.[8] The six weeks following her return were relatively quiet for Texas. The stalemate in peace negotiations did not break until the spring.

Santa Anna released a prisoner, James W. Robinson, who returned to Texas carrying the Mexican's terms for freeing his comrades still held in Castillo Perote. He went directly to Washington-on-the-Brazos to confer with Houston. On April 10 Robinson wrote Santa Anna a letter which many believe to have been dictated by the Texan president himself. Certainly the views expressed were his. Houston preferred peace but was prepared for war and could easily muster an army of 10,000 men if Santa Anna reopened hostilities. The writer noted: "I will not be so presumptuous as to advise your Excellency about anything; but as things have changed . . . I feel bound to inform you of such facts as result from my observation."[9] However, Santa Anna was more impressed by the counsel of U.S. minister Waddy Thompson.

A treaty of annexation had been drafted in Washington, in essence a rephrasing of the proposal rejected by the Senate years before. There was, however, an interesting difference—President Tyler's personal guarantee that Texas would remain inviolate while the United States Senate debated ratification. Houston learned of it in mid-April. On the twenty-second he wrote Joseph Eve, American chargé d'affaires in Texas: "We now begin to see prospects less distant for a consummation than they have heretofore appeared. . . ." His public reaction was less straightforward. He had seen Texan hopes dashed before and was anxious to avoid a repetition. He remained skeptical that the Senate would approve the treaty, given the rise of the Abolitionist movement in the North, but Tyler's promise pleased him.[10]

He remained calm in the face of mounting criticism in both the Texan and American press about his resort to negotiation with Mexico through foreign diplomats for the release of the Mier prisoners. Many in Texas wanted overt war, but as Houston had frequently noted before, she had not the means for the enterprise.

In the second week of May he wrote Charles Elliot, complaining of the American Senate's delay in ratifying the annexation treaty and implying that he was himself not so enthusiastic for the measure:

Texas once evinced a willingness, amounting to unexampled unanimity, to become annexed to the United States. We sought the boon with humble supplications. In this posture we remained in the outer porch of the Capital for many months. Our solicitations were heard with apathy. Our urgency was responded to with politic indifference. Apprised of this, I directed our Minister to withdraw the proposition. This I did from a sense of national dignity. Since that time Texas has not renewed the proposition; and the United States now, in order to get into an attitude . . . that would be creditable . . . desire, no doubt, that Texas should again come forward soliciting the boon. They have not as yet received such indications as they desire. If it were the case, it would place the subject before the political parties of the U.

States, in a position different from that in which it now rests. In that event there would be but one question: Shall the Annexation of Texas take place? As it is, there are two: First, is Texas *willing* to be annexed? Second, in that case, shall it be annexed? This renders the matter more complicated and produces feelings of excitement and irritibility [*sic*] that induce the leading journals of certain sections of the Country to traduce and vilify the authorities of Texas in a very unbecoming manner. This, I presume, is done by way of whipping prominent men into the list of petitioners.[11]

In stating that the initiative for the pending treaty had not been Texan, Houston was shading the truth. Both of his representatives in Washington had indicated Texas' willingness to be annexed. Llerena Friend, in discussing the implications of this letter, proposes that Houston marked it "private" in the hope that its contents would become public—that, presumably, American legislators who dawdled would thus be pressured into support for the treaty, lest Texas fall definitively under British influence. There is no reason to think her estimation mistaken; Houston used every ruse he knew.

On May 25, 1843 Margaret Houston gave birth to a son. Although it had been the president's intention to name the boy after William Christy, the New Orleans merchant who had been so good a friend to him and to Texas during and after the war for independence, Margaret insisted that he be called Sam, Jr. Writing to Ashbel Smith in London two months later, W. D. Miller noted: "You would suppose the President is proud of his boy—and you would not be far mistaken!"[12] Houston, who had always indulged his wife, was now doubly in her debt for having made him the gift of an heir and namesake. He wrote Miller that his son must not become a poet or a "singer of songs," an assertion which probably means that he would not be permitted to emulate his father's youth.

Houston did not allow his joy to obscure his obligations to Texas. In June, William S. Murphy replaced Joseph Eve as Washington emissary and reported to his superiors that the Texan president was under Charles Elliot's thumb, to the extent of actually opposing annexation, which was favored by most Texans. But Houston was seeking peace and did not seem to care how he got it.[13] On June 10 he instructed

Anson Jones to inform Texan ministers abroad that if peace were not concluded before winter, "Texas will assume an offensive attitude, with all the means she can command. . . ."[14] So while suggesting to Washington that he was playing the Europeans' game, he was implying to the Europeans that if peace were not soon arranged, he would solicit American aid to attain the goal. It may seem curious to find bankrupt Texas in a position of such bargaining strength, but this was the case; partly because of its immensity, potential riches, and strategic location; partly because Houston was a good poker player. Neither the Europeans nor the Americans knew what he had in his hand. Whom was he bluffing? After annexation took place, Houston claimed he had always favored it, but there is no serious reason to suppose that had things fallen differently, he would not have been satisfied to see Texas remain an independent nation.

Washington was concerned when, on June 15, Houston proclaimed that an armistice with Mexico had been secured through British offices. It was to continue while negotiations for a lasting peace went on. The news was not well received by all Texans either. A significant faction felt that an aggressive war might bring the country territory reaching the Pacific. Many were irritated with the president at that time because he had stigmatized Commodore Moore; they also accused him of abusing the army, vacillating between support and neglect of the troops. Finally, his enemies alleged that he favored the abolition of slavery in Texas, for no apparent reason except his failure to publicly attack the Abolitionist cause in the American North. Yet Houston was aware that some of its members in the U.S. Senate would have to support the annexation treaty if it were to be ratified. Houston's enemies also pointed to his approval of a protocol with Britain forbidding the importation of slaves from Africa. This agreement was never effectively enforced.

There was much public outcry against the treaty of armistice. A rump convention was called among bellicose Congressmen from West Texas to meet in mid-July to protest Houston's performance as president. The *Telegraph* of July 12 erected a straw man and dutifully knocked it down, suggesting that Britain's price for intercession had been Houston's promise to abolish slavery. The paper assured its readers that Texans would reject a treaty that included secret provisions. There were no grounds for either implication. It was true, however, that Houston had not been very forthright with the public.

But the rump convention had a poor showing; only six delegates appeared.

With peace in prospect, Houston again looked for a solution for relations with the Indians. He had a right to be proud of his temperate stand when compared to the record of savagery left by Lamar. So far his policy had paid off. No effectively coordinated Indian attack had been mounted against Texans during the period of Mexican harassment. Though unpopular with most Texans, his policy of conciliation had proved useful. Late in July, with Margaret, the baby, and Nancy Lea, the president set out for the Trinity River. He was to attend a conference of Indian chiefs, and his family was to spend the rest of the summer with the Bledsoes at Grand Cane.[15]

In early September, Houston announced an agreement with Santa Anna for an exchange of prisoners. It seemed certain that a stable peace was at hand—a conviction nervously shared in the American capital. Isaac Van Zandt wrote that Tyler was contemplating an early submission of an annexation treaty to the Senate.[16] America's plan was to adopt Texas before the nation proved her ability to stand alone. When this intelligence reached Mexico City, it caused some consternation. Santa Anna asserted that if the United States annexed Texas, he would resume the war in earnest.[17] Houston was unaware of developments in Washington until the end of September. He learned of Mexican reaction even later. He left the Texan capital in the middle of that month to take Margaret and little Sam to Grand Cane again, where they remained until just before Christmas. In his absence, W. D. Miller wrote President Tyler another letter restating the points he had made in his communication of January. Action on annexation was urgently needed to prevent Texas from falling into British hands. Like the January letter, this was undoubtedly inspired by the President. Miller could beg; Houston could not.

A month later Houston was able to pause for a time to consider the prospects for Texas. President Tyler proposed conversations about annexation with Isaac Van Zandt, who responded that he was not authorized to discuss the question but would seek permission from Houston. Van Zandt's blandness was intended to distress the Americans; he was playing Houston's game.[18] But what, many wondered, was Houston's game? The man himself symbolized Texas; he was a household name in the United States as well. A friend in Baltimore wrote Anson Jones in late October that Houston would one day rally the dissident elements of the Democratic Party and become President of the United States.[19] Though the prophesy was false, this is the first known suggestion that he might aspire to that office. Was that his goal?

On October 30, while discussing peace with Charles Elliot, Houston stated categorically that "with the independence of Texas recognized by Mexico, he would never consent to any treaty or other project of annexation to the United States, and he had the conviction that the people would sustain him in that determination." Elliot reported this to the British Foreign Secretary, Lord Aberdeen. This vow was never put to the test, for Santa Anna eventually broke off talks that might have led to recognition. The British diplomat told his superior that though he believed Houston, he was not at all sure that a majority of Texans would support him were the United States to ratify an annexation treaty.[20]

Congress reconvened in November. Houston immediately left the capital to make a speaking tour in defense of his policies, especially his dealings with the Indians and England. He probably convinced few. Indeed, he had no better luck with the legislators of the Eighth Congress, who rejected every important measure he submitted. They resented his lack of candor on the annexation question. Yet President Tyler had been extremely equivocal in his message to his Congress of December 5, expressing America's concern to see peace between the Mexicans and Texans, but failing to mention annexation—a matter still too controversial. So Houston had every politic reason for keeping his powder dry. By maintaining an ambiguous pose while others bellowed their thoughts, he remained in a position to force America's hand by seeming to deal seriously with Britain.

Tyler's diffidence was approved by old Andrew Jackson, who wrote in mid-December that when the propitious moment came, Houston would have to support annexation; and if, perchance, his former protégé were to oppose it, Old Hickory thought he could change the Texan's mind. He hoped the goal could be achieved by peaceful means, but failing that, he advocated force: "[T]he safety of New Orleans, the prosperity of the great valley of the Mississippi and our whole union require the annexation of Texas," he wrote.[21]

The second year of Houston's administration ended on a note of doubt. If the state was not yet one of real peace, at least there was no longer a serious menace of great war. Almost everything else of importance, economic and political, was in abeyance. Margaret and little Sam and Nancy Lea made the uncomfortable journey from Grand Cane to be with the president at Christmastime. For that, at least, he was unequivocally grateful.

On January 8, 1844, W. D. Miller, now secretary of the treasury, wrote Daingerfield at The Hague: "There is a great fuss about annexation both in the U.S. and Texas; but however much to be desired such an event might be, I must think its accomplishment highly improbable. If our independence as a Separate Nation is secured—annexation can never take place."[22] If we recall Miller's two strong letters to President Tyler counseling haste to effect annexation, it is difficult not to conclude that he was providing Daingerfield with grist for a European gossip mill at Houston's suggestion, to keep both major factions guessing about the Texan president's true position.

Meanwhile, Houston, realizing that he must have the cooperation of his legislature, delivered a secret message on January 20. Although he did not take a specific stand, claiming it not "becoming in him to express any preference," he called the goal of annexation "desirable." He was surprisingly straightforward for one who had played his cards so close to his chest for two years. He said he feared the failure of the American Senate to ratify the treaty, for this would leave Texas in an awkward position, with only European allies to fall back on. He requested a large appropriation to enable Isaac Van Zandt to represent Texan interests in Washington more effectively. However, he implored members of Congress to keep his words secret, for he wanted it to appear that all important initiatives emanated from Washington, not Texas. "If we evince too much anxiety, it will be regarded as importunity, and the voice of supplication seldom commands, in such cases, great respect."[23]

Three days later he asked the American chargé Murphy to come to the capital from Galveston.[24] The meeting took place in early February. Murphy told Houston that President Tyler might at last be serious in his attempts to persuade the Senate to ratify an annexation treaty. However, as a precaution Houston sent J. Pinckney Henderson and W. D. Miller to Washington to aid Van Zandt, who was instructed on the fifteenth not to "hazard the consequences which might result from rejection." To this end, the minister should also bargain for a treaty of alliance as an alternative. Though Houston persisted in the fiction that he had no personal predilection toward annexation, he wrote Van Zandt: "It would be useless for me to attempt to portray to you . . . the magnitude of the consequences which are to grow out of these transactions."[25]

Despite pressures from all sides, including another letter from Andrew Jackson, Houston refused to make a public statement in favor of annexation. To William Murphy he put the matter most clearly: "The United States must annex Texas—Texas cannot annex herself to the United States. A concurrent action is necessary. And yet, the U. States have adopted no course that could encourage a confident hope on the part of her friends of that measure in this country." Probably no politician of the nineteenth century better analyzed the situation of Texas than Senator Thomas Hart Benton of Missouri, a proponent of annexation who nonetheless deplored Tyler's concession to Houston of what amounted to control of American land and sea forces in the Southwest during the balance of his Presidency. Benton wrote that the American promise of protection had prevented a peaceful settlement of issues between Texas and Mexico in the spring of 1844. Texas would have entered "the union as naturally and as easily, and with as little offence to anybody, as Eve went into Adam's bosom in the Garden of Eden." Instead, however, Tyler sent troops and ships to Texas, making Houston sole arbiter of their deployment:

> This authority . . . was continued in full force until after the rejection of the treaty [by the American Senate], and then only modified by placing the American diplomatic agent in Texas between . . . Houston and the naval and military commanders. . . . During all that time a foreign President was commander-in-chief of a large detachment of the army and navy of the United States. Without a law of Congress— without a nomination from the President and confirmation of the Senate—without citizenship—without the knowledge of the American people—[Houston] was president-general of our land and sea forces . . . with authority to fight them against Mexico with whom we were at peace . . . and we are indebted to the forbearance and prudence of President Houston for not incurring the war in 1844 . . . which fell upon us in 1846.[26]

In only one minor respect can one fault Benton's statement of the extraordinary facts: The eventual rejection by the Senate of the annexation treaty suggests that Houston's extraction of Tyler's guarantee had been wise, however extralegal—and that it had been much easier for Eve to be bedded by Adam than for Texas to seduce the United States.

Houston at last responded to Andrew Jackson on February 16, sending his letter by hand with W. D. Miller. He tried to reassure his old friend: "So far as I am concerned, or my hearty cooperation required, I am determined upon immediate annexation." Houston's skepticism proved wise. As he put it to Jackson in this same letter, "a bride adorned for her espousal" should not be jilted at the altar by the groom.[27]

On February 18 an armistice agreement with Mexico was initialed at Laredo. Its wording, however, contained a significant defect: Texas was described as "a department of Mexico." When the document reached him, Houston rejected it as worthless.[28] For a month nothing of moment happened. A couple of weeks after his fifty-first birthday, a proud father wrote a friend that his son "has no less than four teeth." This is a rare reference to his private life, for Margaret effectively prevented their occasional moments of intimacy from becoming matters of public knowledge. She had borne with imperfect patience and poor health her husband's term as president, and looked forward with growing eagerness to the end of the year, when he would have to leave office. Houston himself complained that "I have been so much employed in public concerns . . . that my private affairs have been woefully neglected."[29] In early April he took his little family to Houston City. His personal plans were uncertain—whether to visit Tennessee to present his wife and son to Andrew Jackson, who was in failing health, or to go to Grand Cane.[30]

At that time W. D. Miller was writing Old Hickory to use his influence with reluctant American Senators who must soon consider the annexation treaty. Should it be rejected, he told Jackson, the backlash in Texas would be dangerous. "[I]f she be spurned from the threshold of the mother, she may look to a better reception from the grandmother."[31] That was a line Houston could have written. The president and his family were still at Houston City on April 14 when he wrote Anson Jones of his exasperation with delay in Washington.[32] He did not know that two days earlier, President Tyler had finally submitted an annexation treaty, with a message to the Senate stressing the benefits to be derived from ratification, not the least of which was the elimination of British influence in so vital an area. Tyler had chosen a bad moment. It was just before the party conventions were to gather to select candidates for the Presidential elections in November. Congress was acutely conscious of constituent opinion—and Senators were not certain where the people stood on Texan annexation.

Soon after its submission to the Senate, it was evident to its supporters that the annexation treaty was to be a political football. Both Whigs and Democrats, jockeying for position in the Presidential race, had hoped to keep the two most controversial national issues, Texas and the Oregon boundary question, out of the campaign. The Whig platform mentioned neither, though it was known that most party members opposed annexation. As midsummer approached, Old Hickory, who presided over the Democrats from the Hermitage with vigorous authority, decided it was time to confront the electorate squarely with the questions of Texas and Oregon. It had been thought that the Democratic candidate would be Martin Van Buren. However, he was an opponent of annexation. Jackson now proposed James K. Polk, loyal Tennessean and friend of Houston's. The slogan that would mark the campaign applied to Oregon: "Fifty-four forty or fight." But Texas was just as important.

It was now plain to Houston that the Senate would take no favorable action on the treaty until after the election. He responded by withdrawing two of his representatives in Washington, taking the precaution, however, to have them remind Tyler of his promise of continuing military and naval protection. He hoped there would not have to be another Texan presidential election.[33] That hope would have dismayed Anson Jones who, much as he favored annexation, also wanted to be the next president of Texas. He had received an endorsement from Houston for the office nearly a year before.

After taking Margaret and their son to Grand Cane, the president was back in the capital on May 24. There were personal troubles at this time. The future of the Bledsoe property was in doubt. Margaret's brother-in-law was in financial difficulties. Title to the land was transferred to Nancy Lea to prevent it from falling into the hands of creditors. It had been suggested that Houston buy it. He was, however, negotiating to buy a piece of land near Huntsville where he had decided to live after his term expired.[34] He left again for Grand Cane in early June. While he was away, the United States Senate rejected the annexation treaty by the wide margin of 35 to 16.

235

On June 10, two days after the Senate vote, Tyler requested a Congressional act that would have had the effect of annexing Texas. Knowing the gesture to be futile, he nevertheless succeeded in keeping the question before the public during the campaign.[35] When Mexico learned of the Senate's action, General Adrian Woll sent Houston word that a state of hostilities between Texas and his country was again in effect. The Texan president's immediate reaction was to assure himself of continuing American protection. When London learned of the failure of annexation, Lord Aberdeen propounded a scheme to persuade Mexico by threat of commercial coercion to accept Texan independence and resolve the boundary dispute.

Houston toyed with the Aberdeen proposal, but not seriously. It was election time; nothing could be solved until the result was known. Though he made numerous speeches that summer, it was only on August 5 that he endorsed Anson Jones's candidacy, little more than three weeks before the election. On September 2, Anson Jones defeated Edward Burleson, though hardly by a landslide. A week later Houston was at Grand Cane, exhausted and ill. He remained there a week, then traveled alone to Washington-on-the-Brazos, reaching the capital in time to learn that Santa Anna had released the last of the Mier prisoners—a fair omen that the Mexicans were not going to make war.[36]

His first days back at work were devoted mainly to Indian affairs. He hoped to leave a legacy of permanent peace between whites and natives. His hopes were futile; the notion of red men occupying good range and growing lands would always prove intolerable to whites.[37] He planned to attend an Indian conference at the end of September, but wrote Margaret on the twenty-eighth that a fever had delayed him. The tone of this letter, in response to one from her, is so different from much of his correspondence that it deserves partial quotation:

> Your favor is so kind and grateful to me I will not leave without sending an answer to it. I will not tell you of my regret at your illness and sorrow. My heart bleeds! It may be twenty-five days before I embrace you and the family. . . . You may fancy what I felt . . . and feel for poor Sam at our separation. I thought when I told you adieu . . . that I had felt the last pang of parting, but I was mistaken. . . . Your last letter, Love, I will take with me, and peruse it often!!! Dearest, give my Love to Mother and family. Press our dear boy to your bosom and tell him it is from me.[38]

236

James K. Polk's Presidential victory was a narrow one, both in popular and electoral votes, and thus a precursor of the division in American politics for the next sixteen years. As soon as the Tyler administration had the word, it sent another missionary to Texas, James Hamilton, who vowed to thwart Houston's purported scheme to keep his country out of the Union.[39] In Washington there was a Whig plan to deny the Democrats the honor of effecting annexation by accomplishing this before Tyler's term expired. It was still in an embryonic stage by mid-November, just three weeks before Houston yielded his place to Anson Jones. On December 9 he made his exit, offering the Ninth Texan Congress and the populace a final sample of the rhetoric for which he was renowned. He had a dream for his country, he said, which should not be destroyed by overconfidence in the goodwill of other nations.[40]

The next day, President Tyler, in the same position as Sam Houston, sent a message to his Congress citing the reelection result as evidence that annexation was the wish of the American people and suggesting a joint House-Senate resolution, a measure requiring simple majorities of votes cast, to grant the country accession to the Union.[41] So it was that the two outgoing presidents set in motion the vehicle which at last conveyed Texas into the United States.

Houston was at Grand Cane to spend Christmas with his family. He wrote Anson Jones that he was glad "that my probation has passed." He noted the unfamiliarity of the new condition, "and strange to say, I find my mind falling back into a channel, where the current flows in domestic peace and quiet, without one care about the affairs of Government, and only intent upon domestic happiness and prosperity."[42] How long he could maintain this posture of detachment would be difficult to say. He was still the central figure of Texas, loved and hated. His enemies in the Congress lost no time in voting a return of the national capital to Austin. Even after Texas became a state, the seat of government would stray no more.

As a Christmas gift, Margaret Houston composed for her husband the following verses:

> Dearest, the cloud hath left thy brow
> The shade of thoughtfulness, of care,
> And deep anxiety; and now
> The sunshine of content is there.

237

Its sweet return with joy I hail;
And never may thy country's woes
Again that hallowed light dispel
Thy bosom's calm repose.

Thy task is done. The holy shade
Of calm retirement waits thee now,
The lamp of hope relit hath shed
Its sweet refulgence o'er this brow.

Far from busy haunts of men
Oh! may thy soul each fleeting hour
Upon the breath of prayer ascend
To him who rules with love and power.[43]

XIX

E VENTS OF greatest significance for Texas were taking place in Washington early in 1845. The election of Polk had further strained Anglo-American relations. A supporter of Texan annexation and of a "satisfactory" solution to the Oregon question, the President-elect seemed a threat to Britain's role not only in the Caribbean but in the American Northwest. The British were alone, however, in their apparent willingness to go to war to prevent annexation and assure an Oregon boundary line they approved of. American proponents of bringing Texas into the Union made effective use of the British attitude to persuade wavering Abolitionists that it was more dangerous for the United States to leave the southwestern nation independent than to incorporate it as a slaveholding state. Outgoing President Tyler's joint Congressional resolution was, however, in trouble. Not waiting for his inauguration, Polk came to Washington to lobby for its passage. Andrew Jackson, dying at the Hermitage, dictated letters to all legislators with whom he might have influence.[1]

Where did Houston now stand on annexation? Ashbel Smith wrote: "To [Houston's] judgment it seemed a grave problem whether it was not better for Texas, better for the cause of liberty and republican institutions, that there should be two great self-governing peoples instead of one." Justin H. Smith, a twentieth-century historian of Texas, thought Houston's motives somewhat different: "Though a patriot, [he] was no idealist. It was far from his intention to sacrifice his personal fortunes for the halo of martyrdom; and no doubt he proposed to manage that, whatever wind should blow, the vessel bearing his pennant should reach port."[2] The imputation of cynicism rings at least partially true. Presented with two possibilities, Houston opted publicly for neither until it was certain which was the likelier of success. He hesitated because it remained problematical what actions the United States would now take. He would not be cornered.

Houston himself kept discreetly silent. There is no surviving letter from Sam Houston's hand for the first three months of 1845. While the great question was debated in Washington, he and Margaret and little Sam moved into a house they called Raven Hill, about fifteen miles from Huntsville. He allowed his wife to think his political career was at an end, and that his plan was to develop his lands, raise a family, and live out his life in peace. Whether or not she believed him is unknown; she took her moments with him as she found them.

On February 28, 1845, four days before Polk's inauguration, Congress consented to the annexation of Texas as a state, subject to that nation's ratification of the act prior to January 1 of the following year.[3] Word of the event reached Galveston March 20. A.J. Donelson had been dispatched to Texas to urge Texan acceptance. On April 2 he wrote the ex-president that he wanted to speak with him on the topic. Houston, traveling through East Texas at the time, declined. Beyond observing that he thought the American resolution ill conceived to attain its end, he would not discuss it in writing. In a second letter, he said it was his conviction that annexation would be agreed to by Texas only when the boundary question with Mexico—the Rio Grande and not the Nueces River—was resolved. This, he observed, could be accomplished only by negotiation.[4] Back at Huntsville April 9, he wrote Donelson yet again, and was somewhat more critical: "I am in favor of annexation, if it can take place on terms mutually beneficial to both countries." One paragraph merits special attention because of Houston's later opinions and actions:

The wish of every American statesman should be to preserve the concord and union of the States, and the desire of every Texian [is] to cede such rights . . . and privileges to the Union as would be just and proper. We should however retain all which would be necessary to us, as an equal member of the Confederacy, and part with none which we should acquire in our new position . . . with the hope of reclaiming them at a future day! Should we entertain such a hope, it might prove fallacious, and be productive of serious and lasting discord. Texas, if annexed, will become a part of the U States, in opposition to the wishes of a large portion of the people of the union and a strong political opposition. If they are vanquished, they will still retain a strong prejudice against the cause . . . or object . . . of their defeat. The party favorable to the admission of Texas may . . . or may not . . . long retain power in the Union. While they retain power, Texas might do well, but if it once passed into the hands of the opposition, she would in all probability fare equally bad.[5]

It would be an overstatement to say that Houston thus foresaw the Civil War, yet those who had opposed annexation did attain power and did create the discord he spoke of in his letter.

Donelson deplored Houston's niggling. "Tell Uncle [Andrew Jackson]," he wrote his wife April 16, "Houston has disappointed me and has not given me the support I expected."[6] One biographer asserts that Donelson visited the Houstons at Raven Hill, but there is no record of it. However, the ex-president learned from his old friend that Jackson was dying and decided to take his wife and two-year-old son on a journey to the Hermitage. They departed at the end of April.[7] By then Donelson noted that Houston's insistence on the need to negotiate with Mexico over the boundary question and to resolve other prickly issues, like Indian raids from American territory, was worth heeding. On May 5 Donelson's aide wrote Polk from Galveston that Houston was on his way to Tennessee. "He now seems willing to have annexation succeed; at least he will not oppose it. . . . He *is now safe* and no apprehension need be feared from that quarter—and he is 'the Power behind the Throne greater than the Throne itself.' " The idea was general that Houston was manipulating Anson Jones; this was not the case, and Jones deeply resented any implication of it.

On May 24 Andrew Jackson wrote Donelson of his joy to learn of Houston's change of view. That very day, Houston, with his wife and son, disembarked at New Orleans where they visited briefly with William Christy before leaving for Nashville. Houston gave a talk to local businessmen about annexation, concluding with this phrase: "I have been accused of lending myself to England and France; but . . . I have only been coquetting with them." This statement, when it reached the ears of Charles Elliot (who had just succeeded belatedly in securing Mexican recognition of Texan independence), displeased him but could not have surprised him. He wrote Lord Aberdeen from Galveston that he feared the Mexican conversion had come too late to prevent annexation.

In early June, the Houstons left for Nashville, unaware that they were now literally in a race with death. While they traveled, Andrew Jackson took an abrupt turn for the worse. On June 6 Polk wrote Houston a jubilant letter expressing the hope that his old political ally would be one of Texas' first Senators. He promised liberal American treatment of outstanding Texan issues. That day, Donelson wrote his uncle that Texas was now safely committed to annexation.[8] On June 8 as the Houstons were en route from Nashville to the Hermitage, Jackson died. At midnight Houston wrote Polk:

> In deep sorrow I address you this hasty note. At six o'clock this evening General Jackson departed this life. He retained his faculties to the very last hour. I lament that I was denied the satisfaction of seeing him in his last moments. . . .
>
> About three hours before his departure he conversed for some time about his family, and took an effectionate [sic] leave of them, as also of his domestics. His physicians represented the scene as most affecting, and remarked that he departed with perfect serenity and with full faith in the promises of salvation through the Redeemer.[9]

The Houstons stayed with Donelson's family at nearby Tulip Grove until after the Jackson obsequies. Then they went to Nashville where, for the remainder of June and much of July, they were regaled by many old friends and others who had, not so long ago, reviled the former Tennessee governor. Old scores were forgotten. Eliza had remarried. Houston was a hero above reproach—at least in the United States. *Niles' Register* reported that old acquaintances found him much "more reserved" than when he had last visited Tennessee and took note of his rather sickly pallor.[10] Some thought his trip more political than sentimental. Among them was Charles Elliot: "Houston is gone to New Orleans and the Hermitage," he wrote June 11, "to sound the depths in those quarters, and calculates his chance of running for President in succession to Polk."[11] While in Nashville, he gave another talk in which he again deployed the word "coquetted" to describe his dealings with foreign diplomats. With Texas all but committed to annexation, it seemed safe enough now to allow the world to think he had favored Texan statehood from the onset.[12]

On June 28 the Texan Congress approved annexation on American terms.[13] With annexation finally settled, the position of Texas' most illustrious citizen became a matter of great interest in the United States. Some politicians thought they perceived in the rise of Houston a replica of Andrew Jackson's ascent and were quite uncomfortable— for though they did not doubt his loyalty to the great principles of the Democratic Party, they had reason to fear his unswerving devotion to all aspects of party policy. As it turned out, this reluctance to be constrained by partisan doctrine may have cost Houston whatever chance he had of being named a Presidential candidate in 1848. On the other hand, there is little evidence to suggest that he thought of himself seriously as a man for that particular season, no matter what others believed.

On July 1, while the Houstons were still at Nashville, Margaret's brother-in-law William Bledsoe died at Grand Cane.[14] Three days later, a convention gathered at Austin to consider the wording of a resolution to be submitted to Texans by which the nation would become an American state. Before adjourning July 28, the members also drafted a new state constitution.[15] Although Houston had been elected a delegate to this convention, he attended none of its sessions. After leaving Tennessee, he and Margaret and little Sam proceeded to Mobile and then to Blount Springs, Alabama, where Margaret hoped to benefit from the baths. Her ill-health had not been improved by two months of travel and festivity.

During their continued absence from Texas, the groundwork for the Mexican War was being established. U.S. General Zachary Taylor reached Corpus Christi with the vanguard of his "army of observation." The American commitment to protect Texas was interpreted by Santa Anna as an act of hostility. He broke off diplomatic relations with the United States. Efforts by American emissary John Slidell to purchase from Mexico the great expanse of land from Texas to the Pacific were suspended.

The Houstons were at Marion for most of September.[16] At the end of the month, the ex-president left his wife and son with her relations and returned abruptly to Texas. Margaret's biographer asserts he did not tell her the reason for this sudden change of plan.[17] His name had been proposed as one of the new state's Senators. He had to go home to advance his candidacy. If he failed to inform her of his plan, the reason seems clear. She had cherished these months with her husband. If he were sent to Washington, and it was hardly conceivable that he would not be, she would have to decide whether to go with him or stay behind in Texas. Neither choice would have appealed to her.

There was some futile opposition to Houston's Senatorial candidacy. For the balance of 1845 and through February of 1846, feverish editors and politicians railed against Houston's record. But he was, as a friend wrote Anson Jones, the one candidate for the Senate on whom public opinion was united. The only question was who would get the second Senatorial seat. Many men were mentioned, only three of them seriously: Henderson, Lamar, and Rusk. J. Pinckney Henderson eliminated himself by being elected first Governor of Texas. Of the remaining two, Houston naturally favored his old friend Rusk.[18]

Texans almost unanimously approved the annexation referendum and the new constitution in October. 1845 ended with the approval by the United States Congress of the document. With this act, Texas gained statehood. The election of Houston and Rusk as Senators was assured. The election of Houston by virtual unanimity was not a surprise. However, it was startling that Rusk trailed him in popularity by a single vote. By the drawing of straws, Houston was designated the junior member of the Senatorial delegation. This meant he would have to seek reelection little more than a year later.[19]

Sam Houston received the news with decorous pleasure at Raven Hill on February 25. Margaret greeted it with a sigh. Her husband gave her three weeks in which to close the house and prepare for the long journey to Washington. By early March, however, she found herself pregnant again, thus furnishing a good excuse for staying in Texas. It seems likely that she would have invented a reason not to accompany her husband to the national capital in any case. For though plans were made for her to follow him later on, she never made that trip during the thirteen years of his tenure as Senator.[20]

Houston and Rusk left Texas for Washington in early March, choosing different routes for the trip. While they traveled, Zachary Taylor moved his army of about 4,000 men gradually from Corpus Christi to the disputed boundary of the Rio Grande. War with Mexico was obviously imminent. Only an incident was needed to begin it. But the Texan frontier was not the only question confronting the United

States that March. The Oregon matter, debated for a year, was at last coming to a vote. Polk gave continuing support to the boundary line of "54:40" on which he had successfully campaigned in 1844, but was willing to settle for the 49th parallel. The British, smarting over their failure to keep Texas out of the Union, refused to negotiate on this basis. The President then instructed Secretary of State James Buchanan to give Britain the necessary one-year notice of America's intention to terminate the agreement for joint administration of the great Northwest Territory. A report circulated that a vote on this issue was being delayed to permit the participation of the new Texan Senators.

Most Texans opposed the Polk measure on the ground that it might lead to war with Britain. Coupled with the near-certainty of war with Mexico, this might place the new state in a condition of greater jeopardy than she had known during the period of her perilous nationhood.[21] However, since the Texan legislature had been unable to agree on instructions for its Senators, Henderson wrote Rusk that he and Houston were free to vote on the measure as they chose.[22] On March 11, waiting at Houston City for a boat that would take him to Galveston and New Orleans, Houston made a speech promising full support to Polk on Oregon.

He left the next day for Washington, having entrusted his wife to the care of her brother Vernal.[23] He traveled up the Mississippi as a great celebrity. From Pittsburgh, Houston took a train to the capital, arriving there March 28. He checked into his old lodgings at Brown's Hotel.[24] He must have contemplated with some wonder all that had happened to him in the fourteen years that had passed since his last visit.

Rusk had reached Washington three days before Houston and taken his place in the Senate March 26, where he was cordially received.[25] The day after his arrival Houston called on President Polk, who recorded the event: "Gen'l Samuel Houston, late President of Texas and now a Senator in Congress, called. I was much pleased to see him, having been with him in Congress twenty years ago and always his friend. I found him thoroughly Democratic and fully determined to support my administration."[26]

Houston was sworn in as Senator March 30. There were many familiar faces in both houses to greet him. At least four Senators were old friends and/or adversaries—Benton, Calhoun, Van Buren, and Webster. In the House, among others, was the aged ex-President and leader of the "Conscience Whigs," John Quincy Adams. Senator Houston felt at ease in his new role.

In early April, Polk learned of Mexico's refusal to negotiate with Slidell, who had been authorized to offer as much as $5,000,000 just in exchange for acceptance of the Rio Grande rather than the Nueces as the Texan boundary. No doubt the movement of increasing numbers of Taylor's troops to the east bank of the disputed river had failed to improve the bargaining climate. On April 10, determined on war, Polk summoned Houston to offer him command of a portion of an expanded army in Texas.[27] It is easy to suppose that the new Senator, eager to see the boundary question settled in his state's favor, was not averse to war, especially since it would be fought and paid for by the government of the United States.[28] However, he did not accept the proffered commission—which may have been politically a fatal mistake. Of the three major commanders in the war that ensued, one became President and another a serious candidate for the office. Another topic almost surely discussed at this meeting with Polk was Oregon's status. Three days later Houston announced his intention to speak on April 15 in the debate on this topic. In the speech he alluded to the country's unpreparedness for war, presumably concerned about the war to come soon against Mexico. "Will we never be prepared until [war] come upon us? Never. It is not in the genius of this people. They are bold, daring, and confident; and until the shock of danger comes, every American is proud of the national character; and, glorying in his individual liberty, each feels that he is indeed a freeman, and therefore cannot be conquered. They cannot realize the necessity of concert and preparation."[29] Then, in supporting the admission of Oregon as a territory which would become, of necessity, a free state, he gained the enmity of many Southerners, who pointed to this vote as an early sign of Houston's sympathy for the Abolitionist cause. At the time, however, his action incurred the reproach of hardly anyone. The Senate supported Polk's position by a vote of 40 to 14. The 49th parallel was accepted as the line between the Oregon Territory and British Columbia. War with Britain was precluded.[30]

Later, Polk requested 50,000 volunteer soldiers and a war chest of $10,000,000 for the impending Mexican conflict. He had the support of both Texan Senators. On April 23 the new Mexican chief of state,

246

Mariano Paredes y Arrillaga, declared war against the United States because American troops had violated his country's territory by taking up positions along the Rio Grande.[31] Thus, Zachary Taylor had furnished the provocation he had sought from Mexico. There had been some indecisive skirmishes before Paredes' declaration, and some immediately followed it—though it would be May 10 before Washington was apprised of the matter.

Meanwhile there was much uneasiness in Texas about one aspect of American maneuvers in the Southwest. This was the movement of federal troops, under General Stephen Kearny, into the Santa Fe Territory so long claimed to be Texan. Though Kearny's troops pushed farther west, the implications of his having established a "temporary" government in the regime caused some apprehension —and rightly. New Mexico was lost to Texas as a result.[32]

But the war was the main event. In early May, a group of Taylor's men was engaged by a Mexican force at Palo Alto. A second encounter occurred at Resaca de la Palma. Neither was conclusive.[33] Not yet aware that war had been declared by Mexico, Houston met Polk on May 9 and 10, urging vigorous action. Cabinet meetings on both days dealt almost solely with that topic. Immediately after the session of May 10, word of Paredes' declaration of war was received. Polk's advisers helped him draft a statement to Congress asking that a state of war be declared. A measure calling for men and money was submitted. On May 11, it was considered by the Senate Military Affairs Committee, of which Houston was a member, and gained immediate approval.[34] On that same day he spoke on the Senate floor in favor of a declaration of war.[35] On May 12, he declaimed at greater length, this time taking Calhoun and others to task for their objection that there was still insufficient evidence that Mexico wanted war. In truth, he said, a state of war had existed with Mexico for the past decade; the only difference was that, since annexation, the United States had replaced Texas as the Mexicans' adversary. The measure passed easily.[36]

Margaret Houston, still at Raven Hill, wrote her husband on the sixteenth that while she approved of his stand on the Oregon question, she was not happy about his advocacy of war with Mexico. Her reasoning was entirely selfish; she feared its effect on their personal lives. She again refused to come to Washington. She was due to give birth to their second child in September. She was not well. She played shamelessly on his sympathies. "But why do I speak of my feelings at all! I cannot describe them. Oh my love if you could look into my heart at this moment, I know you would never leave me again!"[37]

Ashbel Smith reported a movement in Texas to prevent Houston's reelection to the Senate, led by Lamar's people. He predicted its failure. "Their hopes are more than idle. The people of Texas have seen with great pride their Senator take his place with the very foremost of the powerful men in the American Senate. The accounts of your influence and estimation everywhere have come to Texas and strengthened the hands of your friends here."[38] He remained in Washington through most of the summer, as Senate debates on the conduct of the war continued—to Margaret's despair. Houston had informed her of Polk's offer of a command, asking her to decide whether or not he should accept it. Since he had already made his decision, her response was academic, but it is a model of craft:

> Alas, what has always been my decision when my own happiness or the good of the country was to be sacrificed? Have I not invariably ascertained your views and then coincided with them, let my own sacrifices be what they might? And even now, though your personal danger will be far greater than it has been on any previous occasion, since our marriage, I will not express one word of opposition, but I cannot look around upon my widowed hearth and hear my poor boy's plaintive cry, "What makes pa stay so long?" and then tell you that I am willing for you to go. . . . I wish you to be governed entirely by your own judgment, and though the decision may bring misery upon me beyond description, I will try to bear it without a murmur.[39]

When it was deemed necessary to introduce a third commander, the assignment went to General Winfield Scott, not Sam Houston.

Congress finally adjourned August 10. The Senator returned to Texas after writing a friend: "I am most painfully anxious to see my dear Wife . . . and my young Pioneer. I was always fond of home but I now place something like a true estimate . . . upon the source of true happiness—Home." Like so many congenital wanderers, he felt most strongly a desire to be home only when he was away. Before he reached Texas, Ashbel Smith recorded in his diary a conviction that Houston would be President. The notion, which had been stirring in other heads

248

for some time, seemed to have lodged itself more than casually in Houston's thoughts during the summer of 1846.

An indication that his interest was piqued can be discerned from an agreement he had made in Washington with C. Edwards Lester—journalist, minor diplomat, and a cousin of Aaron Burr—to compose a biography. He and Lester had toiled in the capital through most of the spring and summer to produce a volume which, on its first printing at the end of this year, was called *Sam Houston and His Republic.* Lester furnished a prefatory note which was far more inflammatory than the text: "I have lived to see unmeasured calumny poured on the head of an heroic man who struck the fetters from his bleeding country on the field and preserved her by his counsels in the cabinet. And I have lived to do justice to that man and that People by assisting the truth."[40] The author's portrait of Houston was aided by judicious omission of potentially embarrassing material. The book proved very popular; even those predisposed to dislike it because it eulogized Houston were more annoyed by the title than the matter.

Mirabeau Lamar's review of *Sam Houston and His Republic* was scathing: "*His* republic! That is true; for the country literally belongs to him and the people [are] his slaves. I can regard Texas as very little more than *Big Drunk's* big ranch." Lamar described Houston as a "demented monster" whose influence on Polk was nefarious. "Polk is but a poor tool to that malice of that bloated mass of iniquity." This view, as the writer himself conceded, was not the common one in Texas. Yet the fact remained that when Houston's term as Senator expired in March of 1847, he had not yet been reelected by the Texan legislature.[41]

The Senator reached Raven Hill early in September. On the sixth, his second child, Nancy Elizabeth, was born—named for her two grandmothers and always called "Nannie." Margaret's recovery from her confinement was rapid. She was ambulatory within a week of Nannie's birth.[42] There was much talk in the household about the war. Houston supported a plan to establish a protectorate over all of Mexico, a proposal he would reiterate with some frequency more than a decade later. It was, moreover, in harmony with earlier ideas of extending the Texan boundary all the way to the Pacific—something that General Kearny's army was accomplishing with little enemy opposition. By early December, Houston was on his way back to

Washington, leaving his growing family at Grand Cane, for Margaret expressed an increasing dislike for the isolation of the Raven Hill property.

In February, 1847, Margaret became very ill. Charles Power, who appears to have replaced Vernal Lea as head of the household at Grand Cane, summoned a doctor from nearby Liberty. However, because the problem was a swelling in one of her breasts, Margaret refused to let the physician examine her. He left without making a diagnosis.[43] Almost immediately afterwards, however, the swelling burst and bled profusely. Vernal Lea wrote Ashbel Smith to come from Galveston at once to see his friend's wife. Smith responded as soon as he could and detected a tumor which had to be removed immediately. He performed this surgery in early March, with Antoinette Power as his unwilling aide. He ordered the patient to drink whiskey to lessen the chance of shock. He should have known she would refuse. As an alternative, she used a variation of the traditional battlefield technique—biting on a silver coin while the surgeon made his incision.[44] Houston learned of these alarming events long after the danger had passed. As soon as he learned of the situation, the Senator came back to Texas.

He was greatly relieved to find his wife in much better condition than he had feared, and devoted his first days at Grand Cane to her. By the time of his return, she was able to do some walking about the grounds of the plantation.[45] On April 12 Houston wrote Ashbel Smith a letter of profoundest gratitude for having saved Margaret's life. He was at pains to deny greater political ambitions, claiming "but one desire, and that is for home & peaceful retirement, with competency, and social quiet!"[46] A week later, however, he gave a Senatorial campaign speech at San Augustine. To commemorate San Jacinto Day, the twenty-first, he visited Raven Hill and gave another talk at Huntsville. He was at Liberty on the twenty-sixth when he wrote Smith to come examine Margaret, whose condition had deteriorated dangerously.[47] There was infection in the wound. By return letter, the doctor recommended a physician who lived at Liberty, for he himself could not leave Galveston just then. Houston brought this doctor to Grand Cane and Margaret, with her husband present, allowed the man to view her infected bosom and prescribe a remedy.[48] She began to improve at once, thus leaving her husband free to stump the state in support of the war and his candidacy for the Senate.

By the end of the month, Margaret's cure was complete. In June she accompanied her husband and children to Raven Hill—for the last time. Soon after their arrival, he exchanged the property for a house and acreage much closer to Huntsville, satisfying his wife's desire to be nearer medical and clerical solace. His last letter from Raven Hill was written on June 12 to Joseph Ellis, a family friend, calling the Huntsville place "bang-up."[49] He cared little about where he lived, and no matter how much he portrayed himself as a "home man," dutiful husband and father, his record belies these claims.

He remained fairly close to the Huntsville place until December. On the reluctant recommendation of Governor Henderson (who would soon be succeeded by G.T. Wood), Houston's name was submitted to the Texan legislature for reelection to the Senate. Hardin R. Runnels, an ardent Lamar man, wrote his leader on the eleventh: "I hope you will be able to make at least a formidable show of opposition to Houston's election. . . . If there are but ten members . . . against him[,] that opposition should by all means be made to appear in the election—I know not who you can make the most available, but that individual[,] be he who he may[,] should be run: From all that I can learn there will be . . . a respectable opposition if not formidable. It is humiliating to [have] so large . . . a minority in the State succumb to so great a tyrant, without putting to test his real strength." On December 18 Houston was accorded 69 votes, only one less than he had received two years before. Nevertheless, ten years afterward, Hardin Runnels would have his revenge.

His future assured for the next six years, Sam Houston could concentrate on the problems that beset Texas. He was also free to make a move for the Presidency, if he was seriously considering it. The war was virtually won and remained an issue only in the minds of Northern foot-draggers. Texans were more exercised about the boundary question—the Nueces or the Rio Grande—and Indian attacks. The portion of Texas' public debt not absorbed by the United States on annexation was a difficulty being resolved, for the time being, by the sale of land and increasing taxes.

Houston passed Christmas morning at home in the little house near Huntsville. In the afternoon, he went into town to speak at a rally convened in response to a call by Henry Clay, who opposed continuation of the Mexican War. Clay himself had set the example by con-

vening the citizens of Lexington, Kentucky, to express their indigna-
tion at the cost of the conflict and its object. That Houston should have
devoted a portion of his holiday to this meeting is indicative of his
Presidential ambitions. The resolutions in support of the war were
hardly astonishing.[50] Texans thought it merely the final phase of their
war for independence. That the territorial tribute exacted in this
instance should coincide with the policy of Manifest Destiny espoused
by Democrats was no accident. He also introduced the matter of
slavery in this speech. One of the arguments advanced against the
Mexican War by Northern opponents had been that one war aim was
to increase the slaveholding areas of the country, thus upsetting the
precarious balance established by the Missouri Compromise of 1821.
That Houston, who had supported a slave-free Oregon, should defend
the compromise's principle of noninterference was evidence of no in-
consistency. As he would later maintain, he was "a man of the South."
What obtained for Oregon did not necessarily obtain for Texas.
Within two years this question would produce in Congress and in the
nation the most spectacular and divisive debate of the century to date.
But for Houston, this was more a Presidential than a Senatorial enterprise; he hoped his participation at the rally would result in a good
press, North as well as South.

When he was ready to leave for Washington, shortly after Christmas,
he wanted Margaret to come along. She declined. He had the consolation of leaving her in good health, in a house she greatly preferred
to Raven Hill. Though conditions were crowded, they planned additions.[51]

The Democrats thought they had every reason to be jubilant as the
election year of 1848 began. The war was about to end, and with
dazzlingly impressive territorial gains to show for it. The only question
was the identity of the party's candidate. This would be decided at a
convention in Baltimore at the end of May. The Treaty of Guadalupe
Hidalgo was concluded February 2; Mexico ceded to the United States
lands which now comprise most of New Mexico, Arizona, Colorado,
Utah, Nevada, and California, in addition to the disputed space
between the Rio Grande and Nueces. Rarely has a conflict yielded so
vast a bounty.

Late in February Houston delivered a querulous and sometimes
pungent speech in New York's Tammany Hall. One theme was the
Texan boundary dispute, resolved only later on.[52] Another was the title

252

to the Santa Fe Territory. Eventually, Texans would win the former and lose the latter claim. His tone was condescending in reference to the conquered Mexicans: "[T]he Divine Being has been evidently carrying out the destiny of the American race. We give to the Mexican[s] liberal principles; we elevate them far above what their tyrants have done; and the day will come when they will bless the Americans as their friends and liberators until time shall cease."[53] Although such views fell on receptive ears in Northern Democratic strongholds, they were not universally accepted in the North.[54]

It was, however, in the Senate that the first note of gloom was detected by the party in power, especially the Southerners, and most especially the Texans. In March the Treaty of Guadalupe Hidalgo was ratified. It was assumed that the land between the Nueces and Rio Grande would be automatically ceded to Texas. This did not happen. Besides, the much more complicated issue of slavery was reintroduced in debate. The so-called Wilmot Proviso, which would have prohibited slavery in all lands acquired by the United States, though ultimately defeated, reinforced the conviction of Southern Congressmen and Senators that slavery ought to be permitted wherever it was the will of the populace. The Texan boundary issue was right in the center of these debates. The land between the Nueces and Rio Grande had been granted by Mexico to the United States and not directly to Texas. The fact that Texas was a slaveholding state upset the Abolitionists. It could not simply be a question of an old territorial dispute between Texas and Mexico. At issue was the principle established by the Missouri Compromise: Could that portion of land be turned over to Texas? It stood west of the Mississippi and south of the Missouri border.

Added to this complexity was the matter of the Santa Fe Territory which had to be resolved between Texas and the federal government. In the middle of March, the Texan legislature created Santa Fe County, an area embracing most of that portion of modern New Mexico which it had long claimed. Representatives of the state administration were eventually dispatched from Austin to govern the county. They were turned back by federal authorities.

In Washington, argument raged in both houses of Congress to no avail. Only the Presidential election could resolve the difficulties—if they were to be peacefully resolved. An impasse had been reached. Ashbel Smith, who had spoken in support of Houston's Presidential

253

aspirations, wrote him at the end of March that there was a movement among Galveston Whigs to promote the candidacy of Zachary Taylor.[55] Military historians usually ascribed to Winfield Scott, captor of Vera Cruz and Mexico City, the more brilliant role in the Mexican War, but "Old Rough and Ready" was a man for the moment, his eye fixed firmly on the main chance, a slaveowning Whig who could thus appeal to Southern Democrats as well as members of his own party. When political ambitions at last occurred to General Scott, in 1852, the appeal of his successes in battle had lost much of its luster.

On April 13 Margaret gave birth to a second daughter, at Huntsville. She was named for Margaret Lea; they called her Maggie. When writing to her husband of this event, Margaret added news of the progress being made to develop their new property. She would not come to Washington; she was increasingly needed at home as the size of their family increased—acknowledging their mutual loneliness for each other, but pointing out that, after all, the cure for this surely lay more in his power than hers. There were some financial problems, too; not serious ones, but if she journeyed to the national capital, they could hardly supply their table with produce from their own garden, nor would they enjoy the unlimited credit accorded them in Texas.[56] Sam Houston's correspondence with his wife, as it has survived from his lengthy career as a Senator, reveals him to have been at constant pains to assure her of his good habits (he even attended church occasionally) and his desire for nothing more than to be with her and the children. Yet duty constantly demanded that he choose another course. One wonders how often he attempted to distinguish, in his own consciousness, between duty and ambition.

The Democratic convention at Baltimore named Senator Lewis Cass of Michigan as Presidential candidate on the fourth ballot. The Texan delegation had supported him from the beginning, not so much because its members opposed Houston, but as a show of solidarity seemed essential to bolster Cass's chances against the powerful opposition of Zachary Taylor. A splinter party, the Free Soilers, met at Buffalo to nominate New Yorker Martin Van Buren.[57]

In the middle of May, Margaret had decided she had had enough of the overcrowding in the Huntsville house and gone to Cedar Point for some peace and a breath of salt air to relieve her asthma. In the letter recounting her plans, she said nothing to her husband of his Presidential hopes; nor, for that matter, had he discussed them with her. What would be would be. While she basked in the breezes of the Gulf, he remained in the North, mainly to campaign for Lewis Cass. Twice he gave significant attention to the question of statehood for Oregon.

Although Oregon had only a remote connection with the issue of slavery, that shibboleth had been introduced by Southerners who were already at loggerheads with Congressional forces of the North over the question of slavery in the newly acquired Mexican territories. The leader of this faction was Senator John C. Calhoun of South Carolina, twice Vice President of the United States, twice holder of a high Cabinet post, and the principal political philosopher of the movement in the South that supported the rights of the states to nullify any federal acts with which they were not in harmony and, ultimately, to secede from the Union. So far as Oregon was concerned, the slavery question was a red herring, brought up by Calhoun to lay the groundwork for a debate that would begin two years later over what came to be called the Compromise of 1850. The 1848 debate in the Senate began June 2 and ended in the middle of August. Calhoun protested that settlers in Oregon would not be permitted to bring their slaves with them if the principles of the Missouri Compromise were adhered to. Thus he questioned the basis on which states other than Texas had been admitted to the Union since 1820.

Responding to this argument, Houston and Thomas Hart Benton pointed out that few slaveowners would be likely to move to Oregon. Fearful that any tampering with the fragile compromise might menace the integrity of the entire Union, Houston—while declaring himself a man of the South, prepared to defend Southern principles—announced yet again that he was above all for the Union.[58] As ultimately passed by both houses of Congress, the Oregon bill contained a specific prohibition against slavery. The embittered Calhoun, girding himself for the final and most tragic battle of his life, returned home muttering imprecations against the regional betrayal of Benton and Houston, whose two votes on the measure had been the decisive ones in the Senate. A Charleston paper put the position succinctly: "The South has been beaten by the South."[59] For the duration of his political life Houston would be reminded of his defection from the hard-line Southern ranks in the summer of 1848.

On returning to Texas, he spent little time at home, for there was some local fence-mending to be done. While he had succeeded brilliantly in establishing himself as a national political figure, he

255

discovered some erosion of his reputation at home. Many Texans thought, with reason, that he had been playing grasshopper to Thomas Rusk's ant. His vote on the Oregon bill was thought to be symptomatic of the fact that his outlook had altered—was no longer purely Texan nor even purely Southern. His enemies alleged that he meant to use Texas as a base from which to stretch a ladder that one day would lead him to the White House. There was just enough truth in the charge to make Houston feel vulnerable; he *was,* in general, less concerned about local than national issues. William Seale, Margaret Houston's biographer, suggests that the Senator also objected to "the regimentation and the hierarchy within the Democratic party."[60] It seems more probable that he simply resented not having been named his party's choice for the Presidency.

In the end, he should have been grateful for having been passed over in favor of Lewis Cass, who went down to defeat at the hands of Old Rough and Ready and his running mate, Millard Fillmore of Buffalo. Texans, however, remained faithful to Jackson Democracy and voted overwhelmingly for Cass.

Shortly after they learned of the national election results, Houston and Rusk departed for Washington.[61] Hardly was Congress convened before the debate over the Texan boundary was again embroiled with the issue of slavery in the territories acquired from Mexico.[62] Calhoun and other extreme Southerners were soon predicting that if these questions were not satisfactorily resolved, slaveholding states might decide to secede from the Union. Houston found himself drawn into the vortex of this turbulent struggle because, while a Southerner, he was much more strongly a Union man—a position that grew progressively more difficult for him to maintain. Yet maintain it he did, for the rest of his life.

XX

IN JANUARY, 1849, Senator Calhoun, eager to protect the institution of slavery, found an opportunity to fan the flames of secession when Joshua Giddings and Abraham Lincoln introduced a resolution in the House to restrict and ultimately abolish slavery in the District of Columbia. He summoned a caucus of all Southern legislators to discuss plans for a defensive strategy against what he saw as the thin end of the wedge that would eventually split the Union. Of this group, a Committee of Fifteen was selected to draw up what came to be called the Southern Address. Worded by Calhoun himself, the document drew fire from such Southern moderates as President Polk, and Senators Benton, Rusk, and Houston. Rusk was a member of the committee. He offered language changes that brought him into forceful conflict with the aged Calhoun, whose objections to Rusk's alternative wording brought about its defeat. Rusk resigned from the group, yielding his place to Texan Congressman David Kaufman.[1]

While the Committee of Fifteen labored through session after session, other matters pressed, but the drafting of the Southern Address preoccupied the Texan delegation in Washington. At the end of January Rusk wrote, "I yield to none in my devotion to the just and constitutional rights of the southern states but I doubt if they are to be benefited by the formation of a new party, by using threats which are not to be executed, by bringing into disrepute the bonds of our Union, or by an appeal to the fears of any section of the union."[2]

To his closest Huntsville friend, lawyer and historian Henderson Yoakum, Houston expressed himself more colorfully on the subject:

"Ah! we have had a Southron [*sic*] Convention here—a second act (or s intended by Mr. Calhoun) of nullification. Rusk and myself smoke Johnny and would not indorse for him. We are not done with hir yet—but I think he has *nearly done with himself.* Less than half the Soutl would not be a sweet morsel for him. Whiggery has nothing to do wit the question. It is 'the Union,' or 'disunion.' You know I am a unionfier as General Jackson was, and cannot look with one grain c allowance upon any fanatical project while selfish and unholy amb tion is to be gratified at the expense of the Republic. We [Texans] wer among the last to come into [the Union], and being in, we will be th last to get out of it."[3] While this final observation was unwittingl prophetic, Houston had no idea that secession was little more than decade away; he feared it might occur much sooner.

The Southern Address was ratified by forty-eight Southern legisla tors, but it merely applied more heat to a controversy to which ther could be no final solution short of violence. To confuse matters mor Calhoun supported a measure which would have sanctioned slavery i all territories acquired from Mexico. It passed the Senate, after a uproarious and drunken debate that ended early in the morning c Inauguration Day, but was defeated in the House when members ha sobered up.

As the end of the session drew near, Houston prepared a lon statement for his constituents about his position on the Souther Address, knowing that he and Rusk would be bitterly reproached a home for their refusal to subscribe to it. The name of John C. Calhou figured in every significant paragraph; he accused the old Senator c jeopardizing the entire course of American history by his "mad amb tion." Trying to seem evenhanded, he alluded as well to the "ma fanaticism" of the Abolitionists, but there could be no mistaking h conviction that the error lay chiefly with those who had supported th Southern Address. His conclusion was stirring:

> I would lay down my life to defend any one of the States from aggression, which endangered its peace or threatened its institutions. I could do no more for the Union, but I wish to do more; for the destruction of the Union would be the ruin of all the States. A stab in the heart is worse than a cut in a limb, for this may be healed. It is nature that teaches us to cling to the Union. It is the best security against every ill

that the weak have to apprehend. This feeling has been impressed upon my heart by the instruction of the great man whom, when a boy, I followed as a soldier. (I trust I may say with the instinct of patriotism,) and from whom as a statesman I never separated, until I wept over his warm remains at the Hermitage. The great trophy of his history will be the stern purpose with which he maintained the watchword of his administration, "The Federal Union, it must be preserved."[4]

Houston almost surely did not attend Taylor's inauguration. He had no great love for the new President. Along with other Texans, this disaffection grew during the fifteen months of Taylor's survival in office. The Senator went home to pass a quiet spring and summer.[5] The Congress that convened in early December of 1849 was riven by the slavery issue. Henry Clay, absent from Washington for more than six years, had been unanimously returned to the Senate to seek compromise—the art with which his name had been associated for so long. The fiery Calhoun and Mississipian Jefferson Davis were fervently opposed by Lewis Cass and Daniel Webster. The stage was set for a debate that made 1850 one of the most crucial years of the entire century for the United States.[6] The main issues confronting Congress were hazardous ones indeed—slavery in the District of Columbia, statehood for California, the status of New Mexico and Utah, a fugitive slave act, and—of great immediate importance to Houston and Rusk —an ultimate solution to the Texan boundary dispute. All these matters, in Houston's view, embraced the larger issue of the preservation of the Union.

As a Southerner who was also a Whig, Taylor seemed to have little interest in supporting compromise. His reservations about achieving an accommodation with Northerners over these questions were especially strong. He proposed, for example, that California be granted statehood with no provision in its constitution about slavery—that decision was to be made eventually by the state's populace. This was called the "no-action" plan. An avalanche of other solutions was then introduced, some fanciful, some extremely annoying to Texans.

In Texas there were strong feelings against Houston and Rusk for their general outlook and, specifically, for their refusal to subscribe to the Southern Address. The *Texas State Gazette* of early 1850 carried an anonymous letter which typified the drift of opinion among opponents: "[I]f Texas were not so unrepresented and so far behind the time with her elder sisters and advocating her claims [in New Mexico], there would be no failure in Congress. . . . Texas is losing vantage ground. Whatever is done, is done in her disfavor, for every act is a new impediment, or a new rival." However, opinion in Texas, even that of the *Gazette,* was not consistently hostile to the moderation of the state's two Senators.

At the end of January, Henry Clay began the debate on his compromise program—eight pieces of legislation that were the last major work of his long career. On the twenty-ninth and thirtieth he spoke his mind, proposing a middle ground which, while pleasing neither Northerners nor Southerners greatly, was a basis upon which both sides could agree to stand with mutual toleration. This came to be called the Compromise of 1850. Its principal provisions called for the abolition of slavery in the District of Columbia, the admission of California as a free state, the eventual admission of New Mexico and Utah to statehood (whether slave or free to be determined by popular or "squatter" sovereignty), the resolution of the Texan boundary question by the assumption of $10,000,000 of the state's indebtedness and the passage of somewhat more stringent fugitive slave legislation.

With so bright a star as Clay to present the argument for compromise, no less a figure than Calhoun could possibly deliver the rebuttal. A month would pass before the South Carolinian's dramatic and final appearance in the Senate chamber, however.[8] In early February Sam Houston spoke in support of compromise. Llerena Friend notes that in his address of the eighth he anticipated Abraham Lincoln by more than a decade in citing a famous passage from the Bible:

> I beseech those whose piety will permit them reverently to petition, that they will pray for this Union, and ask that He who buildeth up and pulleth down nations will, in mercy, preserve and unite us. For a nation divided against itself cannot stand. I wish, if this Union must be dissolved, that its ruins may be the monument of my grave, and the graves of my family. I wish no epitaph to be written to tell that I survive the ruins of this glorious Union.[9]

Houston left soon afterward for Texas. It seemed a very odd moment for him to leave, given what he himself had characterized as a most critical debate in progress. Yet he offered no satisfactory explanation to his constituents for his abrupt departure. There was, he said, an illness in the family. Besides, he added, nothing of importance was likely to occur in his absence. Although Margaret had sprained her ankle and was again pregnant, there was a matter of far greater moment that required Houston's immediate attention.

Some years before, Margaret's sister-in-law, Mary Lea, had adopted an orphan, Virginia Thorne. Apprehensive that no one would care for the little girl in the event of her death, Mary had exacted from Margaret a promise to look after her. This was willingly given—in part, no doubt, because it had seemed unlikely that Vernal's young wife would die. But she did, and Margaret, true to her word, took the girl into the Houston household. Records are skimpy and contradictory of what ensued.

Virginia Thorne seems to have been willful and demanding. She was also sexually precocious. When the girl was about thirteen, the Houstons hired an overseer, Thomas Gott, in his mid-twenties. Virginia enthralled him very soon after his arrival. It seems that they did nothing more reprehensible than to sit on the Houstons' porch in the evenings—but in Huntsville's Baptist eyes, that was very reprehensible conduct indeed. To so jeopardize Margaret's position in her own church was cause for great anguish. She sent Virginia, fourteen by now, to live with Frances Creath, wife of the local Baptist cleric. The couple eloped soon afterward, Virginia having persuaded Gott that she was eighteen. Thus began a series of legal actions, instigated by Houston's enemies, that caused Margaret the greatest degree of chagrin. One charge lodged by Virginia Thorne and Gott, when they returned to Huntsville, was that Margaret Houston had molested the girl. This allegation apparently never got beyond a grand jury hearing, where it was dismissed. Another, more delicate issue was whether Margaret might have "tolerated" the reckless sexual behavior purportedly occurring beneath her roof. This question was eventually resolved by a committee of the Baptist congregation, which wholly exonerated the Senator's wife. Houston's sudden return to Huntsville almost certainly was occasioned by some phase of the Gott-Thorne case that was so traumatic for Margaret.[10]

While Houston was on his way to Texas, some of his constituents responded hotly to his support for Clay's measures of compromise. J Pinckney Henderson wrote Ashbel Smith: "And now Mr. Clay has the *impudent effrontery* to propose that we shall yield *all* the North now claim of us on [slavery] and calls it 'compromise.' Houston too must outrage his state and the feelings of the whole South by his resolution of *submission* to the dictates of the abolitionists. This is the *damnedes* outrage yet committed upon Texans."[11]

Houston was not on the Senate floor to hear James Mason of Vir ginia read for the failing Calhoun, on March 3, an impassioned speech against the compromise proposals. As soon as the address was finished Calhoun was helped from the chamber. He met Henry Clay in the aisle. These ancient enemies stared at each other briefly; then in tears they embraced and parted, never to meet again. Calhoun was dead within the month. Reports of the Calhoun speech were circulated to wild applause in Texas. Daniel Webster's even more celebrated re sponse, delivered four days later, is customarily described as having ended his Presidential hopes—for in espousing compromise, he dras tically undercut his support among fanatical Abolitionists of New England. Costly though it was to him personally, Webster's March 7 address was extremely influential, even in the South, where opinion began to shift away from Calhoun's extreme position. Support for the Southern Convention, called to meet at Nashville, began to wane.

When Calhoun died on March 31, the secessionist movement, beref of its most spirited leader, faltered temporarily. His demise ended an era, or so the compromisers hoped. It was probably this news that sen Sam Houston scurrying back to Washington. He was at Vicksburg April 6, three days before the birth of his third daughter, Mary Willie A little more than a fortnight later he was in the capital. Though Texans had continued to revile him for his absence, he had been correct in saying that nothing would occur while he was gone. Only in the middle of May did the Compromise bills enter the crucial amend ment stage—the major battle. Houston spoke several times on the measure affecting the Texan boundary. He reproached President Taylor and those participating in the Southern Convention for menacing the integrity of the Union. There were also personal matter disturbing the Senator in the early summer. His sister Eliza died. His sister Mary had gone mad in Tennessee. Vernal Lea was ill with malaria. The Gott-Thorne matter came up again to distress Margaret who evinced almost no interest in her husband's political life except to observe, whenever the topic was raised, that she wished he would stay home more.[12]

Zachary Taylor died of typhoid on July 9, 1850. Millard Fillmore succeeded to the Presidency. The complexion of the debates in the Senate and House cleared almost at once. For Fillmore favored the compromise proposals. Now he was in a much more favorable position to help to implement their passage.

Two days after his inauguration, Fillmore received a letter from Sam Houston in which, among other suggestions, the Texan Senator urged that Daniel Webster be named Secretary of State, an appointment the new President soon made. Though acknowledging himself a Democrat, Houston promised no "factious opposition" to the Whig President's administration. He went on, in this mood of magnanimity:

My object in writing you . . . is to let you know . . . that I feel, as I believe you do & as every other citizen ought this moment to feel. Duties of high moment have by a marked disposition of Providence . . . been devolved upon you. . . . You now have it in your power . . . to render your country more important benefits than have been rendered for the last quarter of a century by any one individual. With your capacity and intelligence, you will I have no doubt perceived . . . that there is but one course to pursue for the attainment of the vast object—peace to the country. . . . To do this you have only to compass the whole and not feel that you are of or belong to any *one* section or another. . . . To accomplish this end it will only be necessary to compromise in such sort as will give quiet to the people by either consummating some plan which has now been suggested or by devising a better and procuring its adoption.

You were elected as a Whig, and I presume no rational man will expect you in party matters to deviate from party principles. Nevertheless, you are elected by the American people and are their President. The present agitations can not be settled by either of the political parties of the country, but it must be done by both parties acting for the Union as a great Union party. . . . For my part, as a Senator & as citizen, I feel . . . that the object of restoring peace . . . and tranquillity to the people of the country . . . rides high above all party considerations and would be worthy of the fame of Washington if he were now on earth. I doubt not . . . but what you will believe me sincere when I assure you that the first . . . and most ardent, as well as the most sincere wish of my heart . . . is to see our country at rest. Nor do I care by whom the great work is accomplished. Party and party influence can never enter into my estimate of the value of the Union, or my country's happiness or prosperity.[13]

Fillmore's succession assured passage of the Compromise of 1850, though not without further struggle by Southern diehards. Some thought Houston's role in the success of the measures was inspired not by a concern for the Union, but by Presidential ambition. Francis Blair, publisher of the *Globe*, wrote Martin Van Buren in mid-July that Houston was "so full of presidential hopes" that he would "do anything in his power" to reach the office.[14] There was some justice in the editor's allegation, but to be right for the wrong reasons is still to be right. Houston reserved his most stinging comments on the compromise bills for a late-July amendment which offered some concessions of territory by Texas in exchange for the $10,000,000 indemnity already proposed. He indignantly rejected the suggestion that his state would accept a bribe for her acquiescence in the remaining portions of the compromise. "It is her boundary she asks—not your millions."[15]

Other measures of the compromise legislation passed the Senate after varying amounts of acrimonious debate, mainly from the mouths of Southerners. The most difficult bill for Northerners to swallow was the new Fugitive Slave Act, ratified by the Senate in the middle of August. Though in the main it restated what was law already, the facts of its necessity enraged the Abolitionists. Yet it provided the keystone to the arch of compromise.

Back in Texas, the performances of both Rusk and Houston in the compromise debates excited great scorn. Houston was in no immediate danger, as his term had four more years to run. Rusk, however, appeared in some jeopardy, for his term ended the following March. In late August the *State Gazette* expressed the thought that there was little point in attacking Houston. "We will only remark, so far as he is concerned, that his ability, enlarged patriotism, and devotion to his duties, have won him a high place among the distinguished men of the Senate."[16] Barely a month later, after the Compromise of 1850 had been passed by the House, the press and people of the South were in full cry

On the boundary settlement there were objections from every corner of Texas. Though the state had gained its primary objective of securing the disputed land between the Nueces and the Rio Grande, it had lost all its claims in New Mexico. "Gold might buy the votes of members of Congress," said the *Gazette* in September, but "we rely upon the uncorrupted and incorruptible people of the Lone Star State for a glorious triumph over abolition artifice and the intrigues of speculators."[17]

Hopeful of gaining support for yet another Presidential run in 1852, Houston made several speeches in the North before returning home in the autumn. He left a favorable impression almost everywhere. The New York *Sun* thought that he alone was "fit to unite all the discordant elements of the [Democratic] party." After offering a brief biography of the Senator, emphasizing his support for the recently enacted compromise legislation, the editorial went on: "Who will refuse to rally to the standard of Sam Houston, the true American patriot, the fearless and brave champion of American institutions—of the country and the rights of American citizens, under àll circumstances—the pupil of the illustrious Andrew Jackson in youth, his bosom friend and councillor in manhood—like him in all the noble qualities that make the true man[?] Such is General Sam Houston the People's Candidate for the next Presidency."[18] The day this article appeared, October 30, Houston and Rusk were speaking at San Augustine in defense of their support of the Texan boundary measure which had been part of the Compromise of 1850, so decried in the state's press.[19] Listeners would have been astounded to read the *Sun*'s unguarded praise of the "People's Candidate." Nevertheless, when the boundary question was submitted to the Texan electorate, it was approved by the unequivocal proportion of 2 to 1.[20]

Shortly after her husband's return to Huntsville, the final phase of the ugly Thorne-Gott case occurred—the examination by local Baptists of Margaret's treatment of the errant girl. Her conduct was found impeccable. Virginia's name was never again mentioned in the Houston household. Margaret now directed her attention to the saving of the Senator's soul; she wanted to see him baptized.[21] Perhaps out of gratitude for the moral support given his wife by Frances Creath, wife of Huntsville's Baptist minister, he had been attending services at a Baptist church in Washington, presided over by George Whitfield

Samson. According to Samson's account (published decades later), Houston confided in him the secret of his failed marriage to Eliza Allen. As Samson sermonized, the Senator whittled.[22]

When he learned in late November that the Texan governor had signed into law the boundary settlement voted by Congress and approved by the people of the state, Sam Houston told his friend, Henderson Yoakum: "I may now retire then, for it is consummation of what I have struggled to attain for eighteen years past." He had no intention of retiring, nor was Yoakum deceived. After the Senator went back to Washington, the Huntsville lawyer recorded a conversation he had had with Houston about the Presidential election of 1852. "He doubtless desires to occupy that high station and believes strongly in his destiny. He is not a man of great reading, but one of the best judges of human nature in the world."[23]

The following year was filled with talk of the election of 1852. Houston was often absent from Washington, leaving the administrative chores to Rusk, while he followed the heady Presidential trail. He was surprised, early in the year, to hear from Margaret that she was considering a trip to Washington to reside with him, provided she were not compelled to live in the capital city. If they could find a house eight or ten miles away, she would have the pleasure of his company without having her treasured privacy constantly interrupted by a flood of political visitors.[24] Nothing came of this. It was as close as Margaret ever came to leaving Texas during her husband's lifetime. He wrote her in late winter that he was to be baptized March 6 by Mr. Samson.[25] Though this ceremony evidently occurred, it did not satisfy his wife; she insisted on a repetition, before her eyes.[26]

Politics occupied most of Houston's time. Several New England papers supported his Presidential hopes for the next year. One of them stated that as President, he would "unite the democracy, North and South, East and West, more thoroughly than any other candidate." The *Texas State Gazette,* however, reported that Washington Democrats were seeking to arrange a ticket of Cass for President and Houston for the Vice Presidency. A New York friend wrote him that there was a plan to support a combination of Cass and James Buchanan in that city; he urged an immediate visit to further his interest.[27] That Houston should, instead, have returned to Texas for the summer indicates a contrariness that amounts to perversity in his outlook toward the Presidency. From Huntsville in May he wrote Senator Nicholas Dean of New York: "I do not talk of politics, I have not written of them, and if you will believe me, I think but little about them. . . . I have not written a letter on politics since we parted, nor will I, unless I intend it for the public eye, and I do not·expect to write any for that purpose!!!"[28]

This was close to the truth. Houston wanted the Presidency without seeming too eagerly to seek it. But rarely has that office sought the successful candidate. He was alone at Huntsville during June; Margaret had taken the children to Cedar Point in search of quiet and the sea air to ease her asthma. But in the middle of July they were together again, and Houston was writing that while the topic of politics was "quite ripe" in Texas, he took no part in talk of it.[29] "I am anxious to get out of public life, and remain in quiet the residue of my days."[30] In his letter to Senator Dean of the previous May he had been even more resolute, vowing that he would not even finish his current term in the Senate, for it would keep him from home too long.[31]

We must not place any confidence at all in this sort of statement, however often reiterated. It was part of a gambit—like the adage about the girl who runs from a boy until she catches him. To his cousin John Houston, the Senator wrote in the fall of 1851: "[O]thers have had their day, and *mine is to come!* Should I live!"[32] He did return to Washington for the final weeks of the Senatorial session. Just before Christmas he gave his colleagues his reasons for rejecting a proposal that the entire Compromise of 1850 be subjected to Congressional reaffirmation—a Southern move prompted by the hope that it might this time be voted down. He denied that his position related to his Presidential aspirations, but even the most careless reading of these remarks discloses it to be a campaign speech.[33] On Christmas Day Margaret took to her bed at Huntsville and remained there intermittently until the termination of her fifth pregnancy. Houston was in the North, speaking in early January at Tammany Hall and at Hartford, Connecticut. The topic for his Hartford speech was the North American Indian. Whatever benefit he thought to derive from this choice of themes, it did not sit well in Texas. The *Gazette* of January 24, citing a dispatch in the New York *Sun,* reported his Hartford talk of January 5 thus:

General Sam Houston gave a lecture on the subject of the North American Indian. . . . The object of the lecture was to arouse feeling in favor of the Indians. Houston claimed that in their contacts with the whites, the latter were almost always the aggressors, and that the Indians, in a body, never broke their treaties. A single Indian, or two or three combined, might sometimes kill a white for plunder, but that in such cases, an appeal to the chief would secure the surrender of the murderers. He said that the United States were now expending [$]6,000,000 per year to preserve peace with the Indians on the Texas and New Mexico frontiers, and that it was for the most part useless. He said that he would guarantee peace throughout the entire frontier for $100,000 per year if he could appoint the leaders and select the kind of men for the troops. General Houston went on to explain that many times the Indians were cheated and wheedled into making treaties by dishonest and designing men. The whole lecture was a eulogy on the American Indian.[34]

This speech could not have gained him a single vote. Even the Abolitionists of Hartford hated Indians. We have no recorded indications of his motives in selecting this topic for an audience basically friendly toward him. Perhaps the murder of The Bowl and Texas' subsequent refusal to honor any of the treaties solemnly negotiated with tribes of the Southwest still stuck in his craw. This, added to current and continuing difficulties wherever whites and Indians came into contact with one another, may have prompted him to speak his mind at Hartford where, at any rate, he would not be hooted off the rostrum. But it was politically an unwise speech.

On January 20 Antoinette Power Houston was born at Huntsville.[35] Her father, who had hoped for another son, was not home until late the following month. He would have gone sooner, but was committed to speak to a temperance rally in New York. The reporter for the *Herald* was overwhelmed by his performance: "He has sounded all the depths and shoals and quicksands and snags and sandbars of the waters of destruction. . . . His case is a living example of the power of an inflexible will in support of a good resolution . . . and the manly fortitude with which he has stuck to the pledge, among all the temptations of Washington, commends him to the applause of all men." There was a danger, all the same, that in adopting the "cold-water" cause of temperance, Houston might lose the support of the drinking classes, which certainly outnumbered the "dries" in the electorate. But he was making an impact on important men. Senator Charles Sumner, the powerful New Englander and true father of emancipation, recorded in early February: "I was won very much by Houston's conversation. With him the antislavery interest would stand better than with any man who seems now among the possibilities. He is really against slavery, and has no prejudice against Free Soilers. In other respects he is candid, liberal, and honorable. I have been astonished to find myself so much of his inclining."

Southerners would have been depressed to learn that Houston was opposed to slavery. In fact, he opposed its spread to the West, not out of principle, but because it was divisive. He was content, however, to allow Abolitionists like Sumner to see him as an opponent of slavery—at least for the time being. Thomas Rusk, having been reelected to the Senate with Houston's aid, endorsed his old friend's Presidential candidacy—while deploring his frequent absences from Washington. By late March the *Gazette* expressed the belief that only Senator Stephen A. Douglas of Illinois was likelier than Houston to secure the Democratic Presidential nomination.[36] Houston's increasing fever of ambition, as convention time approached, was not wildly cheered by Margaret. William Seale believes that the prospect of her husband as President appalled her. The idea of having to play the role of First Lady was repellent to this shy, withdrawn woman.[37]

We must at this point attempt the impossible—to read Houston's mind, for he was apparently of two persuasions with respect to the Presidency. He acted the part of candidate to perfection, was a proven vote-getter and probably more acceptable to the North than any other Southern Democrat—and not so hated in his own part of the country that a Northerner could defeat him there. But he had reservations—or at least he expressed them in correspondence. They are difficult to reconcile with his behavior. Even with those closest to him he made only occasional and modest references to the campaign, and these were self-deprecatory: He wanted to stay home with his wife and children. But he also wanted desperately to be President. Perhaps he knew intuitively that the office would never be his, and he guarded himself against disappointment by seeming indifferent. It seems to come down to the fact that he was a Southerner with views considered to be

Northern. He was Sisyphus; he knew he would never succeed in pushing the rock to the top of the incline, but he could not help himself from continuing the effort.

In early April Tennessean Andrew Johnson wrote: "In respect to Houston, there is but one opinion with friends and foes—all agree that if he could get the nomination ... he could be elected by a greater majority than any other person now spoken of in connexion with the presidency and that he is the only man in our ranks that can defeat General Scott if he is the candidate of the Whig Party."[38] As it happened, another Democrat did defeat Winfield Scott in 1852. However, Johnson put his finger exactly on Houston's political difficulty—that the Democrats were unlikely to nominate him. For every friend he had made in one section of the nation, he had made an enemy in another. He was thought unstable. He was clothed in an aura of eccentricity, impetuousness and even mystery; to Democrats who worshipped the memory of Andrew Jackson, Sam Houston was a cynosure. But there was a younger generation of voters and legislators who looked back on Old Hickory's era with some distaste and misgiving. It had been too baldly Populist. Moreover, the Democrats, especially in the South, were not so rigidly organized as the Whigs. The party was something of a catch-all, not overprincipled in most matters. Embracing the urban agglomerations of the North with their increasing numbers of recent immigrants, the party was inclined to splinter on many issues. In the Deep South, there had been no need for the party to create a hierarchy; it survived because there was no rival. This, of course, would soon change.

Houston was not revered in Texas. In late April former Governor J. Pinckney Henderson wrote that he favored Thomas Rusk for the Presidency if only because he was not seeking it. "I *hate* an office seeker and have no respect for one who shapes his course, not by reason or conviction of right, but by considerations of self interest. I *fear* that Cass & Buchanan are influenced by those considerations—I *believe* that such are the motives which actuate Douglas and I *think* I *know* that such are the motives of Houston's actions. Therefore I cannot & shall not vote for Douglas or Houston & do not believe I shall vote for either of the other two should either of them be nominated. I have for some time believed that no one of the aspirants would be nominated and I hope they will all be disappointed." Henderson's judgment of Houston was inspired by a personal animus. Houston, in Henderson's view, did not merit the name of hero. But his evaluation of the impending convention was uncanny. None of the major figures he discussed was given the nomination.

The Democratic convention began in early June. From the first ballot, on June 3, to the last, the experience of waiting for the outcome was disillusioning for all those thought to be front runners. The initial vote reflected the moods of the state delegations: Cass and Buchanan led the rest of the pack by a wide margin; Houston ran a poor fifth with only eight supporters. During the 48 ballots that followed before agreement was reached, the largest number of votes he received was 14. When the dust settled, the candidate was Franklin Pierce of New Hampshire, former Congressman and Senator, whose most recent service to the nation had been as a political general in the Mexican War. Though the words must have stuck in his throat, Houston was quoted as calling Pierce "an excellent choice; it will unite the whole Democracy."[39]

Though the campaign could not get fully under way until the Whigs had named their man, Houston and other Democrats began stumping the country immediately after the long and bitter gathering at Baltimore had ended in the middle of June. He remained in the North for most of the summer, interrupting his speaking tour only long enough to attend the funeral of the great Henry Clay in early July. His family spent some weeks at Grand Cane; there, Vernal Lea was dying at the age of thirty-seven, leaving a new young wife and a plantation that was at last proving successful.[40] In letters home, the Senator made no allusion to the angry sorrow in his heart over his failure to receive the nomination. He also made no reference to his reason for campaigning so hard for Pierce, more of a nonentity by far than the maligned Millard Fillmore: There was, after all, going to be another election in 1856.

Houston was home in October, having spoken often along the way from Washington at torchlit gatherings and barbecues, in churches and courthouses. He expressed pleasure to learn of Pierce's election, but his private feelings must have been mixed.[41] If Pierce made a success of the office, Houston's chances for nomination in 1856 would be dim indeed. As it happened, Franklin Pierce was undoubtedly the worst President the country had ever elected. While not personally corrupt, he countenanced corruption in his administration; while conciliatory by nature, he allowed domestic rifts to develop by his refusal to veto the catastrophic Kansas-Nebraska Bill and the repeal of the Missouri Compromise. His foreign policy, if he could be said to have one, was predicated on the sound Democratic principle of Manifest Destiny—except that during his period in office, its only manifestations were an abortive raid on Cuba, an alienation of the British, and the Gadsden Purchase—mitigated only slightly by the opening of the door to the Far East. No one, of course, could perceive in Pierce the origins of the Civil War; he had been elected because the Whigs were divided in the North whereas the Democrats were not divided in the South.

The only cause for elation that Margaret Houston might have felt that autumn was the fact that her husband was not the President-elect. Everything else seemed to be going wrong for members of her family. Her brother Henry had died at Marion, Vernal Lea at Grand Cane. The prosperous Charles Power saw his fine plantation near Galveston devastated by hurricane, and his wife, Antoinette, had given birth to a sickly child. The Powers moved to Independence, where the indestructible Nancy Lea was established. Taking all these things into account, 1852 had not proven a very good year for the Houstons.[42]

In January, 1853, Sam Houston was elected to his second full term as Senator by substantial margins in both legislative houses, indicating that whatever wrath he had incurred in the past was now forgotten.[43] He passed an uneventful winter in Washington, annoyed that Pierce had failed to give enough patronage to Texans—after having advised the President to act with "irreproachable and unapproachable integrity."[44] He returned to Huntsville in the spring to learn that Margaret had decided to move the family to Independence; the presence there of Nancy Lea and the Powers being the main inducement. Houston himself had no strong feelings, since he was away from home more often than not. He would, however, miss the occasional companionship of Henderson Yoakum, who had become almost as intimate a friend as Ashbel Smith.[45]

During that summer, a Presidential commission bargained with Indians living north and south of the Kansas River for a tract of 13,000,000 acres—the Kansas and Nebraska territories. As always, the

Indians lost, agreeing in the end to cede the land in exchange for gold that was never fully remitted and reservation areas to be created for them by the government—from which they would later be driven. These dealings would soon take on great significance in the career of Sam Houston and in the life of the nation, when the Kansas-Nebraska Bill was debated in the Congress. Another foreshadowing of events to come is found in a letter of June 30, 1853, from Houston to W.D. Miller, in which he sharply criticized President Pierce for his insensitivity to Texan patronage needs and for his naming of James Gadsden to deal with Mexico over a disputed piece of land along its border with New Mexico and Arizona. Houston planned to do battle with Franklin Pierce.[46]

It was in this rather ugly frame of mind that the famous Texan Senator allowed himself to be drawn into one of the least appealing political movements to flourish in the nineteenth century—Know-Nothingism. The Know-Nothing faction had its origins prior to the Mexican War, when the influx of immigrants, particularly Irish and German Catholics, had led to election frauds inspired by Protestant suspicions of Catholics' loyalty to an alien Pope. The war eclipsed the movement before it had attained major political significance. However, after 1850, with the renewed flood of Irish escaping the famine in their land and Germans fleeing the collapse of uprisings in theirs, it enjoyed a resurgence. When queried, partisans would respond that they knew nothing of it. They had previously been known as "nativists," proponents of candidates for office who had been born in the United States. They supported a law which required as much as twenty-five years of residence before citizenship (and therefore voting rights) could be obtained. By 1853, Know-Nothingism began to emerge. The American Party evolved from it, attracting Whigs who were apprehensive of foreign enclaves in the major Northern cities. By the Presidential election of 1856, the Know-Nothings had cut so deeply into the ranks of Whiggery that the Democrats, more or less intact in the South, and solid in the North, could not be defeated.

To what degree Houston subscribed to Know-Nothingism is difficult to ascertain. Curiously, its impact was greater in the South than in the North, in terms of votes cast. However, in the off-year elections of 1854, the candidates of the American Party prevailed in Massachusetts, Delaware, Maryland, California, and almost in New York—where

Millard Fillmore had allowed his name to be associated with it in his quest for the governorship. Many members of Congress were dependent for their success that year on Know-Nothing support. Yet it seems accurate to state that the party's principal accomplishment was the destruction of the Whigs as a national organization. In 1856, disgruntled Whigs who had supported Know-Nothingism in 1854 created a new party, the Republicans. Modern American politics dates from this year. We may suppose that Houston was drawn to Know-Nothingism in part because he was disaffected from the Democrats. He saw himself to have been rejected by them in favor of Pierce, whom he despised. We must also sadly conclude that he thought the American Party the right bandwagon to jump on in his pursuit of the nation's highest office. In this he sorely erred.

Before the year 1853 was out, the eagerness of settlers to occupy the land filched from the Indians of Kansas and Nebraska was so intense that Missouri Senator David Atchison proposed that it be declared open to homesteaders, with the provision that "all citizens of all states, slave or free, might settle on equal terms."[47] This meant, in effect, that the Missouri Compromise would be ignored. Once again the fate of the slavery issue was thrown into the legislative fire. The matter was to come up for debate in the next session of Congress—resulting in the Kansas-Nebraska Bill.

The Houstons moved to Independence in September, renting their Huntsville house to an Alabamian family known to the Leas. The Senator told W.D. Miller that he planned to remain in his new home for the rest of his life.[48] They had acquired a piece of land somewhat larger than the one at Huntsville with a satisfactory house on it. Houston thought the town offered his children the best opportunity for education in all of Texas. Baylor University was situated there. Rufus Burleson was president of the university and soon a friend of Houston's. He was a Baptist minister of great force with whom the Senator argued constantly about theology.[49]

Although he reached Washington just after Christmas, it was not until the middle of February that Houston made his first major speech of the session. He opposed the measure introduced by Stephen Douglas that implemented Senator Atchison's initial proposal, leaving the territories of Kansas and Nebraska open to slavery. The bill was popular among Southerners. Houston was virtually the only

Southerner to object, arguing that the bill violated the spirit and purpose of the Missouri Compromise and that, because it antagonized even some moderate Northerners, it would prove a significant force for disunion. On February 15 he concluded his remarks with a warning of the agony that would soon beset the Union he so cherished:

The day, I fear, must come in the progress of our country—though God forbid that it ever should—that great trials and emergencies would grow up between the North and the South. The South is a minority. She cannot be otherwise. The laws of nature and of progress have made her so. If the South accede to the violation of the compact [the Missouri Compromise] as sacred as this, they set an example that may be followed on occasions when they do not desire it. If you take away the sanctity of the first compromise after the formation of the Constitution, why not take away the last [the Compromise of 1850]; and if others grow up, why not sweep away all compromises from your statutes, and from the policy of the country? If you disregard one, and treat it with levity, impair its importance and its weight in the public mind, you prepare the way for a disregard of all. If you regard it as a sacred instrument, one to be esteemed and adhered to, you will find that its benefits will inure to you. But if you tear it up and scatter it to the winds, you will reap the whirlwind; you will lose the benefit of the compacts. Sir, I most fervently and devoutly trust that the Missouri compromise may remain. If the South is to get nothing by its repeal but an abstraction, she does not want it. So far as I can represent her, she has not demanded it. It is an afflictive gratuity which will be of no benefit to her.[50]

In early March, he spoke with even greater fervor against repeal of the Missouri Compromise and passage of the Kansas-Nebraska Bill—which some have called the greatest legislative blunder of the century. His conclusion was melodramatic, but he had never spoken with clearer vision: "The events of the future are left in the hands of a wise Providence; and, in my opinion, upon the decision which we make upon this question . . . must depend *union or disunion.*"[51] The amount of rage engendered by Houston's stand on this issue can be measured by a report in the *Enquirer* of Richmond, Virginia. "What objects Mr. Houston has in view, and what excuses he may have to gratify them, I know not. Nothing can justify his treachery; nor can anything save the

275

traitor from the deep damnation which such treason may merit. It will, however, effect no injury; and its impotency will but add to its infamy."[52]

Passage of the measures could not be prevented. A coalition of the entire Southern delegations in the House and Senate with the "moderates" from the North, led by Douglas, was not to be stopped. Why, then, did Houston oppose them with more vigor than he had manifested on any other subject ever to come before the Senate? Since he had everything to lose by his stand, the conclusion is inevitable that he spoke with utter honesty to his principles and convictions. He feared absolutely for the future of the Union. Any hope that he might now gain important Southern support for a Democratic Presidential candidacy was banished by these speeches. The South could perhaps forget his significant part in the ratification of the Compromise of 1850, but it would never forgive his vote against the Kansas-Nebraska Bill and its consequent negation of the Missouri Compromise.

The Senate's passage of the measure stirred up so great an outcry in the North that a group of more than 3,000 clergymen petitioned that body for the right to air its views to the legislature. Accused of misuse of their spiritual offices for political purposes, these ministers—all Protestants, incidentally—were denounced by Stephen Douglas and his Southern allies. On March 14 Houston rose to defend the petitioners, describing them as "harbingers of peace to their fellowmen." He prayed that there would never again be a need for such a protest. "But for the necessity or cause, which originated in [the Senate], this memorial would never have been laid upon your table. This is but the effect; the cause was anterior to it. If we wish to avert calamitous effects, we should prevent pernicious causes."[53]

When Houston returned to Independence in the spring, Margaret was well along in her sixth pregnancy and sickly. She was also anxious for her husband's safety, so great was the anger in Texas against his vote on the Kansas-Nebraska Bill. Reaction, however, was not uniformly negative. The *Gazette* observed: "Notwithstanding our objections to his course . . . we should regret to see him leave the Senate at this time. Texas has large interests in many questions likely to arise in Congress during the present session, and his great abilities and enlarged experience would materially aid in securing them. We hope that he only intends a short visit to his family, and does not design permanently vacating his seat in the Senate."[54] A constituent wrote Thomas Rusk (who had supported the Kansas-Nebraska Bill) that Texans were "down on old *Sam.* . . . But yet you know how they will cry out against him and turn right round and vote for him."[55]

Sam Houston never showed the least regret over his stand on this issue. He told Rufus Burleson that though his vote had been the most unpopular of his long career, it had also been the wisest. Passage of the measure would have a terrible effect on the country. "[I]n 1856, the Free Soil party will run a candidate for president, and the whole vote will be astounding. In 1860 the Free Soil party, uniting with the Abolitionists, will elect the president of the United States. Then will come the tocsin of war and clamor for secession. . . . But, alas! I see my beloved South go down in the unequal contest, in a sea of blood and smoking ruin."[56] If for "Free Soil party" we read "Republican," Houston's forecast was truly prophetic.

While he was on his way back to Washington, the House passed the Kansas-Nebraska Bill. This began an era of six years that would be known as the period of "Bleeding Kansas." The guerrilla war between advocates of slavery and free soil that occurred in the region was a curtain-raiser for the greater drama that began in the winter of 1860. His direst apprehensions were to be realized.

During Houston's absence, his second son, Andrew Jackson Houston was born on June 21 at Independence. He had despaired of having another man-child, and was delighted by the news.[57] Though he remained in the North until the early days of September, he accomplished little, traveling to cities near Washington to speak on topics mainly related to Texas, the Kansas-Nebraska Bill and the larger issues that distressed the nation. He was well received everywhere, and hoped his immediate popularity had larger implications. Back home to see his new son and mend fences as well as he could, he was doubtful of the future. However unpopular as he was in the South, his star appeared to rise in the North. In October the Democratic General Committee of President Pierce's home state, New Hampshire, endorsed him as successor to the native son. To implement this proposal, "San Jacinto Clubs" were to be opened across the country.[58]

Margaret Houston, imperfectly reconciled to whatever course her husband decided to follow, was determined that he would not leave Independence again without being baptized properly—that is, in her presence. Houston was reluctant; for one thing, he had already been baptized twice—the first time as a Catholic at Nacogdoches, the second time by Dr. Samson in Washington. Yet a combination of wifely pressures and clerical arguments prevailed. On the morning of November 19, 1854, in his sixty-second year, Sam Houston allowed Rufus Burleson to immerse him totally in the chilly waters of Rocky Creek, on the outskirts of Independence. Hundreds of his friends and neighbors looked amusedly on, as the man whom so many had called "pagan," "savage," and "Big Drunk," submitted to the Baptist rite.[59]

XXI

IT HAS been written that the Civil War began not in the harbor of
Charleston, South Carolina, but in Lawrence, Kansas, in 1855, as
squatters from North and South disputed territory and policy. That
Sam Houston had predicted this did not enhance his reputation at
home.[1] It was believed that he had become closely associated with the
American Party, if not actually a member. He was in sympathy with its
basic tenets, and he appreciated the interest of its leaders, who were
looking seriously in his direction as a Presidential candidate for 1856.
By his vote on the Kansas-Nebraska Bill, he had burned his boats as a
Democrat at the state and national levels. Thus he may have
concluded that he had little to lose by a connection with the Know-
Nothings, who now numbered some prominent former Whigs and
Northern Democrats in their ranks.[2]

It was a year of divisions. The Whigs were ruined. The Democrats
were in peril just when they were beginning to organize themselves
systematically in the South as they had long since done in the
North—though the party did hold together through the election of
1856. At Ripon, Wisconsin, a group of dissident Whigs and Free Soilers
who were not apostles of Know-Nothingism would proclaim the formation of the Republican Party. There was another filibustering venture, this one against Nicaragua. The railroad builders were beginning
to appreciate the extraordinary riches which were being thrust upon
them by politicians eager for their states to be linked with the
Northeast.

In Sam Houston's deportment during the next eighteen months one may detect elements of his despair of ever achieving the Presidency. Evidence of his confusion of ideals and ambition abounds. In a speech of late January, he took delight in denouncing the Pierce administration for having failed to protect the Texan frontier against the Indians, while at the same time deploring the treatment by whites of the beleaguered tribes. He spoke again on this theme of white treachery in mid-February.[3] A bit later, replying to advice that he not address the Anti-Slavery Society of Boston on Washington's Birthday, he wrote: "I must go on. Under the circumstances General Jackson would have done so. To be honest and fear not is the right path. I would not conceal an honest opinion for the Presidency. If I did, I could not enjoy the office, and worse than that, I should blame myself. I know well that it is a risk, but it is for the harmony of the Union, if perchance I may benefit it."[4] In essence, this speech in Boston was a defense of the principle of compromise and a vigorous assault against the Kansas-Nebraska Bill. He also offered a rationale of the institution of slavery in Southern terms which he hoped his potentially hostile audience would understand:

We found slavery in our country. We use slaves but we do not abuse them. One race or the other must give way. If slavery were to give way the [textile] spindles of the North would stop. It may be objected that I am appealing to the cupidity of the Northern people. I am appealing to their common sense and experience, and they may give it what name they please that object to it. Look to Jamaica. Has the slave advanced with all the advantages of emancipation, after passage through all the stages of apprenticeship? No, he has deteriorated. He is lower than when he was a slave. His labor is unproductive; he is not profitable to himself or to any other. How would it be in the South? Turn them loose and they could not set up in business. Land could not be appropriated to them; and if it were they could not work it. They would be as they are in Bermuda and everywhere else where they have been thrown upon their own resources. They are listless, inert, lazy, living on the fruits of the earth where they can be had, but never will they be industrious. . . .[5]

It is necessity that produces slavery; it is convenience, it is profit . . . that creates slavery; though often the owners are not as much benefited by it as it is thought. It is true that labor must be performed, and when foreign labor has become reduced to a standard . . . at which it was cheaper than that of slaves . . . with the capital invested in them, you [Northerners] employed foreigners, and turned off your slaves. Had there been such an influx of foreign emigration at the South, do you believe they would have continued to hold slaves? No! they would have constructed ships . . . to transport [the blacks] back to Africa, rather than to have them among them. These are the things the North should look at. Your slaves became unprofitable here, and they are thrown off. Labor and institutions, too, are governed by convenience and necessity to a great extent, without canvassing the morality or immorality of the institutions. Now, wherever the South should employ foreign labor, if it were possible to do it, it would depreciate the value of slave labor, slaves would become worthless, and, if possible, it would get rid of them.

I have given an honest exposition of my sentiments tonight. I have not sought to be censorious nor to reflect on any; I have told you the truth, and how, by necessity of our condition, we are forced to act as we have done in regard to slavery. I trust, though a misunderstanding may have arisen between the two sections [of the country], no deplorable result may arise, such as has been prognosticated.

Our country is too glorious, too magnificent, too sublime in its future prospects, to permit domestic jars of political opinions to produce a wreck of this mighty vessel of state. Let us hold on to it, and guide it; let us give it in charge to men who will care for the whole people, who will love the country for the country's sake, and will endeavor to build up and sustain it, and reconcile conflicting interests for the sake of prosperity. This can be done, and let us not despair and break up the Union.[6]

This speech was surprisingly well received in Boston, partially because Houston was such a persuasive, polished orator. Also, his comparison between foreign and slave labor struck a Know-Nothing nerve, trading one set of prejudices off against another. What would finally destroy the American Party was its waffling on the slavery issue. Reports of this address in Texas failed to record Houston's casuistic defense of slavery. Simply the fact that he had been welcomed and applauded by an Abolitionist audience was held against him.[7]

When he returned to Independence in the spring, he received a copy of Lester's revised edition of his memoirs, now newly titled: *The Life of Sam Houston: The Only Authentic Memoir of Him Ever Published.*[8] The additions contained the author's enthusiastic support for Houston as a

Presidential candidate—the reason, of course, for the republication of the work. Though Houston remained in Texas for several months, he was not often home, for he spoke often in defense of his record. He had a debate at Nacogdoches with Thomas Rusk in which the two old friends aired their differences amicably. Houston denied, characteristically, that he had hopes for higher office: "I have been accused of catering to the Presidency. Why need I want the Presidency? I have twice been President, and although not on as large a theatre as the United States, yet the future will show that no President of the United States has ever had the opportunity of doing as much for his country ... as I could have done for Texas."[9] He alleged that it was his intention soon to retire from public life. There was nothing to it; no one was deceived.

The idea prevailed in American Party circles that a revival of Jacksonian Populism, in a Know-Nothing guise, could project Houston into the White House. Houston himself half believed in this possibility; he certainly wanted to believe in it. But hardening views about economics, opening territories, and slavery on both sides of the Mason-Dixon line decreed the extinction of the American Party, which refused to take a stand on the slavery issue for fear of dividing itself. Ironically, the party became divided because of this omission.

In June, when the American Party held a convention in Texas, Houston thought it wise to identify himself with the views he thought most of its delegates shared, thinking to win their support. Instead, they named a former Democrat to be their candidate for governor. Stunned, the Texas Democrats staged a "bombshell" convention to drum the traitor out of their ranks. This caused a split within the intimate political structure of Texas which could only harm Sam Houston, who remained dependent on the state's Democracy for his grassroots support. Yet, with typical perversity, he doomed his own chances of regaining Democratic favor with a speech in late July. He defended the platform of the Know-Nothings; it was not intended to suppress Catholicism but to prevent that church from suppressing Protestantism. *"I believe the salvation of my country is only to be secured by adherence to the principles of the American Party."*[10] He was attacked by Texan Democrats who predicted what Houston already knew, that he could not be reelected to the Senate. Their object was to undermine his position in the nation as well as the state. If he were in trouble at home, he would be useless on the national level. The *Gazette* accused him of seeking to exchange the philosophy of the South for votes in the North in his lust for the Presidency: "Gen. Houston has not yet, and God knows never will supplant the Pantheon with a toadstool—the old Hickory tree . . . with a Jonah's guard of a single night! When he talks of the pulsations of the American heart, we will point to the vote of his own town and that of his own state! The voice of America is the voice of its cherished Democracy!" The Know-Nothing candidate for governor was thrashed in August. Houston's political prospects seemed moribund.[11]

In October the Houstons returned to Huntsville. Independence was apparently too hostile after the election.[12] Margaret offered no objection to the change. But there was hostility to the Senator everywhere in Texas. He spoke repeatedly through the autumn, denying that he had betrayed Southern principles. The real traitor, he said, was Franklin Pierce.[13] The *Gazette* coyly observed that Stephen Douglas, no friend of the South in most matters, had refused to speak to the Anti-Slavery Society in Boston that Houston had been so warmly received by. The Texan legislature officially censured him for his vote on the Kansas-Nebraska Bill. The Dallas *Herald* wondered why he retained a seat in the United States Senate, which he had morally forfeited by so misrepresenting his constituents.[14] He was in a defiant frame of mind when he started his return to Washington, pausing in late December at Nacogdoches, where he spoke partly in defense of his actions and partly to attack a current measure that proposed to ease the naturalization process. This talk contains one brief passage which is among the least attractive he ever uttered:

> Europe is emptying her vials of wrath upon us in the shape of thousands of her worst population, and it is time that a more cautious policy should be adopted. There are honorable exceptions, but the mass is a vile compound of all the dangerous tendencies of trans-Atlantic society. The South found herself powerless to check the evil, and it gave way. I could not do it, and whether I am to stand alone . . . or not, I will always be found resisting the encroachments of foreign influence upon our government.[15]

It seems strange that the Know-Nothings did not realize they were cutting their own throats by such pronouncements, which had the effect of galvanizing the Democrats of Texas and the entire nation into a much more efficient political machine than ever before. The refugees of famine and tyranny in Europe had by now acquired American citizenship and represented a formidable array of voters, especially in the cities. The politically astute Houston ought to have perceived the error of the line he was taking. All he could discern, however, was that he had made important new enemies in Texas and that he had better establish himself as a national figure if he meant to pursue a career beyond his present term in the Senate. So he chose to play the demagogue.

The Know-Nothings staged their convention at Philadelphia in February, 1856. From the beginning, it was a scene of regional strife. When balloting for a Presidential candidate began, the man in commanding position was Millard Fillmore, who had come close to capturing the New York governorship for the party in 1854. He was at the time on a trip to Europe. Houston's largest number of supporting votes was 6; on the final tally, he had only 3. Fillmore was a nearly unanimous choice, with A. J. Donelson as his running mate. National reaction to the American Party's ticket was almost cosmic boredom. Rusk wrote his brother that Houston was embittered and would probably not support Fillmore and Donelson.[16] The Senator was half right; Houston's support was offered late and was less than wholehearted. In early spring he wrote that he had no regrets: "I was glad that I was not nominated . . . by such an incongruous body."[17] He toyed with the idea of running as an independent. Such a naïve notion is amazing in a man who had been on the national political scene for thirty years. By April he had reconciled himself to the idea that he would not be the next President. He wrote his wife:

> I often jest to my friends about having the doors of the "White House" widened and yesterday I was there and told the doorkeeper that he must keep the house in good order as I might have to take it over for the next four years. He is an Irishman, and was much delighted. He played it off quite handsomely. So you see my Dear, I am not very sensitive on the subject, worn out as it may [be]. I comment at times about the pretty play grounds for the children! I never think of our humble home, but what emotions of deep and abiding affection swell my heart.[18]

By the end of May, the Houstons were staying with Margaret's relatives at Independence. Houston was suffering from a bronchial condition which he had difficulty throwing off.[19] The newly created Republican Party nominated John C. Fremont as its standard-bearer, and the Democrats named James Buchanan. Buchanan's election was assured by the division of the Whigs into two factions—Know-Nothings and Republicans. Noting Houston's publicly expressed skepticism about the chances of the American Party's slate, the *Gazette* accused him in early July of having turned "state's evidence" against Fillmore. The writer went on: "No man has ever played a more desperate game for the Presidency than Houston, and none have ever been more rightfully rebuked by disappointment. He is the last man to talk about 'selfish politicians.' "[20] By the time this article was printed, Houston was in Washington, campaigning feebly for Fillmore. It was not so much that he favored the Know-Nothings as that he despised their opponents. Texas supported Buchanan by a substantial margin in the November election; his victory, coupled with the defeat of the Know-Nothings (who fared surprisingly well in the South, however), altered the texture of national politics in the United States. The Democrats remained the only major party. But given the increasing ill temper of the times, the composition of the party was not strong enough to preserve it intact even for four years. Houston's letter to Rusk on November 8 was prophetic: "I dread the success of the Black Republicans."[21]

All around him, Texans were dividing along new partisan lines—Calhoun Democrats or Houston Democrats. The leader of the state's official Democratic organization predicted in December, 1856, that the Senator would seek the governorship the following summer, a prophecy which was to a degree self-fulfilling; the decision was being made for him by the splitting up of his state.[22] He felt he must give leadership to the Texans who shared his convictions about the sanctity of the Union, and there were many of them—far more than in most other states of the Deep South. There was no other man for the task, since Rusk had been all but immobilized by the death of his wife.[23]

In early March, soon after Congress adjourned, the Supreme Court handed down the most fatefully inauspicious decision of the decade, a ruling against Dred Scott's application to keep his status as a free black. Thus those provisions of the Missouri Compromise not nullified by the Kansas-Nebraska Bill were declared unconstitutional. Once a slave, always a slave. The precarious balance of the Union was irrevocably upset. There is no direct record of Houston's reaction to the

Dred Scott decision, though he can only have deplored it for its effect of consolidating the Abolitionist ranks of the "Black Republicans."

By mid-April the main topic of political conversation in Texas was the coming gubernatorial election.[24] For a while Houston disclaimed any interest, but not for long. Certain that the state legislature would refuse to reappoint him to the Senate when his term expired in 1859, and still eager for the Presidency, he felt he must firmly establish the idea that while professional politicians despised him, he was still the darling of the "sovereign folks." On May 21 he let it be known that he would be a candidate. He wrote Rusk that day: "You will be surprised, as I believe, for you know it was my intention to retire . . . to private life.`. . . The people want excitement, and I had as well give it as any one." His opponent was the incumbent, Hardin R. Runnels. Houston announced that he would debate the governor or his running mate, Francis Lubbock, in any of the twenty-four communities where he was to appear through early July.[25]

It was a vile campaign. With no organization and little money, Houston stumped the state in a red buggy which he shared with its owner, Ed Sharp, a plow salesman. Sharp recalled a visit to Nacogdoches where Houston was to debate Thomas Rusk. "[B]oth senators approached the Speaker's stand, met each other, embraced, and sobbed like women. Without uttering a word, Rusk took Houston by the hand, led him to his carriage and to his home. Neither was seen again that day." Several times in the next weeks, partisans of Runnels asked Rusk to side publicly against Houston or risk discrediting his own image among organization Democrats. But, as Rusk acknowledged, there was "little or no difference politically" between his own position and Houston's—though he promised to vote for Runnels. Whether or not this assertion meant that Rusk now regretted his vote against the Kansas-Nebraska Bill was an open question. It obviously meant that his support for Runnels was merely dutiful; his heart was with Houston. But in different ways, the tether was running out for both men.

For the first time in his long career, Houston was apprehensive about the outcome of an election. The campaign ended for him in San Antonio on July 28; defeat was a virtual certainty, though naturally he claimed victory. The following day, Thomas Rusk killed himself. When he heard this news, Houston claimed that the activities of the state Democratic Party were responsible for his friend's suicide.

However, Rusk had never fully recovered from the death of his wife; politics probably had nothing to do with his untimely death. The election took place on August 3. Runnels defeated Houston by a vote of 32,552 to 28,678.[26]

A week later Houston learned of the outcome. He was at Huntsville. He walked to his bedroom and quietly closed the door behind him.[27] Although Margaret had been at his side, it was a misery he was unwilling to share even with her. That the citizens of *his* republic, *his* state, should have repudiated him was unthinkable. Yet it had happened. In late August, the *Gazette* trumpeted: "He never again will crow on this side of Mason and Dixon's line."[28] This political obituary was issued prematurely. By the time it had appeared, Houston wrote Ashbel Smith:

> The fuss is over, and the sun yet shines as ever. What next? Will the spoils be equal to the wants of the spoils seekers? I fear not. Will the late victory be equivalent to the State . . . & the Country . . . for the murder of Genl. Rusk? I should say not. There are matters of vast import now on hand, and I would like to see you in relation to them. While I am a proscribed man, I do not like to put my thoughts on paper. . . .
>
> In the result of the election I am cheered, and were it not for my friends, I assure you, I wou'd rejoice at the result, if I am spared to take my seat in the Senate. I will, as the Frenchman said, "have some fish to fry." Had I been elected, I would have had "other fish to fry."
>
> If you come to see me, I bind myself to make you laugh.[29]

Despite his economical mode of transportation during the campaign, Houston had incurred debts of such magnitude that he found it necessary to sell the Huntsville house to satisfy his creditors. The Houstons returned to Independence, where they still had property and a house. Many Texans urged him not to resume his Senate seat, arguing that his defeat had discredited him.[30] But as he had indicated to Ashbel Smith, he had no plans to retire. With the convening of the Texan legislature, there was talk of humiliating him by naming his successor nearly two years before this was necessary, to emphasize his lame-duck status. The members had to elect a replacement for Rusk. This was J. Pinckney Henderson. The unanimous and gleeful choice to succeed Houston was Judge John Hemphill. The *Gazette* deplored

Houston's insistence on completing his designated term. Its issue of November 14 savaged him:

It must indeed be a sad Spectacle to witness Gen. Houston again in his seat at the present session of Congress. . . . He stands there deserted and alone—his own party denying him and scrambling to all corners for shade and obscurity. Look, then, at him, and ask ourselves, what must be the sadness of this spectacle, when with this picture of evident distrust and dissatisfaction—this unyielding determination of the people of Texas to condemn him—he still holds on to the barren office and sits in his place among fellow Senators to receive his *per diem allowance.*[31]

Only Ashbel Smith offered consolation: "The new Senators do not displease me. Gen. Henderson was my choice from the East; and if there has to be a change in the West [at the expiration of Houston's term in 1859], Judge Hemphill is greatly preferable to most of the persons spoken of from this district. I should have been deeply mortified . . . had one of the itinerant pedlars of politics been chosen."[32] In Washington by early December, Houston met Francis Blair, who wrote to Martin Van Buren: "[Houston] has a beautiful leopard skin turned into a waistcoat—Laying hold of it, I inquired whether it was a wildcat's, a panther's, or a tiger's coat. He said neither—but a leopard—which I have chosen to wear next to my bosom because the scripture says 'a leopard cannot change his spots.' "[33] His next-to-last Christmas as Senator was perhaps made lonelier by his recent rejection at the polls. He missed Margaret and may have worried over the news that she was pregnant again.

He observed in a letter to her of January 20, 1858, that the South was more and more secession-minded, especially her native state of Alabama.[34] Four times in February Houston spoke against proposals to increase the size of the standing army. The apology advanced by proponents of the measure was that more troops were needed to deal with the Indians who were resisting efforts to compress them into smaller and smaller enclaves where survival was barely possible. Houston believed that state militias like the Texas Rangers were better suited to the task. However, he offered no impassioned defense of the Indians to inflame his constituents. The Indians were beyond help.[35] So too was Kansas. The Dred Scott decision, in conjunction with the repeal of the Missouri Compromise, had had the effect of making Houston's position on the Kansas-Nebraska Bill now appear impeccable. As he wrote his wife at the time, "facts vindicate the course taken by me!"[36]

On February 15 Houston proposed for the first time a resolution calling for the creation of a protectorate over Central American countries. His rationale was stated in the opening sentences: "[T]he events connected with the numerous efforts of the people of Mexico . . . and of Central America . . . to establish and maintain order and good government, since their separation from [Spain], have so far resulted in failure and consequent anarchy, and demonstrated to the world [their] inability . . . to effect an object . . . so desirable and so indispensable to their welfare and prosperity." He spoke of this proposal again the next day, assuring his colleagues that its aim was not to extend America's hegemony. However, if the United States failed to act, European countries might be tempted to. Though this measure received virtually no support, Houston refused to allow it to drop. He brought it up again and again.[37]

His record of speeches on other issues during this spring session was active but not exciting. He addressed himself mainly to domestic matters. On April 17 he wrote a friend of his current mood: "I am truly glad that I will soon retire from all the care of public life. The grapes are not sour! I have no doubt from events in Texas many think the grapes are sour. . . . God has granted us six fine children, and there is another in the shuck for June, and for these I wish to be at home and render all the aid in my power."[38]

On April 20, in offering an amendment to his protectorate scheme, Houston appeared to imply that if Texas were not given her way in this, she might secede. Her situation, he said, differed from that of other states. She had voluntarily joined the Union after having been a separate and independent nation; therefore, she could voluntarily secede.[39] We cannot measure the sincerity of the threat, but may conclude from his later conduct that it was totally cynical. He remained a Union man to the core, and had probably been aroused by the rhetoric of fellow Southerners who talked of secession for different reasons. At Huntsville, on May 25, a third son and seventh child, William Rogers Houston, was born.[40] The curious may well wonder after which member of the Rogers family the boy was named.

In early June, Houston spoke in the Senate yet again about the protectorate scheme. If the federal government refused to act, Texas might move on its own.[41] Just what his colleague, J. Pinckney Henderson, made of this fantastic proposition is uncertain. He had been ill since reaching Washington. On June 4 he died. The following day Houston delivered a eulogy.[42] The *Gazette,* commenting on these remarks, accused him of being a slanderer and a hypocrite who had no right to speak so kindly of a man whom he had vilified during the recent gubernatorial campaign. The harshness of the denunciation was significant. Had Houston been as dead politically as the *Gazette* suggested, the need for such vituperation would not have existed. But there was thought in Texas that he would run for governor again in 1859.[43]

Home for the summer, he saw his new son and helped Margaret make arrangements for the departure to Independence following the sale of the Huntsville property.[44] He was gratified to note that however preposterous his protectorate proposal had been considered in Washington, there were Texans who took it seriously. Seven newspapers, including some that had been generally hostile to him approved the plan, noting that Mexico's British creditors seemed disposed to accept the idea as a solution to their predicament.[45] It was not much of a surprise to Margaret, therefore, to discover that her husband's help in moving was less and less available as the summer progressed. He went off on several speaking tours. After a barbecue in August, he stated flatly that the protectorate was official federal policy—a completely false assertion.[46] The protectorate was not his only theme. He said at Hempstead that if the South were to secede from the Union, it would not make its will effective.[47] The power of the North and West was overwhelming. Many of his listeners believed this campaign designed to influence the legislature to elect him Henderson's successor.[48] By September, when he was still traveling and speaking, everyone in the state was convinced that this was his purpose, though he had little support in the press or the legislature.

In October, his finances slightly improved, he arranged to buy more land and a new house at Cedar Point, for summer use. He discussed with Ashbel Smith the practical aspects of sheep raising, a plan he had for his retirement.[49] After the Houstons finally made the move to Independence, in November, the Senator began his final trip to Washington.[50] Matthias Ward had been named to take Henderson's place. Guy Bryan, one of the two Texan Congressmen, received a letter from a constituent in late December with this comment: "It seems understood that Genl. Houston will 'fight his battle o'er again next summer—and that he will give the Democracy some trouble.' "[51] Whether the retiring Senator had decided at this point to seek the governorship is questionable, but his speeches in Texas had kept his name before the public.

With only a few weeks of his term left, Houston did not overwork himself. In the course of one debate, he took occasion to reprimand his Northern colleagues for inflammatory statements that served only to exacerbate relations with the South. "As a Union man, I have ever maintained my position, and I ever shall. I wish no prouder epitaph . . . than this: 'He loved his country, he was a patriot; he was devoted to the Union.' If it is for that I have suffered martyrdom, it is sufficient that I stand at quits with those who have wielded the sacrificial knife." His new associate, Matthias Ward, said he would rather see the Union dissolved than countenance a violation of Southern rights. Houston's reproach was gentle: "I hope [Ward] does not suppose I would submit to an infraction of our rights. Our rights are rights common to the whole Union. I would not see wrong inflicted on the North, or on the South, without any 'if' in the case; and my motto is, 'it shall be preserved.' "[52]

One wonders if Margaret was deceived by her husband's letters of January in which he suggested that all he wanted now was tranquility and "petticoat rule."[53] She must have been dismayed by a paragraph in his communication of January 29:

> At this moment, I need your society and advice more than I have ever done, but as it is not at hand, I will make no decision . . . whatever . . . until I can see you on the subject. *In confidence,* I tell you that the matter relates to the "Protectorate." I can entertain no proposition, with any pleasure, that even blinks at a temporary separation from you. I hope you will not desire it. And I am sure that you will not be willing, tho' you might consent to it. . . . You will be able, from what I premise, to form some idea as to the subject on which I wish to see you, & confer with you about.[54]

This furtive reference was clarified soon afterward. It related to an oblique proposition made to Houston to lead a filibuster into Mexico. Financed by British funds, the offer contained significant guarantees of long-term assistance to his widow and children should he perish in the enterprise. Whatever Houston decided, it was obvious that, one way or another he meant to remain active in public life. Though Margaret would object, she would naturally abide by his decision. If he planned to seek the governorship of Texas, at least he would be nearer home than in Washington or Mexico.

When his term expired, Houston returned home. The *Southern Intelligencer*, copying an editorial from the San Antonio *Herald*, applauded "feeling in behalf of the Old Hero Patriot," and added the hope that the people of Texas were "waking up, that the scales are dropping from their eyes, that their great error is coming boldly up to their view and that upon reflection they will remember the injustice done [Houston] and will place him in that position due him for past services."[55] Though he had yet to declare for the governorship, his brother-in-law Charles Power wrote Ashbel Smith on April 1: "I think the Old Dragon will run again, that he can make the race this time, the reaction in his favor is wonderful."[56]

On June 3 Houston wrote George Pashcal of the *Southern Intelligencer* at Austin: "On yesterday I yielded my own inclinations to the inclinations of my friends, and concluded, if elected, to serve the people as Executive of the State." His only platform would be the "Constitution and the Union. . . . They comprehend all the old Jackson National Democracy I have ever professed, or officially practised."[57] One by one, papers previously opposed to him changed their views. Although the bandwagon for Houston could not be stopped, he did have opposition. The incumbent, Hardin R. Runnels, took a position of extreme Southern nationalism which was stronger stuff than most Texans were willing to accept at that point.[58] The secessionist movement in Texas was not nearly as powerful as in other Southern states. Mexico and Indians were topics nearer the voters' hearts.[59]

One published letter and one public address at Nacogdoches constituted the entire Houston campaign. He spent most of the summer with Margaret and the children at Cedar Point, where they now owned 4,000 acres. Willie, their youngest, was a sickly child; they bathed him in the warm Gulf waters and were relieved to see a rapid improvement in his health. The candidate then returned to Independence with his family. The final six months of 1859 were a joy for Margaret. Her husband was with her almost constantly without the duties of an office to preoccupy him. It was the longest uninterrupted period of undiluted connubiality in their nineteen-year marriage.[60]

The election occurred August 1. Houston defeated Runnels handily, 35,227 to 27,500—an almost exact reversal of the 1857 result. Most editors attributed the election to Houston's personal popularity. Even his vote on the Kansas-Nebraska Bill had been turned to his advantage by events taking place as a result of the measure's passage. He was, moreover, an elder statesman come home to pass his final public years at the helm of the state he had helped to create.

XXII

HARDLY WAS the result of the election known before some papers began promoting Houston's name for the Presidency. The governor-elect avoided all semblance of seeking the office, though he still wanted it above all else. He stated that he would be governor of Texas, nothing more. He had plenty to do before moving into the post. He made a few public appearances, had a private secretary to handle his correspondence, and spent time with his wife and children. He was again the great man of the state. There was some talk of reelecting him to the Senate. He refused to become a candidate.

In early December, before his inauguration, the country and the Congress were in turmoil over John Brown's October raid. It required two months of furious debate for the House in Washington to select a Speaker, and in both branches there were almost daily threats of secession. Nor was all peaceful at Austin. Yet, by December 8 Houston and his family were installed in the governor's mansion.[1] Because, it was said, there was so much animosity toward him in the legislature, Houston staged the inaugural ceremony on the steps of the capitol. He spoke briefly and sensibly, mainly addressing himself to state matters. However, he could not resist the urge to stress once more his conviction that only in union was there strength. He concluded: "Half the care—half the thought which has been spent to meet sectionalism with sectionalism, bitterness with bitterness, and abolition by disunion, would have made this people, today, a happy, united and hopeful nation."[2] Though the speech was warmly received, especially in the North, the conception of Union to which Houston was so devoted had been doomed by the sectionalism he condemned. Some optimists thought it might yet be preserved by a successful Presidential candidate who could inspire confidence on both sides of the Mason-Dixon Line, and many believed Houston to be the man; but there were too few of them and the election of 1860 was too late.

Houston's term as governor began with enough domestic difficulties to consume much of his energy. There were increasing Indian incursions. More significant, in the light of his plan to establish a Central American protectorate, there were uprisings in Mexico, led by Benito Juárez. Juan Cortinas, whom many considered no better than a bandit, had captured the border town of Brownsville. This gave the Texas Rangers an excuse to take countermeasures that would both assist Juárez and divert Texans' attention from the issues that were destroying the Union. But the timing was wrong; the secession was too pressing to be concealed by this regional embarrassment.[3]

Houston also discovered what it was like to be the head of a large family. Of his seven children, only young Sam was away at school. Margaret's asthma confined her to her bed—and she was pregnant again. So Houston received the added responsibility of managing a large household—a role he did not savor.

On December 27 a combined force of Texas Rangers and regulars of the United States Army drove Juan Cortinas from Brownsville.[4] The next day, however, the governor felt it necessary to issue a proclamation declaring illegal the formation of armed bands, for filibustering expeditions.[5] His order was ineffectual. The filibuster impulse was too powerful, the lure of Mexico too bright. Houston's speeches in favor of a protectorate were partially to blame. Indeed, Walter P. Webb, author of a history of the Texas Rangers, thought this plan essential to Houston's campaign for the Presidency: "To be President of the United States, to be the savior of the Union, and to establish a protectorate over Mexico were the principal features of one grand plan. In this trinity of his ambition, the protectorate . . . seems to have been the central figure which supported the other two."[6] If Webb's judgment is correct, Houston mistakenly appraised the mood of the entire nation. This appears unlikely. The Abolitionists were already crying that the protectorate scheme was no more than an excuse to introduce slavery into Mexico. Its basic appeal was local, designed to keep Texas in the Union. The rest of the South was to be placated by compromise. Compromise could only be achieved by a man whose record of support for the Union was impeccable. Houston saw himself as that man. For the moment, however, he would lie low.

On January 21, 1860, he transmitted to the legislature a copy of resolutions drafted in South Carolina defending the right of a state to secede. In his message accompanying these resolutions, Houston attacked the premise.[7] Perhaps in view of the certainty that he would veto a bill in support of the South Carolinian measure, the Texan House and Senate refused to follow the example of other Southern states. The fever over the Mexican situation helped to distract Texan attention from the secession debate. Thirty-two militia brigades were authorized, comprising 10,000 men in all. In mid-February, the governor sent a representative to Washington to warn Buchanan and Secretary of War John Floyd of the menace on the Rio Grande. He hoped more federal troops would not be required, but wanted it known that the possibility existed.[8] Houston had allowed the Mexican situation to be blown out of all proportion to its national significance. The question is whether his motives were self-serving or whether he thought to save the Union by creating an apparent external threat. Houston gave no clues that would answer this.

There is another mystery that Houston had alluded to in the letter to his wife of a year before—the British proposal that he lead an expedition against Mexico. In conversations with her following his return to Texas, he apparently dismissed the idea. But in February, 1860, he responded to a letter from General Elkanah Greer, a soldier of fortune and commander of the "Knights of the Golden Circle," a leftover of Know-Nothingism. The matter of a semiofficial filibuster had come up again, and Houston wrote, "I have neither money, arms, nor munitions!" The conclusion of this letter was somewhat equivocal: "The want of grain as well as grass, on the route to the Rio Grande, would render the advance of a force at this time . . . impracticable."[9] Yet the lure of financial security for his family must have been tempting to a man of sixty-seven who had amassed no considerable assets and who had a young wife with seven children and another "in the shuck."

Such matters could not be kept secret. The day Houston wrote Greer, President Buchanan demanded to know if he was seriously considering an invasion of Mexico. Texan Congressman Forbes Britton replied that the governor would make that decision when he had a better appreciation of the military situation. Buchanan replied that he himself did not oppose the move. However, he would have to contend with a hostile House, whose members must approve the sending of arms and troops to Texas. Britton approached John Floyd to inquire if the War Department would oppose a purely Texan force that might cross the Rio Grande. In a letter to Houston of early March, Britton reported the Secretary's reply: "No Sir, but I would stand upon this side [of the river] & clap my hands and holler hurrah." [10] On March 8 Houston wired the President that while Texas would do nothing to disgrace the nation with respect to Mexico, the state required supplies with which to defend itself.[11] He requested 5,000 troops along with arms for 5,000 Texas Rangers.[12] He assured John Floyd that he had done nothing to worsen the Mexican situation. However, he did not exactly deny that he had ordered the Rangers to the Rio Grande or that he hoped for a war.[13] On March 14 the governor had his answer: Since the Cortinas menace had passed, Texas could expect only $5,000 in military aid from Washington.[14]

At about this time, a Houston-for-President movement began among the regular Democrats of Texas.[15] The national convention was to meet at Charleston toward the end of April. The best strategy was to start a bandwagon in his home state that would sweep the country.[16] While Texan Democrats met at Austin, however, the governor acted in a way his backers questioned. He declared a recent filibuster into Mexico illegal. Furthermore, in a proclamation of late March he stated that while there remained a danger on the border, obligation to protect it was a federal rather than a state concern. To give weight to this pronouncement, he ordered Ranger companies pulled back and instructed officers to muster out any trooper who showed reluctance to follow orders.[17] None of this was likely to fan a grassfire in his favor.

Yet he had certainly not abandoned Presidential hopes. On March 25 he indicated a willingness to be the Democratic candidate, stipulating only that his nomination not be obtained by "connivance, trick, or management." He added, "If my name should be used in connection with the Presidency, the movement must originate with the people themselves, as well as end with them." [18] That statement was for public consumption; he knew very well how candidates were named. For Houston, April was the cruelest month. When the Democrats convened at Charleston, the leader of the Northern faction, Stephen Douglas, called for a platform that incorporated a popular-sovereignty clause for territories destined for statehood. This was tantamount to creating one more "Bleeding Kansas" after another. The delegations from Texas and seven other Southern states withdrew without naming a candidate. The rift between North and South was total. Yet a second convention would be held at Baltimore before the break was perceived to be irrevocable. Houston had declined to go to Charleston; it would be indecorous, and there were vital state matters to attend to.

On April 21, the twenty-fourth anniversary of the Battle of San Jacinto, a gathering of veterans and patriots heard a speech proposing the candidacy of Sam Houston as a man above party—one who would "arrest the growth of the spirit of disunion" in the land.[19] This did not catch fire even in Texas. Nevertheless, a Houston campaign was started that day. But it was too late to affect the deadlock in Charleston; too late, indeed, to affect the outcome of the November election.

At Baltimore, in the second week of May, a Know-Nothingish Constitutional Union Party, a group which had been improvised in a matter of weeks, opened a convention to create a diversion from the main contest between Democrats and Republicans. The name of Sam Houston was placed before the gathering by Erastus Brooks, editor of the New York *Express*. He assured delegates that Houston would respect the "Constitution and the laws." Others mentioned were John Bell and Edward Everett, the latter considered the greatest public speaker of his era. On the first ballot, the Tennessean, Bell, led with 68½ votes to Houston's 57. The matter was resolved on the second, when Bell was accorded 125 votes, Houston 69. Everett became the Vice-Presidential candidate.[20] The most that can be said for this fiasco was that it was the closest the Texan had ever come to a party nomination.

On May 17 Houston responded to the talk of his candidacy. He would run, he wrote, if drafted by the people. He declared that the placing of his name in nomination at Baltimore had been unauthorized. His conclusion was essentially a reiteration of his remarks of March 25—good reading but unrealistic politics: "The people alone have the nominating power, as they have that of election. If they declare for me, I desire that they do so without aid of 'contrivance, trick, or management,' on the part of my friends."[21] How much confidence he really felt in the power of the people to prevail against that of the parties is debatable. So long a loyal Democrat, he could not have failed to appreciate the capacity of an organization to get out the vote. But with the Democrats in fatal disarray, he may have sensed the possibility of successful candidacy as a man "above party."

William Brown, a Douglas Democrat, suggested that when his party's convention next met at Baltimore, the "Little Giant" should step aside in favor of Houston or another Southerner.[22] On May 24 the governor of Texas restated his willingness to serve as "People's Candidate."[23] Houston's wildcat candidacy disturbed many Southern politicians, among them Charles W. Russell, who observed: "The folly of General Houston in announcing himself a candidate . . . is another movement that tends to add to the complications, and will have the effect of further distracting the South. I suppose he will take off Texas [from the regular Democratic vote], and thus weaken us, to that extent, even if we shall harmonize at Baltimore on a ticket."[24] That Houston's present role in the campaign posed difficulties was irrefutable. There was a rally in New York on May 20, attended by a large crowd—attracted, perhaps, by the promise of fireworks, music, and a throng of well-known speakers. The *Herald* recorded the resounding approval of a resolution describing Houston as a figure who "has a hold upon the sympathies and confidence of the people possessed by no other living statesman."[25] This presumably included Abraham Lincoln, just nominated by the Republicans at Chicago.

Having contemplated political suicide at Charleston a few weeks earlier, the Democrats committed it at Baltimore in June. The Northern faction settled on Douglas and Herschel V. Johnson. Shortly after at Richmond the Southern Democrats selected John C. Breckinridge of Kentucky and Joseph Lane. The rupture of the Democratic Party brought little joy to Texas. There was not much organized enthusiasm for any of the national candidates, not even Sam Houston. A friend wrote him: "[W]e did all we could for you. . . . You are good for our own state and I believe for the entire South, but how will it be in the North? Can any good come out of Nazareth?"[26]

By the end of June the choices to be placed before the electorate had been determined. With the largest number of candidates since the election of 1824, it seemed to some that the election might again have to be settled in the House of Representatives.[27] From the balcony of Kelly House, a Houston City hotel, Houston gave a talk in mid-July in which he failed to refer to his own candidacy, though he defended his record, saying that the Kansas-Nebraska vote was the best of his career.[28] It seemed that he thought he could win the national election as he had won the Texan governorship, without campaigning. Or had he finally acknowledged to himself that he had no chance? The single intimation of his private feelings is to be found in a letter of the twenty-fourth to Ashbel Smith: "I am with politics as Falstaff was with strong Potations. I will let the world wag, and if it does well, & suits others, it will suit me! I am as easy as an old shoe, and have come to the sage conclusion . . . that if the people can do without my services, I am sure I can do without their suffrages. So you see I still retain a share of common sense!"[29]

He had nothing to lose by remaining in contention; for Texas, like much of the South, was in a condition of political perplexity. The only certainty was opposition to Douglas and, above all, to Lincoln. Because of her pregnancy and her general outlook, Margaret Houston had not expressed much interest in her husband's political adventures. On August 12 their eighth and last child, Temple Lea Houston, was born at Austin.[30] If the governor rejoiced, he concealed his rapture. In a letter from the state capital two days after Temple's birth, he elaborately outlined his views of the four other men who sought the Presidency and found them all wanting.[31] This document must be read as a request to support the Houston candidacy. Yet only four days later, the governor published a statement asking that his name be withdrawn from consideration as a candidate and that it not appear on the November ballot.[32]

This decision was reached on a day when a group of important Southern politicians were meeting at Galveston to discuss the retirement of Bell from the campaign in favor of a fusion with Douglas and Houston.[33] How this could have been successful, given the unacceptibility of Douglas in the South and that of Houston to many Northern Democrats, is difficult to imagine. But it is ironic that Houston was now thought the stronger candidate. Had he known of this gathering in advance, he might have remained in the race and perhaps attained his goal. The primary object of the Galveston conference was to devise a strategy to stop Lincoln. Of all those seeking the Presidency, Houston could have given the hated Republican the most serious challenge in a two-man race.

Why Houston chose this day for his withdrawal, we do not know. A clue may exist in a letter to a friend of August 27, in which he noted that since the birth of Temple, Margaret had been more seriously ailing than usual. As a result, he had been unable to undress for sleep during the previous ten days, "so you may think that I have had a protectorate at home to claim my attention."[34] He had written that his

301

bowing out of the campaign was intended to help restore harmony to the Union.[35] Yet his earlier writing suggests that he did not believe harmony could be restored at this point.

By early September he was worried about more than secession. He wrote a denunciation of the policy of some Southern states to gather arms and ammunition in preparation for war; as an alternative, he proposed constitutional remedies and announced that he had had his name removed from the ballot "in support of a Union ticket of all parties to defeat Lincoln."[36] The issue, which had many ramifications, was that of states' rights. Less than three weeks later, on September 22, he addressed a mass meeting at Austin which took place against the backdrop of the total demise of the national Democrats and the certain election of Lincoln. Yet Houston asserted that all talk of secession was treasonous, even if Lincoln became President: "the Union is worth more than Mr. Lincoln, and if the battle is to be fought for the Constitution, let us fight it in the Union and for the sake of the Union."[37]

So predictable was the election's outcome that South Carolina's Governor William Gist kept his legislators in session so that when Lincoln's success was officially announced, his state might have the honor of being the first to secede. On October 5, while Houston was still speaking for harmony, Gist sent a letter describing his plan to all his Southern counterparts except the governor of Texas.[38] Until the end of October, Houston was on the trail of every possible vote to save the Union. His proclamation to the people of October 27 summarized the line he had been taking:

> Providence has ever guarded the people of these United States. He has sustained the hope of our struggling fathers until they gained the liberty that we now enjoy. He gave them the wisdom and the prudence through which our government was formed. For Eighty four [sic] years the Same Providence has shielded us, and amid danger from without and dissention from within, He has encircled us with His protecting Arm and has preserved our liberties intact. Let us in the hour of Prayer . . . implore Him to shield us still in the time of peril, that we may be preserved a United people, free, independent, and prosperous.[39]

It is not clear which of the candidates Houston urged his followers to support—given his plague-on-all-their-houses letter of a few months before. All we know is that they were strictly enjoined against voting for Lincoln. Certainly, there was hysteria in Texas. Arson was reported in several towns and was ascribed to infiltrating Abolitionists—though how many were in the state that autumn is problematical. Fear that slave insurrections would proliferate in the wake of the Lincoln election was common gossip-fodder, even though there had been no significant uprising of blacks in the South since Nat Turner. The Knights of the Golden Circle declared themselves in favor of secession. Their wizard, George Bickley, spoke at Austin to proclaim that the objective of the order was to foster and protect slavery against all its enemies.[40]

For all the fury of the rhetoric that flourished in the final weeks before the election, it was quiet on election day in Texas. Not a single voter, if the figures are to be credited, cast his ballot for Lincoln. Only 410 supported Douglas; 15,463 opted for Bell, and Breckinridge was accorded a handsome majority of 47,548. In a letter of November 7 to his eldest son, Sam Houston commented on the Texan election result: "The fire eaters got their chunk put out. The price of liberty is blood, and if an attempt is made to destroy our Union, or violate our Constitution, there will be blood shed to maintain them. The Demons of anarchy must be put down and destroyed. The miserable Demagogues & Traitors of the land . . . must be silenced . . . and set at naught."[41]

According to William Seale, the governor and his wife were together at Austin when the final election returns were announced. Secessionists were not long in seeking to exploit Southern dismay over Lincoln's victory. Almost at once the Knights of the Golden Circle offered to set upon Mexico. Houston's private reaction to this idea may well have been mixed, for though a filibuster might distract Texans from the implications of the recent poll, he was still an advocate of constitutional procedures. He called for calm. But secessionists hoisted the Lone Star banner of the old republic over several county courthouses. The atmosphere in Texas was very tense.[42]

By November 10, only four days after the election, Houston was importuned to convene a special session of the legislature to permit Texas to join her sister states in seceding. He resisted with every legalistic and constitutional device at his command.[43] There were Texans who opposed a hasty decision, but their numbers dwindled in the hurricane that ensued. The secessionist attitude was squarely put in a post-election editorial in the Navarro *Express:* "The North has gone overwhelmingly for *Negro Equality* and Southern Vassalage! Southern men, will you submit to the degradation?" The pressures on Houston to summon the legislature and to convene a constituent assembly were enormous; he continued to turn them aside. On November 20 he announced that Lincoln's election had been totally constitutional and that Texans must accept it. If, however, after the new President's inauguration, he were in some way to violate his oath, revolt might be an appropriate action; but for the time being, the state was safer remaining part of the Union.[44] That day, Ashbel Smith arrived from Galveston bearing a petition asking the governor to bring the legislature to Austin. With regret, he turned his dear friend away.

There were some reports (which persisted well into 1861) that Abraham Lincoln, anxious to prevent secession, was considering an invitation to Houston to become Secretary of War.[45] There is no evidence that such an offer was ever made. Had it been, Houston would probably have turned it down. He was a Texan and would follow the fate of Texas. Moreover, Lincoln was his bane. Yet he continued to refuse to call the legislature. At the end of November it was believed that if the Congress of Texas were assembled and did vote to secede, Houston would resign in favor of Lieutenant Governor Edward Clark.[46] There is no substantiation for this suggestion. To the contrary, on November 28, he sent each Southern governor a copy of a statute passed in 1858 by the Texan legislature calling for a consultative assembly of the South to resolve the differences that separated them from the North.[47] This delaying tactic also failed.

In early December a petition was circulated throughout the state demanding a special election to name delegates to a secessionist convention to meet at Austin January 28, 1861. Since he recognized that this effort would prove successful, Houston decided to convene the legislature on January 21. He was at Galveston on December 8. A reporter found him "whittling pine keepsakes." The governor "had found Texas in a very bad condition a number of times, out of which he had gotten her, but . . . she was old enough now to take care of herself, and if she was bent on her own destruction by secession, he would not go with her . . . but thanked the Lord he could resign any time he thought proper."[48]

As soon as he issued the call for a special session of the legislature, the editors of the *State Gazette* published an extra edition in which extracts were printed from the governor's speech to a crowd gathered outside his official residence. One line ascribed to him was that he would "teach the people that he would have his own way; that the people would have to follow him for a while." When he saw this statement in print, Houston is supposed to have said to a friend, "The scoundrels! They would contaminate Christ's sermon on the mount if they could!"[49]

On December 20 South Carolina seceded, to be followed in fairly rapid order by Mississippi, Florida, Alabama, and Louisiana. When Governor Iverson of Georgia learned that Sam Houston would oppose Texas' following suit, he suggested that the man be assassinated.[50] However Houston personally regarded the issue, he could not overlook the need to send representatives to the inauguration of the Southern states' president. On December 27 he ordered their election, dividing Texan election districts up in a fashion that he hoped might produce two or three delegates of a unionist persuasion.[51] This effort, too, was in vain. Too much was at stake emotionally, economically, and politically. The state he had helped to shape was no longer recognizable to him. Even its population was boggling to a man who had known Texas when there were barely 20,000 whites within her ill-delin ated boundaries. The census figures now showed almost 431,000 whites and 182,000 slaves. The investment in blacks alone dictated Texan adherence to the new cause.

Early in the new year Ashbel Smith came to Austin again, hoping to convince his friend of the need to concur with the secessionist movement. On New Year's Day, at Waco, Houston had already stated his willingness to bow to the will of the people in the matter. However, if Texas did secede, he hoped she would not join the Confederacy, but would again become the "Republic of the Lone Star" which she had been from 1836 to 1845. This address had not proved wholly acceptable to his listeners. According to one witness they offered three cheers for South Carolina and none for Sam Houston and his renewed republic.[52] Nor could the governor find any solace in the Texan press, which was almost unanimously for secession.[53]

In a letter to Alabamian J.M. Calhoun, who had come to Texas to drum up support for secession, Houston stated how he might yet prevent his state from joining the Confederacy, whether or not she seceded from the Union. He would march Texan troops into Mexico, thus precluding their participation in the civil war that must necessarily follow the destruction of the Union:

It will be but natural that [Texans], feeling that they must look to themselves . . . will prefer a separate nationality . . . to even an equal position in a Confederacy, which may be broken and destroyed at any moment . . . by the caprice or dissatisfaction of one of its members. Texas has views of expansion not common to many of her sister states. Although an empire within herself, she feels that there is an empire beyond, essential to her security. She will not be content to have the path to her destiny clogged. The same spirit of enterprise that founded a Republic here . . . will carry her institutions Southward and Westward.[54]

Whether or not Houston believed sincerely in his alternative cannot be determined. The thought of a French occupation of Mexico was repugnant to him; he hoped he could attract his people to a policy of preventing its success. But only *his* eye seemed now to be on that sparrow.

The Texan legislature convened January 21. Houston's message was a plea for cool deliberation. He begged the members to consider the state's unique situation, with her long Mexican border. This made her vulnerable to foreign interlopers who might attack and try to reconquer Texas if secession took place. "The Executive has not yet lost hope that our rights can be maintained in the Union, and that it may yet be perpetuated. Between constitutional remedies and anarchy and civil war he can see no middle ground." There was none.[55]

In one of her rare references to her husband's official activities, Margaret wrote that day to her mother at Independence: "Truly the present appearance of things is gloomy enough. . . . General Houston seems cheerful and hopeful through the day, but in the still watches of the night I hear him agonizing in prayer over our distracted country. . . . I cannot shut my eyes to the dangers that threaten us. I know that it is even probable that we may be soon rendered to poverty, but oh, I have such a sweet assurance in my heart that the presence of the Lord will go with us wherever we may go."[56]

The first act of the legislature was to reject Houston's ruling that the recent election of delegates to the state secession convention had been illegally arranged. A resolution was passed authorizing the gathering to meet at Austin January 28 to prepare a document to be submitted for popular approval. Because he had made his view of secession so clear, the reception offered Houston by members of the convention was hostile.[37] On the second day, delegates drafted a referendum to the effect that Texas should secede. It was to be placed before the voters on February 23. If approved, it would take effect March 2, to coincide with the twenty-fifth anniversary of the declaration of Texan independence—Sam Houston's sixty-eighth birthday.[38] The vote for this resolution was 166 to 8. On February 4 Houston reluctantly approved the convention's acts.

On February 18, with a delegation of seven Texans on hand, Mississipian Jefferson Davis was inaugurated President of the Confederacy at Montgomery, Alabama—little more than a fortnight before Lincoln took his oath in Washington. Houston campaigned relentlessly against popular approval of the secession referendum. Never had his opinions been less acceptable to Texans. Yet, though his health and morale were poor, and though the Houstons' personal future appeared bleak, he maintained an attitude of calm and common sense in all his public appearances, seeming not to be ruffled by the antagonism of the crowds he addressed.

Well-intentioned friends had allowed a rumor to circulate that privately the governor supported secession. On February 20 the *Southern Intelligencer* reprinted a portion of a letter from Houston to its editor, George Paschal, that could not have been more lucid:

> You say that I am for secession. Ask those who say so to point to a single word of mine authorizing that statement. I have declared myself in favor of peace, of harmony, of compromise, in order to obtain a fair expression of the will of the people. . . . I am determined that those who would overthrow the law shall not learn the lesson from me.
>
> I still believe that secession will bring ruin and civil war. Yet, if the people will it, I can bear it with them. I would fain not be declared an alien in my native home in old Virginia, and to the scenes of my early toil and triumph in noble Tennessee. I would not of my own choice give up the banner beneath which I have fought, the Constitution which I have revered, or the Union which I have cherished as the glorious heritage bequeathed to me by my fathers. Sixty-seven years of freedom, the recollection of past triumph, and past suffering, the memories of heroes whom I have seen and known, and whose venerated shades would haunt my footsteps were I to falter now, may, perhaps, have made me

too devoted to the Constitution and the Union, but be it so. Did I believe that liberty and the rights of the South demanded the sacrifice, I would not hesitate. I believe that far less concession than was made to form the Constitution would now preserve it. Thus believing I cannot vote for secession.

I have hesitated to say anything on this topic, because I desire the people to act for themselves. My views are of record. Yet, it is, perhaps, but right that my old friends should know that the charge that I am for secession is false. If I err . . . my countrymen will forgive me, as they have forgiven me for many other things I have done. I am willing, even, to be called a submissionist. . . .[59]

Only one statement in this letter is untrue—that he had hesitated to speak of his opposition to secession. For the past three months he had done almost nothing else.

On February 23 secession carried the day. The vote was small, given the vitality of the issue—46,129 to 14,697. The convention met again at Austin on March 2.[60] On the fourth, as Lincoln became President of the United States, Sam Houston announced officially that his state had seceded from that Union. What he refused to proclaim, however, was that secession meant joining the Confederacy.[61] The members of the convention were enraged by this ploy. By a vote of 109 to 2, they declared the governor in error. Houston refused to accept their authority to make such a judgment. He pointed out that there had not been a word in the referendum submitted to the electorate to suggest affiliation with the Confederacy. It was a quibble, and he knew it, but in this way he set the stage for his final act of defiance.

There was no way to keep Texas out of the Confederacy. However, on March 13, Houston composed a long letter to LeRoy Pope, Confederate secretary of war, observing that Texas was too proud to be "annexed to a new government without the state's knowledge and consent."[62] Then, on March 14, the Texan convention made their move. The members adopted a resolution to continue in office the entire present state administration with the proviso that each man must take an oath of allegiance to the Confederacy.[63] The next day, George W. Chilton was delegated to inform the governor that he had until noon of the sixteenth to comply.[64] He delivered this message on the evening of the fifteenth. Nannie Houston, who was about fifteen at this time, recounted the hours that followed Chilton's departure:

The family had their usual dinner and when the negro servants had removed the food and soiled dishes, Mrs. Houston brought the family Bible and placed it before the General at the head of the table. The negroes brought in their rawhide bottom chairs from the kitchen and the servants quarters and arranged themselves along the back wall of the dining room. The General then read a chapter from the Bible, made appropriate remarks, and they all knelt in family prayers as was the usual custom. . . .

After bidding his family goodnight the General left positive instructions with Mrs. Houston that he must not be disturbed under any circumstances and that no visitors were to be admitted to the mansion. He then went to his bedroom on the upper floor, removed his vest and shoes and remained alone throughout the night during which he did not sleep. Instead he walked the floor of his bedroom and the upper floor in his sock feet, wrestling with his spirit as Jacob wrestled with the angel until the purple dawn of another day shone over the eastern hills. He had come through his Gethsemane, and the die was cast.

When he came down and met Mrs. Houston, he said, "Margaret, I will never do it." That meant that he would not take the oath of allegiance and had reconciled himself to be deposed to go into political exile rather than violate his conscience or sacrifice his principles.[65]

There remained only the ultimate confrontation. Houston had forced the issue. Late in the morning of March 16 he appeared at the capitol, where other public officials were eagerly assenting to the required vow. Only one other man refused: E.W. Cave, secretary of state. The Reverend William Baker, a Presbyterian opposed to secession, left an account of this critical hour in Houston's life. The governor awaited the summons from the convention to take the oath; he was seated in the basement of the capitol building. "The officer of the gathering upstairs summoned the old man three times to come forward . . . [B]ut he sat silent, immovable, in his chair below, whittling steadily."[66] He was deposed, but he did not remain silent for long. On the day of his expulsion, he published a strong denunciation of the convention's act, declaring it invalid:

I PROTEST IN THE NAME OF THE PEOPLE OF TEXAS AGAINST ALL THE ACTS AND DOINGS OF THIS CONVENTION, AND I DECLARE THEM NULL AND VOID! I solemnly protest against the act of its members who are bound by no oath themselves, in declaring my office vacant, because I refused to appear before it and take the oath prescribed.

It has accomplished its mission, and its chief object has been fulfilled. If to drive me from office and to defeat the will of the people . . . is an honor, it may wear it. To prevent my having an opportunity to send a message to the Legislature, which meets on Monday, March 18th, I am required to appear at its bar today and take the TEST OATH. Even Shylock granted the full three days ere he claimed his three pounds [*sic*] of flesh. The Convention prescribed that time as the limit, but the President has been less gracious than even Shylock, and clamors for the bond ere two days are gone. If I am thus deprived of the poor privilege of putting upon record my sentiments, through a refusal of the Legislature to receive my message, I will lay the same before the people, and appeal to them, as I declared I would do in my inaugural.[67]

Lieutenant Governor Edward Clark was named Houston's successor, taking the required oaths March 18. The defrocked governor submitted a message to the legislature in which he decried the convention's usurpation of the Congressional right in declaring his office vacant and claimed that constitutionally he was still governor. However precise his reasoning, his words were unheeded. On the nineteenth, while the Houstons and friends were beginning to pack the family belongings, a group of armed citizens appeared outside the mansion. Their intention was to prevent his expulsion from office. Houston's reaction, as recorded much later by a witness, was as forceful as his denunciation of the men who had voted to expel him:

My God, is it possible that all the people are gone mad? Is it possible that my friends should be willing to inaugurate a war that would be infinitely more horrible than the one inaugurated by the secessionists? Do you know, my friends, that the civil war now being inaugurated will be as horrible as his Satanic Majesty could desire? And after condemning them for their folly and their crimes, would you be willing to deluge the capital of Texas with the blood of Texans, merely to keep one poor old man in a position for a few days longer? No. No! Go tell my deluded friends that I am proud of their friendship, of their love and loyalty, and I hope I may retain them to the end. But say to them that for the sake of humanity and justice to disperse, to go to their homes and to conceal from the world that they would have been guilty of such an act.[68]

The Houstons remained at Austin until about March 30. Then they began moving slowly south. Though there had been threats against his life, the ex-governor made several speeches in which he restated his well-known position, calling the impending war "the fearful harvest of conspiracy and revolution."[69] Yet, just before quitting the capital, he had told an officer of the United States Army that he had no desire to be reinstated in office and maintained there with the protection of federal troops.[70] He spoke at Brenham on March 31, at Galveston April 19, and at Independence May 10. By then the Civil War had begun.

Though he feared it and had done his best to prevent it, he was a Texan and would support the Southern cause: "A good citizen, who has been obedient to law and civil authority, always makes a good soldier. I have ever been a conservative; I remained conservative as long as the Union lasted; I am now a conservative citizen of the Southern Confederacy, and giving to the constituted authorities, civil and military, and to the Government which a majority of the people have approved and acquiesced in, an honest obedience, I feel I should do less than my duty did I not press upon others the importance of regarding this the first duty of a good citizen."[71]

EPILOGUE

WHEN HE reached Independence in May, 1861, Sam Houston had a little more than two years to live. He passed this time quietly. His eldest son enlisted against his father's advice—but to his pride as well as to his distress—and was badly wounded at Shiloh. The tranquility of life for which he had so often expressed a desire proved not wholly satisfying. Had he ever really wanted it, of course, he would have chosen it before it was so rudely thrust upon him.

There were some financial difficulties. In order to pay war taxes Houston sold much of the timber off his Cedar Point land. He had never accumulated savings. On his death, his estate was valued at $89,000, most of it in real property. In December of 1862 the Houstons acquired a new house at Huntsville. The old man grew increasingly feeble, so he lived on the ground floor to avoid the need of climbing stairs.[1] After returning for a time to study at Baylor, young Sam rejoined the army. He was sent on a mission to Mexico with his uncle, Charles Power.

On the day after his seventieth birthday, Houston wrote E.W. Cave, now a Confederate officer, that though he could not help thinking about politics, he had no intention of involving himself again.[2] There were many who did not believe him. He made a gentle speech at Houston City in mid-March, and returned to Huntsville where Margaret immediately put him to bed with a fever. On April 2 he drew up and signed a will in which he duly listed all liabilities and assets and, after bequeathing his earthly goods appropriately, expressed the wish that his sons "be early taught an utter contempt for novels and light reading."[3] To his daughter Nannie, a fortnight later, he sent a warning to avoid the appearance of love scrapes, for he had heard that the girl was writing letters to Confederate soldiers.[4] In June he went to Sour Lake, where it was hoped the salt springs would alleviate the pain occasioned by his old war wounds.[5] Margaret wrote him from Huntsville that she hoped God would spare him; she was gratified to have received word that his health was improving.[6] When he passed through Houston City on his way home later in the month, a reporter was pleased that his appearance was so good.[7]

As July began, all the Houstons except young Sam were together at Huntsville. On the seventh word came of Grant's victory at Vicksburg. Though Houston was not surprised, having predicted the defeat of the South in the war, the news depressed him. His condition declined so markedly that Margaret wrote Ashbel Smith, caring for the wounded at Galveston, that she now feared for her husband's life. Two local physicians agreed on a diagnosis of pneumonia.[8] Smith came a few days later, remaining only long enough to confirm the other doctors' opinion and to tell Margaret that there was nothing to be done. She spent every waking hour at the invalid's side, reading to him suitable passages from Holy Writ during his fitful periods of consciousness. On Sunday evening, July 26, 1863, Sam Houston died in his sleep.

E.H. Cushing, editor of the *Telegraph*, who had opposed Houston on most major policies for years, did the decent thing in the paper's edition of July 29. His obituary notice was mercifully wanting in false sentimentality. Among other things he wrote, "He has not always been right, nor has he always been successful, but he has always kept the impress of his mind upon the times in which he acted."[9]

NOTES

CHAPTER I

1. George Wilson Pierson, *Tocqueville and Beaumont in America*, 607–615. Marquis James, *The Raven*, 3–8. James, *op. cit.*, 9–10. James, *op. cit.*, 11–12. Llerena Friend, *Sam Houston: The Great Designer*, 5.
2. C. Edwards Lester, *The Life of Sam Houston . . .*, 18.
3. James, *op. cit.*, 14–15.
4. James, *op. cit.*, 24–25.
5. Friend, *op. cit.*, 6.
6. Lester, *op. cit.*, 21–22.
7. John Reynolds, *My Own Times . . .*, 119.

CHAPTER II

1. James, *op. cit.*, 19.
2. Blount County (Tennessee) Records, Maryville.
3. James, *op. cit.*, 20.
4. Lester, *op. cit.*, 23.
5. James, *op. cit.*, 21–22. Friend, *op. cit.*, 6.
6. James, *op. cit.*, 26–27.
7. Josephus Conn Guild, *Old Times in Tennessee . . .*, 290. Marquis James, *The Life of Andrew Jackson.*
8. Friend, *op. cit.*, 6. Lester, *op. cit.*, 21–22.

9. James, *The Raven*, 29. Thomas H. S. Hamersly, *Army Register*, 521.
10. James, *op. cit.*, 29–30.
11. Lester, *op. cit.*, 27.

CHAPTER III

1. James, *op. cit.*, 31.
2. James, *The Life of Andrew Jackson*, II, 16.
3. James, *The Raven*, 31–32.
4. Friend, *op. cit.*, 7. James, *op. cit.*, 32.
5. Lester, *op. cit.*
6. James, *op. cit.*, 32–35.
7. James, *op. cit.*, 36.
8. Lester, *op. cit.*
9. Amelia W. Williams and Eugene C. Barker, editors, *The Writings of Sam Houston*, I, 1. [Hereafter listed as *Writings*.]
10. *Writings*, I, 4.
11. James, *op. cit.*, 37. Friend, *op. cit.*, 7.
12. *Writings*, I, 6.
13. Guild, *op. cit.*, 262.
14. Friend, *op. cit.*, 7.
15. John Spencer Bassett, Editor, *The Correspondence of Andrew Jackson*, II, 296.
16. James, *op. cit.*, 39–40.
17. Friend, *op. cit.*, 7.
18. Friend, *op. cit.*, 8. Jack Gregory and Rennard Strickland, *Sam Houston with the Cherokees*, 17–18. John P. Brown, *Old*

Frontiers: The Story of the Cherokee Indians from Earliest Times to the Date of Their Removal to the West, 1838, Kingsport, Tennessee, 1938, 463–477. Emmett Starr, *Cherokee "West" 1794–1839,* Claremore, Oklahoma, 1910, 9–22. ———, *An Early History of the Cherokees,* Kansas City, 1916, 114–179. Charles Keppler, Editor, *Indian Affairs, Laws and Treaties,* Washington, 1903, 140 *et seq.* Cherokee Nation, *Laws of the Cherokee Nation Adopted by the Council at Various Times,* Tahlequah, Cherokee Nation, 1852, 41–50.

19. Gregory and Strickland, *op. cit.,* 18. Keppler, *loc. cit.* Cherokee Nation, *loc. cit.*

20. Gregory and Strickland, *op. cit.,* 18.

CHAPTER IV

1. James, *op. cit.,* 43 *et seq.*
2. Brown, *op. cit.,* 476–477. Charles C. Royce, "The Cherokee Nation of Indians," *Fifth Annual Report,* Smithsonian Institution, Bureau of American Ethnology, Washington, 1887, 209–223. Grant Foreman, *Indian Removal: The Emigration of the Five Civilized Tribes of Indians,* Norman, Oklahoma, 1936, 229–312. Gregory and Strickland, *op. cit.,* 19.
3. Friend, *op. cit.,* 8.
4. James, *op. cit.,* 45.
5. Gregory and Strickland, *op. cit.,* 18–19.
6. *Writings,* I, 8.
7. Gregory and Strickland, *op. cit.,* 144.
8. James, *op. cit.,* 47.
9. Friend, *op. cit.,* 8.
10. N.M. Ludlow, *Dramatic Life as I Found It . . .,* 166.
11. Friend, *op. cit.,* 8–9. Lester, *op. cit.,* 42 *et seq.*
12. Gregory and Strickland, *op. cit.,* 106.
13. James, *op. cit.,* 48–49.
14. Friend, *op. cit.,* 9.
15. Alexander Hynds, "General Sam Houston," 494–506.

16. Gregory and Strickland, *op. cit.,* 106.
17. Friend, *op. cit.,* 9.
18. Gregory and Strickland, 146.
19. *Writings,* I, 13.
20. *Writings,* I, 14.
21. *Ibid.,* I, 16.

CHAPTER V

1. *Writings,* I, 19.
2. *Ibid.,* I, 22.
3. *Ibid.,* V, 1.
4. *Ibid.,* I, 24.
5. *Ibid.,* II, 9.
6. George Ticknor Curtis, *Life of James Buchanan,* I, 514. Friend, *op. cit.,* 11.
7. *Writings,* V, 2.
8. *Ibid.,* VIII, 1.
9. Friend, *op. cit.,* 13.
10. *Writings,* I, 28.
11. *Ibid.,* I, 37.
12. *Ibid.,* I, 61.
13. James, *op. cit.,* 56.
14. Friend, *op. cit.,* 15.
15. *Writings,* IV, 4.
16. Joseph Howard Parks, *Felix Grundy, Champion of Democracy,* 166–73. Friend, *op. cit.,* 14.
17. *Writings,* IV, 5.
18. *Ibid.,* IV, 8.
19. Bassett, *op. cit.,* VI, 485–486.
20. Friend, *op. cit.,* 15.
21. *Writings,* I, 65.
22. *Ibid.,* I, 71.
23. James, *op. cit.,* 58–59.
24. *Writings,* VII, 1.
25. *Ibid.,* I, 112.
26. James, *op. cit.,* 67–69.
27. Friend, *op. cit.,* 14.
28. *Writings,* IV, 9.
29. *Ibid.,* I, 115.
30. *Ibid.,* I, 121.
31. Friend, *op. cit.,* 17.
32. Friend, *op. cit.,* 18.
33. James, *op. cit.,* II, 154.
34. *Ibid.,* II, 163.

CHAPTER VI

1. A. W. Terrell, "Recollections of General Sam Houston," 113–136. Gregory and Strickland, *op. cit.,* 4.
2. James, *The Raven,* 73.
3. *Writings,* II, 10.
4. James, *op. cit.,* 74.
5. *Ibid.,* 72.
6. Friend, *op. cit.,* 19.
7. James, *op. cit.,* 75.
8. *Ibid.,* 138, 443.
9. Friend, *op. cit.,* 271.
10. James, *op. cit.,* 139.
11. Gregory and Strickland, *op. cit.,* 5.
12. Friend, *op. cit.,* 22–23.
13. *Writings,* I, 130.
14. Lester, *op. cit.*
15. Friend, *op. cit.,* 22.
16. James, *op. cit.,* 139.
17. Gregory and Strickland, *op. cit.,* 5.
18. *Writings,* I, 131.
19. Bassett, *op. cit.,* IV, 23. Friend, *op. cit.,* 21. Gregory and Strickland, *op. cit.,* 157.
20. *Niles' Register,* XXXVI (May 5, 1829). James F. Perry Papers. Henry A. Wise, *Seven Decades of the Union: The Humanities and Materialism,* Philadelphia, 1872, 148.
21. Friend, *op. cit.,* 22.
22. Lester, *op. cit.*

CHAPTER VII

1. James, *op. cit.,* 79. Friend, *op. cit.,* 23.
2. Lester, *op. cit.,* 49.
3. Gregory and Strickland, *op. cit.,* 5–6.
4. *Ibid.,* 72–73. *Ibid.,* 157.
5. Bassett, *op. cit.,* IV, 21. Friend, *op. cit.,* 24.
6. *Writings,* I, 132.
7. Gregory and Strickland, *op. cit.,* 7.
8. Lester, *op. cit.,* 50.
9. Gregory and Strickland, *op. cit.,* 9–10. Lester, *op. cit.,* 51.
11. Gregory and Strickland, *op. cit.,* 142.

12. James, *op. cit.,* 83.
13. Lester, *op. cit.,* 52. *Ibid.,* 53–63.
14. Gregory and Strickland, *op. cit.,* 15–17.
15. *Ibid.,* 70.
16. *Ibid.,* 61–62. Terrell, *op. cit.*
17. Gregory and Strickland, *op. cit.,* 29. Owen P. White, *Texas: An Informal Biography,* New York, 1945, 70. Gregory and Strickland, *op. cit.,* 146. *Ibid.,* 143.
18. Henderson Yoakum, *History of Texas . . . ,* I, 307. Friend, *op. cit.,* 50.
19. *Writings,* I, 134.
20. Gregory and Strickland, *op. cit.,* 39–40.
21. Yoakum, *op. cit.,* I, 281.
22. James, *op. cit.,* 177.
23. *Writings,* I, 139–140.

CHAPTER VIII

1. Yoakum, *op. cit.,* I, 281.
2. James, *op. cit.,* 126–127.
3. Grant Foreman, *Indians and Pioneers . . . ,* 284. Friend, *op. cit.,* 26.
4. *Writings,* I, 143.
5. James, *op. cit.,* 129.
6. *Writings,* I, 144.
7. Gregory and Strickland, *op. cit.,* 158.
8. Alfred M. Williams, *Sam Houston and the War of Independence in Texas,* 403. Gregory and Strickland, *op. cit.,* 30–31. *Ibid.,* 97–98.
9. *Writings,* I, 146.
10. Friend, *op. cit.,* 52.
11. *Writings,* I, 147.
12. *Ibid.,* I, 149 footnote.
13. James, *op. cit.,* 133.
14. Guild, *op. cit.,* 270–272. James, *op. cit.,* 141.
15. *Writings,* I, 149.
16. *Ibid.,* I, 151.
17. Gregory and Strickland, *op. cit.,* 107–108.
18. *Writings,* I, 152.
19. *Ibid.,* I, 155.
20. *Ibid.,* V, 4.
21. *Ibid.,* I, 157.
22. *Ibid.,* I, 177.

23. Gregory and Strickland, *op. cit.*, 46 *et seq.*
24. *Ibid.*, 37–39. *Ibid.*, 44–45.
25. *Ibid.*, 34 *et seq.*

CHAPTER IX

1. Foreman, *op. cit.*, 285–286. Friend, *op. cit.*, 29.
2. Gregory and Strickland, *op. cit.*, 28. *Ibid.*, 102.
3. Papers of Matthew Maury, Alderman Library, University of Virginia, Charlottesville. Friend, *op. cit.*, 29.
4. *Writings*, I, 196. *Ibid.*, 195.
5. Friend, *op. cit.*, 30.
6. *Ibid.*, 4.
7. Gregory and Strickland, *op. cit.*, 101–102.
8. *Writings*, I, 199.
9. James, *op. cit.*, 163–164.
10. *Writings*, I, 202.
11. James, *op. cit.*, 167. Charles H. Ambler, Editor, *The Life and Diary of John Floyd*, Richmond, 1918, 181.
12. Friend, *op. cit.*, 31–32.
13. *Writings*, I, 203.
14. *Ibid.*, I, 207.
15. James, *op. cit.*, 172.
16. *Writings*, I, 230.
17. Gregory and Strickland, *op. cit.*, 129.
18. *Writings*, I, 260.
19. *Ibid.*, I, 263.
20. James, *op. cit.*, 183.
21. Gregory and Strickland, *op. cit.*, 163.
22. *Ibid.*, 48.
23. *Ibid.*, 81.

CHAPTER X

1. *Writings*, I, 267.
2. *Ibid.*, VI, 1.
3. *Ibid.*, I, 271.
4. Friend, *op. cit.*, 56.
5. Lester, *op. cit.*, 65.
6. *Writings*, V, 34.

7. *Ibid.*, I, 274.
8. Friend, *op. cit.*, 57.
9. James, *op. cit.*, 199–201.
10. *Ibid.*, 202.
11. Friend, *op. cit.*, 54.
12. Lester, *op. cit.*
13. Friend, *op. cit.*, 59–60.
14. Emmett Starr, *History of the Cherokee Indians*, Oklahoma City, 1921, 187 –224. Gregory and Strickland, *op. cit.*, 152. Varina Howell Davis, *Jefferson Davis* . . . , 156–157. Friend, *op. cit.*, 60.
15. *Writings*, I, 289.
16. *Ibid.*, I, 290. James, *op. cit.*, 207.
17. G. W. Featherstonhaugh, *Excursion through the Slave States* . . . , II, 161.
18. Friend, *op. cit.*, 60–61.

CHAPTER XI

1. Friend, *op. cit.*, 61.
2. Eugene C. Barker, Editor, *The Austin Papers*, II, 1075.
3. *Ibid.*, 1007.
4. *Writings*, I, 294.
5. Friend, *op. cit.*, 61–62.
6. *Writings*, I, 298.
7. *Ibid.*, 302.
8. *Ibid.*, 303.
9. Friend, *op. cit.*, 65.
10. *Ibid.*, 63.
11. *Telegraph and Texas Register*, November 7, 1835.
12. James, *op. cit.*, 214–215.
13. Barker, *op. cit.*, III, 238.
14. C. A. Gulick, and others, Editors, *The Papers of Mirabeau Buonaparte Lamar*, VI, 173. Friend, *op. cit.*, 63.
15. James, *op. cit.*, 216–217.
16. *Writings*, I, 307.
17. Friend, *op. cit.*, 65.
18. Ashbel Smith Papers. Friend, *op. cit.*, 109.
19. James, *op. cit.*, 218–219.
20. *Writings*, I, 315.
21. Friend, *op. cit.*, 65.

CHAPTER XII

1. *Writings*, I, 334–335.
2. *Ibid.*, I, 337.
3. *Ibid.*, I, 339.
4. *Ibid.*, I, 340.
5. *Ibid.*, I, 344.
6. Barker, *op. cit.*, III, 298–299. Friend, *op. cit.*, 65–66.
7. James, *op. cit.*, 282.
8. *Writings*, I, 355–360.
9. Friend, *op. cit.*, 66–67. William Fairfax Gray, *From Virginia to Texas, 1835...*, 121.
10. *Writings*, 360.
11. James, *op. cit.*, 279.
12. James, *op. cit.*, 228.
13. Friend, *op. cit.*, 68.
14. *Writings*, IV, 17.
15. *Ibid.*, I, 367.
16. *Ibid.*, I, 373.
17. *Ibid.*, I, 377.
18. James, *op. cit.*, 233–234.
19. *Writings*, II, 23.
20. *Ibid.*, IV, 21.
21. *Ibid.*, I, 380.
22. James, *op. cit.*, 235 *et seq.*
23. *Writings*, I, 384.
24. *Ibid.*, I, 388.
25. *Ibid.*, I, 389.
26. *Ibid.*, I, 390.
27. *Ibid.*, I, 399.
28. James, *op. cit.*, 241.
29. *Writings*, I, 412 footnote.
30. Friend, *op. cit.*, 69.
31. James, *op. cit.*, 242–243.

CHAPTER XIII

1. *Writings*, 419.
2. *Ibid.*, 416.
3. *Ibid.*, I, 415.
4. Friend, *op. cit.*, 70.
5. *Writings*, I, 416.
6. Thomas Jefferson Rusk Papers. Friend, *op. cit.*, 70.
7. *Writings*, I, 425.
8. J. F. H. Claiborne, *Life and Corre-*spondence of John A. Quitman, I, 193–194. Friend, *op. cit.*, 71.
9. *Writings*, I, 428.
10. Friend, *op. cit.*, 71.
11. Barker, *op. cit.*, III, 360–361. Friend, *op. cit.*, 117–118.
12. Friend, *op. cit.*, 71–73.
13. James, *op. cit.*, 259.
14. *Writings*, I, 430.
15. Friend, *op. cit.*, 72.
16. *Writings*, I, 431.
17. Friend, *op. cit.*, 73.
18. James, *op. cit.*, 260.
19. *Writings*, IV, 22.
20. *Ibid.*, IV, 23.
21. James, *op. cit.*, 261–263.
22. *Ibid.*, 265.
23. *Writings*, I, 436.
24. Friend, *op. cit.*, 74–75.
25. Barker, *op. cit.*, III, 428.
26. James, *op. cit.*, 266. Friend, *op. cit.*, 76.

CHAPTER XIV

1. James, *op. cit.*, 277–278.
2. Friend, *op. cit.*, 79.
3. Gulick, *op. cit.*, I, 528.
4. *Writings*, I, 451.
5. *Ibid.*, I, 453.
6. Homer S. Thrall, "Sam Houston."
7. *Writings*, I, 456.
8. Friend, *op. cit.*, 84.
9. *Writings*, I, 487.
10. *Ibid.*, I, 495.
11. James, *op. cit.*, 278–279.
12. Friend, *op. cit.*, 119.
13. *Writings*, II, 28.
14. Francis Richard Lubbock, *Six Decades in Texas...*, C. W. Raines Editor, 74–75. Friend, *op. cit.*, 82.
15. *Telegraph and Texas Register*, March 21, 1837. Friend, *op. cit.*, 87.
16. *Writings*, II, 74.
17. *Ibid.*, IV, 29.
18. *Ibid.*, II, 82.
19. James, *op. cit.*, 294.
20. *Writings*, II, 107–115.
21. James, *op. cit.*, 289–292.

22. Erasmus Manford, *Twenty-five Years in the West*, Chicago, 1875, 53. Friend, *op. cit.*, 88.

23. Eugene C. Barker, "The Annexation of Texas," 55-57. Friend, *op. cit.*, 120.

24. *Writings*, II, 147.

25. James, *op. cit.*, 296-297.

26. *Writings*, II, 150.

27. Friend, *op. cit.*, 38-39.

28. *Writings*, II, 180.

29. Friend, *op. cit.*, 90-91.

30. *Writings*, II, 189.

31. Ashbel Smith Papers.

32. Friend, *op. cit.*, 91. *Telegraph and Texas Register*, February 24, 1838.

33. *Writings*, II, 240.

34. Herbert Gambrell, *Anson Jones, the Last President of Texas*, 138. Friend, *op. cit.*, 120-121.

35. *Writings*, II 277 *et seq.*

36. *Ibid.*, II 289.

37. James, *op. cit.*, 302-303.

38. Anson Jones, *Memoranda and Official Correspondence Relating to the Republic of Texas...*, 139-140. W. S. Red, "Allen's Reminiscences of Texas, 1838-1842," 295. *Telegraph and Texas Register*, December 12, 1838. Friend, *op. cit.*, 92-93.

CHAPTER XV

1. Friend, *op.cit.* 85.

2. *Writings*, II, 310.

3. *Telegraph and Texas Register*, February 20, 1839. *Ibid.*, May 14, 1838. Jones, *op. cit.*, 135. Friend, *op. cit.*, 93.

4. William Seale, *Sam Houston's Wife: A Biography of Margaret Lea Houston*, 10. *Ibid.*, 11-13.

5. *Writings*, II, 313.

6. Seale, *op. cit.*, 14.

7. James, *op. cit.*, 307.

8. Seale, *op. cit.*, 6-7. *Ibid.*, 30. *Ibid.*, 16.

9. Friend, *op. cit.*, 94.

10. James, *op. cit.*, 309.

11. Gulick, *op. cit.*, III, 79. Friend, *op. cit.*, 95.

12. Ashbel Smith Papers. Friend, *op. cit.*, 93.

13. James, *op. cit.*, 313.

14. Gambrell, *op. cit.*, 181-182. *Austin City Gazette*, November 27, 1839. Friend, *op. cit.*, 95.

15. *Writings*, II, 322.

16. James, *op. cit.*, 311.

17. Friend, *op. cit.*, 85.

18. *Texas Sentinal*, January 15, 1840. *Telegraph and Texas Register*, February 5, 1840. John Salmon Ford Memoirs, II, 213. Friend, *op. cit.*, 95-96.

19. Gulick, *op. cit.*, III, 304. Seale, *op. cit.*, 31. *Ibid.*, 36.

20. *Writings*, II, 350.

21. Seale, *op. cit.*, 17-18.

22. *Ibid.*, 31. *Ibid.*, 18-19. *Marion (Alabama) Herald*, May 16, 1840.

23. *Telegraph and Texas Register*, July 1, 1840. Seale, *op. cit.*, 32-33. Ashbel Smith Papers.

CHAPTER XVI

1. James, *op. cit.*, 299. *Ibid.*, 314. Ashbel Smith Papers. Friend, *op. cit.*, 97.

2. Seale, *op. cit.*, 38-40.

3. *Telegraph and Texas Register*, July 1, 1840. Friend, *op. cit.*, 97-98.

4. Ashbel Smith Papers. John Salmon Ford Memoirs. Friend, *op. cit.*, 98.

5. Seale, *op. cit.*, 42-43.

6. *Writings*, II, 352.

7. Seale, *op. cit.*, 44-45.

8. James, *op. cit.*, 317.

9. Seale, *op. cit.*, 45-51.

10. James, *op. cit.*, 315-316.

11. Friend, *op. cit.*, 100.

12. *Writings*, II, 365.

13. Seale, *op. cit.*, 51-52.

14. James, *op. cit.*, 317-319.

15. Seale, *op. cit.*, 54-55.

16. *Writings*, II, 369.

17. Harriet Smither, "Diary of Adolphus Sterne," *Southwestern Historical Quarterly*, XXXII, 178. Seale, *op. cit.*, 59-60.

18. Ashbel Smith Papers. Friend, *op. cit.*, 101.

19. *Writings*, II, 390.

20. *Ibid.*, 392 *et seq.*

21. Seale, *op. cit.*, 65.

CHAPTER XVII

1. Maurice Garland Fulton, Editor, *Diary and Letters of Josiah Gregg*, I, 109–110. *Daily Bulletin* (Austin), December 14, 841. Friend, *op. cit.*, 102–103.
2. *Writings*, II, 401.
3. Seale, *op. cit.*, 66–67.
4. James, *op. cit.*, 321–322.
5. *Writings*, II, 430.
6. Friend, *op. cit.*, 107.
7. Gambrell, *op. cit.*, 232. Friend, *op. it.*, 121–122.
8. *Writings*, II, 484. Seale, *op. cit.*, 68.
9. Smither, *op. cit.*, 161. Friend, *op. cit.*, 04. Seale, *op. cit.*, 68–69. *Writings*, II, 84–485.
10. *Ibid.*, IV, 76.
11. Friend, *op. cit.*, 85.
12. *Writings*, II, 490–491.
13. *Ibid.*, II, 495.
14. *Ibid.*, II, 503.
15. James, *op. cit.*, 323.
16. *Writings*, II, 508.
17. *Ibid.*, II, 527.
18. *Ibid.*, II, 537.
19. *Ibid.*, II, 539.
20. James, *op. cit.*, 324.
21. Ashbel Smith Papers. Friend, *op. it.*, 104.
22. *Writings*, III, 24.
23. *Ibid.*, III, 31.
24. *Ibid.*, III, 37.
25. *Ibid.*, IV, 100.
26. *Ibid.*, III, 154.
27. *Ibid.*, III, 58.
28. Jones, *op. cit.*, 169–170. Friend, *op. it.*, 105.
29. *Writings*, III, 74.
30. Jones, *op. cit.*, 192.
31. *Writings*, III, 84.
32. Yoakum, *op. cit.*, II, 345–347. Friend, *op. cit.*, 122.
33. *Writings*, III, 112.
34. *Ibid.*, III, 116.
35. *Ibid.*, III, 137.
36. *Ibid.*, III, 138.
37. Ashbel Smith Papers.
38. Friend, *op. cit.*, 106.
39. *Writings*, IV, 136 *et seq.*

40. *Ibid.*, III, 145.
41. Seale, *op. cit.*, 72–73.
42. James, *op. cit.*, 328.
43. *Writings*, III, 360–361.
44. Seale, *op. cit.*, 74–75.
45. *Writings*, III, 170.
46. *Telegraph and Texas Register*, October 19, 1842. Friend, *op. cit.*, 108.
47. *Writings*, III, 191.
48. *Ibid.*, III, 199.
49. *Ibid.*, III, 201.
50. *Ibid.*, III, 203.
51. Friend, *op. cit.*, 83.

CHAPTER XVIII

1. Ashbel Smith Papers. Friend, *op. cit.*, 109.
2. *Writings*, III, 280.
3. Seale, *op. cit.*, 80 *et seq.*
4. *Writings*, III, 304.
5. *Ibid.*, III, 299.
6. Washington D. Miller Papers. Friend, *op. cit.*, 122–123.
7. *Writings*, III, 311.
8. *Ibid.*, III, 323.
9. *Ibid.*, III, 351.
10. *Ibid.*, IV, 181.
11. *Ibid.*, III, 385.
12. Washington D. Miller Papers. Seale, *op. cit.*, 86.
13. George Lockhart Rives, *The United States and Mexico*, New York, 1913, I, 559. Friend, *op. cit.*, 125.
14. *Writings*, III, 407.
15. *Telegraph and Texas Register*, August 8, 1843. Ashbel Smith Papers. Friend, *op. cit.*, 110–111.
16. *Writings*, III, 427. Friend, *op. cit.*, 126.
17. Jones, *op. cit.*, 261–262. Friend, *op. cit.*, 163.
18. *Ibid.*, 271.
19. Ephraim Douglass Adams, *British Diplomatic Correspondence . . .*, 271–273. Friend, *op. cit.*, 126.
20. *Ibid.*, 111.
21. Bassett, *op. cit.*, VI, 249. Friend, *op. cit.*, 126–127.

22. *Ibid.*, 128.
23. *Writings*, III, 521.
24. *Ibid.*, IV, 233.
25. *Ibid.*, IV, 238. *Ibid.*, III, 541.
26. Thomas Hart Benton, *Thirty Years' View* . . . , II, 644. Friend, *op. cit.*, 131–132.
27. *Writings*, IV, 260.
28. Oren M. Roberts Papers.
29. Friend, *op. cit.*, 112.
30. Seale, *op. cit.*, 93.
31. Bassett, *op. cit.*, VI, 276 *et seq.* Friend, *op. cit.*, 135.
32. *Writings*, IV, 297.
33. *Ibid.*, IV, 327.
34. Seale, *op. cit.*, 93–94.
35. Friend, *op. cit.*, 139–140.
36. Seale, *op. cit.*, 94–95.
37. *Writings*, IV, 369 *et seq.*
38. *Ibid.*, IV, 373.
39. Friend, *op. cit.*, 143–144.
40. *Writings*, IV, 401.
41. Friend, *op. cit.*, 147.
42. *Writings*, IV, 408.
43. Seale, *op. cit.*, 96–97.

CHAPTER XIX

1. James, *op. cit.*, 211.
2. Ashbel Smith, *Reminiscences of the Texas Republic*, 69–70, 80. Friend, *op. cit.*, 116. Justin H. Smith, *The Annexation of Texas*, 98–99. Friend, *op. cit.*, 117.
3. *Ibid.*, 148.
4. *Writings*, VII, 11–12.
5. *Ibid.*, IV, 414.
6. Andrew Jackson Donelson Papers. Friend, *op. cit.*, 153.
7. *Writings*, IV, 422 *et seq.*
8. J. Franklin Jameson, Editor, *Correspondence of John C. Calhoun*, 1030–1031. James K. Polk Papers. Friend, *op. cit.*, 154. Adams, *op. cit.*, 487–493. Friend, *op. cit.*, 151. James K. Polk Papers. Friend, *op. cit.*, 155.
9. *Writings*, IV, 424.
10. James K. Polk Papers. Friend, *op. cit.*, 157. *Niles' Register*, July 12, 1845. Seale, *op. cit.*, 103.

11. Friend, *op. cit.*, 271–272.
12. Adams, *op. cit.*, 503. *Ibid.*, 466.
13. Friend, *op. cit.*, 156. Gambrell, *op. cit.*, 403–404. Friend, *op. cit.*, 158.
14. Seale, *op. cit.*, 103–104.
15. Friend, *op. cit.*, 158–159.
16. *Alabama State Review*, September 17, 1845. Seale, *op. cit.*, 104.
17. *Ibid.*, 107.
18. *Telegraph and Texas Register*, October 10, 1845. Jones, *op. cit.*, 496–497. Friend, *op. cit.*, 165.
19. *Telegraph and Texas Register*, March 4, 1846. Friend, *op. cit.*, 167–168.
20. Seale, *op. cit.*, 109.
21. Friend, *op. cit.*, 173.
22. Thomas Jefferson Rusk Papers.
23. *Niles' Register*, April 4, 1846.
24. New York *Tribune*, March 31, 1846.
25. Friend, *op. cit.*, 168–169.
26. M. M. Quaife, Editor, *The Diary of James K. Polk* . . . , I, 309.
27. Quaife, *op. cit.*, I, 327. Friend, *op. cit.*, 172–173.
28. James, *op. cit.*, 361–362.
29. *Writings*, IV, 451.
30. Friend, *op. cit.*, 174–175.
31. *Telegraph and Texas Register*, April 29, 1846. *Ibid.*, May 13, 1846. *Ibid.*, January 1, 1847.
32. Friend, *op. cit.*, 193.
33. Ashbel Smith Papers.
34. Friend, *op. cit.*, 176.
35. *Writings*, IV, 475.
36. *Ibid.*, IV, 476.
37. Seale, *op. cit.*, 114.
38. Ashbel Smith Papers. Friend, *op. cit.*, 185.
39. Friend, *op. cit.*, 179.
40. Lester, *op. cit.*
41. Gulick, *op. cit.*, IV, Part I, 165. Friend, *op. cit.*, 183.
42. Seale, *op. cit.*, 120–121.
43. *Ibid.*, 124.
44. Ashbel Smith Papers.
45. Seale, *op. cit.*, 125–126.
46. *Writings*, V, 10.
47. *Telegraph and Texas Register*, May 3, 1847. Friend, *op. cit.*, 184. *Writings*, V, 11.

48. Seale, *op. cit.*, 127.
49. *Writings*, V, 13.
50. *Ibid.*, VI, 18.
51. Seale, *op. cit.*, 129.
52. Friend, *op. cit.*, 196–197.
53. *Writings*, V, 35.
54. Friend, *op. cit.*, 274.
55. Ashbel Smith Papers.
56. Seale, *op. cit.*, 131–132.
57. Friend, *op. cit.*, 190. *Ibid.*, 275.
58. *Writings*, V, 53, 58.
59. *Telegraph and Texas Register*, November 21, 1848.
60. Seale, *op. cit.*, 138–140.
61. *Writings*, V, 62.
62. Friend, *op. cit.*, 138–140.

CHAPTER XX

1. Friend, *op. cit.*, 194.
2. Thomas Jefferson Rusk Papers.
3. *Writings*, V, 70.
4. *Ibid.*, V, 78.
5. Henderson Yoakum Diary. Seale, *op. cit.*, 140–141.
6. Friend, *op. cit.*, 200.
7. *Texas State Gazette*, January 12, 1850. Friend, *op. cit.*, 201. *Telegraph and State Gazette*, January 26, 1850. *Ibid.*, February , 1850. Friend, *op. cit.*, 202.
8. James, *op. cit.*, 376–377.
9. *Writings*, V, 119–144. New York *Tribune*, March 2, 1850.
10. Friend, *op. cit.*, 203–204.
11. Ashbel Smith Papers.
12. Seale, *op. cit.*, 154.
13. Millard Fillmore Papers.
14. Martin Van Buren Papers. Friend, *op. cit.*, 276–277.
15. *Writings*, V, 204.
16. *Texas State Gazette*, August 24, 1850. Friend, *op. cit.*, 210.
17. *Texas State Gazette*, September 21, 1850.
18. Friend, *op. cit.*, 277.
19. Friend, *op. cit.*, 212–213.
20. Henderson Yoakum Diary.

21. Seale, *op. cit.*, 153.
22. *Ibid.*, 141.
23. Henderson Yoakum Diary. Friend, *op. cit.*, 213.
24. Seale, *op. cit.*, 143.
25. Friend, *op. cit.*, 215.
26. James, *op. cit.*, 381.
27. *Texas State Gazette*, April 26, 1851. *Ibid.*, July 19, 1851. Friend, *op. cit.*, 278.
28. *Writings*, V, 297.
29. Seale, *op. cit.*, 158.
30. *Writings*, V, 302.
31. *Ibid.*, V, 297.
32. *Ibid.*, V, 316.
33. *Ibid.*, V, 317.
34. *Ibid.*, V, 337.
35. Friend, *op. cit.*, 218.
36. *Texas State Gazette*, March 6, 1852. Nacogdoches *Chronicle*, March 13, 1852. Friend, *op. cit.*, 280–281. Edward L. Pierce, *Memoirs and Letters of Charles Sumner*, III, 278. Friend, *op. cit.*, 284. *Texas State Gazette*, March 13, 1852. Friend, *op. cit.*, 282. *Texas State Gazette*, March 20, 1852. Friend, *op. cit.*, 282.
37. Seale, *op. cit.*, 157–158.
38. Andrew Johnson Papers.
39. Friend, *op. cit.*, 284. Thomas Jefferson Rusk Papers. Friend, *op. cit.*, 285. David Rusk Papers.
40. Seale, *op. cit.*, 158–159.
41. Friend, *op. cit.*, 219–220.
42. Seale, *op. cit.*, 160.
43. *Texas State Gazette*, January 20, 1853.
44. *Writings*, V, 370.
45. Seale, *op. cit.*, 161.
46. *Writings*, V, 450.
47. Friend, *op. cit.*, 227.
48. *Writings*, V, 455.
49. Georgia Jenkins Burleson, Editor, *Life and Writings of Rufus C. Burleson . . .*, 114.
50. *Writings*, V, 469.
51. *Ibid.*, 504.
52. *Telegraph and Texas Register*, May 13, 1854. Friend, *op. cit.*, 228.
53. *Writings*, V, 523.
54. *Texas State Gazette*, April 4, 1854.

55. Friend, *op. cit.*, 232. Thomas Jefferson Rusk Papers.
56. Burleson, *op. cit.*, 579.
57. Friend, *op. cit.*, 233.
58. *Ibid.*, 289.
59. Seale, *op. cit.*, 268–270.

CHAPTER XXI

1. James, *op. cit.*, 386.
2. Friend, *op. cit.*, 290.
3. *Writings*, VI, 111–159.
4. *Ibid.*, VI 166.
5. *Ibid.*, VI, 171.
6. *Ibid.*, VI, 176.
7. *Texas State Gazette*, March 31, 1855. *Ibid.*, May 5, 1855. Friend, *op. cit.*, 291.
8. *Ibid.*, 289.
9. *Writings*, IV, 180–184.
10. *Ibid.*, IV, 192.
11. *Texas State Gazette*, August 18, 1855. Friend, *op. cit.*, 292.
12. Seale, *op. cit.*, 172–173.
13. *Writings*, VI, 204.
14. *Texas State Gazette*, October 20, 1855. Friend, *op. cit.*, 240. Dallas *Herald*, December 8, 1855. Friend, *op. cit.*, 242–243.
15. *Writings*, VI, 236.
16. David Rusk Papers. Friend, *op. cit.*, 294.
17. *Writings*, VI, 299.
18. Seale, *op. cit.*, 182.
19. Ashbel Smith Papers.
20. *Texas State Gazette*, June 7, 1856. Friend, *op. cit.*, 296.
21. *Writings*, VI, 384.
22. Thomas Jefferson Rusk Papers. Friend, *op. cit.*, 246.
23. Seale, *op. cit.*, 184.
24. Oren M. Roberts Papers. Friend, *op. cit.*, 248.
25. *Writings*, VI, 444.

26. Dallas *News*, April 4, 5, 1892 Friend, *op. cit.*, 248–249. Thomas Jefferson Rusk Papers. Friend, *op. cit.*, 250 Thomas Jefferson Rusk Papers. Friend *op. cit.*, 252.
27. Seale, *op. cit.*, 188.
28. *Texas State Gazette*, August 22 1857.
29. *Writings*, VI, 447.
30. *Southern Intelligencer*, September 9 1857. Friend, *op. cit.*, 298.
31. *Texas State Gazette*, November 14 1857. Friend, *op. cit.*, 255.
32. Ashbel Smith Papers. Friend, *op. cit.*, 254.
33. Martin Van Buren Papers. Friend *op. cit.*, 256.
34. Seale, *op. cit.*, 186.
35. *Writings*, VI, 466 *et seq.*
36. *Ibid.*, VI, 486.
37. *Ibid.*, VI, 508.
38. Friend, *op. cit.*, 261.
39. *Writings*, VII, 97.
40. Seale, *op. cit.*, 187.
41. *Writings*, VII, 131.
42. *Writings*, VII, 140.
43. *Texas State Gazette*, August 21 1858.
44. Friend, *op. cit.*, 259–260.
45. Dallas *Herald*, July 10, August 21 1858. *Southern Intelligencer*, July 14, August 11, 1848. Friend, *op. cit.*, 300.
46. *Southern Intelligencer*, August 18, 25 1858. Friend, *op. cit.*, 261.
47. *Writings*, VII, 181.
48. Dallas *Herald*, August 21, September 1, 1858. Friend, *op. cit.*, 262.
49. *Writings*, VII, 189.
50. Seale, *op. cit.*, 188.
51. Guy M. Bryan Papers. Friend, *op. cit.*, 262.
52. *Writings*, VII 194.
53. *Ibid.*, VII 219.
54. *Ibid.*, VII 224.
55. *Southern Intelligencer*, March 30 1859. Friend, *op. cit.*, 322.
56. Ashbel Smith Papers.
57. *Writings*, VII, 339.
58. Friend, *op. cit.*, 269.

59. *Ibid.*, 325.
60. Seale, *op. cit.*, 191.

CHAPTER XXII

1. Charles A. Culberson, "General
am Houston and Secession," 585.
riend, *op. cit.*, 327. Seale, *op. cit.*, 191.
2. *Writings,* VII, 384.
3. Walter Prescott Webb, *The Texas
'angers . . . ,* 197–203, 212–213. Friend,
b. cit., 301–304.
4. *Ibid.*, 328.
5. *Writings,* VII, 389.
6. Webb, *op. cit.*, 197. Friend, *op. cit.*,
97.
7. *Writings,* VII, 441.
8. *Ibid.*, VII, 473.
9. *Ibid.*, VII, 495.
10. Friend, *op. cit.*, 305.
11. *Writings,* VII, 502.
12. *Ibid.*, VII, 506.
13. *Ibid.*, VII, 521.
14. Friend, *op. cit.*, 306.
15. *Ibid.*, 312.
16. *Ibid.*, 305–306.
17. *Writings,* VII, 541.
18. *Ibid.*, VII, 545.
19. E. W. Winkler, Editor, *Platforms of
'olitical Parties in Texas,* 86. Murat Hal-
:ead, *Caucuses of 1860: A History of the
'ational Political Conventions of the Current
'residential Campaign,* Columbus, Ohio,
860, 104–120.
20. Friend, *op. cit.*, 315–316.
21. *Writings,* VIII, 58.
22. Stephen A. Douglas Papers, Uni-
ersity of Chicago Library. Friend, *op. cit.*,
16.
23. *Writings,* VIII, 66.
24. Charles H. Ambler, "Correspon-
lence of Robert M. Hunter." American
Iistorical Association *Annual Report,*
916, 332. Friend, *op. cit.*, 317.
25. New York *Herald,* May 30, 1860.
26. Friend, *op. cit.*, 318.
27. New York *Herald,* June 25, 1860.
'riend, *op. cit.*, 319.
28. *Writings,* VIII, 102.

29. *Ibid.*, VIII, 109.
30. Friend, *op. cit.*, 309.
31. *Writings,* VIII, 118.
32. *Ibid.*, VIII, 121.
33. William Pitt Barringer Diary.
Friend, *op. cit.*, 319.
34. *Writings,* VIII, 126.
35. *Ibid.*, VIII, 121.
36. *Ibid.*, VIII, 129.
37. *Ibid.*, VIII, 145.
38. Howard K. Beale, Editor, *The
Diary of Edward Bates, 1859–1866,* IV of
American Historical Association *Annual
Report,* 1930. Washington, 1933, 87.
Friend, *op. cit.*, 329.
39. *Writings,* VIII, 173.
40. Dallas *Herald,* October 31, 1860.
Friend, *op. cit.*, 330.
41. *Writings,* VIII, 184.
42. Seale, *op. cit.*, 201.
43. James, *op. cit.*, 405.
44. *Writings,* VIII, 199.
45. Dallas *Herald,* November 21, 1860.
Friend, *op. cit.*, 341.
46. Oren M. Roberts Papers. Friend,
op. cit., 331.
47. *Writings,* VIII, 197.
48. *Texas Republican,* December 15,
1860. Friend, *op. cit.*, 333.
49. John Salmon Ford Memoirs.
50. James, *op. cit.*, 405–406.
51. *Writings,* VIII, 225. *Texas Republican,* January 1, 1861.
52. Friend, *op. cit.*, 333–334.
53. Culberson, *op. cit.*, 590.
54. *Writings,* VIII, 230.
55. *Ibid.*, VIII, 251.
56. Friend, *op. cit.*, 335.
57. Seale, *op. cit.*, 205.
58. Friend, *op. cit.*, 336.
59. *Writings,* VIII, 263.
60. E. W. Winkler, *Journal of the Secession Convention . . . ,* 88. Friend, *op. cit.*, 337.
61. James, *op. cit.*, 411.
62. *Writings,* VIII, 268.
63. Winkler, *op. cit.*, 178 *et seq.*
64. Friend, *op. cit.*, 338.
65. Address by Temple Houston Morrow.

66. Friend, *op. cit.*, 338-339.
67. *Writings,* VIII, 271-292.
68. *Ibid.,* VIII, 293.
69. Friend, *op. cit.,* 349.
70. *Writings,* VIII, 294.
71. *Ibid.,* VIII, 305.

EPILOGUE

1. Seale, *op. cit.,* 223-224.
2. *Writings,* VIII, 326.
3. *Ibid.,* VIII, 339.
4. *Ibid.,* VIII, 344.
5. James, *op. cit.,* 431.
6. Seale, *op. cit.,* 230.
7. James, *op. cit.,* 432.
8. Seale, *op. cit.,* 231.
9. *Writings,* VIII, 348.

SELECTED

BIBLIOGRAPHY

CHARLES FRANCIS ADAMS, ed., *Memoirs of John Quincy Adams from 1795 to 1848.* Philadelphia, 1874–1878.

EPHRAIM DOUGLASS ADAMS, *British Diplomatic Correspondence Concerning the Republic of Texas, 1836–1846.* Austin, 1917.

———, *British Interests and Activities in Texas, 1838–1846.* Baltimore, 1910.

O. F. ALLEN, *The City of Houston from Wilderness to Wonder.* Temple, Texas, 1936.

Arkansas Advocate, Little Rock, 1831.

Arkansas Gazette, Little Rock, 1826–1833.

Austin City Gazette, 1839, 1842.

Austin *Daily Bulletin,* 1841.

WILLIAM PITT BALLINGER, Diary. Archives Collection, University of Texas Library, Austin.

EUGENE C. BARKER, "The Annexation of Texas." *Southwestern Historical Quarterly,* L (1946/47).

———, ed., *The Austin Papers.* Austin, 1927.

———, *The Life of Stephen F. Austin, Founder of Texas, 1793–1836: A Chapter in the Westward Movement of the Anglo-American People.* Nashville, 1926.

———, "The Private Papers of Anthony Butler." *The Nation,* June 15, 1911.

AMELIA BARR, *All the Days of My Life: An Autobiography, the Red Leaves of a Human Heart.* New York, 1913.

JOHN SPENCER BASSETT, ed., *Correspondence of Andrew Jackson.* Washington, 1926–1935.

———, *The Life of Andrew Jackson.* New York, 1916.

BERNARD BEE, Papers. Archives Collection, University of Texas, Austin.

THOMAS HART BENTON, *Thirty Years' View; or, A History of the Working of the American Government for Thirty Years from 1820 to 1850.* New York, 1854–1856.

ALFRED HOYT BILL, *Rehearsal for Conflict: The War with Mexico, 1846–1848.* New York.

JAMES G. BLAINE, *Twenty Years of Congress: From Lincoln to Garfield. With a Review of the Events Which Led to the Political Revolution of 1860.* Norwich, Connecticut, 1884–1886.

CHAUNCEY S. BOUCHER AND ROBERT P. BROOKS, eds., *Correspondence Addressed to John C. Calhoun, 1837–1849.* Sixteenth Report of the Historical Manuscripts Commission, pp. 125–533 of American Historical Association *Annual Report,* 1929. Washington, 1930.

HENRY BRUCE, *Life of General Houston.* New York, 1861.

GEORGE S. BRYAN, *Sam Houston.* New York, 1917.

GUY W. BRYAN, Papers. Archives Collection, University of Texas Library, Austin.

AUGUSTUS C. BUELL, *History of Andrew Jackson: Pioneer, Patriot, Soldier, Politician, President.* New York, 1904.

EDWARD BURLESON, Papers. Archives Collection, University of Texas Library, Austin.

GEORGIA J. BURLESON, comp., *The Life and Writings of Rufus C. Burleson, DD, Ll. D., Containing a Biography of Dr. Burleson by Harry Haynes.* Waco, 1901.

Cincinnati *Daily Commercial,* 1856.

J.F.H. CLAIBORNE, *Life and Correspondence of John A. Quitman.* New York, 1860.

MARGARET COIT, *John C. Calhoun.* Boston, 1950.

DIANA FONTAINE MAURY CORBIN, comp., *A Life of Matthew Fontaine Maury.* London, 1888.

WILLIAM CAREY CRANE, *Life and Select Literary Remains of Sam Houston of Texas.* Philadelphia, 1884.

GEORGE CREEL, *Sam Houston: Colossus in Buckskin.* New York, 1927.

CHARLES A. CULBERSON, "General Sam Houston and Secession." *Scribner's Magazine* XXXIX (May, 1908).

GEORGE TICKNOR CURTIS, *Life of James Buchanan.* New York, 1883.

Dallas *Herald,* 1855–1861.

Dallas *News,* 1892.

VARINA HOWELL DAVIS, *Jefferson Davis, Ex-President of the Confederate States of America: A Memoir by his Wife.* New York, 1890.

ANDREW JACKSON DONELSON, Papers. Library of Congress, Washington.

SARAH BARNWELL ELLIOTT, *Sam Houston.* Boston, 1900.

G. W. FEATHERSTONHAUGH, *Excursion through the Slave States, from Washington on the Potomac to the Frontier of Mexico.* London, 1844.

MILLARD FILLMORE, Papers. Buffalo and Erie County Historical Society, Buffalo.

SUE FLANAGAN, *Sam Houston's Texas.* Austin, 1964.

JOHN SALMON FORD, Memoirs. Archives Collection, University of Texas Library, Austin.

———, *Rip Ford's Texas,* ed. by Stephen B. Oates. Austin, 1963.

CAROLYN THOMAS FOREMAN, Letters. "Arkansas File Box," Indian Archives. Oklahoma Historical Society, Oklahoma City.

GRANT FOREMAN, Letters. "Arkansas File Box," Indian Archives, Oklahoma Historical Society, Oklahoma City.

——, *Indians and Pioneers: The Story of the American Southwest before 1830.* New Haven, 1930.

——, *Pioneer Days in the Early Southwest.* Cleveland, 1926.

LLERENA B. FRIEND, *Sam Houston: The Great Designer.* Austin, 1954.

MAURICE GARLAND FULTON, ed., *Diary and Letters of Josiah Gregg.* Norman, Oklahoma, 1941–1944.

FRÉDÉRIC GAILLARDET, *Sketches of Early Texas and Louisiana.* Translated with an Introduction and Notes by James L. Shepherd, III. Austin, 1966.

Galveston *News,* 1856.

HERBERT P. GAMBRELL, *Anson Jones, the Last President of Texas.* Garden City, New York, 1848.

——, *Mirabeau Buonaparte Lamar: Troubadour and Crusader.* Dallas, 1934.

PHILIP GRAHAM, *The Life and Poems of Mirabeau B. Lamar.* Chapel Hill, 1938.

WILLIAM FAIRFAX GRAY, *From Virginia to Texas, 1835: Diary of Col. Wm. F. Gray Giving Details of His Journey to Texas and Return in 1835–1836 and Second Journey to Texas in 1837.* Houston, 1909.

THOMAS JEFFERSON GREEN, *Journal of the Texian Expedition Against Mier.* New York, 1845.

JACK GREGORY AND RENNARD STRICKLAND, *Sam Houston with the Cherokees, 1829–1833.* Austin, 1967.

JOSEPHUS CONN GUILD, *Old Times in Tennessee, with Historical, Personal, and Political Scraps and Sketches.* Nashville, 1878.

C. A. GULICK AND OTHERS, *The Papers of Mirabeau Buonaparte Lamar.* Austin, 1921–1927.

THOMAS H. S. HAMERSLY, *Complete Regular Army Register of the United States for One Hundred Years, 1779–1879.* Washington, 1879.

JAMES A. HAMILTON, *Reminiscences of James A. Hamilton; or, Men and Events, at Home and Abroad, During Three Quarters of a Century.* New York, 1869.

JIM DAN HILL, *The Texas Navy in Forgotten Battles and Shirtsleeve Diplomacy.* Chicago, 1937.

A. M. HOBBY, *Life and Times of David G. Burnet, First President of the Republic of Texas.* Galveston, 1871.

WILLIAM RANSOM HOGAN, *The Texas Republic: A Social and Economic History.* Norman, Oklahoma, 1946.

ANDREW JACKSON HOUSTON, *Texan Independence.* Houston, 1938.

SAM HOUSTON, *The Autobiography of Sam Houston,* Donald Day and Harry Herbert Ullman, eds., Norman, Oklahoma, 1954.

——, Biographical File. Barker History Center, University of Texas Library, Austin.

——, Papers. Sam Houston Biographical Files and Grant Foreman Typescripts, Reference Library, Thomas Gilcrease Institute, Tulsa.

SAMUEL RUTHERFORD HOUSTON, *Brief Biographical Accounts of Many Members of the Houston Family.* Cincinnati, 1882.

ALEXANDER HYNDS, "General Sam Houston." *The Century Magazine* XXVII (August, 1884).

Washington Irving, *Journal of Washington Irving,* William P. Trent and George S. Hellman, eds., Boston, 1919.

———, *A Tour of the Prairies.* annotated by Joseph B. Thoburn and George C. Wells. Oklahoma City, 1955.

———, *Western Journals of Washington Irving,* Francis McDermott, ed., Norman, Oklahoma, 1944.

Andrew Jackson, Papers, Series I and II. Library of Congress, Washington.

Marquis James, *The Life of Andrew Jackson.* New York, 1938.

———, *The Raven, A Biography of Sam Houston.* New York, 1929.

J. Franklin Jameson, ed., *Correspondence of John C. Calhoun.* Vol. II of American Historical Association *Annual Report,* 1899. Washington, 1900.

John Holland Jenkins, *Recollections of Early Texas,* John Holmes Jenkins, ed., Austin, 1958.

Andrew Johnson, Papers. Library of Congress, Washington.

Anson Jones, *Memoranda and Official Correspondence Relating to the Republic of Texas, Its History and Annexation, Including a Brief Autobiography of the Author.* New York, 1859.

———, Papers. Archives Collection, University of Texas Library, Austin.

George Wilkins Kendall, *Narrative of the Texan Santa Fe Expedition, Comprising a Description of a Tour through Texas and across the Great Southwestern Prairies. . . .* London, 1844.

Ralph Ketcham, *James Madison: A Biography.* New York, 1971.

Richard C. King, ed., *Victorian Lady on the Texas Frontier: The Journal of Ann Raney Coleman.* Norman, Oklahoma, 1971.

C. Edwards Lester, *Life and Achievements of Sam Houston, Hero and Statesman.* New York, 1883.

———, *The Life of Sam Houston: The Only Authentic Memoir of Him Ever Published.* New York, 1855.

———, *Sam Houston and His Republic.* New York, 1846.

Francis Richard Lubbock, *Six Decades in Texas; or, Memoirs of Francis Richard Lubbock, Governor of Texas in War Time, 1861–63: A Personal Experience in Business, War, and Politics,* E.W. Raines, ed., Austin, 1900.

N. M. Ludlow, *Dramatic Life as I Found It: A Record of Personal Experience, with an Account of the Rise and Progress of the Drama in the West and South.* St. Louis, 1880.

Wilson Lumpkins, *The Removal of the Cherokee Indians from Georgia.* New York, 1865.

Prairie View Malone, *Sam Houston's Indians.* San Antonio, 1960.

Robert Mayo, *Political Sketches of Eight Years in Washington.* Baltimore, 1839.

Thomas L. McKenney, *History of Indian Tribes of North America.* Philadelphia, 1865.

Return Jonathan Meigs, Papers. Grant Foreman Typescripts, Indian Archives, Oklahoma Historical Society, Oklahoma City.

Edmund T. Miller, *A Financial History of Texas.* Austin, 1916.

Washington D. Miller, Papers. Archives, Texas State Library, Austin.

GEORGE FORT MILTON, *The Eve of Conflict: Stephen A. Douglas and the Needless War*. Boston, 1934.

JAMES MONROE, Papers. Library of Congress, Washington.

TEMPLE HOUSTON MORROW, "Address by Temple Houston Morrow." *Senate Journal*, 49th Texas Legislature, reg. sess., February 27, 1945.

OREN F. MORTON, *A History of Rockbridge County, Virginia*. Staunton, Virginia, 1920.

JOSEPH MILTON NANCE, *After San Jacinto: The Texas-Mexican Frontier, 1836–1841*. Austin, 1963.

The National Intelligencer. Washington, 1844–1845.

ALLAN NEVINS, *Ordeal of the Union*. New York, 1947.

New York *Herald*, 1860–1861.

The New York *Times*, 1858.

New York *Tribune*, 1846–1850.

Niles' Register. Baltimore, Washington, and Philadelphia, 1811–1849.

JOSEPH HOWARD PARKS, *Felix Grundy, Champion of Democracy*. Baton Rouge, 1940.

JAMES PARTON, *Life of Andrew Jackson*. Boston, 1889.

GEORGE W. PASCHAL, "Last Years of Sam Houston." *Harper's New Monthly Magazine* XXXII (1865/66).

EDWARD L. PIERCE, *Memoirs and Letters of Charles Sumner*. Boston, 1877–1893.

FRANKLIN PIERCE, Papers. Library of Congress, Washington.

GEORGE WILSON PIERSON, *Tocqueville and Beaumont in America*. New York, 1938.

JAMES K. POLK, Papers. Library of Congress, Washington.

KENNETH WIGGINS PRUCHA, *American Policy in the Formative Years*. Cambridge, Massachusetts, 1962.

M. M. QUAIFE, ed., *The Diary of James K. Polk during His Presidency, 1845 to 1849*. Chicago, 1910.

W. S. RED, "Allen's Reminiscences of Texas, 1838–1842." *Southwestern Historical Quarterly* XVIII (1914/15).

JOHN REYNOLDS, *My Own Times, Embracing Also the History of My Life*. Belleville, Illinois, 1855.

OREN M. ROBERTS, Papers. Archives Collection, University of Texas Library, Austin.

JOHN ROGERS, Papers. Grant Foreman Typescripts, Reference Library, Thomas Gilcrease Institute, Tulsa.

DAVID RUSK, Papers. Stephen A. Austin State College, Nacogdoches.

THOMAS JEFFERSON RUSK, Papers. Archives Collection, University of Texas Library, Austin.

EDWARD L. SABIN, *With Sam Houston in Texas*. Philadelphia, 1916.

San Antonio *Daily Herald*, 1859.

RICHARD G. SANTOS, *Santa Anna's Campaign Against Texas*. Waco, 1968.

WILLIAM O. SCROGGS, *Filibuster and Financiers: The Story of William Walker and His Associates*. New York, 1916.

WILLIAM SEALE, *Sam Houston's Wife: A Biography of Margaret Lea Houston*. Norman, Oklahoma, 1970.

Marilyn McAdams Sibley, *Travelers in Texas, 1761–1860.* Austin, 1967.

Stanley Siegel, *A Political History of the Texas Republic, 1836–1845.* Austin, 1856.

Ashbel Smith, Papers. Archives Collection, University of Texas Library, Austin.

——, *Reminiscences of the Texas Republic.* "Historical Society of Galveston Series," No. 1, December 16, 1875. Galveston, 1876.

Justin H. Smith, *The Annexation of Texas.* New York, 1941.

William Ernest Smith, *The Francis Preston Blair Family in Politics.* New York, 1933.

The Southern Intelligencer. Austin, 1856–1860.

The Telegraph and Texas Register. San Felipe, Harrisburg, Columbia, Houston, 1835–1850.

A. W. Terrell, "Recollections of General Sam Houston." *Southwestern Historical Quarterly* XV (1935/36).

The Texas Sentinel. Austin, 1840–1841.

The Texas State Gazette. Austin, 1849–1856.

Lately Thomas, *The First President Johnson.* New York, 1968.

Homer S. Thrall, "Sam Houston." *Round Table* IV (July, 1892).

W. S. Tisdale, ed., *Know-Nothingism Almanac and True American's Manual for 1856.* New York, 1856.

Martin Van Buren, Papers. Library of Congress, Washington.

Ernest Wallace, *Texas in Turmoil.* Austin, 1965.

Cephas Washburn, *Reminiscences of the Indians.* Richmond, Virginia, 1869.

Walter Prescott Webb, *The Texas Rangers: A Century of Frontier Defense.* Boston, 1935.

Walter Webber, Papers. Biographical Files, Indian Archives, Oklahoma Historical Society, Oklahoma City.

John Edward Weems, *Dream of Empire: A Human History of the Republic of Texas, 1836–1846.* New York, 1971.

Alfred M. Williams, *Sam Houston and the War of Independence in Texas.* Boston, 1893.

Amelia W. Williams and Eugene C. Barker, eds., *The Writings of Sam Houston.* Austin, 1938–1943.

—— and Bernhardt Wall, *Following General Sam Houston.* Austin, 1925.

E. W. Winkler, ed., *Journal of the Secession Convention of Texas, 1861.* Austin, 1912.

——, ed., "Platforms of Political Parties in Texas." *University of Texas Bulletin No. 53.* Austin, 1916.

Marion Karl Wisehart, *Sam Houston: American Giant.* Washington, 1962.

Albert Woldert, "The Last of the Cherokees in Texas, and the Life and Death of Chief Bowles." *The Chronicle of Oklahoma* (June, 1923).

Henderson Yoakum, *History of Texas, from Its First Settlement in 1685 to Its Annexation to the United States in 1846.* New York, 1855.

——, Papers. Archives Collection, University of Texas Library, Austin.

INDEX

335

War of 1812, 13, 27, 28–29, 31 ff.
Washington, George, 59
Washington, Martha, 59
Washington: burning of, 36; abolition of slavery in, 257 ff.
Washington-on-the-Brazos, 148, 150 ff., 177, 218–19, 226, 236
Weatherford, Bill, 32, 34
Webb, Walter P., 296
Webber, Walter, 96
Webster, Daniel, 58, 217, 246, 259, 262, 263
Western Cherokees. *See* Cherokees, Western
Wharton, John A., 51–52, 76, 92, 95, 116, 125, 128, 133
Wharton, William H., 66, 76, 125, 126, 128, 133, 135, 141, 149, 153, 164, 174, 176, 187

Whigs, 64, 235, 237, 270 ff., 279
White, Edward Douglas, 38
White, Owen P., 90
White, Gen. William A., 61–62, 68
Wigwam Neosho, 102 ff., 107, 109, 117
Williams, Amelia W., 61
Williams, Col. John, 32, 38
Williams, Col. Willoughby, 80, 81, 83
Wilmot Proviso, 253
Woll, Gen. Adrian, 218, 219, 220, 236
Wood, G. T., 251
Wounded Knee, 16

Yoakum, Henderson, 257, 266, 272

Zavala, Lorenzo de, 148, 150, 164